Nonprofit
Internet Strategies

*Best Practices for Marketing,
Communications, and Fundraising Success*

TED HART
JAMES M. GREENFIELD
MICHAEL JOHNSTON

WILEY

John Wiley & Sons, Inc.

Library of Congress Cataloging-in-Publication Data:

Nonprofit internet strategies : best practices for marketing, communications, and
    fundraising / [edited by] Ted Hart, James M. Greenfield, and Michael Johnston.
        p.   cm.
    Includes index.
    ISBN 0-471-69188-7 (cloth)
    1. Internet marketing—Computer network resources.   2. Nonprofit organizations—
Computer network resources.   3. Internet.   4. Telecommunication.   5. Fund raising—
Computer network resources.   I. Hart, Ted, 1964–   II. Greenfield, James M., 1936–
III. Johnston, Michael W., 1963–
    HF5415.1265.N65 2005
    658'.054678—dc22

                                                                    2004025805

contents

CHAPTER 14

CHAPTER 17
Institutional Support: Foundation and Corporate Giving   236
Bob Carter   *Ketchum*
Kristina Carlson, CFRE, ePMT   *FundraisingINFO.com*

CHAPTER 18
ePhilanthropy Regulation and the Law   254
Bruce R. Hopkins   *Polsinelli Shalton Welte Suelthaus P.C.*

CHAPTER 19
Evaluating ePhilanthropy Programs   285
James M. Greenfield, ACFRE, FAHP   *J.M. Greenfield & Associates*

When my friend Mike Johnston asked me to write the foreword for this book, I was happy to help. After all, it was his firm Hewitt & Johnston Consulting (now HJC New Media) that got *The NonProfit Times* up and running on the Web many years ago.

When I started to read the manuscript, I couldn't get an old Monty Python routine out of my head. In a scene titled "The Miracle of Life" in the classic comedy movie *The Meaning Of Life,* the doctors helping to deliver a baby were impressed with "the machine that goes ping!" Of course, none of them knew what it actually did, other than it went *ping*. And, because it was the most expensive machine in the hospital, they just had to have it for the procedure.

Another thought was triggered while reading the breathless accounts of money being raised on the Internet by some of the planet's largest organizations. I wondered how in the world a nonprofit in New York City was able to raise the couple of million a year it needs when an old friend of mine who is the development director there doesn't even have e-mail access on the job.

There you have it. The divine versus the ridiculous. Too much horsepower or none at all. Who really needs all of the bells and whistles? And, does something a Brazilian organization uses to generate income translate to Abilene, Texas? Maybe, maybe not. That's why the first rule of fundraising is to test.

Technology is a wonderful thing. But, there are some simple truths that have to be dealt with before diving onto the World Wide Web. There are basic truths of fundraising and advocacy, no matter what they are now called in this era of e-donors.

These are some of the questions that nonprofit executives have to answer while reading this tome. First, who are your donors, and how do they want to be contacted? Is brand really such a big deal? What are the privacy issues? How about the costs?

Not only are donors as different as snowflakes (did I just write that?) but techniques used abroad just might be pointless in the United States. For example, online fundraising and advocacy are gangbusters in Europe compared to the United States. One reason is that mailing lists are considerably better in the United States, so charities hit the snail-mail trail. Privacy rules in Europe make mailing very expensive and getting productive lists a difficult chore.

Europeans also adopt personal technology much faster than Americans. For example, you can buy a soda from a vending machine via cell phone in Europe. You can't do that in the United States. But when Americans do get comfortable with a new technology, the United States is an immense market that turns quickly, like those annoying Blackberries, an adult answer to Nintendo. That's why testing is vital.

Let's face it. For all of this talk about personal freedom, Americans are prudes. Sure, we go to the beach, but there is only one Rio, and it ain't in New Jersey. You'd never see any of that on a U.S. shoreline. It's a privacy and legal issue. It's the same thing with solicitation. There are electronic strategies that simply can't cross borders.

Do donors really know how much information can be captured about them when they provide an e-mail address? Will you tell them? Will you prevent your in-house geeks from tracing donor footprints on that virtual beach in Rio? Will you put in writing for your donors what you will and won't do to get information?

All sorts of select information such as credit card purchases, how long the donor has owned a house, etc., are run against lists of names in an attempt to find a great donor. The fact that you've bought something from a catalog or used a credit card is semi-public information. But, should the charity be dipping into a donor's electronic cookie jar? Absolutely not.

Todd Baker, who contributed a chapter to this book, once remarked about a mutual acquaintance, "He's brilliant, but sometimes he uses it for evil." The same can be said for technology.

There are no spam filters on a mailbox. The donor makes the ultimate choice of whether or not to open an envelope. That can also be true of e-mail. You just have to take the additional step of getting people to opt-in to future solicitations and contacts. And yes, the donor probably found you online, since e-mail lists are expensive and, in the case of non-business e-mail addresses, not very reliable.

Everyone has a mailbox, but not everyone has high-speed Internet access. A lot of the nation—and the world—is still on dial-up. The initial message on the Internet must be crafted for everyone, despite the claim that it can easily be tailored.

Remember, this foreword is being written by someone whose computer programmer pal refers to as *"geek"* when he calls. It's a mocking gesture. *Ludite* would be more appropriate and accurate.

Of course, all costs have to be considered when making technology decisions. The consultants tout that shipping off an e-mail is so much less expensive than sending out a direct mail piece. Is it? Sure, a direct mail piece has creative costs, printing, and postage. Well, so do e-mails. While you can actually send an e-mail for pennies, it probably cost more than $100 an hour each for several hours for the techies to develop the e-mail blast message.

Tim Mills-Groninger makes several excellent points in his chapter on staffing. There comes a point when outsourcing technology is no longer cost-effective. His blueprint for making those decisions is terrific.

The authors make the point that a Web page is a 24/7 window to your organization. So, it's two o'clock in the morning and some teenager in Des Moines hacks into your Web site for grins. Will a service provider be able to alert you or block the attack? There have been numerous cases of hacked sites. You have to decide how to handle the situation. Technology is not something that can be completely controlled.

This again begs the question of whether you need in-house IT staff. At that point, it's not an issue of technology. It's an issue of damaging your brand. I thought it was interesting that the authors used Ivory Snow, Levi Strauss, and Ford as examples. Each survived their share of image attacks—one's spokeswoman became a porn queen, another moved work offshore and had to financially reorganize, and the other has had a couple of incidents of its product literally blowing up.

They remain American icons, so charities should have little problem, right? Wrong. Americans don't really trust big business. All they have to do is look at the shrinkage in their 401(k) retirement plans to get the chills—particularly if those plans included stock in Enron and WorldCom.

Americans expect charities to do good work. They may still buy Asian-stitched jeans from Levi Strauss, wash them with Ivory Snow, and drive to the store in a re-stored Pinto, but they'll never give to you again if jilted.

It's this growing, cynical donor base that will lose its trust of charities quickly if the organizations don't follow ethical rules online.

It's estimated that roughly $2 billion was donated online last year. That's a spit in the ocean of $240 billion donated to charity during 2003. The authors of this book learned from the technology bust of the middle-1990s. Instead of technology being the be-all and end-all, they explain that it's just one element of fundraising.

Finally, common sense prevails.

Paul Clolery
Vice President/Editorial Director
NPT Publishing Group/The NonProfit Times

introduction

The first e-mail was sent in March 1972. The origins of the Internet began in the 1960s and evolved over the next 10 to 15 years. By April 1993, the World Wide Web made it possible for corporations, government entities, and nonprofit organizations to create a presence to the world on the Internet. It is estimated that in the year 2000, there were 475 million e-mail boxes worldwide, through which 500 to 600 billion e-mail messages flowed. Approximately 1.4 million belong to nonprofit organizations. A communications device this extensive holds great potential for philanthropy and fundraising. The editors of this book and their authors provide an excellent guide for the various ways in which philanthropy can be developed using electronic means.

Less than a decade ago, ePhilanthropy was all the rage. With technology companies driving the equities market and capturing the imagination of U.S. industry, developing philanthropy over the Internet to gain not only the attention of this new breed of philanthropist but the American people in general held great promise. Many nonprofit organizations saw ePhilanthropy as a quick fix to their problems. Internet Web sites allowed nonprofit organizations to list themselves on Web sites in return for a fee or percentage of any contributions collected. Organizations developed Web sites as a way to collect contributions. There was an "If we build it, they will come" mentality. But they didn't.

Research, such as the December 2003 *Philanthropic Giving Index* of the Center on Philanthropy at Indiana University, has shown that while 30 percent of organizations predict they will have success with Internet fundraising within the next six months, only 18 percent indicate success currently. Nonprofit organizations think that success with the Internet is right around the corner, but the corner may be farther away than most people think. There are notable exceptions. It is estimated that within the first six months after 9/11, $150 million in contributions came over the Internet. The American Red Cross alone received an unprecedented $64 million online after 9/11. For the Red Cross, online giving spikes after disasters, and many times the donors live far beyond the region affected by the disaster. Tech-savvy colleges and universities are using e-mail to solicit gifts from alumni. However, ePhilanthropy did not turn out to be the effort-free, magical solution to increased funds for an organization that many thought it would be.

So why write this book, and why should you read it? First, you should read it because long-term ePhilanthropy will have a major impact on our organizations. Pierre Omidyar proved through eBay that you could create trust, build community, and change the buying habits of people around the world. As use of electronic media to communicate becomes more prevalent, our constituents will expect us to offer the same possibilities for philanthropy. And we need to be prepared to take advantage of these possibilities or be left behind by colleagues who embrace ePhilanthropy and learn how to integrate it into their evolving fundraising programs.

Second, you should read this book because, while there is no magic, ePhilanthropy provides great potential for our organizations. Using electronic media for fundraising to generate ePhilanthropy requires the same intentional behavior on the part of nonprofit organizations that organized, intentional fundraising without electronic media requires. Communication, constituency relations, involvement, use of volunteers, and soliciting the gift are part of both processes.

Research has repeatedly shown that people make gifts when they are aware of a need, believe in the need, are engaged in organizations that satisfy the need, and see themselves in the clients being served. The editors and authors of *Nonprofit Internet Strategies: Best Practices for Marketing, Communications, and Fundraising Success* provide nonprofit organizations with an excellent guide to using the Internet in deliberate and intentional ways for support and expansion of their fundraising programs. But we must be willing to do the work required for success. The contributors show us how we can enhance, not replace, our communications, constituency relations, and fundraising efforts with the Internet.

The Internet is a useful tool for communicating with our constituents, telling our story, and receiving feedback. It is an excellent marketing tool. It has possibilities for efficiently engaging constituents with the organization and with each other—helping organizations with not only outreach efforts but also scaling challenges and opportunities. It is a way to project the image of our organizations not only to our constituents but also beyond—regionally, nationally, and globally. It is a way to inspire and mobilize our constituents and even provide opportunities for volunteers to assist us without leaving their homes. The chapters in this book tell us how.

The authors remind us that we must be strategic in developing our plans for ePhilanthropy and that we must hire professional staff to implement our plans just as we would hire professional staff to implement other aspects of our fundraising. They give us tips for getting our Web site recognized through search engines and for using our own databases and other databases available electronically over the Internet.

They offer us separate chapters on marketing, brand building, and visitor relationship management. In addition to a special chapter on building an integrated fundraising strategy, there are separate chapters on various aspects of our fundraising programs. The authors apply use of the Internet to annual giving, planned giving, special events and sponsorships, and foundations and corporate giving.

Finally, they offer us insights into the regulatory environment relating to ePhilanthropy and ways to evaluate the success of our philanthropy programs. The title promises best practices. The authors present us with ideas and principles backed up by successful programs and projects, by stories that make the ideas and principles come alive—yet they avoid the typical hype that many Internet-based plays suffer from.

ePhilanthropy is not a magical solution to our fundraising needs. It will not produce the funds our organizations need without effort on our part. It is not the final solution to our marketing and communications needs. But *Nonprofit Internet Strategies: Best Practices for Marketing, Communications, and Fundraising Success* can help us develop thoughtful and methodical Internet strategies and initiatives that will enhance our current fundraising, marketing, and communications efforts and prepare us for the brave new world in ePhilanthropy that lies ahead.

Eugene R. Tempel

Executive Director
The Center on Philanthropy at Indiana University

Thomas K. Reis

Program Director
W. K. Kellogg Foundation

ePhilanthropy Strategy: Where Relationship Building, Fundraising, and Technology Meet

Ted Hart, ACFRE, ePMT
ePhilanthropyFoundation.org

ePhilanthropy techniques have brought to the nonprofit world an unprecedented opportunity to leverage technology for the benefit of the charity and convenience of the donor.

Although fundraising and relationship building have always been dynamic endeavors, no change has demanded or received more attention in the past several years than the arrival of *ePhilanthropy,* or the use of the Internet for philanthropic purposes. During this time much has been tried, theorized, and learned. What is certain is that to succeed using the Internet as a fundraising vehicle requires strategy.

In the beginning, some nonprofit professionals thought, hoped, or just fantasized that ePhilanthropy represented quick and easy money for charities. It was unrealistic to ever think that would be the case. However, through careful planning, ePhilanthropy has been shown to add efficiency, reach, options, and success to traditional fundraising and relationship-building efforts.

The book *Fundraising on the Internet: The ePhilanthropyFoundation.org's Guide to Success Online* introduced many tools and options for developing an online presence. This book, *Nonprofit Internet Strategies,* is dedicated to helping take those tools and marry them successfully with offline, traditional fundraising into an Integrated ePhilanthropy Strategy (IePS).

The growth of ePhilanthropy has required even the most seasoned professionals to learn new skills and to reevaluate how they approach nearly every aspect of fundraising. This is not to suggest that ePhilanthropy has taken the place of any traditional fundraising methods—actually, it is the opposite. ePhilanthropy tools add a new dimension of efficiency and require high levels of integration with every *offline* approach to attracting philanthropic support. Although some would relegate ePhilanthropy as

1

a specialty area to be administered separately, much in the way some offices might have a prospect-research or planned-giving specialist on staff, doing so diminishes the overall effectiveness and denies the opportunity to fully benefit from these tools. This chapter will provide an overview of ePhilanthropy strategy and techniques that non-profits can use to cultivate and steward relationships, communicate and invite advocacy for their cause, and solicit contributions online.

The true strength of ePhilanthropy-based methods lies in their ability to do more than simply functioning as a novel way in which to send messages or raise money. When integrated with off-line efforts, the Internet provides an ideal platform from which to reach, inform, and engage potential donors, many of which may be beyond the reach of normal communication and fundraising channels alone.

Charities seeking success online should approach the Internet as a communication and stewardship tool first and a fundraising tool second. Any seasoned fundraiser will tell you that when you can build and enhance a relationship with a prospective donor, you have a much higher chance of successfully soliciting a gift.

DEFINING ePHILANTHROPY

ePhilanthropy is a set of efficiency-building Internet-based techniques that can be used to build and enhance relationships with stakeholders interested in the success of a nonprofit organization.

ePhilanthropy is the building and enhancing of relationships with volunteers and supporters of nonprofit organizations using the Internet. It includes the contribution of cash or real property or the purchase of products and services to benefit a nonprofit organization, and the storage of and usage of electronic data and services to support relationship building and fundraising activities.

CREATING AN INTEGRATED ePHILANTHROPY STRATEGY (IEPS)

ePhilanthropy is not about a quick (or click) hello and a request for money. It's about building and enhancing stronger relationships with supporters. With the steadily increasing market penetration of Internet, wireless, and broadband Internet access, charities have more opportunities than ever to communicate, educate, cultivate, and solicit their supporters.

Five strategies are fundamental to the online success of nonprofit organizations. Taken separately, these strategies may appear too simple. Combining them and integrating them throughout the organization will create a momentum that helps nonprofits meet the dual goals of *friend raising* and *fundraising*.

1. Integrate all supporter messages.
2. Give supporters a reason to visit you online.
3. Interact with supporters; don't just send messages.
4. Communicate using multiple methods.
5. Assess and improve performance.

Integrate All Supporter Messages

In the *always-on* online philanthropy world, the job of the development professional is a lot tougher. Gone are the days when synchronized tone and manner and consistent look and feel were the benchmarks of successfully coordinated campaigns. Today, the coordination of experiences across both online and offline activities requires three steps:

1. Integrate technologies, systems, organizations, and processes to enable your organization to deliver meaningful experiences to deepen supporter relationships. The efficient and effective use of e-mail—while an incredible boon to nonprofits—is best utilized in concert with and integrated into a strategy that includes outreach through traditional methods of print, phone, and face-to-face communication and fundraising.
2. Synchronize information across various communication channels to deliver relevant and consistent experiences at the right time and in the right place.
3. Integrate data from all over your organization to optimize supporter experiences.

In short, if you don't integrate data and activities in new ways, it will be difficult to apply the next four strategies successfully; your efforts are likely to fall short when you treat the Internet as just another communications or donation medium, as opposed to a relationship channel. To be successful, your organization will need to implement organizational and organization process changes to create and manage effective supporter experiences.

Give Supporters a Reason to Visit You Online

The supporter controls the mouse—and therefore, controls the interaction and the relationship. When the supporter dictates the rules, charities earn loyalty and contributions when they deliver value to those supporters. Many Internet-based strategies fail because they never offer a reason for someone to go online and fail to use all their resources in concert with one another to enhance and deepen relationships with supporters.

To create a sustainable ePhilanthropy strategy, charities must deliver the right experiences to the right supporters. This requires understanding both the supporters' needs and their likelihood of making contributions over a sustained period of time.

To identify value for the supporter, you must assemble data to significantly increase your understanding of your supporters. Why and how do they use the Internet? What online information and opportunities could they use that would open the door to a deeper relationship?

Four online categories usually define value for the supporter:

1. Access to information about the organization's mission and services
2. Increased convenience/saved time in philanthropic transactions (making a donation, volunteering, or advocacy)

3. Ability to expand support to others through use of online tools that aid in supporting the mission (making it possible for family, friends, and colleagues to be informed about your charity directly by your current supporters)
4. Online stewardship and information on accountability

The key is determining what will have the biggest impact on supporters' interest and satisfaction, while increasing value for your organization. As you gather information to gain insights into these topics, you can simultaneously identify the value of supporters and prospective supporters, measured by current and potential contributions. With analysis and prioritization complete, you can deliver the information, experiences, and services that meet supporter needs most effectively and efficiently.

Interact with Supporters—Don't Just Send Messages

Your supporters *read* newspapers, they *watch* television, but they *use* the Internet. The Internet's value is measured by its ability to give convenient and quick access to what supporters want when they want it, and by what it empowers supporters to do. Although a basic strategy of ePhilanthropy would be to collect e-mail addresses and send out messages to supporters, your strategy should NOT look like an electronic version of a high school public address system, where all communication is blasted out to the entire audience and all communication is one way.

The Internet enables charities to initiate dialogues, invite two-way communication, and enhance relationships. The value of ePhilanthropy is not solely determined by the design of a Web page, but by providing supporters with convenient access to what they want when they want it, and by providing useful tools allowing them to accomplish their interest to support the organization's work and to share their support with their personal and business networks.

A good example is an online service that helps donors reach out to friends, family, and colleagues to solicit funds in support of a race or walk. By focusing on ways to truly interact with your supporters—giving time-starved professionals instant access to easy-to-use tools—your strategy is to develop the charity as a partner geared toward enhancing the ability of supporters to share your message with others. Studies show that by putting such tools in the hands of online supporters, nonprofits will raise much more money from many more contributors than the traditional offline "pass around the pledge form" approach.

Communicate Using Multiple Methods

Getting information and services into the hands of the right supporters at the right time and in the right place is as important to ePhilanthropy success as creating the message itself. This makes distribution a critical component of ePhilanthropy.

Key to a successful ePhilanthropy strategy is thinking about your online and offline presence as a series of experiences that intersect with your supporters' activities and preferences. Conduct research to understand where and when your organization is of greatest relevance to supporters and prospects. Armed with this supporter insight, your strategy should emphasize a series of services that can be distributed to your supporters as distinct messages across various methods of communication (e-mail, Web site, direct mail, telephone, print, etc).

For example, an organization that traditionally has a gala/auction event would benefit greatly by offering e-invitation options to supporters to aid in selling more tickets; online registration to cut down on staff time updating attendee rosters; and an online auction to expand the number of donors beyond those able to attend the event. By offering these tools and promoting them both online and offline, the organization does not alter its message yet expands its audience and reach.

Assess and Improve Performance

ePhilanthropy is more than conceiving and implementing innovative strategies that meet the demands of supporters and the objectives of organizations. It is also about continuously measuring and improving results for your supporter and your organization.

When optimizing online services such as content or online donation functionality, the vital measure is the return on supporter time—how well you enable supporters to quickly get the information they want to execute their desired tasks. When reviewing data on Web activities and e-mail donor or advocacy campaigns, it is critical to measure both the immediate actions taken by those receiving the message, as well as their long-term impact on future supporter activity. Therefore, you should track, assess, and act on results across multiple time horizons.

Although it is more difficult to get this information regarding the opening and reading of direct mail or newsletters, what is learned in the online world about your supporter interests and preferences should be used to help enhance the offline services. This sharing of learned experiences will enhance efforts to build an Integrated ePhilanthropy Strategy (IePS).

Be certain you build into every program ways to measure, analyze, and adjust. For example, the data you receive from a single online e-mail campaign will allow you to understand how many received, read, forwarded, and discarded the message, but by looking at longer time horizons, you can learn the long-term effect of such messages on event registration, donations, and Web site traffic. You will be able to plan future campaigns based on an analysis of where and how you acquired the most valuable supporters, rather than on acquisition data that do not factor in links between long-term supporter value and short-term online activity.

Be certain you measure performance on an integrated basis across all media both on- and offline, not in channel silos. True optimization can come only from understanding your supporters' activities across various avenues—offline drive traffic, Web site campaigns, direct mail, e-mail campaigns, newsletters, the content you provide to other Web sites through partnership agreements, telephone outreach, and special events.

After all, ePhilanthropy is less about simple fundraising—that is too easy—and more about creating an always-on interface between your organization and your supporters. You will need to understand and influence technology platforms, and you will want to integrate with systems, databases, and data flows that will enable experiences. Likewise, in building performance-tracking systems you will need to integrate multiple data sources, both online and offline, to ensure a comprehensive, integrated view of your supporters' behavior and their activities with your brand.

You Can Do It

Marketing today is not about saying hello and making an offer, as it was at the turn of the twentieth century. It's about enabling supporters to never have to say goodbye. Now companies can always be connected, and your interface with supporters can always be on. So, success will hinge on how well connected you are with your supporters. Will you always be on for them? Will you conceive and deliver relevant services to them? Will the services be valuable to both your supporter and your organization? Will your attempts at advertising be embraced as welcomed services or rejected as intrusive annoyances? Will you rigorously optimize the supporters' experience, as well as your marketing budget? Will you integrate your organization, your processes, your channels, and your data in new ways that enable you to take advantage of the Internet's power? Follow the five strategies just described and you will ultimately prevail in the *always-on age.*

DONORS MUST BE ASKED

Whether the solicitation for support comes via news broadcasts reporting on a tragic event or in the form of an e-mail message from a charity, donors must still be asked for support if organizations expect to receive it. These would-be ePhilanthropists are much more likely to be inspired to contribute based on the mission, the stated need, and the opportunity to give, presented by a charity they have likely already supported offline. But to obtain their support, *they must be asked!*

Local and national charities that do not offer their supporters the opportunity to communicate and contribute online fail to do so at their peril. Every nonprofit has the opportunity to reach out to more donors and prospects than they could ever afford to using traditional methods of direct mail, telephone or personal visits, but they must cultivate an online relationship before asking for support. This cultivation and solicitation must be part of an integrated fundraising program that includes both online and offline fundraising techniques.

BACK TO THE FUTURE

This is not the first time that nonprofit organizations and fundraisers have had to adapt to new technologies. Radio, television, newspapers, telephone, fax machine, computers, electronic databases, and direct mail have all affected the way we raise money. Some of the new methods that have evolved are more successful; others have been used with less success.

Each new advance in technology has created a particular set of challenges for nonprofits and their donors; each has triggered a corresponding set of fundraising norms. For nonprofit organizations, the Internet provides an unprecedented and cost-effective opportunity to build and enhance relationships with supporters, volunteers, clients, and the communities they serve. Connecting with supporters online provides a new means for converting interest in a mission to direct involvement and support.

In March 2001, Harvard's Professor James Austin wrote,

> . . . *make no mistake; the ePhilanthropy revolution is here to stay, and it will transform charitable giving in as profound a way as technology is changing the*

commercial world. Charities that have dismissed ePhilanthropy as a fad, or run from it in confusion, will, sooner or later, need to become reconciled to it. If they don't, they risk losing touch with donors and imperiling the vitality of their work.[1]

In order to harness the power of ePhilanthropy, nonprofit organizations must remember two things:

1. ePhilanthropy should be seen as a set of relationship-building tools first and fundraising tools second.
2. Nonprofit Web sites and use of e-mail for promotional purposes will succeed when integrated into every other form of communication used by the nonprofit (e.g., direct mail, brochures, planned giving, newsletters, telephone, radio, print media).

SIX CATEGORIES OF SERVICES

The Internet gives donors easy access to numerous philanthropic choices. Increasingly, as the ePhilanthropy revolution builds steam, more and more people have turned to the Web to fulfill their charitable intentions. As ePhilanthropy has emerged, organizations have discovered that one of the keys to success is consistent and deliberate e-mail communication driving traffic to the organization's well-organized and informative Web site.

Years of experience in the offline world have taught fundraisers that attention to detail, privacy, security of information, and honesty in reporting are key components to any successful solicitation of support, whether that support comes in the form of volunteerism, advocacy, or contributions. Through the appropriate use of permission-based e-mail, a nonprofit can provide its donors with increased access to information and more timely details regarding the stewardship and solicitation of their charitable support. Increased access and detailed information help strengthen the relationship and trust between the nonprofit and supporters. To earn this trust, nonprofit organizations will become accustomed to increased levels of scrutiny and demands for evidence that the charity is well managed and provides service consistent with its mission.

Building a Web site is not enough. Success on the Internet requires an integrated strategy that embraces standards for protecting and preserving donor relationships. For-profit vendors have developed a wide array of services to help power nonprofits' Web sites. Many of these services are cataloged on the Nonprofit Matrix at *http://www.nonprofitmatrix.com*. See Exhibit 1.1.

As charities look at various services, they should start by understanding the strategic objectives for their Web site. It is not necessary to have all the bells and whistles before engaging prospects and donors online. It is advisable, instead, to start small and build slowly. Begin with collecting e-mail addresses, communicating via e-mail, and offering the opportunity to give online via an encrypted Web page.

Taking the time to plan ahead can often mean the difference between merely using the Internet and developing a successful ePhilanthropy strategy. The exact mix of strategies and techniques are as varied as the number and types of nonprofits that deploy them.

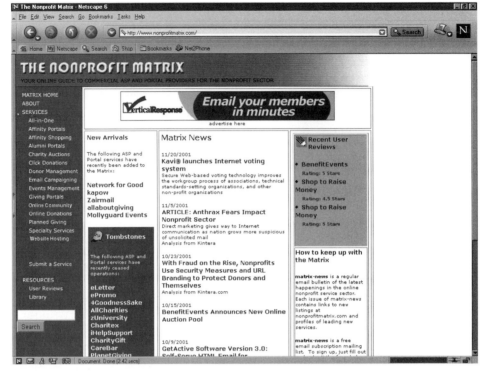

EXHIBIT 1.1   Home Page for Nonprofit Matrix

ePhilanthropy techniques fall into six categories:

1. Communication/education and stewardship
2. Online donations and membership
3. Event registrations and management
4. Prospect research
5. Volunteer recruitment and management
6. Relationship building and advocacy

The particular mix of tools and services for each organization will vary widely; organizations should always evaluate options and test assumptions. Incremental improvements and additions of services will help supporters and staff become accustomed to using the new technology and communicating via the Internet. Only by testing can the organization learn which techniques perform the best.

COMMUNICATION/EDUCATION AND STEWARDSHIP

The first step toward using the Internet to build online donations, expand the volunteer base, and better communicate the organization's mission with a larger audience is to identify who you want to reach, what you want them to do, and what will inspire them to accept the organization's invitation to take action, volunteer, or give.

Use of the Internet as a stand-alone solution is not effective. Although some have predicted that ePhilanthropy will replace many traditional approaches to soliciting support, this will not be the case. Just as television failed to kill radio, yet changed it significantly, so, too, will the Internet change traditional forms of fundraising, not by eliminating them but by changing their utility and increasing their effectiveness.

Just as there are no shortcuts to long-term success offline, there are no shortcuts online. ePhilanthropy methods permit an organization to communicate and engage supporters, not only through a Web site, but directly through e-mail, which can direct attention back to the organization.

As part of an integrated communication and fundraising strategy, ePhilanthropy offers effective and efficient opportunities for nonprofits to communicate with a much wider audience than they might otherwise have the resources to do. Direct mail, telephone, radio, television, personal visits, and other traditional means of communication with supporters all have significant personnel, printing, postage, or other costs associated with them.

The organization's Web site should reflect the mission of the organization; outdated content on a Web site indicates there is nothing new to share. The Web site must be a true resource for information related to the charity's mission and must provide ample opportunities to support and communicate with the charity.

Supporters who begin or maintain an online relationship with an organization have expectations of communication different than their offline counterparts. In most cases, those who communicate via the Internet will expect to receive an automatic electronic response.

Integration

Promotion of online resources and services through integration with traditional marketing and communication channels significantly increases the effectiveness of overall operations while providing additional options to supporters:

- *Direct mail/ telemarketing.* Every direct mail and telephone appeal should provide the opportunity for supporters to give by mailing in the response form or by making a gift or pledge online. In the case of telemarketing, those who might be at their computer when the call is placed could be directed to an online audio or video message that can enhance the telemarketer's message and could then be prompted to give online.
- *Print material and literature.* Every publication and printed item should include the organization's Web address. This address should appear anywhere the address and/or phone number for the nonprofit would be printed. Large and expensive to produce publications like an annual report can be posted on a Web site as a pdf file (*www.Adobe.com*). Directing donors and supporters to download and print the file not only saves money but also expands the number of people who can access the report.
- *Brand building: promotional opportunities.* Public service announcements (PSAs) and paid advertising and marketing efforts on television, radio, and in print are often some ways organizations share their message with a wider audience.

By directing those hearing or viewing these messages to a Web site, the nonprofit is able to make a more comprehensive appeal for support of their mission.

- *Press.* Press conferences, television and radio appearances, and public speaking engagements are prime opportunities to promote online resources. Nonprofits should establish an online pressroom, providing in a downloadable format background information, press releases, photos, and other material of interest to the media. This will give the press an opportunity to learn about the organization at any time, day or night.

Getting the Word Out

The online environment offers several opportunities to communicate with potential supporters. There are several essential aspects to getting the word out online:

- *E-mail.* This is the most powerful and cost-effective online communication tool available to nonprofit organizations. In accordance with the ePhilanthropy Code of Ethics, it is important that supporters *opt in* to nonprofit e-mail lists. This means that they give permission to receive e-mail from the nonprofit; permission should never be assumed. Even after permission is granted, supporters must be given the option to have their names removed from the e-mail list at any time, known as *opt out.*
- Several vendors have developed services that make it easy for organizations to use e-mail and the Internet for soliciting donations, outreach, education, and advocacy strategies. The integration of the organization's Web site (content and encrypted online donor forms) and e-mail (pushing the message to supporters), along with direct mail/ telephone and other campaigns, not only provides additional options for donors but also gives them the opportunity to become more informed and engaged donors.
- *Search engines.* Each has its own criteria for cataloging the resources of the Internet. Yet no single search engine provides reference to more than 16 percent of the Internet. Therefore, it is important to register the organization's Web site with several of the leading search engines (e.g., Google, Yahoo!, Lycos, AltaVista, Hotbot).
- *"Pass-along" marketing.* Although it is highly unlikely that anyone receiving a direct-mail appeal from a charity will make several copies, address envelopes to their friends and family, and mail copies of the letter urging they also support the organization, it is very likely this activity will take place online. Also known as *viral marketing,* it is a method of asking the recipient of an e-mail to send the message along to other people they know who might be interested. Within a few seconds, the message can be sent along to scores of people on their personal e-mail list. Very important to the success of this method is the fact that the message is now being sent by a friend or family member, thereby increasing the chances of it being read.
- *Send to a friend.* Those who visit a nonprofit organization's Web site are often looking for expert information related to the mission of that organization. By offering the option to "send-to-a-friend" an article or link to a Web page on the site to a friend, the utility of the Web site's content is further enhanced. Once again, the power of this feature is that the recommendation is coming from a trusted friend or family member.

ONLINE DONATIONS AND MEMBERSHIP

Most visitors to a Web site go there because they know or care something about an organization or its mission, and they are seeking information. Effective sites offer multiple opportunities for visitors to support the organization through advocacy, volunteerism, or donations, often on each page of the Web site.

William Park, the chief executive of the marketing firm Digital Impact, talking about e-mail marketing in an interview with *The New York Times*, said, "It's the most measurable marketing vehicle of all time."[2] Response rates are more quickly and accurately measured than in other media. This combination of price and response makes e-mail, particularly e-mail newsletters, very attractive to nonprofits.

Online Donations

The technical details of establishing and owning a secure e-commerce server can be overwhelming; however, with so many vendors and several free services available for processing online gifts in accord with ethical and security standards, it is inadvisable that most nonprofits undertake the creation of a *home-grown* online donation solution. According to the ePhilanthropy Foundation's *Tips for Online Giving*, charities should offer Web sites that use encryption technology to ensure appropriate security for online donations and data transmission. Before entering any information the donor should be able to verify that the page requesting your credit card information is secure (encrypted). The letters https:// (rather than http://) should precede the page's URL, and/or there should be an unbroken key or padlock symbol located in the corner of the Web browser.

Planned Giving Online

Planned giving can often seem complicated to both donors and nonprofits. For donors, education is an important component to learning how they can match their charitable intentions with their estate plans. Nonprofit organizations are faced with the challenge of identifying those who may support their missions with planned gifts—and provide them with the details they need to choose the right planned giving vehicle. For both large and small nonprofits, and for donors and prospects, the Internet is increasingly becoming both a strong marketing tool for planned giving and a great resource for information. The Internet can be an effective vehicle to promote and enhance planned giving efforts, allowing nonprofits to provide detailed information regarding tax-wise giving to more of their donors and prospects.

The Internet provides many opportunities to reach out to colleagues and professionals who share an interest in most any topic of ePhilanthropy. There are several services that allow others to learn from colleagues and share experiences.

Information

It is relatively easy for most nonprofits to put planned giving information on their Web sites; keeping the site updated and legally accurate is more difficult. Several services provide Internet-ready tools that are regularly updated and kept compliant with changing tax laws. These tools represent a cost-effective way to provide compelling and effective planned giving content.

Many donors are turning to the Internet to investigate for themselves how a planned gift would work, instead of calling an adviser or asking a charity for a planned giving illustration.

To meet the needs of these donors, charities can include online tools such as a gift-planning calculator on their Web sites. This information makes available to donors information and resources that had once been the exclusive purview of accountants, lawyers, and planned-giving professionals. Providing these tools gives another reason for donors to visit the Web site.

Marketing

Once planned giving information is available on the charity's Web site, it is time to invite donors and prospects to visit. Most board members and staff members hesitate to discuss planned giving with donors and prospects for fear they will be asked questions they can't answer. The Web site provides a valuable tool in reaching out to these donors by providing self-explanatory planned giving pages. Local attorneys, financial planners, and other advisors should be contacted and made aware of the content and services available. These advisors are often asked by their clients if they know of reputable organizations they might support via their will or planned giving vehicle. Advisors not wanting to appear to have a conflict of interest will often offer several options. They are much more likely to advise in favor of organizations they think are prepared and understand the concepts and topics on which they are asked for advice.

Event Registration and Management

ePhilanthropy special event management makes event registration easier for nonprofits and event attendees. Online services are available to send event invitations, organize volunteer activities, maintain income and expense records, and provide high-quality registration and attendee services. Golf tournaments, walks, and silent and live auctions each have specialized registration and item organization needs. Several online services have been developed to address one or more of these specific requirements.

Surveying the participants from the prior year's event can enhance special event planning. An online survey form can be e-mailed to participants to obtain their feedback. There are several free and fee-based online survey tools available.

PROSPECT RESEARCH

Although an incredible amount of information about fundraising prospects is available online, it's important to pay close attention to the management and use of information gathered. Whether you subscribe to the Association of Professional Researchers for Advancement (APRA) (*www.aprahome.org*) code of ethics or develop your own privacy policy, it is important to protect sensitive and confidential information.

Some Internet resources regarding online privacy issues include the following:

Online Privacy Alliance: *www.privacyalliance.org*
Electronic Frontier Foundation: *www.eff.org/privacy.html*
Electronic Privacy Information Center: *www.epic.org*

Manual Prospect Research

Although it is estimated that the Internet comprises more than half a trillion Web pages (growing daily), the challenge is to determine what is most likely to support fundraising. Indexed Web sites offer an easier approach to finding helpful databases. These sites have been developed to aid access to information databases and Web sites.

Internet Prospector (www.internet-prospector.org) is the very best customized nonprofit site for doing manual prospect research over the Net (see Exhibit 1.2). The site is set up as a roadmap to resources that have direct bearing on gathering information on prospects. Staffed by a national network of volunteers, this nonprofit site provides a unique service that mines the Internet to report on resources of use to prospect researchers.

Electronic Screening

The Internet makes it possible for charities of all sizes to obtain helpful information regarding the capacity of their key prospects to make a major gift. There are several free and paid access databases available to nonprofits seeking to identify prospects with wealth. Several companies have developed services that make it possible to match a charity's prospect database to specific information about known persons with private wealth, philanthropists, inside stock traders, private company owners, high-net-worth professionals, as well as corporate and foundation executives and trustees.

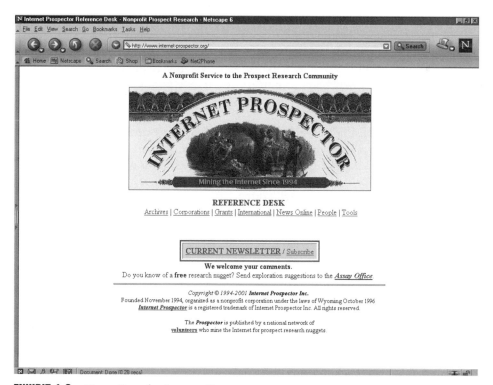

EXHIBIT 1.2   Home Page for Internet Prospector

VOLUNTEER RECRUITMENT AND MANAGEMENT

Volunteers are important to any successful nonprofit program or fundraising endeavor. The Internet provides tools that can enhance relationships and improve communication. Recruiting volunteers online is an excellent way to reach nontraditional volunteers, including populations that might be underrepresented in an organization's volunteer ranks (seniors, ethnic minorities, people with disabilities, etc.).

Several online resources are available that can help with technical assistance, resource sharing, training, and consultation. Organizations interested in posting volunteer opportunities online have several options to obtain help in locating volunteers, tracking them, and managing their activities. One of the largest is SERVEnet (*www.servenet.org*); another is VolunteerMatch (*www.volunteermatch.com*).

Virtual Volunteer Management

The Internet can be used to increase communication, coordination, education, and collaboration with and among volunteers. The Internet can help volunteers, particularly those that work away from direct supervision, feel more connected to the work and mission of the organization. Here are five examples:

1. E-mail is an easy and free way to communicate with volunteers quickly and provide them opportunities to communicate easily with nonprofit staff.
2. An online *ask a peer* discussion group for your volunteers is an ideal tool to help them collaborate, share what they have learned, and increase teamwork.
3. Regular e-mail updates on important organizational news and volunteer activities can help in volunteer retention.
4. Volunteer manuals, guidelines, statistics, and other information helpful to volunteers can all be posted online, making them available anytime.
5. Online calendars can help volunteers remember important assignments and deadlines.

For an extensive list of free and fee-based services, check out Web Hosting Forum Services at *www.thinkofit.com/webconf/hostsites.htm*.

According to the Virtual Volunteering Project (*www.serviceleader.org/vv*), "virtual volunteering means volunteer tasks completed, in whole or in part, via the Internet." This combines technology with offline volunteer recruitment and management efforts. Organizations can expand their reach by attracting volunteers from new areas and increasing their level of participation.

Privacy Concerns

When an organization asks donors or members for demographic and personal contact information, it is implicitly asking them to trust that it will not misuse the information they provide. Organizations must address privacy concerns. Information will not be given and donations will not be made online if they don't trust that their information will be used responsibly.

To increase the likelihood that the trust supporters have for the charity will be transferred to the online environment, charities should do the following:

- Publish their privacy policy on the Web site and at other places where such data is requested or required.
- Review and strengthen internal security and use of confidential data.
- Ensure that supporters can control the information collected about them, including removing their name from lists for future online communication and/or solicitation.
- Respond promptly to complaints and all forms of electronic communication.
- Consider seeking certification from one of the well-known privacy trust marks such as trustee or BBB Online.

Shopping and Bidding

Shopping sites, auction sites, and others can give supporters an opportunity to show their support by encouraging them to shop or bid to benefit the charity of their choice. Few of these options have raised significant revenue for charities. The appropriate allocation of staff time would place an emphasis on improving the Web site, developing an effective e-mail communication program, and integrating these efforts into traditional forms of fundraising. Even though such services have failed to generate quick and easy money for nonprofits, it is appropriate to use these services as additional options on a charity's Web site, only when the items being sold or the auction event is somehow tied to the mission of the organization.

RELATIONSHIP BUILDING AND ADVOCACY

For some organizations the promotion of their mission through e-mailing an elected official, signing an electronic petition, receiving electronic *action alerts,* or forwarding e-mail messages to friends, co-workers, and family serves an important role in building and enhancing online relationships.

An online advocacy campaign can serve as a successful way to rally support and an excellent way to build an e-mail database. Making effective use of the organization's Web site and e-mail database requires careful planning. The messages in the action alerts should match those of print media and the Web site. It is important to identify specific goals for online advocacy.

Follow-up to these prospects or donors through traditional direct mail or other methods should refer to the initial e-mail contact. An example might be: "Last month you joined with 75,000 other dedicated Americans who are joining the fight for tougher drunk driving laws. Today, we are writing to ask for your help."

To support the details of this effort, several online services have been developed.

Because their initial contact was on the occasion of an advocacy campaign, it is important to provide appropriate follow-up. Charities might consider proposing additional advocacy activities, an invitation to volunteer, or suggestion to make a charitable gift to support going efforts related to the initial advocacy request. The purpose is to turn potential donors acquired during an online activism campaign into donors.

CONCLUSION

ePhilanthropy techniques have brought to the nonprofit world an unprecedented opportunity to leverage technology for the benefit of the charity and convenience of the donor. In every organization, time and resources are spent on recruiting and retaining charitable support. This support is based on relationships built and missions fulfilled. Hundreds of options exist to develop solutions for each of the six categories of ePhilanthropy outlined in this chapter. Use of the Internet enhances these efforts by providing efficient and effective communication tools tied to robust secure online services. These services empower donors to utilize information and support charitable causes anytime and anywhere.

ABOUT THE AUTHOR

Ted Hart, ACFRE, ePMT, is an Internet and fundraising strategist with close to 20 years of experience in communications, fundraising, and nonprofit management. He is founder and president of the international ePhilanthropy Foundation (*http://ephilanthropy.org*), the global leader in providing training to charities for the ethical and efficient use of the Internet for philanthropic purposes through education and advocacy. He is the former CEO of the University of Maryland Medical System Foundation and chief development officer at Johns Hopkins Bayview Medical Center. Mr. Hart is frequently invited to lecture on fundraising, nonprofit management, ethics, and the Internet throughout North America. You can e-mail Ted at tedhart@ephilanthropy.org.

ENDNOTES

1. Kellogg Foundation Report on e-Philanthropy (2001).
2. "Charities Turn to Email Experts," *New York Times* (August 21, 2000).

CHAPTER 2

It All Begins with Strategy: Using the Internet as a Strategic Tool

Anthony J. Powell, CFRE, ePMT
Blackbaud Consulting Services

From an organizational standpoint, the degree to which online activities complement and communicate other activities within the organization is more important than leading-edge technology or the number of Web visitors.

The Internet has the potential to revolutionize philanthropy. However, it should not fundamentally change the way nonprofits develop and implement organizational strategy. Strategy provides an organizationwide roadmap that determines the activities an organization should carry out. Although the Internet is an effective tool for achieving goals and supporting organizational mission, the Web is not a unique functional area in and of itself, and simply having a Web site is not a strategy. In order to effectively deploy an ePhilanthropy strategy, nonprofits should first assess their missions—each organization's purpose and reason for being—and then develop a dynamic, organization-specific strategy that aligns key processes and programs with Internet activities.

A COMMON SITUATION

Jane walked into the board meeting confident and proud. As the director of development for a regional Midwestern symphony orchestra, she had a strong relationship with the board, and she enjoyed the challenging assignments they gave her. A year ago, she completed a five-month project to roll out the symphony's first Web site—one of the board's major initiatives. Although Web traffic was slow at first, over time she and the board came to regard the project as a success: hundreds of visitors came to the site each month, and she had received a good deal of positive feedback on the online program guide.

The board, though pleased with the Web site, wanted to expand the symphony's online presence to make it more dynamic. One of the members had seen another symphony's site—it had online ticketing functionality and a "Donate Now" button to accept electronic donations. Shouldn't they have that as well? Building the site had cost money, and the recurring hosting and maintenance fees were adding up. They wanted to be sure they were using the Internet to its full potential.

The board began asking Jane what her plans were for the site: "Can we raise money online? . . . what about selling tickets? . . . event registration and customer service? . . . online communities and Web casts of performances? . . . real-time customer service? . . . more graphics and animation? . . . what about a charity auction feature like on eBay?"

Jane was pretty sure the symphony could carry out each of these activities online, although she was uncertain which of these ideas, if any, they should now implement. The symphony wanted to take its Web presence to the next level, but neither Jane nor the board knew the best way to approach this task.

EARLY RETURNS ON ePHILANTHROPY

Jane's situation is very familiar to nonprofits exploring Internet technology. The Internet is a dynamic, interactive environment for engaging constituents in meaningful ways, and it provides access to larger, more advantageous demographics inaccessible through offline means. Online credit-card processing increases ease and flexibility of payment for Web visitors, and the broad reach of the Internet provides a high-volume, low-dollar means of accepting donations. Over the past few years, these advantages have driven impressive results: On average, online donations are larger and the transaction costs are significantly lower than through more traditional channels.[1] Who hasn't been impressed by the $63.4 million in online donations the American Red Cross (ARC) received[2] at *www.redcross.org* in the wake of September 11, 2001, or the $6 million Heifer International received at *www.heifer.org* in the fourth quarter of 2002?[3]

Fundraising success online is not limited to larger organizations like ARC and Heifer. Online giving was estimated to be a staggering $1.9 billion in 2003, an amount growing at a rate of nearly 50 percent a year.[4] Needless to say, thousands of other nonprofits have found success online as well. However, the majority of nonprofits have yet to leverage Internet technology to its full potential. A relatively small number of nonprofits have taken the lion's share of online donations, while hundreds of others struggle to design, implement, and execute successful campaigns using the Web. After investing in market-leading Web technology, many otherwise highly successful nonprofits have received little traffic and few, if any, donations. Many painstakingly planned, perfectly executed e-mail campaigns have yielded unsatisfying returns. Why have so many nonprofits had so much trouble?

ORGANIZATIONAL STRATEGY

In each of these situations, organizational strategy—not just Internet technology—was the key to a successful use of the Internet. The American Red Cross's mission is to "help people prevent, prepare for and respond to emergencies." Because of a long-standing history of crisis response, people naturally turn to the American Red Cross after times of crisis. The organization's Web site serves as a conduit for quickly and efficiently accepting support and distributing information. The key to the ARC's on-line results was not its Web site, but its strong, nationwide brand presence and long history of providing disaster relief services, without which its online donations probably would not have been noteworthy.[5]

Although one of the leaders of the ePhilanthropy movement, Heifer International had been successfully raising money for almost 55 years when it built its first Web site in 1998. The site was deployed in conjunction with larger marketing and public relations efforts. A popular children's book about the Heifer's efforts was featured on *The Oprah Winfrey Show*, and the organization was mentioned on the popular television program *The West Wing*. These high-profile appearances on national media helped to raise visibility and create interest, and individuals wanting to learn more gravitated to Heifer's site for more information.[6] In Heifer's case, the Web provided a complementary means of marketing the organization's mission to reach a larger market segment. The Web leveraged longstanding efforts, rather than supplanting them.[7]

Although the Internet played a key role in each organization's success, it was part of an orchestrated, organizationwide strategy that involved offline programs and activities that supported the mission, goals, and objectives as much as a Web site and e-mail. Although it might be true that having a Web site is more important than being listed in the phone book,[8] simply having a Web site or e-mail address is a far cry from successfully raising money or engaging constituents online. When it comes to nonprofit Web sites, the line from the movie *Field of Dreams*, "If you build it, they will come" proves false more often than not. And, while e-mail is often described as "cheap, quick and simple,"[9] it can overwhelm constituents, dilute communications, and potentially turn away donors if not deployed in an organized, concerted fashion. Although the drive to get ahead in ePhilanthropy is well intentioned, it can be fraught with significant risk if not integrated with organizational strategy.

The reality is that developing an Internet strategy independent of organizational strategy is essentially treating a Web site as an end in itself—which is why many non-profits have a "Donate Now" button but a disappointing amount of online donations. ARC and Heifer employed Internet technologies in support of their efforts as a whole, developing Web activities that specifically reinforce offline efforts in support of their mission, and vice versa. Organizations that have conducted Internet activities with less than satisfactory results generally lack this comprehensive, organizationwide strategic approach—which is often the largest barrier to successful fundraising, communication, and marketing over the Web.[10]

DEVELOPING AND ALIGNING STRATEGY

Jane came out of the board meeting feeling overwhelmed. The board members had a wide variety of ideas, all of which seemed good, but it would be far too expensive to implement them all. Additionally, although the ideas seemed good in theory, Jane was unsure if they would actually work in the real world. And what if there were more ideas they hadn't yet considered? The symphony lacked direction and focus, and before it could start using the Web, it would need to develop a strategy.

More than a set of tactical plans or a step-by-step recipe for success, strategy is a clearly articulated, mission-driven, and organization-specific roadmap that aligns activities, programs, and communication channels. Strategy provides direction, helps to set priorities, and ensures that each department work together to create the right activities to serve the organization as a whole and support its mission. This *strategic fit* between previously independent activities exponentially increases results, making the sum of activities more valuable than individual parts.[11]

In regard to the Internet, this means that organizations must ensure that online efforts work in close synchronization with more traditional programs to support the organization's mission. Lacking the knowledge for integration of Internet technology and its potential for engaging constituents, many nonprofits have understandably treated the Web as a separate, fundamentally different functional area than the more traditional forms of outreach. Although the Web is a new technology for most non-profits, strategy expert Michael Porter notes that the Internet is essentially "an enabling technology—a powerful set of tools that can be used, wisely or unwisely, in almost any industry and as part of almost any strategy."[12]

Rather than an independent functional silo, the Web is a technology with the potential to leverage efforts across departments and functional areas. When it comes to the Internet, nonprofits must focus not on how to develop an Internet strategy, but on how to integrate the Internet as part of an organizational strategy.

THE FUNDAMENTALS OF STRATEGY

In order to develop a strategy that served the symphony as a whole, Jane looked to the board. They had a number of strong ideas to begin with, and their role as a governing body could help them understand the wants and needs of departments throughout the organization, not just those of her development office. Although the different offices within the symphony rarely worked together, the board assembled a cross-functional team including members from every department: ticketing, operations, administration, and marketing, as well as Jane's development team. While brainstorming ideas at their first meeting, the strategy team realized that a true organizational strategy would reach across all functional areas. A strategy that leveraged the Internet would benefit them all.

From an organizational standpoint, more important than leading-edge technology or the number of Web visitors is the degree to which online activities complement and communicate other activities within the organization. Strategies are effective when they create a synergy between activities to provide specific and valuable services to constituents—a compelling reason for donor interest, support, and ongoing loyalty.[13]

As seen in Exhibit 2.1, strategy begins and ends with the organizational mission—every nonprofit's reason for being. The mission determines the divisional goals that, in turn, determine the coordinated constituent-centric activities that provide information to and gather support from donors—the foundation of fundraising and relationship building. The impact of executing strategy-driven, constituent-centric activities is twofold:

1. Support-gathering activities fulfill the mission.
2. The results of the activities provide the feedback necessary to making informed decisions about divisional goals and objectives.

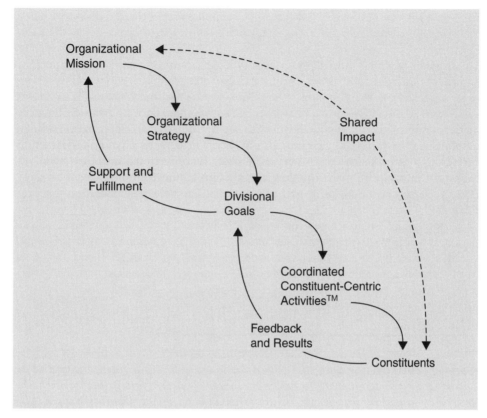

EXHIBIT 2.1 The Waterfall Strategy Model

Source: © 2004 Blackbaud, Inc. All rights reserved.

Because every nonprofit is different—with a specific mission, goals, resources, and constituencies—there is no one strategy that will work for all organizations. The degree to which a strategy is unique sets an organization apart by providing key differentiation from similar and potentially competing organizations. In other words, the unique fit of a strategy to an organization is essential to its success. On the most fundamental level, this involves the consideration of the specific mission, goals and objectives, and constituency of an organization.

MISSION, OBJECTIVES, AND ACTIVITIES

Each department was conducting activities critical to the symphony's mission: "to enrich the cultural life of the region by presenting a diverse range of artistically superior performances." Fulfilling this mission required a number of activities and programs. Marketing promoted the world-class performers featured at the symphony, primarily through advertising and events. The operations team managed the complexities of ticketing and volunteer management—both mission-critical activities. Development was responsible for raising the funds necessary to bringing in quality talent—a task accomplished primarily through an annual benefit concert and direct mail. Together, the strategy team brainstormed about how they could use the Internet to enhance each of these mission-critical activities or carry them out more efficiently.

Strategic planning should always begin with organizational mission—the purpose and reason for being of every nonprofit. *Mission* dictates the activities and programs of an organization, both on- and offline. Mission clarifies the "business" a nonprofit is in—that is, the scope of what an organization wants to accomplish—and strategy determines the activities that will be used to support the mission. Some organizational missions require promoting awareness, providing services, conducting programs, or carrying out other activities. Properly deploying the Internet requires viewing an organization holistically, with fulfilling the mission as the paramount goal of every activity, department, and program. Mission articulates the *what*; strategy provides the *how*.

Additionally, every activity should be accompanied by clear, quantifiable objectives to measure the relative success of efforts, as well as to demonstrate return on investment. Developing a strategy is often the ideal time to revisit goals and objectives to ensure they are still timely, accurate, and relevant to the mission.

CONSTITUENCY

As the strategy team brainstormed, they realized all of their ideas had one thing in common—the involvement of the patrons, donors, volunteers, members, and other constituents who supported the symphony. Internally, the strategy had to serve the symphony's mission. But, it also had to serve an external audience—the wants and needs of the people most important to the organization.

Nonprofits must identify and respond to the wants and needs of constituents in order to build and sustain a loyal donor base. Just as with direct mail, operational activity, marketing, or any other offline activity, Web presence must closely match constituent needs, and building an effective strategy requires knowing and understanding the values, attitudes, and behaviors of constituents in order to tailor Web content and services. Information must be relevant and timely, services must be useful, and the overall experience must be user-friendly and valuable. When it comes to relationship building, organizations must conduct coordinated, constituent-centric activities in order to attract and maintain the attention and support of the public. Having a Web site that lacks timely and interesting content or helpful services, for instance, will discourage visitors from returning.

Of course, these elements are both interdependent and subject to change, making strategy a living, constantly evolving process. To be effective, the use of technology must be revisited from time to time as the activities evolve to ensure all aspects of the organizational strategy are being supported. The impact the Internet will have on fundraising and the nonprofit community is far from certain, and nonprofits will need to adapt their strategy to take advantage of ever-improving technology and online marketing practices. The process of crafting a strategy is often iterative. The results and feedback from strategically planned activities inform and drive decision-making going forward, a self-tuning approach that vastly increases results over time.

APPLYING STRATEGY—SAMPLE CASE

After assessing the symphony's mission, the activities of each department and the needs of their constituents, the team began drafting a strategy. From a strategic standpoint, making decisions regarding the board's suggestions was much easier.

The team recognized two primary objectives for the symphony: optimizing internal business processes and conducting bidirectional communication with constituents. After identifying these objectives, they could focus on how to use the Internet to support, expand, and deepen the symphony's existing mission-critical activities.

Fundraising was integral to the sustainability of the symphony's operations and was one of the initial reasons for investing in a Web site. Accepting online donations would be convenient and easy to use for donors and could automate gift entry and processing, reducing the burden of administration and freeing staff to work on more valuable activities. Additionally, e-mail campaigns could complement the symphony's successful direct mail efforts. The strategy team discussed these options with the board, and everyone agreed they should move forward with these initiatives. Although the symphony held a silent auction fundraiser every year the team realized that online auctions were beyond the scope of the symphony's mission.

A significant portion of the symphony's constituent-facing activities took place through the ticketing department, and the Web offered a number of opportunities to improve service and increase value to the public. Online ticketing would make attending performances more convenient, and online customer service features—including a "Contact Us" Web form and a list of FAQs—could help the symphony better serve patrons while reducing the number of incoming calls. These options could provide convenient alternatives for visitors in addition to the traditional ways of contacting the symphony.

The marketing department began a publicity drive that would take advantage of the inherent benefits of Internet communications. They added the symphony's Web address to all of its printed materials to drive traffic to the site and began publishing high-quality, Web-only content to keep site content fresh and encourage first-time visitors to return to the site. Rather than investing in more graphics and animation for the site, the team decided to repurpose print content for the Web—an approach that would save time and money, as well as provide an ongoing resource for people interested in the symphony and its performers. Although having online communities and Web casts of performances were initially interesting ideas, these ideas failed to hold up under closer strategic scrutiny. The team decided that the time and resources required to build these features would be better spent elsewhere. However, the team agreed to reconsider these ideas in the future when revisiting their strategy.

The marketing and development teams also worked together to take advantage of the Web for a benefit concert with the symphony's jazz quartet at a popular local venue. The jazz quartet had broad appeal and, historically, jazz events had been one of the symphony's top fundraisers. This year, the symphony wanted to expand the event to include an even broader audience. The strategy team recognized that the Internet—with more efficient processing, 24/7 availability, and appeal to a younger demographic—could potentially help to achieve this objective.

In order to reach a broad demographic, the symphony promoted the concert through partnerships with local rock and popular radio stations. In addition to of-

fering tickets through the symphony's traditional ticketing office, the symphony began offering tickets online. Each radio advertisement mentioned the symphony's Web address and encouraged people to buy tickets and donate online. To further encourage online traffic, the symphony offered two-for-one coupons for online ticket buyers. Additionally, demographic information from online donations and ticket purchases—including e-mail addresses—was captured and logged into the donor database for use in future e-mail campaigns.

The initial results from the benefit concert were very encouraging—the broad appeal of the quartet combined with the reach of popular radio stations drew a record crowd, as well as provided a great jump start for the Web site and a substantial pool of e-mail addresses for future communications. The key to this success was the strategy team's recognition that e-mail functionality, e-ticketing, and Web-based communication and support could not replace their traditional offline counterparts. Executing the strategy improved the results of these activities and deepened value to constituents—a key to any successful strategy.

CONCLUSION

The preceding case study, although fictitious, illustrates the leveraging power of the Internet as a tool to support organizational strategy—from optimizing ticket sales and improving the value of customer service to expanding marketing efforts and deepening constituent interaction.

Jane's success derived from the articulation of an organizational strategy and the subsequent implementation of appropriate goals and activities. In regard to Internet, most organizations are little different than Jane's, and nonprofits that want to benefit from the advantages of the Internet must first create a strategy.

ABOUT THE AUTHOR

Anthony J. Powell, CFRE, ePMT, vice president of consulting services, is responsible for Blackbaud's 160-employee consulting and technical services division. Tony joined Blackbaud in 1998 as a fundraising system consultant and has helped consulting services mature into one of the company's fastest-growing divisions.

Before joining Blackbaud, Tony spent 10 years in the nonprofit sector building his expertise in business process improvement, prospect moves management, and major gift solicitations as a major gifts officer at the Smithsonian Institution, assistant vice president for the Greater Baltimore Medical Center Foundation, and VP and COO for The Wesbury Foundation.

Tony is a graduate of Allegheny College, where he began his fundraising career as assistant director of the Annual Fund. A five-time CASE Faculty All Star, Tony is a frequent speaker at national and international industry conferences. You can e-mail Tony at tony.powell@blackbaud.com.

ENDNOTES

1. Fundraising is only one way in which nonprofits can use the Web. Many nonprofits have used the Internet to automate labor-intensive back office tasks through automatic inventory control, services management and similar tools. While constituent engagement has been the focus of much publicity surrounding the Internet, internal optimization has historically demonstrated lasting results for both businesses and nonprofits. A discussion of the benefits inherent to business-to-business (B2B) applications of the Internet, however, is beyond the scope of this book.
2. Nicole Wallace, "Online Donations Make Gains," *The Chronicle of Philanthropy* (June 12, 2003).
3. Nicole Wallace, "Charities Tally Year-End Online Gifts," *The Chronicle of Philanthropy* (January 21, 2003).
4. *NonProfit* Times study, February 17, 2004. Available online at *http://www.nptimes.com/ enews/Feb04/news/news-0204_3.html*.
5. *www.redcross.org.*
6. Nicole Wallace, "Charities Tally Year-End Online Gifts," *The Chronicle of Philanthropy* (January 21, 2003).
7. *www.heifer.org.*
8. Reed Abelson, "Business to Business: Charities See Web's Potential, but Are Finding It Hard to Afford," *The New York Times* (29 March 2000), Section H, p. 30.
9. *www.virtualpromise.net.*
10. Blackbaud Consulting Services 2003 study.
11. Michael E. Porter, "What is Strategy?" *Harvard Business Review* (November–December 1996), 70.
12. Michael E. Porter, "Strategy and the Internet," *Harvard Business Review* (March 2001), 64.
13. Michael E. Porter, "What Is Strategy?" *Harvard Business Review* (November-December 1996), 64–68.

CHAPTER 3

Multichannel Marketing

Marcelo Iñarra Iraegui, ePMT
Greenpeace International

Human beings use different kinds of thought mechanisms to understand different kinds of situations.

MARKETING WITH A CHEF'S HELP

Think about your favorite dish for a few seconds. Ready? Now think about the ingredients that make this dish so special for you—its unique taste, the aroma and special texture, the mixture of colors, or the sound it makes while cooking. This exercise will surely have whetted your appetite, but restrain your desires to rush off to your favorite restaurant. We are here to discuss how marketing will better your fundraising program by using the different offline media integrated with the online world. So let's go back to the kitchen. As I can't make an analysis of your favorite dish, I'll do so for mine.

Spaghetti with Seafood Sauce

What makes this dish so special for me? The texture of freshly made spaghetti, the tomato sauce with red crayfish, mixed with fresh green herbs, and the unique aroma of chopped garlic in olive oil all produce expectations and anticipation of an unmistakable taste. This dish awakes all my senses, and this synergy of sensations makes it my chosen dish from among hundreds. This dish naturally uses multichannel marketing.

As fundraisers, we need to use multichannel marketing to combine traditional media with the Internet, just as a chef mixes ingredients with artistic flair and knowledge to create our favorite dish.

Multichannel marketing grew on a worldwide scale in the commercial sector during the 1990s, but without a doubt, this great revolution is a result of the incorporation of the Internet as a channel that modified the way of understanding and doing business. Today, it seems impossible for a company not to plan a sales campaign in an integrated online/offline way, whether we are talking about a mass consumer product such as soap powder, or a luxury item such as the most expensive car in the world. This is a tremendous opportunity for the nonprofit sector, because there aren't many such organizations using the mass media or more segmented media such as direct mailing or telephone fundraising with an online component.

A CHEF IN A VIRGIN LAND

I started as fundraising director for Greenpeace Argentina in 1995. Argentina was then an almost virgin market in professional fundraising, with all the advantages, challenges, and inconveniences that a new market presents. Instead of copying the established models, we ran multiple tests to find out which was the most appropriate form of media for Greenpeace Argentina. We incorporated integration of online media in 1996. We had our first donor through our Web page *www.greenpeace.org.ar* in the same year. Our Web site has subsequently transformed itself into a response channel whereby a third of new donors join Greenpeace Argentina (see Exhibit 3.1).

The Greenpeace Argentina case began to be published and presented in the main international conferences, without our seeking this out, because of the diverse and successful strategies we have been working with since the middle of the 1990s.

Following Jules Verne's thought that "by knowing your village you will know the world," we systemized the general teachings of the "Seven Elastic Rules of Online Fundraising":

1. Change organizational culture, or how to make bytes an integral part of your existence.
2. Use the Web site as a response channel.
3. Develop a strong e-mail fundraising program.

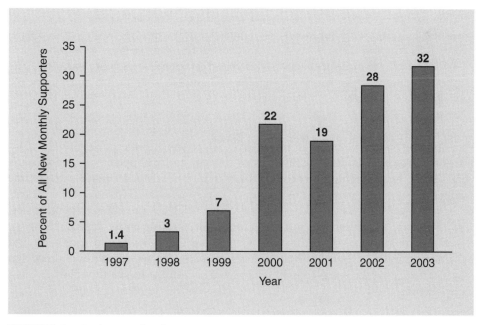

EXHIBIT 3.1   Evolution of Online Donors

Source: Greenpeace.org.ar

4. Integrate online and offline media.
5. Communicate from your Web site the opportunity to "live" the experience of being part of your organization.
6. Use online media to foster the relationship with donors.
7. Test. The history of online fundraising is being written and boundless discoveries are there to be made.

In this chapter, we shall be looking in detail at some of these rules, relevant to the theme of this chapter.

KNOCKING DOWN WALLS

Human beings use different kinds of thought mechanisms to understand different kinds of situations. One such mechanism is separating a complex problem into its distinctive parts in order to understand them. By analyzing these parts, we can understand the whole.

As fundraisers, we often propose strategies that employ this thought mechanism, but sometimes we get stuck in the middle of this process without reintegrating each component into the whole. This is one of the consequences of how some organizations structure their fundraising department, somewhat like a silo. They have an area of direct mail, another of telemarketing, another of major donors and yet another of bequests, and there is a very low level of integration between the divisions.

This management structure was carried into fundraising, using only one medium, without at least testing the different integration possibilities with one or more media. The Internet has done more than just knocked on fundraising's door, however; it has the tools to demolish walls!

The online strategy is a transversal component that cuts across all areas and poses a big challenge to these areas. A challenge that is even more complex in big organizations where structures are more specialized resulting in more isolation.

The solution to these problems is varied and different for each organization. The important thing is to knock down these walls, and the entire team must share the same motivation to reach a common goal.

Integrating Traditional Media with Online Media

Integrating the Internet into the fundraising strategy has to happen in the fundraiser's head. This integration has more to do with a change of attitude toward using online media than massive investment of resources. It is fundamental to break down resistance, such as "This won't work," "It's not for us," "Things are different in our country," and many other barriers and fears, too numerous to mention here.

There are hundreds of reasons in this book, backed up with solid arguments and evidence, that prove that the Internet has arrived in the world of philanthropy to stay. Strategically, the integration of offline media with the Internet involves two big components:

1. Using the Web site as a channel where donors respond to campaigns
2. Providing the opportunity to consolidate the reasons why people should support our organization, and acting as the point of "closing" for appeals

Going in through the Screen

To be able to use your Web site as a response channel, it is advisable to ask yourself some questions:

- How would I respond to being asked for a donation?
- What channel would I use to respond?
- Would I prefer to respond by telephone?
- Would I prefer to send a fax?
- Would I like to fill in a coupon to be sent by mail?
- Would I want to make my donation online using a Web site?

In my experience of working on a global level, from the 1990s up to now, having contact with fundraising professionals from all over the world, I have seen a strong and growing trend in the use of online media as a response channel.

In fundraising programs where a choice of options to make donation is given, including online, there has been a significant increase in the number of people who respond via the Internet, in detriment to traditional channels, such as by post, fax, or telephone.

This trend will continue to rise over the next several years. Demographic changes have shifted the power to kids—who are practically born with a PC in their crib. These will be the core targets of most organizations (see Exhibit 3.2).

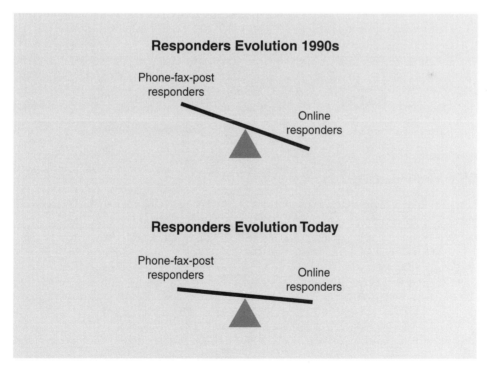

EXHIBIT 3.2　Tracking Core Targets

Source: Greenpeace Argentina

Let's analyze a case from a quantitative point of view.

In Greenpeace Argentina's January 2000 multimedia campaign (see Exhibit 3.3) against whaling in the Antarctic, 25 percent of total supporters who responded preferred to make their donation via our Web site, even though our messages were transmitted from various offline media such as television, radio, billboards, and press ads, among others. Thus, 75 percent of donors responded through *offline* channels, such as telephone, fax, or mail.

The results obtained in that campaign has established guidelines and standards that are still used today. Some results obtained were as follows: 21 percent of total donors who saw a 36-second television spot preferred to join through our Web site, and the most surprising, 34 percent of donors who heard our message by radio joined via the Web site.

Let's analyze this campaign from the viewpoint of online donors. What media had more influence on these donors? Was it the offline ones, such as a 36-second TV spot, newspapers, magazine and posters advertisement, those by radio, or the online ones with an intensive banner campaign in the main portals? Which ones would you bet on? If you bet on the offlines—then you've won. Of total online donors, 67 percent had seen our appeal for donation through the offline medias. The other 33 percent responded to our intensive banner and article campaign with Web site links. This is not a surprising result given that we spend most of our lives living our "material world" offline.

Let's look at what these *online donors* thought about their online experience. From a qualitative point of view, it is interesting to note the comments of some of these donors, who later formed part of a focus group on satisfaction. Some of their com-

APPEAL	Response Channel %	
	Online	Offline
TV spot	21	79
Web + Portals + Banners	73	27
Press ads	17	83
Radio	34	66
Billboards	26	74
PR	17	83
Newspapers and magazine inside	62	38
Inserts	16	84
Free postcards	5	95
Spontaneous	0	100
TOTAL	25	75

EXHIBIT 3.3 Whaling Campaign 2000—General Results

Source: Greenpeace Argentina

ments, in relation to the response channel, were surprising: "It is so easy, you just fill in the form on the site and you donate right away." "It was the only way to join. If it hadn't been so simple, I would have never joined."

This research proves that they would not have made their donations if there hadn't been the option of donating via our Web site. This result is also backed up by our daily experience in our Supporter Service Area.

Another fundamental reason to integrate your Web site as a response channel is that it allows you to attend to hundreds of requests per second. This makes any campaign that uses a mass-media strategy such as DRTV—Direct Response Television— a natural partner to online response mechanisms.

Television spots generate a huge volume of "calls/hits/requests" in the first few seconds of an appeal, be this a 60-second spot or a telethon of various hours. People respond impulsively and immediately. A Web site allows you to process a volume of transaction that is impossible for any traditional call center to attend to in the same space and time.

The UK Comic Relief Case, *www.comicrelief.com* shows that in their 2002 yearly telethon, they succeeded in processing 47,000 online transactions between 9:30 P.M. and 10:30 P.M.

That is 783 per minute!

Using your Web site as a response channel, when responding to offline medias, also has other fundamental attributes. It is open 24 hours, 365 days a year. This advantage was fully utilized in a 2003 Pan Regional Greenpeace International campaign covering 23 Latin American countries, that I ran, combining the use of satellite television and the Internet as the response channels, running a series of messages on a rotative basis, covering the different time zones and effective use of nighttime and early hours.

One remarkable fact is that online donations have a higher average than those made offline. In the case of one-off gifts, online donations have been 50 percent more than offline, as in the September 2001 Telethon case, "America: tribute to heroes," where average offline gifts were $100 (U.S. dollars), while online gifts were $150.

In my experience of working with monthly and automatic donations, online donations are between 10 percent and 20 percent more than offline.

Welcome to . . .

The second strategic component in the integration of media is the possibility to consolidate the reasons why people should support our organization. Our Web site has the job of "closing" our offline request.

The Internet offers tools that fundraisers have dreamed about: to be able to penetrate the mind, inspire, and seduce people into how worthy it is to support our cause. A Web site can use almost all the creative resources of other mass media, amply surpassing their normal effectiveness when used interactively.

Let's look at some examples: A direct-mail pack can be made more powerful by being combined with an unforgettable online experience. The contents of a press ad, or a radio or television spot can be amplified to a degree that is impossible to communicate on a page or otherwise in a few seconds.

There is also one vital point to be noted. A Web site offers the chance to start a dialogue that can last for life. If we invite visitors to the site to leave their e-mail address, we will have found a channel of communication at a cost per contact, which was impossible a few years ago.

You only have to visit the American Red Cross's site *http://www.redcross.org/* in order to see effective use of these resources. The Red Cross has been a pioneering organization in the effective use of communication in emergencies, and likewise in the functionality of their site, orientated toward maximizing the flow of visitors to their different donation pages.

Apart from far outweighing the communication potential of offline medias, the Internet has made the possibility of a world of new offers, relevant to the needs and requests of prospective new members a reality. Sites that offer their donors "special services" through a section accessible to members only include Greenpeace Argentina and Greenpeace Brazil—*www.greenpeace.org.ar* and *www.greenpeace.org.br*.

Members can exchange personal details, take part in chats, read the electronic version of our newsletter, make contact with other supporters in our supporter area in real time, and download screensavers, among other benefits, in the members-only section.

The United Kingdom's Royal Society for the Protection of Birds (*www.rspb.org.uk*) attracts the attention of visitors to its site by offering what birdwatchers most want: being able to see a bird in its nest in real time through a Web cam, from the comfort of their own home.

There are many good examples of organizations providing expected services, such as the possibility of participating, electronic gifts, and other resources for donors or prospective donors. This makes an organization's proposal attractive.

Integration and Media Planning

Media planning must follow a horizontal management strategy, a concept presented by Tim Matthews, of the Pilgrim Communications, Australia, at the 2003 International Fundraising Conference in Holland. This concept has helped me to systemize a concept I have used for years, based on incorporating the online response channel by integrating all our offline communication—DRTV, direct mail, radio, press ads, billboards, free post cards, and all other media that can include a mechanism of direct response.

Planning should also include a vertical management strategy, which integrates all communication with our donors, once they have become members.

We have tested the most diverse media in Argentina, with results on differing levels (see Exhibit 3.4). However, it is the synergy created among the different channels that maximizes the results and multiplies return on investment.

When planning has been adequate for our target, reports on campaigns have shown that donors had seen our campaign in more than one media. In response to open questions online, researching how donors had arrived at our site, many answered that they "had seen our campaign on TV, radio and on billboards," or simply that they "had seen them everywhere."

Although integration of all media is fundamental in planning, I want to concentrate on three only: DRTV, radio, and direct mail.

DRTV

Television is, without a doubt, the engine that drives any multimedia campaign. It generates a high volume of leads and consequently a high volume of online donors. The

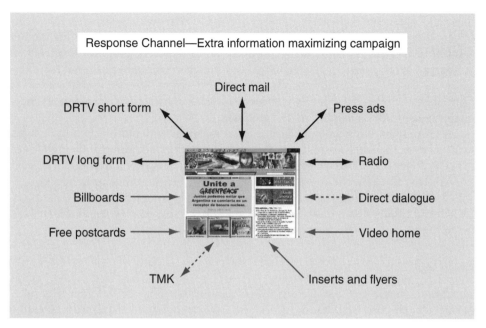

EXHIBIT 3.4   Recruitment Integration Map

Source: Greenpeace Argentina

cost of production and publicity campaigns has to be carefully studied, depending on the country where the campaign is developed.

In the United States, Canada, and many Latin American countries, environmental and social organizations that transmit DRTV program format longer than an hour, with spots of 60 seconds or less, have succeeded in increasing their online responses in recent years.

In Greenpeace Argentina, average response from DRTV programs of half an hour format is between 15 percent and 20 percent of total monthly donors per transmission, with an average gift of more than 10 percent to 20 percent higher than that of an offline donation.

Radio Days

At the end of the twentieth century, radio was the Cinderella of media planning. However, it now has a place of prominence thanks to the Internet, transforming itself into an effective tool. It is a passive medium, which permits the doing of more than one activity at the same time. Millions of people work at their computer while listening to the radio, or listen to their favorite radio program at home via the Internet, thanks to wireless connections or broadband.

It is thus not surprising that there is a growing use of radio–Internet interactive communication between program presenters and their listeners. Listeners who usually make their comments by telephone are now communicating more and more by e-mail.

There are at least two ways to use radio: the traditional radio spot and interviews. The use of radio spot in our campaign allows us to divide the audience into segments, thus making our campaign more cost effective. A PR campaign based on live interviews of people from our organization has given very good results. The explicit mention of an offer to visit our Web site is still not seen as a commercial plug. If the offer is an attractive one, it generates a large number of hits. It is recommended that the interviewee be well prepared with a script, so that she doesn't improvise at the moment of mentioning the offer. This strategy can also be used on television, although the chances of getting a live transmission are less frequent.

Radio audience is segmented into sectors, so you have to plan very carefully with many stations to make sure that you are appealing to the right group at the right time, in order to achieve a high volume of responses.

In many countries it is possible to get PSAs (public service announcements), which are easier to place on radio than on more competitive medias such as television. The cost of production and transmission in radio are usually low, and PSAs make it much lower, with a consequential higher return on investment.

Direct Mail

Integration with direct mail has degrees of significance that are different from integration with the media previously mentioned. Direct mail is not a mass media like radio or television. Its integration follows the same basic principles for online/offline integration, which is by using the online channel as a response and closing channel. However, e-mail enables direct mail to take on a much stronger role.

A method that I have used with success is shown in Exhibit 3.5. In December 2000, we sent a direct mail requesting an upgrade in monthly donations, taking advantage of the presence of our ship *MV Artic Sunrise* in Argentina to go on a tour to stop pollution. The direct mail package was aimed at current supporters who we were asking to increase their monthly donation. The pack included traditional response mechanisms, to which we added a special URL, where supporters could increase their donations with only two or three clicks, and without having to give sensitive information such as credit card number. Response via our Web site was about 15 percent. Later we sent a very simple and emotive follow-up e-mail in .txt format, using the successes achieved during our tour in defense of the environment, aimed at donors who gave their e-mail address (about 40 percent of base total). The response rate to this e-mail was 4 percent, and return on investment (ROI) was 1:1,240 in the first year, taking into account that they were monthly and automatic donations.

Hundreds of integration combinations are possible with direct mail and the Internet. However, it is indispensable that advance work be done to build a database of e-mail addresses. Clear targets should be set about the number of e-mail addresses to be gathered, both in direct marketing campaigns and in the dealings in the supporter service area. This will yield good short-term results in recruiting new donors and reducing the attrition rates.

ONE WAY OR TWO WAYS

We always think about the relationship between the online and offline worlds from a one-directional point of view—from outside offline to inside online. There are good examples of how online can, for example, give added value to our offline activities.

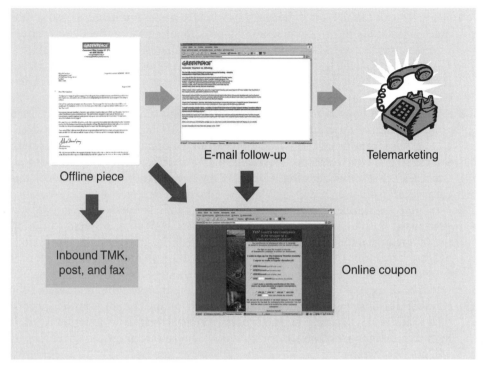

EXHIBIT 3.5 Basic Direct Mail Integration Chart

Source: Greenpeace Argentina

Spanish and Latin American social and environmental organizations are taking advantage of the possibility of building telemarketing base from their Web site. The response from outbound telemarketing continues to match hot list rates.

Various Greenpeace offices in Latin America are successfully implementing *Call Me Button* in their online donation Web pages. Another online/offline case is *www.moveon.org*, a U.S. political action organization that tries to permanently mobilize people from its Web site. One of its more creative proposals has been the launching of a competition for ideas for TV publicity called "Bush in 30 seconds," with the prize being the broadcast of the ad as a part of its campaign. This is an excellent example of an online promotion having a strong impact on offline media.

CREATIVITY FOR BETTER RESULTS

Creativity is a key element in integration. What follows are some common rules for the development of a multimedia campaign, which integrates the online component.

- *Be coherent in your online and offline communications.* The communication design should be coherent in its design of the distinctive online and offline parts such as the Web site or the e-mail. This will empower the synergy between both media, working to the advantage of our message.

- *The URL is a fundamental part of the publicity piece, not just a dressing.* It is much more common to commission advertisement agencies. Publicity creators have the pre-conceived idea that the response mechanism dirties their creativity. But don't be fooled! Response rates are directly proportional to the amount of time that our URL stays on screen, or how much the offer to visit our Web site is emphasized.
- *A URL should be easy to remember.* This seems an obvious point, but it often happens that fundraisers do not define a campaign 100 percent because they don't have 100 percent power. It is not unusual for an organization to appear with a URL such as *www.savetheforestsandseasofcostarica.org*. It is advisable to always ask oneself this question: Can I use my organization's main URL for this campaign?
- *Long live the simple, creative, and direct site!* Web site designers who are not specialized in fundraising and interactive marketing Web pages tend to put all the creativity that they can't use with commercial clients into the designing of non-profit organizations' Web sites. Creative briefs must follow a clear line, relevant to objectives. The creativity of the site must be aimed toward the "closing" of our appeal, using all interactive resources to make the site solid, honest, and the simplest possible, to enable donors to get to the online coupons. In the spirit of "All roads lead to Rome," for fundraisers, Rome is the online donation form! If high-tech designs are too flashy or do not appeal to the target audience, visitors will go elsewhere.
- *Use digital bridges.* This might be the most advisable of the general rules, but don't forget the basis of fundraising. The heartbeat of an organization depends on the generosity of its donors, despite us being connected by a digital bridge.

DONOR RELATIONSHIP ONLINE: EFFICIENT, FAST, AND CHEAP

A new chapter on integration of online and offline media opens when donors join our organization. Online donors who join via our Web site are more anxious to receive online proposals.

In my experience, the basic rule for cultivating online relationships with these donors is to incorporate online communication tools into the donor relationship cycle, in a way that will create an integrated message beyond the medium being used.

Exhibit 3.6 shows a practical example that Greenpeace Argentina has been using for many years. The photo shows a protest against GM foods. It was necessary to count on volunteers' participation in order to have this protest. We counted on a wide group of donors who had expressed their willingness to participate.

But let's retract a bit. These people had already learned about the issue and arguments of this campaign through articles published in our newsletter, where they were invited to visit our Web site to get more information and take part in cyberactions. A few days before the protest, we invited them to attend via e-mail, asking them to confirm their participation. In that e-mail we communicated to them that if they wanted to get more information about the protest, they should enter the donor space in the site, or extranet, which they could access by using the username and password sent to them in the welcome mail.

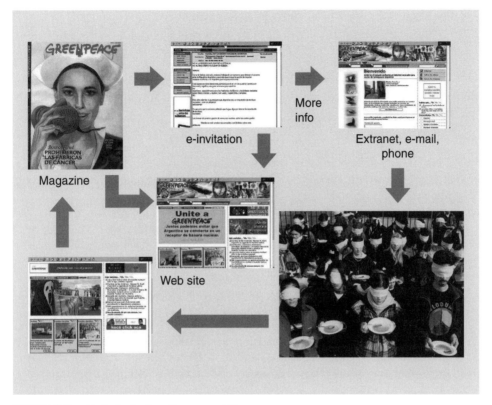

EXHIBIT 3.6 Cycle in Action: Protest and Events

Source: Greenpeace Argentina

The group of donor activists who responded to this request participated en mass in the protest. The cycle continues when we offer each donor an invitation card during the protest—and, for that matter, during any other event—which allows him or her to download a digital photograph of themselves as a reminder of their participation in the event, which they will find in a photo album located in our member section. A photo of this group is published in the next newsletter, as a testament of their participation, and also beginning a new cycle.

In certain events, the photo download rate has surpassed 50 percent of the number of participants. This in itself is an interesting and relevant point.

CONCLUSION

Why integrate online and offline medias? Because they offer us many of the things fundraisers love, such as:

- Increasing our return on investment
- Increasing the rate of response

- Establishing stronger links with our organization
- Having a low-cost channel of communication with our donors in the palm of our hand

Going back to my favorite dish mentioned at the beginning of this chapter, I hope this chapter has whetted your appetite for preparing your future campaign in a manner that integrates traditional with the new medias.

Bon appetite!

ABOUT THE AUTHOR

Marcelo Iñarra Iraegui, ePMT, is an International Fundraising Manager at Greenpeace International, and has 18 years of experience in the nonprofit sector.

Marcelo was fundraising director in Greenpeace in Argentina where he has developed a very successful fundraising program combining direct marketing and online fundraising. Marcelo was a pioneer in online fundraising worldwide getting his first donation online in 1996.

He lectures in the United States, Europe, and Latin America about fundraising. Marcelo is also a board member of AEDROS, the Argentinean Association of Fundraising Executives, and is an ePhilanthropy master trainer of the e-Philanthropy Foundation. From 2004, he is also working as international consultant. You can e-mail Marcelo at Miniarra@ar.greenpeace.org.

CHAPTER 4

Staffing ePhilanthropy

Tim Mills-Groninger
IT Resource Center

Having a plan that identifies communications, development, and technology goals is critical.

Wanted: ePhilanthropy director. Nonprofit organization seeks a qualified ePhilanthropy director to spearhead online fundraising, advocacy, marketing and communications efforts. Successful candidate will possess the technical skills of a Vint Cerf or Bill Gates, the business insight of Warren Buffett or Jack Welch, and the commitment to social justice and values of Mahatma Gandhi or Mother Theresa. Duties include all aspects of planning, implementing, delivering, and evaluating income-producing and mindshare-improvement services. Early stages will involve fundraising for start-up funds and developing a comprehensive business plan. Pay in low to mid twenties, depending on experience.

While a little fanciful, the preceding job advertisement is not as far-fetched as you might think. Depending on the size of the organization, the executive director, development director, or human resource department might have an ePhilanthropy plan in hand when they write a job description like this. Without truly understanding the work to be done, they will assemble a list of attributes on paper and hope for the best. In this chapter, we will take a broader and, hopefully, more realistic look at staffing an ePhilanthropy effort and examine some common problems in attracting and keeping the right people for the job.

HAVING THE RIGHT FOUNDATION

Before you start hiring, it is necessary to know what that person (or those people) is (are) going to do. Our assumption is that you will have carefully read the rest of the book and possess some idea of the media and messages you plan to use, the audience you hope to engage, and the actions you want them to take. To simplify matters a bit, we will break the ePhilanthropy plan into three broad areas: development, communications, and technology. Although responsibility can shift between these departments, and new areas might be added, these three tend to cover the major tasks you will need to staff in your overall effort.

Breaking your ePhilanthropy plan into smaller sections mirrors the departmental structure of many nonprofits and helps clarify reporting and support functions. The key requirements of each type of plan are as follows.

Development Plan

The *development plan,* sometimes called the *institutional advancement plan,* describes the function, methods, and goals of the fundraising effort. Knowing both the direction of the fundraising effort and the frequency and types of transactions allows you to identify where human intervention—and staff time—should be allotted.

To better organize the work, many development offices are divided into two divisions: fundraising and advancement services. The fundraising part of the shop directs the donor-facing activities such as developing the message, targeting different segments, and planning the types of appeals and actions most compelling to donors. This is what most people think about when they hear the word *fundraising.*

The advancement services division addresses the "back of the shop" side of fundraising. *implements* the plans developed by the fundraising side. Activities (and often job titles) include gift processing, prospect research, report writing, volunteer tracking, database maintenance, and related tasks. Even the smallest fundraising office will have advancement services tasks, even if the tasks are being performed by fundraisers.

Communications and Marketing Plan

Admittedly, separating communications from development can be difficult. We recommend treating them as distinct activities when planning for staff allocations. Based on the size and independence of the effort, along with other organizational concerns, we give them a distinct place in the agency hierarchy.

Your communications plan can address multiple messages and channels. In addition to good writing skills, you will have to deploy and manage graphic design, layout, image editing, and other technical activities.

Likewise, in addition to packaging message content (whether it is in print, Web pages, e-mail messages, or faxes), communications staff often take responsibility for delivering them.

Technology Plan

Whether it is its own department or a component of another division, *information services (IS)* is going to play a significant role in supporting ePhilanthropy. The technology plan is the *de facto* charter for IS. In addition to addressing core infrastructure and support issues for your agency in general, as well as the specific needs of your ePhilanthropy effort, a good technology plan effectively addresses the people side of the equation. This encompasses mundane tasks of unpacking desktops and connecting them to the network as well as the more subtle needs of managing work groups, the applications and the files staff need to do their work.

Staffing infrastructure support is more complex than for development and communications. Although the work product, if not the results, of communications and development staff can be quantified—new content created, gifts processed—the most efficient infrastructure is never seen. A good network is just there when you connect. Developing the right staff size to effectively create infrastructure support is a challenge: understaffing will eventually cause problems as software bugs combine with hardware failures in a cascade that shuts the system down for long periods. Inversely, over-staffing wastes money that could be better spent on mission.

It is difficult to determine when a well-functioning system is overstaffed and when levels are appropriate to activity. Similarly, a downsized support effort might function well until failures begin to overwhelm staff skills and time.

THE ISHIKAWA FISHBONE

The *Ishikawa fishbone analysis* is a process design tool that can help you analyze ePhilanthropy procedures and begin identifying staffing needs. Exhibit 4.1 shows the process design of an online registration. It is named after Kaoru Ishikawa (1915–1989), who pioneered quality management processes in Japan. It is often used as a brainstorming tool in solving problems, but it is also useful in micro (analyzing a specific task) and macro (working with a department-level initiative) process design.

Simply put, the fishbone analysis takes a task or activity, such as processing registrations for a benefit dinner, and identifies four primary components—usually method, materials, money, and manpower. (There is a charming tradition of alliteration; the titles and number of ribs can vary according to need.) To create the fishbone, make the task a horizontal line, representing the backbone. From the spine draw two diagonal lines upward and two downward. These are the ribs, and represent the four components. On each rib you can add additional branches representing sub-components.

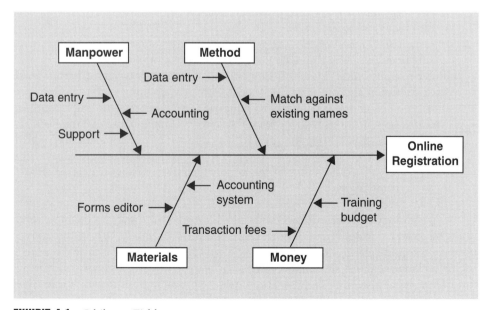

EXHIBIT 4.1   Ishikawa Fishbone

For our event registration example, we can list direct and indirect costs on the money rib—the method will describe the steps that a registration goes through once the user presses *submit* on the Web page. The materials can include the Web and local software applications used in processing the registration. On the people side, we are able to list the steps that require human intervention and the amount of time that each transaction requires. The selection of software might have eliminated the need to type in an attendee's name, but it might still fall to a clever human to make the final determination of who is who. Therefore, determining the need for and level of human intervention must be understood before you start your staffing plan.

Working at the macro level, you will have an idea of where staffing is required (development, communications, or IS) and some estimate of the time involved. At the micro level you can pinpoint the actual business process.

DEPARTMENTS, TEAMS, AND TITLES

Once you have identified staff tasks within development, communications, IS, and possibly other departments, it is time to identify job descriptions and titles. The nonprofit world has a long tradition of elaborate and ambiguous job titles. The technology world is not immune from this affliction.

Keep two things in mind when identifying job descriptions and titles:

1. *Group related tasks together.* In matching related tasks, remember that outputs can be very different from process. For example, in the past, your volunteer recruitment effort may have involved deciphering hand-written interest cards collected at events. The person performing data entry from these cards may have developed super-human powers in handwriting analysis. With online volunteer recruitment, volunteers type their interest information into your system. There is still an important role for interpretation, but the skills, and perhaps the person, are different.
2. *Use established job-title conventions.* New job titles should be consistent with existing positions. Creating a new IS *director's* position—when other staff with similar responsibilities and authority are called managers or coordinators—will create confusion and potential resentment. Similarly, creating an IS assistant's position with power and accountability equal to a program director will have risks. Typically, organizations with more established development and communications programs will have existing job titles such as director of development, major gifts officers, advancement services director, and so on. Technology positions have only recently become requirements in the nonprofit universe, so there are fewer traditions to draw upon.

As technology has become more ingrained into the full range of business functions, the need for technology support has grown proportionally. Where the ratio of technical support staff to PC users used to be 1 to 50, the average is now closer to 1 to 30. Technical support staff maintain the hardware, software, and basic infrastructure. They might also provide basic software support and conduct training sessions for new employees on new and established software programs. On the technology side of the shop, who does what will be determined by project complexity and organizational size. The larger the organization or the ePhilanthropy project, the more specialization is required. With a larger staff, you will need to include more traditional supervision and management.

TECHNOLOGY JOBS

The nonprofit sector has substantial experience when it comes to hiring and managing development and communications staff. For your ePhilanthropy effort, the challenges are on the technology side of the equation. ePhilanthropy is uncharted. Nonprofits can follow established guidelines in the areas of development and communications, but you should expect longer *start-up* time and expense in the technological aspects, and more pitfalls in the *operations* phase as you put your plan into action.

One metaphor we use to distinguish *start-up* from *operations* issues is the hobby of model railroading. This pastime often involves two distinct personality types—some railroaders like to build, others like to operate.

For model railroad *builders*, creating the layout, attaching track, connecting switches and otherwise planning and assembling the components is the attraction. These hobbyists love to solve problems and receive great satisfaction from making their vision a reality. Once in operation, the hobby is not as satisfying, and so the enthusiast begins planning the expansion or redesign of the elaborate diorama. Technicians enamored with the start-up phase are driven in a similar way.

The model railroad *operator* loves to run trains. Once the layout is complete, the operator is attaching engines to cars and starting complex schedules of trains running sophisticated circuits. Operational efficiencies are the primary draw, and the greatest satisfaction comes from making things run well. Likewise, some people are more attracted to making the technological side of the organization run smoothly.

The psychological profile of the model railroader is exaggerated for clarity, but it does exist and is paralleled in the technology world. Understanding this mindset will affect how you hire and keep technical staff. Recognizing the motivations and interests of builders and operators will help you in managing them on an ongoing basis.

Keep in mind that builders tend to gravitate to consulting positions and operators crave administrative jobs. It seems obvious, but because many nonprofit technology staff tend to gravitate into their roles, they might not realize their preferences for a long time. As an ePhilanthropy manager, you may have to intervene when you notice that the network administrator is happy only when replacing the server—or, by contrast, fights every upgrade as being unnecessary.

The practical solution when you have staff in the wrong position is to help builders become more project oriented and to hire additional help for major implementations or upgrades. When hiring new staff, think about the type of personality that would be the best fit, and ask the kinds of questions that help you understand where a candidate would fit in.

Depending on your organization's current infrastructure and the complexity of your ePhilanthropy plan, your staffing plan may require both builders and operators. Typical building chores include server installation and upgrades, network expansion and enhancements, including firewalls, security, and application development. Operations and maintenance chores include keeping those things working smoothly adding and deleting users, running backups and protecting the system from viruses, as well as managing e-mail bounces. Building and operations jobs also extend into the traditional development/advancement services and communications/marketing arenas.

IN-HOUSE VERSUS OUTSOURCING

One serious question to ask is, "How do I hire all of these builders and keep them happy?" The answer is either "Don't," or "Hire on a project basis with the understanding that the employee will move on after completion." This second answers implies that the builder's manager is aware of and is assisting the employee's career path.

Not hiring is synonymous with outsourcing. *Outsourcing* is the practice of contracting with a provider to supply staff and services for a specified business function. Hiring a moving company to relocate file cabinets from one end of your office to the other is an example of outsourcing. You could do the job yourself, but the contractor provides skill and tools that you might not have. Contracting with a janitorial service to empty the wastebaskets and vacuum the floor is also outsourcing. The janitorial service supplies, manages, and pays staff to come to your office and perform a mutually agreed upon set of tasks.

For technology projects that require building or installing new applications and systems, outsourcing can be an attractive option. You are hiring a company (or person) to perform a job that needs to be done only once. Their day-to-day job is to perform the miracles that you will need only occasionally. Operations tasks, like the janitorial service, put the contractor in charge of chores that you and your staff don't have time to do and that don't contribute directly to your mission. The most common task outsourced in an ePhilanthropy effort is in hardware and infrastructure support. Typically, this involves engaging a firm to install, maintain, and replace all desktop and possibly server hardware on a regular basis. Depending on the size of the agency, this can vary from one or two days per week for one person to full-time staff working at your office.

However, there is a dark side to outsourcing. The principal risks are overpaying and losing control. The key element to success here is management involvement and understanding. Overpaying for a system implementation project almost always originates from scope creep—the expansion of the goals of the project beyond the original understanding. Overages in ongoing contracts are defined as paying more for the service than you could hire for and manage on your own.

The best way to manage scope creep is to have negotiated a comprehensive range of work that is measurable against the original plan. From a staffing perspective, it is important to have someone internally who understands the plan, is connected to your agency's mission, and who knows the work being performed. The first two are fairly simple characteristics to look for in developing a successful liaison. Developing staff expertise may seem counterintuitive—why spend time learning what you are paying someone else to do? However, not being able to understand what your agency is buying means that you could be held hostage to a contractor who is not necessarily committed to your best interests.

Similarly, not knowing what an outsourced builder or operator is doing means that you might not have control of the work. Again, the answer is in knowledge. Developing management skills in the business and technology of ePhilanthropy will help you maintain control over operations and make sure the work is connected to your mission. These skills can be gained through hiring the right manager or through developing a learning plan for existing staff. Skill development can originate from traditional sources such as classes and seminars, but it can also be achieved from peer learning, contractors, and expert staff. Most contractors, and indeed regular employees, enjoy teaching their colleagues about their expertise. Make training responsibilities part of all job descriptions.

Contractors and Employees

The further a task is from being essential to the ePhilanthropy project, the more likely it can be outsourced. Hardware maintenance, back-office transaction processing, and other activities are some of these. For some tasks central to the project, potential employees might ask if they can work as contractors. Often, these are people who have learned their skills on the job and are trying to advance their careers by becoming consultants. It can be an attractive arrangement: the bookkeeping of paying a contractor might be easier than issuing a tax receipt to an employee. There is also the perception that a contractor can be terminated more readily. Finally, your staff increases while the official staffing budget stays unchanged.

There is a legal risk to classifying a position as a contract slot instead of as an employee. The test for this focuses mainly on control. When you specify work hours location, and provide close supervision, the position is more likely to resemble that of an employee. However, when contractors supply their own tools (computers, software tools, etc.), provide a product that is either accepted or returned, and determine the manner of work, the position is appropriately classified as contractual.

For smaller ePhilanthropy projects, deciding whether a position is employment based or contractual will not make a great deal of difference. As long as the job description is appropriate to the task and there is adequate management and evaluation of the work, your ePhilanthropy effort will have the human resources necessary for the goals you have set. U.S. law has a slight bias toward classifying jobs as employment based. Employment laws in other countries will vary. In either case, when considering contractors, particularly for ongoing or operations tasks, it is prudent to seek qualified counsel in making the final determination. Remember, it is better to invest time and money up front to make the correct classification than to read about your mistake in the newspaper.

MANAGING

Hiring

Where you advertise depends on the job description. More and more metropolitan areas have nonprofit-focused employment services, both print and Web-based. Advertising your job opening in a nonprofit environment means that you will be more likely to attract applicants who understand the ethos and exigencies of the nonprofit world. EPhilanthropy job descriptions should be consistent with the rest of your agency's positions. The description should indicate the tasks to be performed, physical requirement necessary, and whom the position supervises and reports to.

In terms of physical requirements, many infrastructure support positions will require the ability to lift computers and monitors, as well as crawling around with cables and patch cords. By contrast, gift and payment processing, programming, and copy production may have no physical demands at all. Such positions can be a good way for your agency to increase overall diversity. In addition, staff familiar with adaptive technology, such as screen readers, either through necessity or as an additional skill, can help make your Web and overall communications plan more accessible to all users.

You may not have the background or experience to adequately evaluate a candidate's technical skills during an interview. However, you can ask to see examples of work they accomplished in previous positions. Similarly, asking about technical expertise is an appropriate question when checking references. Finally, you might ask a technically qualified co-worker, friend, or volunteer (ask one of your board members if their organization can loan you someone for final interviews) to sit in on the second interview. When interviewing internal candidates who might not have experience with the selected ePhilanthropy solution, it is important to assess how well they can master new tasks. Indeed, the solutions that you have selected will soon be obsolete, so your entire ePhilanthropy team will need the ability to learn new things and apply them to the goals of the plan.

Keeping Employees Fresh

Lifelong learning is a key objective for all employees in the nonprofit world. In addition to a staff member's capacity to learn and use new ideas and technologies, it is important for the organization to provide learning opportunities. Classroom and online learning events can help keep staff up to date. Many ePhilanthropy vendors provide specific training on their products. Likewise, you can find commercial (and even nonprofit) training on general technologies such as SQL Server or Java. It is much better to provide training to staff and improve their skills than to assume that they can figure it out on their own. Whenever possible, build the training cost for users and administrators into the implementation budget for any ePhilanthropy solutions.

Another way to keep staff fresh is to allow time for them to participate in user groups and peer learning. Having time to question colleagues in the same agency or at different organizations can provide a broad perspective and may introduce new ideas when they are needed. When face-to-face user groups are not practical, there are a number of online communities where staff can communicate with one another and provide a range of problem solving and support activities.

CONCLUSION

Having good people on your ePhilanthropy team puts the soul into your work. The best plan, the most modern software, and state-of-the-art technology are meaningless without people committed to your mission and knowledgeable about the tools. You may apply a combination of approaches—hiring new people, developing talent from within, or engaging contractors—each approach has risks and benefits. Although your ePhilanthropy projects may be bringing new technologies and ideas into your nonprofit or NGO, the best practices of human resource management remain unchanged.

Having a plan that identifies communications, development, and technology goals is critical. The plan might only indicate that a project manager needs to be hired, but it will ultimately outline job responsibilities and tasks that must be accomplished in order for the project to be successful. Those tasks and responsibilities form the basis of the job description and subsequent evaluation of the work performed. The technical skills required this month might be obsolete the next, making each staff member's ability to learn and translate new ideas their most important asset. There will always be challenges in hiring and supervising technical employees, but by focusing on how people fit into the process along with materials and money, you can effectively populate your ePhilanthropy plan.

ABOUT THE AUTHOR

Tim Mills-Groninger is the associate executive director of the IT Resource Center, a 20-year-old Chicago-based nonprofit MSO providing computer planning, assessment, training, and technical support services to the nonprofit and government community. His 25-year career in nonprofit technology has involved numerous teaching, staff, and board positions in local and national initiatives. Among his national roles, he was the chairman of the Technology Resource Consortium during the planning and consolidation process with the Nonprofit Management Association and Support Centers of America into the National Alliance for Nonprofit Management. He was part of the National Strategies for Nonprofit Technology (NSNT) project that became the Nonprofit Technology Enterprise Network (N-TEN). He is a contributing editor to the *NonProfit Times*; and he has been a grant reviewer for the Department of Commerce's TIIAP/TOP program, the Ericsson Erica Awards, and other technology grant programs.

He writes and speaks frequently on nonprofit technology issues with a focus on fundraising databases and their role in improving advancement services. He has recently completed a series of workshops demonstrating how different commercial applications solve common fundraising problems. Information about the IT Resource Center is available at *http://www.itresourcecenter.org/*; the *NonProfit Times* is at *http://www.nptimes.com*. You can e-mail Tim at timmg@itresourcecenter.org.

CHAPTER 5

Integrating Online and Offline Databases to Serve Constituents Better

Jeff Gignac, CFRE, ePMT
JMG Solutions, Inc.

Pamela Gignac
JMG Solutions, Inc.

A nonprofit must analyze their database regularly for information to build strategies and directions in order to meet short-term and long-term fundraising objectives.

INTRODUCTION

It is critical that nonprofits plan for the strategic development of the information they capture by various methods. Through this strategic development, the information can be effectively implemented into fundraising activities. The data are gathered in areas as diverse as prospect research, donor development, moves management, database mining, two-way Internet data exchange, and strategic analysis and evaluation. This chapter will touch on these information-gathering areas, where many nonprofits need to spend more time to help develop a better overall fundraising plan.

In many areas of fundraising, technological innovations are used to improve technique, as well as give nonprofits the ability to have a more involved relationship with their donors.

Technology is inspiring nonprofit organizations to offer donors their choice of communication—through the Internet, telephone, regular mail, or person-to-person. Nonprofits can get back to donors faster and more accurately (if they have concerns, questions, or comments) than ever before. They have more opportunities to communicate with donors—and donors with them. Overall, nonprofits are beginning to know more about their constituents.

Today there are few valid excuses to fundraise with a cold, generic, or mass marketing approach.

The building blocks for improved, personalized fundraising lie with the use of databases and the Internet. Databases are becoming more powerful and capable of creating stronger relationships with nonprofit donors by uncovering the motivations underlying actions, needs, and desires.

Nonprofit managers need to understand what these databases are capable of doing before they can use them to improve and, in some cases, revolutionize their fundraising practices.

Fundraising and Technology

Many fundraisers are aware that nonprofits need to go beyond using database systems to capture only names, addresses, and giving histories. But not everyone knows that we should be thinking about the strategic development of the information captured, and how to implement this new and powerful source in fundraising activities. Good strategic development is the same as what makes a good database: donor development; prospect research; segmentation of data; solicitation tracking; monthly donor programs; electronic funds transfer; bar code scanning; telemarketing, and the Internet.

Technology (and especially database use) is enabling nonprofits to understand how a donor relates to an organization, starting from a number of entry points, such as volunteer, event participant, newsletter subscriber, monthly donor, Internet e-mailer, or Web site newsletter subscriber. Nonprofits need to adopt values, initiatives, and fundraising practices that recognize this fact. If fundraisers understand the basics, best practices, and advanced abilities of databases and the Internet, then nonprofit managers will be ready to understand what a donor wants. The result is an intimate, knowledgeable, and stimulating relationship.

Databases and the Internet

Today, most nonprofit organizations are in a fiercely competitive fundraising environment, so their donors will be receiving fundraising appeals from other organizations that understand how to use a database to treat donors in a personal and appealing manner. Most donors have a limited budget when it comes to philanthropic spending, so nonprofits need to understand how their database can help secure and keep current and future donors.

With e-commerce, the Internet has become a new solicitation vehicle. When a donation is made over the Internet, it is usually processed immediately, and in some cases, an electronic tax receipt is sent out via e-mail. You could also program the output from your Web page to create a file that could be imported into your fundraising management system. This would save having to manually enter the information into the system. It would also reduce entry errors. At the same time, since the donor is entering the information on your Web site, you could ensure that the donor enters the correct information into a standard format, thus ensuring accuracy and uniformity.

In addition to name and address details, one is able to capture Web site and e-mail addresses. Many companies and some foundations have their own Web sites and many more are being developed all the time. More nonprofits are also developing very sophisticated Web sites. As a result, more and more people have their own organizational and staff e-mail addresses.

Many of today's charities are using e-mail addresses to keep donors up to date, as well as to communicate with board members. It is quick and nearly immediate, depending on how often they check for messages. It is no secret that this method of communication can be more cost-effective than using faxes, couriers, or regular mail.

AN ONLINE DATABASE VERSUS AN OFFLINE DATABASE

There are many different types of databases in the nonprofit world. Some are considered online and others are considered offline: some are both. An *offline database* is software installed and maintained on the nonprofit's own computers and systems in the office. One can think of it as an *in-house database,* versus an online database, which is controlled and managed *out of house.*

Most offline or *in-house* databases are within physical proximity. They arrive in the office on CDs and are installed on the network so everyone in the team can access it. Offline databases can include systems that have been used in the past, such as an old legacy system or customized Microsoft Access databases. The following is a list of specific nonprofit sector offline databases:

- Banner
- Donor Perfect
- eBase
- Millennium
- Pledge Maker
- Raiser's Edge

An online, or out of house, database is one where, generally, the access to it is via the Internet. The database itself is located outside of the nonprofit's office. One usually has secure entry to it through any computer connected to the Internet. The information usually belongs to the nonprofit, but the management and control of the database itself belongs to the service provider of the system. The following is a list of online databases:

- Artez Interactive
- Convio
- Etapesty
- Kintera

WHICH DATABASE IS RIGHT FOR ME?

This is a question asked by many nonprofits, and it can be a daunting and complex one to answer. For example, would a widely available program such as an Excel spreadsheet or a Microsoft Access database be all that is needed? Or does one go with a specialized, and perhaps, more costly solution? If one decides on more specialization, and can justify a more significant investment of time and money, then how does one decide which one is better: an offline database or an online database? They both have advantages and disadvantages.

When selecting new software, you should review all options and determine if an offline database or online database is best. As with any new product, you should review all the features and functions required, and then compare your analysis with the different software packages and what they have to offer. One should think about key organizational needs in creating a functionality wish list. These are some of the key areas:

- Base price
- Additional modules and their cost structure
- Training
- Support

HOW DOES MY DATABASE INTEGRATE WITH MY WEB SITE?

All nonprofits need to build closer and longer-term relationships with current donors and supporters, as well as create a greater awareness with and accessibility for the public. Most utilize a selection of traditional fundraising methods such as direct mail, special events, cultivation events, planned giving, and corporate and foundation fundraising to accomplish this. It is more important than ever to look at the Internet and how one can present image, mission, and goals in an easily accessible format. An organization can achieve this by reviewing data from their Web site, discovering who visits it, and then developing opportunities to find out more about these visitors.

When current or future supporters visit a nonprofit's Web site, they are looking for information about mission, service, programs, general information, and perhaps products that might be for sale, such as Christmas cards or T-shirts. One wants to look at ways of capturing information about them, as well as provide them with the information that they are seeking. One can use a database to integrate the flow of information directly from the Web site into the nonprofit's own system. This will provide you with a more detailed picture about donors and supporters in one central location—the database.

Capture of E-Mail Address

One of the easiest ways to use the Internet and a database is to begin building a relationship with donors and prospects by capturing their e-mail addresses. This can be achieved by setting up a link or other vehicle directly on the Web site that the visitor can select in order to join an e-mail list. One can set up the Web site to help them join the e-mail list and thereby capture information through one of the following methods:

Web site visitors can click on a link to open a default e-mail program (such as Microsoft Outlook) in order to send an e-mail asking to join the list.

The designated Webmaster (the person responsible for the Web site's set up, update, and review) can create a way to save the information, either directly to a database or in XML format; this can later be used to import into the main fundraising database system.

Yahoo Groups™ (or other listservs) can be used to request and store e-mail information. Yahoo Groups is a free service provided by Yahoo.com (groups.yahoo.com). Yahoo Groups will manage the e-mail list. It provides a two-way communication vehicle between the organization and its members.

E-Mail Rules

It is important to follow best practice and establish some basic e-mail rules with regards to what the objectives are for this information and at the same time, respecting the visitor's privacy. The ePhilanthropy Code of Ethical Online Philanthropic Practices (*http://ephilanthropy.org/ethics*) requires nonprofits to post a privacy policy that, at a minimum, discloses why they are collecting e-mail information, what they will do with the e-mail addresses and who has access to it. Many organizations are also disclosing how often the visitor should expect to receive e-mail from the organization.

As spam and viruses become more prevalent, people are more concerned about providing information such as an e-mail address. As a result, some organizations are looking at establishing written rules as to what they will do with e-mail addresses. By stating clearly and precisely what it is going to do with this information, the nonprofit shows that it respects its subscribers and supports their privacy, and it expresses that it will be accountable with regards to e-mail addresses.

One organization that has taken the time and consideration to present its e-mail rules is the AIDS Resource Center of Wisconsin (ARCW).

Case Study: AIDS Resource Center of Wisconsin (ARCW)

ARCW (*www.arcw.org*) provides HIV prevention training and education, access to comprehensive services for people affected by HIV disease, clinical research on HIV treatment, and HIV advocacy through nine statewide offices.

When people go to the ARCW Web site, they find a "Join E-List" on their main page, which, when clicked, takes viewers to the Join E-List page. On this page, interested viewers have the option of joining ARCW's e-list. By clicking on the Join ARCW's e-mail list link, it is possible to send an e-mail to its Yahoo Groups' e-mail list. ARCW is using Yahoo Groups' e-mail list facility to implement and activate its specific e-mail list information.

ARCW also gives its subscribers some information about its list, including the following basic details (see Exhibit 5.1):

- It specifies when you should expect e-mails from ARCW.
- Its list is secure and e-mails are not traded.
- E-mail will never contain advertisements.
- Only the Webmaster e-mails the group.
- Users can unsubscribe to the mailing list both via e-mail and via the Web.

Alumni Tracking

There are several ways to keep track of alumni by integrating the Web site with the current fundraising system. Some of these techniques include exchanging or sending information about current events and stories, as well as access to alumni directories.

E-Mail Current Events and Stories

E-mail provides development directors with a great alumni-tracking tool. It is an easy and effective way to get them to exchange information with the nonprofit. The nonprofit can encourage alumni to e-mail about their own current events, such as where

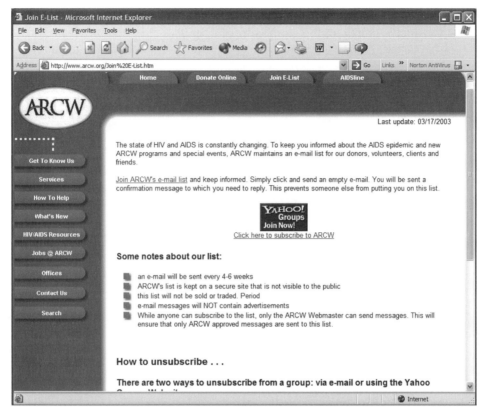

EXHIBIT 5.1   ARCW Join E-List Page

they are working, recent weddings, or baby news. This information can then be integrated, stored, and tracked in the fundraising database. Then when it is needed for outreach, such as for an alumni magazine, all the information is up to date and, literally, right at one's fingertips.

Institutional Alumni Directories

Most major institutions have their own alumni directory, which is usually accessible through their *alumni-only* section of their Web site. This is a secure area of the Web site with restricted access rights. In order to have access to this area and to initially set it up, subscribers need to prove they are actual graduates.

Once they have access, they can usually update their address, search for other alumni, or whatever else the nonprofit lets them do. If they make any changes to their address or personal information, this can be automatically updated into the fundraising system.

The aim is to eliminate as much duplication of effort and manual work as possible. If the alumni directory does not integrate directly with the fundraising system, it should be set up so that the nonprofit can be provided with an electronic file, which is then imported directly into their database.

External Alumni Directories

As an alternative or in addition, nonprofits can purchase information about the organization's alumni through external alumni directories. Two major alumni directory providers are

1. Harris Internet Services (*www.alumniconnections.com*)
2. Net Directories (*www.netdirectories.com*)

You can request that the information be provided in an electronic file, which can then be imported into the organization's database.

Case Study: Toronto Arts Council (TAC)

The Toronto Arts Council (*http://www.torontoartscouncil.org*) is an arm's-length funding body that supports the development, accessibility, and excellence of the arts in Toronto, offering grants programs to the city's arts organizations and professional artists. The Toronto Arts Council Foundation (TACF) was established in 1995 as a sister organization to TAC to allow individuals, foundations, and corporations the opportunity to support a broad spectrum of arts disciplines in the City of Toronto through tax-deductible contributions. TAC/TACF have formed the Toronto Arts Coalition. The Toronto Arts Coalition is an integral part of a recently launched new initiative called Great Arts/Great City—a major 10-year plan aimed at permanently eliminating the arts sector revenue gap. The Coalition is an Internet-based group of arts supporters, dedicated to raising arts awareness and increasing the resources available to Toronto artists and arts organizations.

Individuals and organizations with an interest in the arts are encouraged to join the Toronto Arts Coalition. When someone joins the coalition, all membership information is managed from the Toronto Arts Coalition Web site. One can become a free member or pay $25. Payment can be done directly by credit card or invoiced directly by e-mail. When the e-mail goes out, the invoice is attached in a PDF format, which can be in a secure format. All credit card information entered on the Web site is validated in real time (without any delay) with a third party credit card processor. All membership information is then stored in a secure online database.

When a member joins who is from the city of Toronto, TACF also provides the ability for members to send an e-mail to their city councilor. The online form automatically discovers which ward (electoral district) the member lives in, and from that determines who the city councilor is. Ward and councilor information is stored in an online database, to which this online form is connected.

Periodically, TACF will import the information directly into its fundraising management system. A customized utility automatically checks for duplicates before adding new data. The utility also adds a transaction for either the credit card payment or a pledge requiring an invoice. A transaction is also added for free members. Along with name, address, and e-mail, other biographical information is also captured by TACF. This information includes how the member heard about the coalition, which city ward the person belongs to, the date joined, and a code for the members who do not want to be listed on TACF's Web site.

Once a month, TACF e-mails all the coalition members who have an active e-mail address in the fundraising database. Through its fundraising management system,

TACF creates the e-mail and sends it to all coalition members. The e-mail provides updates on TACF activities and has links to specific articles on the TACF Web site. TACF then tracks which articles are read. Each e-mail also has a link at the bottom to allow readers to unsubscribe if they wish. An automatic function in the fundraising management system notifies TACF that members received the e-mail.

INTEGRATING ASPS WITH YOUR CURRENT FUNDRAISING DATABASE

Application service providers (ASPs) are Internet-based providers of functionality for specific activities such as fundraising, events, and donation processing. It is very important when selecting an ASP that one looks at how the information they are storing interfaces with the nonprofit's current fundraising system.

ASPs give nonprofits greater flexibility with respect to the functions they want to perform. Whether it is for special events tracking or taking donations online, they provide a cost-effective solution for many nonprofits.

When you use an application service provider, software does not need to be loaded onto a nonprofit's computer as it's accessed through the Internet. An ASP sells the use of its software on a subscription basis, and no software has to be acquired by the nonprofit. The vendor maintains it and the nonprofit manages its prospects and donation processing by accessing the software over the Internet.

ASPs provide a low-cost (and, in some cases, free) alternative to traditional software. Some advantages of using an ASP are as follows:

- Assurance that the latest technology is being used (automatic receipt of the benefit of upgrades without having to purchase additional software or pay costly annual service fees)
- Secure encryption of data for increased security in making donations online
- Ongoing database management (clean-ups, patches, fixes)
- Reduced need for technology staff onsite at a nonprofit's offices
- Provides increased accessibility of the data from home, business trips to visit clients, or whenever one is outside the office
- Possible lower costs overall, depending on what the objectives and needs are
- No need to make a capital investment to upgrade to advanced software or hardware

The following ASPs provide these services:

- Artez Interactive (*www.artez.com*)
- Convio (*www.convio.com*)
- Etapestry (*www.etapestry.com*)
- Kintera (*www.kintera.com*)

For more information on ASPs and their services, visit The Nonprofit Matrix at *http://www.nonprofitmatrix.com.*

WHAT IS DONOR DEVELOPMENT?

Donor development is about moves management, relationship building, and more. It has the following characteristics:

- Used to support capital campaigns, as well as other fundraising activities such as major gifts and corporate fundraising
- Designed for top donors and prospects
- Based on techniques practiced in the United States, as well as the United Kingdom and elsewhere
- Used to track more information about donors, such as interests, likes, dislikes, hobbies, who their friends are, colleagues
- Builds a two-way, evolving relationship with a nonprofit's key donors in order to guide them to the next level of giving, preferably for longer periods of time, and then through to a planned gift
- Is an integral part of *all* fundraising activities and ways that one reaches out to people, through projects and communications, allowing donors to feel personally involved
- Focused on getting to know people better while giving them an opportunity to know the nonprofit better

Building Relationships

The best prospects are those who have given already and are considered to be warm to the nonprofit and its work. As part of overall donor development, it is imperative that one builds longer-term relationships with donors by doing the following:

- Thanking them promptly and more than once
- Keeping them informed
- Sharing with them the impact of their gift and how it made a difference
- Making sure to approach the right donors at the right time
- Researching in order to match their interests to a nonprofit's work
- Researching to determine their capacity, inclination, and accessibility
- Developing an approach strategy designed specifically for each donor based on his or her interests and capabilities.

Top Prospect Lists

A nonprofit can use its database to produce research lists of prospects and donors, which can then serve as the basic tool for securing information to identify top prospects. To find hidden nuggets within your database, as well as adding new prospects, you can look at the following potential prospect pools:

- Past and current donors
- Contacts of past and current supporters
- Donors to similar campaigns and charities
- Major corporate and community donors
- Prospects with stated interests that match your work

- Companies, organizations, and individuals previously approached for nil return
- Wealthy individuals and high-profile individuals

PROSPECT RESEARCH

Whether one is in a capital campaign, major gifts campaign, or in planned giving, a nonprofit needs to have good prospect research. Finding, capturing, and tracking information on donors and prospects in your database will help save time and increase support.

In fact, prospect research is the cornerstone of the fundraising operation. It is estimated that research represents more than 80 percent of the work involved in securing a larger-than-average gift. This applies to individuals, companies, and foundations.

However, overall research supports all fundraising activities and leads to more successful solicitations. It is the basis for identifying prospects and the appropriate approaches to reach them. It also helps a nonprofit find the common ground between the organization and a potential donor.

Research and Your Database

Research is, in part, about doing one's homework as quickly, efficiently, and cost effectively as possible. But what it's *really* about is getting back to people and finding out more about them to match their interests with the nonprofit's work. The database is the key to realizing the potential of building relationships with supporters.

It is important to develop and implement a consistent use of reporting systems and the infrastructure to ensure two-way communication between all levels of an organization: locally, regionally, and nationally; from staff to volunteers to board members. Added to this is the opportunity to have two-way communication with donors, supporters, and the community itself. The structures a nonprofit establishes should take this into account, including utilizing the Internet and the gathered information for tracking purposes on the organization's database.

It is crucial to quickly collect and collate the captured information, and to ensure that legal guidelines and regulations are followed. One must remember to be accountable for the details captured and entered on the database, especially since it can include personal information such as contact data, interests, and information about a donor's close circle of family, friends and colleagues. The ideal is to capture and track all the information you can find about the nonprofit's donors and prospects in order to get beyond contact and giving details. Although it's often tempting to want to capture this deeper level of detail for all of your constituent records, it is not always practical to do so. Your nonprofit's needs will better be met by segmenting records and growing information strategically.

It can be challenging to capture all of the information on one central database and to keep it up to date. This avalanche of data includes ongoing input and maintenance and update of the information held on a relational database—all critical for targeting and analyzing prospective and current donors.

Looking at ways to use vehicles such as the Internet and the organization's Web site to capture and update information on the database, provided that it is done carefully and strategically, can make this challenge a little less difficult. It also opens up the opportunity to track and capture e-mail addresses for a greater number of records than your nonprofit might normally be able to do. You can look beyond what would traditionally be the core segment of donors and prospects that would be considered for additional information capture.

Remember that all databases are only as good as the information put into them and the people who know how to get the information out in the most effective way.

Five Top Ways to Use Your Database

The organization's computer, and in particular its database, are fundamental tools to support prospect research and fundraising. Databases can be useful in the capture and utilization of information gathered from:

- Internet research (e.g., *Internet research*. The nonprofit's database provides a valuable tool for. . . .)
- Market research
- Statistics
- Strategic targeting
- Prospect documentation

Analysis of Your Database

A nonprofit must analyze the database regularly for information to build strategies and directions in order to meet short-term and long-term fundraising objectives. It will need to manage and regularly update information to be able to coordinate, facilitate, and search for links through relationships for prospects and donors, as well as to avoid blind duplicate approaches. A regularly updated database system should be used for coordinating, facilitating, and searching for links through relationships for potential prospects and known donors.

The nonprofit's prospect research and fundraising information, including prospect backgrounds, approach strategies, contact, actions, links and relationships; should be tracked on the database and developed on an ongoing basis.

Prospect Research Service Providers

There are specific service providers who provide information designed to meet the needs of the nonprofit sector and fundraising in particular. Each of them has proprietary information that is accessible through secure entry to their online databases. You can use this information to develop profiles and briefing documents, as well as to match names against your nonprofit's donor base and to look for new matches and prospects. The following is a sample list of service providers to help with prospect and grant research:

Company Name	Web Site	Country Served
BIG Online database	*www.bigdatabase.com*	USA/Canada
Canadian Centre for Philanthropy	*www.ccp.ca*	Canada
Foundation Center	*www.fdncenter.org*	USA
Foundation Search	*www.fdncentre.org*	USA/ Canada
PRO Online (iWave)	*www.iwave.com*	USA/Canada

DATA MINING AND DATA OR PROSPECT SCREENING

Data mining and prospect (or data) screening are all about what it is called knowledge discovery. Many organizations are taking a closer look at their own donors to find their "golden prospects"—those for whom specialized approach strategies should be designed. Databases are usually searched for donors for one of the following three reasons:

1. Direct marketing
2. Major gift prospects
3. Planned gift prospects

Data mining and prospect (or data) screening is one of the key fundraising tools and techniques being implemented today. It is considered "hot and new," and for some, it is becoming a must-have. However, it is usually a significant investment, so your nonprofit should carefully consider whether it is right for the organization. You should try not to do it just because it's the latest thing.

Here a few common comments from some organizations that have performed prospect screening:

- "It was a huge investment for us and we didn't know what to do with it."
- "Make sure you plan in advance exactly what you are going to do with the results."
- "The final report sat in a drawer for ages (a couple of years even) without being fully utilized, and now the information is stale although still useful for us."
- "It was a good indicator as to whom we should ignore for now and who we should focus on."
- "It's helpful to decide if you are looking at annual or campaign donors and prospects."
- "It confirmed what we already knew about our donor base."
- "It can show that you are heading in the right direction."

What Is Data Mining?

According to Microsoft, the definition of data mining is as follows:

An information extraction activity whose goal is to discover hidden facts contained in databases. Using a combination of machine learning, statistical analysis, modelling techniques and database technology, data mining finds patterns and subtle relationships in data and infers rules that allow the prediction of future results.[1]

Data mining also has these characteristics:

- It is the starting point on the road to knowledge discovery—finding out more about your donors and potential prospects.
- It can be used to interrogate and analyze customer databases based on a set of statistical facts and numbers.
- It provides a broader look at a database from a broad perspective.

- It is usually more effective with larger numbers of records and databases.
- It includes an electronic screening that provides you with a map of raw data and numbers.

Data Mining Results

Data mining provides nonprofits with reports based on averages, selected statistical information, and criteria. A detailed report is provided based on these averages. It is not an exact science. It provides superior information for making qualified decisions with regards to who one should be approaching. It doesn't provide finished prospect research reports or even partial profiles. In fact, it usually requires additional research to flesh it out in order to match strategic objectives. The results of data mining should, however, point an organization in the right direction, (e.g., closer to identifying which prospects warrant additional research). For example, an organization has a donor database of 50,000 names. One goal of an electronic screening could be to identify which are the best 1,000 prospects out of a total database, based on the donor's wealth indicators and matched against specific statistical information such as zip code or postal code.

Data or Prospect Screening

Data screening is much more than averages and statistics. Just because someone has a certain level of wealth indicated by the data mining process does not mean that they will necessarily support your work. Data or prospect screening takes this idea to the next level. It takes the technique of data mining and fine-tunes it for a more appropriate application for use by the nonprofit sector.

Prospect screening is considered a more holistic and specialized approach to the analysis of results found in searching a database and donor records. The questions this process seeks to answer are much more sophisticated, specialized and customized than those asked during general data mining. As a result, the information found is more applicable and can be implemented quicker.

Even for those who have invested in prospect screening of their database, a bigger challenge remains—taking the results and strategically implementing them. Sometimes the report ends up as a large document put away in a file drawer. Thus, using a specialized service provider for the nonprofit sector might ensure that this valuable information is put to good use quickly and efficiently. As this is a relatively new area for fundraising, the number of providers and their services will continue to grow. The following is a sample of some current prospect screening companies.

A Sample of Nonprofit Prospect Screening Companies

Company Name	Web Site	Country Served
Blackbaud	*www.blackbaud.com*	USA/Canada
P!N	*www.prospectinfo.com*	USA
Wealth ID	*www.wealthid.com*	USA
Target America	*www.tgtam.com*	USA
Charity Consultants UK	*www.charityconsultants.co.uk*	UK
Factary	*www.factary.co.uk*	UK

Company Name	Web Site	Country Served
Fundraising Research Consultancy (FRC)	*www.frandc.co.uk*	UK
JMG Solutions Inc.	*www.jmgsolutions.com*	Canada/USA/ UK

Prospect Screening in the United Kingdom

In the United States, personal information is more readily available than in many other countries and, although current and potential legislation may restrict some access to it, there is still a great deal that you can find out about potential supporters. However, in many European countries such as the United Kingdom, access is much more limited, as is the capturing of certain types of information due to current and potential legislation. This is also the case for Canada, where privacy issues and respecting donor rights are a regular topic for many professional fundraisers. As a result, prospect screening criteria and outcomes vary greatly from country to country.

There are many lessons that nonprofits can learn from each other, no matter where organizations are located or what they do. In the United Kingdom, there are three prospect research companies that specialize in nonprofits; all offer unique prospect-screening services. These companies are Charity Consultants Ltd., The Factary, and the Fundraising & Research Consultancy Ltd.

These companies have been doing extensive research on major individuals, companies, and foundations since the 1980s. They have tracked information with the purpose of having it used to develop specialized approach strategies to secure larger and/or longer-term commitments from prospects and donors. Each of these companies tends to take a more holistic approach to prospect research and data screening. That means that they take into account all aspects of a nonprofit organization, including, of course, strategic objectives. They work with each nonprofit to ensure that the information they have is deep, as they aim to match potential interests.

Finding Gold Prospects

Charity Consultants Ltd. is based in Oxfordshire, England. Andrew Thomas, chief executive, has been fundraising for more than 20 years and was the head of one of the country's largest major gift campaigns, The Prince's Trust. He relates his experience in the area:

> In our experience, a typical database contains 1 to 2% gold prospects and high value donors that are capable of giving £5,000 (approximately $10,000) or more to a ceiling of around £5 million (approximately $10 million). In fact, many have a particular type of gold prospect that they did not realize were there—those who are company directors.
>
> Many nonprofits overlook the fact that these people could open the door to their company and securing a corporate gift in addition to their personal one. Particularly in terms of securing a major gift from the company, and even others that they work closely with, provided that you approach them at the right time with the right project. Just one such gift could more than pay for the service itself.

One of the UK's top charities had such an individual on their database where he was giving a regular donation and was an established donor. This donor was in fact the Chief Executive for one of the top 5 companies in the UK and could quite well not only give a larger personal donation but also could lead them to corporate support from his company. He could certainly open doors for them that perhaps they would be unable to access or would take longer to get to. He could be our champion and assist us in securing a higher-level gift from his company. It truly is all about "networking" connections and extending beyond the initial donor.[2]

Donor Development and Prospect Screening

Prospect screening is much more than an exercise of number crunching. It can be part of a nonprofit's overall donor development program. It is also a way to identify initial top prospects with which an organization can build closer relationships. One can take a more holistic approach to screening and look even closer at what you can find out about one's donors. Here is what Kay Holmes-Siedle, a UK-based consultant, has to say about her extensive experience in prospect research and fundraising:

Many charities recognize the opportunity of a major donor development program as a means of developing long-term key relationships with its supporters and others close to the organization. The first phase of any such program is to locate, research, and provide biographical profiles including influence and wealth for the potentially most generous and influential individuals, particularly in relation to companies and trusts. A major research audit is carried out to select from all their lists and their database the best 1,000 with the intention of finding the very best, say 100 to 120 people.

The mere matching of possible wealth and influence alone is only a very small part of what is needed. A successful major donor development campaign requires research that:

1. Is based on much more than the mechanistic matching of one whole database against another
2. Does not treat all supporters as equal
3. Asks intelligent fundraising questions about where the best donors/ supporters might be located, selecting some of the best people for the establishment of the program
4. Checks the value and quality of the selected records before it starts the profiling. Data [are] often incorrectly input (mechanistic matching misses opportunities that are much less likely to be missed by 20 years of experience of activity with wealthy people).
5. Bespoke research to locate and choose, one by one the very best prospects based on value, warmth, and influence.

Most organisations are astounded when they find out just who their donors are. [3]

Data Screening Is a Research Process

Taking data mining and prospect screening to the next level for donor development comes from focusing on initial top donors. It is part of an overall research process. One should take the information beyond the statistical data provided and look deeper at the donors. Vanessa Hillman and Chris Carnie from The Factary in the United Kingdom provide a useful perspective on this area:

> Data screening is a research process to identify the top percentage of wealthy and powerful donors on a nonprofit database. This process is excellent for identifying prospects for major gift campaigns or removing potential elite donors from mainstream fundraising campaigns for a more individual personal approach.
>
> Geographic and demographic information is used to classify people into "types" for targeting purposes. By segmenting your database in this way you can understand more about your donors' characteristics and behavior. This could include the type of housing they live in, how they shop, car ownership, how they spend their leisure time, their financial situation, the media they use and so on.
>
> Statistical information can include geo-demographic as well as life-stage and lifestyle data to produce different people types that go beyond zip or post code. Examples of lifestyle criteria include numbers of children, pet ownership, interests, charity concerns or type of donation. As the classification is at an individual level, direct mailings can be targeted more effectively, mailing to specific groups.
>
> With database screenings the nonprofit's database is compared with a database of wealth, well-connected and influential individuals. This type of screening is distinguished from others by the fact that it will not classify every individual on the database, but will select a much smaller subset for in-depth examination. At The Factary, we frequently work with a nonprofit's database to identify not just major gift prospects, but people who have useful connections, who can lobby on the charity's behalf or who have an influence in particular regions or sectors.[4]

PRIVACY BEST PRACTICES

Fundraising and prospect research relies on donors and the information that nonprofits find and capture about them. In order to respect the privacy of donors, as well as adhere to current and future privacy legislation, one should be guided by the following points:

- A nonprofit will come across some very personal information.
- Be wary, as some of it will be gossip—do not add to it or spread it further.
- Make sure that the nonprofit is accountable and ethical about what it knows about donors and prospects.
- Respect the privilege of what information brings to the organization.
- Abide by relevant laws and regulations regarding privacy and information.

- Be aware that in most countries, people have a right to see all that the nonprofit has recorded about them.
- Set up the organization's "best practices." Do not record in any format, whether on paper or computers, any information that might be considered to be libelous or detrimental according to laws and regulations.
- Prepare guidelines regarding the sharing, capturing, and tracking of information, and follow a research and fundraising code of ethics and standards. Refer to organizations that have codes that can be used as a guide to develop your own or to adopt directly.
- Make sure that everyone—staff, volunteers, board members—agree to abide by these rules.
- Just because information is found on the Internet, that doesn't mean that the information should be captured on the nonprofit's database or elsewhere.

CONFIDENTIALITY AND YOUR DATABASE

It is extremely important to develop ethical rules and guidelines surrounding information and confidentiality. This is becoming increasingly important as donors count on nonprofits to respect their privacy, as well as their wishes regarding donations. Donors' wishes not only include anonymity but also where they might like their donation to be directed.

Remember that the information the nonprofit keeps on its database could potentially be viewed by that person or organization. In other words, any donor could ask to see what a nonprofit has on them, and the organization is responsible to provide precisely what is kept on file. Therefore, do not use codes to "hide" any information, since this could be considered against the law. If it can be determined that the nonprofit is in the possession of a derogatory or libelous comment, it could damage the organization in many ways. Therefore, be aware of what information you possess.

A database should be set up so that users' information can be accorded different levels of security. This is not only to ensure data integrity, but also controls who should have access to see what types of information. Security rights should be set up for users who are able to do a combination of the following:

- Some nonprofit employees should have access to look up or view data but not change it.
- Certain employees of the nonprofit organization should have the right to make changes to the database.
- A small number of well-managed and trained users should have rights to delete records from the database.
- Two people should have supervisory rights (one to take the lead, the other is a backup person).

More secure areas might be set up under a specific username and password, such as the name of a pet, so that whenever users are logged in as "Spot" they are in an extremely sensitive area, and they need to be careful about what they do. Data can be altered, added, or deleted at this point, and it is imperative that the changes are accurate.

SHARING INFORMATION

A nonprofit needs to establish procedures around the sharing of information with staff members as well as with key volunteers who will be seeking advice about how to make approaches on behalf of the nonprofit. Lists of names should be kept highly confidential and within sight of senior management—literally. Never leave them with volunteers. Although they are probably all honest people, they may help another nonprofit (where they might also volunteer) with the organization's list. That is not in the best interest of the nonprofit or the donors' best interests. And it does happen. The same rules should apply to profiles prepared about prospects and donors.

Whatever the guidelines are, the nonprofit needs to consider ways to ensure that it has an effective flow of information to avoid the possibility that staff might treat a VIP or top donor inappropriately. It helps to use the database to identify these VIPs. That way, if they happen to call, the staff they are speaking to will know roughly who they are, and will be able to pass them to the appropriate staff person.

USING YOUR OFFLINE DATABASE ONLINE

Some development professionals are spending a significant amount of time outside of the office. Increasingly, they are using the Internet to access and print off their donor information offsite.

Many of today's major software programs have an online version. Usually, the online software has most of the same functionality as the regular (or client) version, although it might have a few limitations.

With the online version, nonprofits have real-time access to donors, prospects, and all transaction information. This can be useful for the following:

- Giving development staff on the road visiting prospects and/donors the ability to update call reports and the database from the road, hotel, or at home
- Updating notes from a meeting they just attended
- Changing address or other donor specific details
- Allowing access from chapters or branches from around the country or around the world
- Giving volunteers limited access to the database to look up information
- Allowing volunteers or students the ability to help clean up the database
- Enabling older (legacy) computers to continue in use

CASE STUDY: THE CHILDREN'S WISH FOUNDATION OF CANADA

The Children's Wish Foundation of Canada (CWF) (*http://www.childrenswish.ca*) is dedicated to working with the community to provide children who have high-risk, life-threatening illnesses the opportunity to realize their most heartfelt wish.

They have 12 chapters across the country, as well as their National Office. Most of their chapter offices are staffed by a small number of individuals.

When CWF was looking for new fundraising software to replace its custom Lotus notes application, one of the requirements was to be able to have access to its fundraising system from all the chapters around the country. The new fundraising software it implemented allows for online access to their database. Users in the other chapters can do data entry, run reports, print tax receipts, and send thank-you letters.

This allows The Children's Wish Foundation of Canada the ability to use their offline database online.

THE VAST GALAXY OF THE INTERNET

The Internet will continue to be an unlimited source of information. As the number of Web sites is growing by the minute, so are the sources of information available to find out more about your donors and prospects through researching the net. Many sites offer free information, some require you join but charge no fee, and still others charge fees for access to their information.

An organization can find out prospect information on people, companies, governments and foundations, not only in their home country but also around the world, wherever your prospects might have interests. By checking out international sites (including international newspapers and periodicals online) you might be able to find out information about prospects that might have appeared to be only active in your own country. You can learn other addresses for them or visit the websites for companies or foundations they might have involvement in around the world.

THE CHALLENGE

There is such a galaxy of information available for fundraisers and prospect researchers, that it could become a black hole that absorbs a lot of a nonprofit's time and resources. It is crucial that the processes one puts in place includes the transfer of information into the organization's own database.

To date, worldwide legislation has been relatively limited with regards to the treatment of personal information, accountability, access and data protection. Countries in Europe, having started with their collective Data Protection Act, are now looking into regulating the Internet.

Regardless of developments in legislation, nonprofits have a moral responsibility to ensure that they are responsible and accountable to donors and those who are provided with services. Most of all, they need to respect donors' wishes and stay fair and reasonable as further online activities are undertaken.

The Internet has so much more to offer for both Web site fundraising as well as prospect research. The challenge will be to keep up on this ever-changing environment and capture it all in these emerging database systems.

SUGGESTED READINGS

Burk, Penelope. *Thanks! —A Guide to Donor-Centred Fundraising.* Burlington, Ontario, Canada: Burk & Associates Ltd, 2000. ISBN: 0968797806.

Burnett, Ken. *Relationship Fundraising—A Donor-Based Approach to the Business of Raising Money.* 2nd ed. San Francisco: Jossey-Bass, 2002. ISBN: 0787960896.

Carnie, Christopher. *"How to Guide"— Find the Funds—A New Approach to Fundraising Research.* London: Directory of Social Change, 2000. *www.dsc.org.uk*. ISBN: 1900360543.

Carnie, Christopher. *Fundraising from Europe.* London: Directory of Social Change, 2003. *www.dsc.org.uk*. ISBN: 1903293081.

Greenfield, James M. *The Nonprofit Handbook of Fundraising*. 3rd ed. The AFP/ Wiley Fund Development Series. New York: John Wiley & Sons, Inc., 2001. ISBN: 041403040.

Greenfield, James M. *The Nonprofit Handbook of Fundraising*. 3rd ed. The AFP/Wiley Fund Development Series, 2002 Supplement. New York: John Wiley & Sons, Inc., 2002. ISBN: 0471419397.

Johnston, Michael, ed. *Direct Response Fund Raising—Mastering New Trends for Results*. The AFP/Wiley Fund Development Series. New York: John Wiley & Sons, Inc., 2000. ISBN: 0471380245.

Johnston, Michael. *The Non-Profit Guide to the Internet*. The NSFRE/Wiley Fund Development Series. New York: John Wiley & Sons, Inc., 2000. ISBN: 047132857.

Joyaux, Simone P. *Strategic Fund Development—Building Profitable Relationships that Last*. Gelatt, James, ed. Aspen's Fund Raising Series for the 21st Century. Gaithersburg, Md.: Aspen Publishers Inc. ISBN: 0834207966.

Lake, Howard. *Direct Connection's guide to Fundraising on the Internet*. London: Aurelian Information Ltd., 1996. ISBN: 1899247068.

Nichols, Judith. *Pinpointing Affluence: Increasing Your Share Of Major Donor Dollars*. Bonus Books, 2002. ISBN: 1566251656.

Sloggie, Neil. *Tiny Essentials of Fundraising*. Merland, France: The White Lion Press Limited, Kermarquer, 56310, 2002. ISBN: 0951897152.

Sprinkel Grace, Kay. *Beyond Fund Raising—New Strategies for Nonprofit Innovation and Investment*. The NSFRE/Wiley Fund Development Series. New York: John Wiley & Sons, Inc., 1997. ISBN: 0471162329.

———. *High Impact Philanthropy: How Donors, Boards, and Nonprofit Organizations Can Transform Communities*. New York: John Wiley & Sons, Inc., 2000. ISBN: 0471369187.

———. *Over Goal: What You Must Know to Excel at Fundraising Today*. Medfield, MA: Emerson & Church Publishers, 2003. ISBN: 1889102148.

Warwick, Mel, Theordore Hart, and Nick Allen. *Fundraising on the Internet: The ePhilanthropy Foundation.Org Guide to Success Online*. 2nd ed. San Francisco: Jossey-Bass. ISBN 0787960454.

Wyman, Ken, Joyce Young, and John Swaigen. *Fundraising for Nonprofit Groups*. 5th ed. Self Counsel Press—Business Series. ISBN 1551802619.

ABOUT THE AUTHORS

Jeff Gignac, CFRE, ePMT, is founder and president of JMG Solutions Inc. Jeff has worked with a variety of more than 500 local and national nonprofits across Canada since 1992. Jeff is a Certified Fundraising Executive (CFRE), an ePhilanthropy Master Trainer (ePMT), a volunteer, and a regular speaker at International conferences and seminars. He is also an instructor at Humber College Institute of Technology and Advanced Learning's Fundraising and Volunteer Management program, including Donor Relations Management and Computer Applications. He is also a member of the Humber program's advisory board, Association of Fundraising Executives and the Association of Professional Researchers for Advancement.

Jeff has contributed chapters to popular nonprofit-sector, books including Mike Johnston's *Direct Response Fund Raising: Mastering New Trends for Results w/CD-ROM* and James Greenfield's supplement to his *The Fundraising Handbook: Fundraising*, 3rd Edition. You can e-mail Jeff at jeff@jmg solutions.com.

Pamela M. Gignac, vice president of JMG Solutions Inc., became inspired in 1985 in Vancouver, Canada, while volunteering for Rick Hansen's Man-In-Motion worldwide tour in his wheelchair to raise funds for spinal cord research. Since then, Pamela has worked with a variety of local, national and international nonprofits in Canada and the United Kingdom including the Prince's Trust, British Red Cross, University of Bristol, Canadian Red Cross, St. Michael's Hospital, University of Toronto and Alzheimer Society of Canada.

Pamela is a member of the Association of Fundraising Professionals (AFP), the Association of Professional Researchers for Advancement (APRA), and the Institute of Fundraising (InstF) in the United Kingdom. She is a regular speaker at International conferences and seminars and is currently an instructor for Humber College Institute of Technology and Advanced Learning's Fundraising and Volunteer Management program, including Donor Relationship Management and Prospect Research. Pamela has also developed the first online prospect research course, which runs regularly throughout the year. Together with her partner, Jeff, and two young sons, Pamela is extremely proud to be both a member of her profession and a mother. You can e-mail Pamela at pamela@ jmgsolutions.com.

ENDNOTES

1. Claude Seidman, *Data Mining with Microsoft SQL Server 2000 Technical Reference*, Microsoft Press; 2001.
2. Based on a telephone interview with Andrew Thomas, chief executive, Charity Consultants Ltd., *www.charityconsultants.co.uk* in October 2003.
3. Kay Holmes-Siedle, Fellow of the Institute of Fundraising in the United Kingdom, consultant for Fundraising & Research Consultancy Ltd. *www.frandc.co.uk*.
4. Vanessa Hillman and Chris Carnie, Fellow of the Institute of Fundraising in the United Kingdom, The Factary. *www.factary.co.uk*

CHAPTER 6

Online Community Building

George Irish, ePMT
HJC New Media

Getting yourself noticed in this milieu takes more effort than just sticking up a notice on the neighborhood bulletin board.

—Marshall McLuhan

THE NATURE OF THE NET

When Marshall McLuhan looked forward from the 1960s to the world that he saw taking shape around the new electronic media, he foresaw a global village where everyone around the world would be able to interact with the ease and closeness that comes with living in the same cozy neighborhood. But what McLuhan didn't realize was that as the world has become more connected and "closer," it has also become more crowded, more noisy, and more confusing—more like a big, clogged, chaotic city than a village. Getting yourself noticed in this milieu takes more effort than just sticking up a notice on the neighborhood bulletin board. Finding like-minded people who will support your organization requires a careful strategy matched with focused action, and, sometimes, dogged determination.

Nonprofit organizations that are planning online marketing initiatives should begin from a clear understanding of the nature of the Internet and how it differs from other forms of media such as print, radio and television.

We have heard many times how millions of people are connected to the net, but, in fact, the Internet is actually a poor medium for reaching large audiences. It's not a broadcast medium at all (*broadcast* in the way network TV or radio signals are sent out from a single source, and reach a large audience within their zone of coverage). The Internet is really a *narrowcast* medium, where the information you put online is available to everyone around the globe, but in fact it is only going to be accessed by a very small percentage of that overall audience. That audience has to make a conscious decision to *tune in* to the message you are offering, whether it's through the Web or e-mail or online video or other format.

That means that the prime challenge of online marketing is to establish that connection between your organization and your specific individual audience members. You can invest as much as you want in building a flashy, fancy Web site with all the bells and whistles, but unless you put an equally significant effort into developing your marketing strategy, you won't reach anything near your potential online audience.

THE BASICS OF ONLINE MARKETING

Online marketing has emerged in just the past few years, but already numerous books have been written on how to harness the power of the Internet for promoting your particular brand or cause. Here, we're going to look at a few basic principles of online marketing that every organization should keep in mind.

Make Your Organization Findable

There are already people on the Internet who are looking for your organization, but they haven't yet been able to find you. Some of these people may already know about your organization, and may be looking for the information that you can provide. One of your prime marketing tasks is to make your organization as visible as possible.

There are a couple of key steps you can take to increase your organization's *find-ability*.

Search Engines

Somewhere between half to three-quarters (the statistic on this vary considerably) of all people surfing on the Internet rely on search engines like Google, Yahoo!, and MSN to locate the information they are seeking. Getting your organization well placed on prominent search engines will help ensure that those who are looking for your information online will be able to find you.

Search engines are well-established services of the Internet, and they are big business—both for the companies that run them and for the specialized online marketing companies that promote their clients' sites as prominently as possible. Fortunately, nonprofit organizations don't really compete in the high-stakes commercial search engine market, and it's possible for most organizations to achieve very good search engine placements without spending a lot of money. I will outline here a basic approach to search engine optimization and registration that is within the means and know-how of many organizations.

1. *Placement review.* A placement review can give you a good benchmark to measure your optimization success. Start by making a shortlist of five or six key words or phrases associated with your organization that you would like to achieve high search placement on, then visit the major search engines like Yahoo! and Google, and try doing searches for those key words, making note of where your Web site shows up in the list (if at all). The specific goal of the search engine optimization is to improve those results.

2. *Optimization.* Optimizing your Web site to achieve a higher ranking in the search engines involves making subtle changes to your Web site's design, content, and, in some cases, the behind-the-scenes programming, to improve the ranking assigned by the search engines when they evaluate your Web site. You will need the assistance of your Web master to carry out most of the following basic optimization procedure:

- Start by looking at the <TITLE> tag in your homepage, and other significant pages on your site. The <TITLE> tag should contain the full name of your organization, along with a three- to five-word phrase that contains one or two of your keywords.

- There is a hidden set of tags in your Web pages called <META> tags. There is one <META> tag called *keywords* that should contain the most important keywords for your organization. A second <META> tag is called *description* and should have a one- or two-sentence description of your organization, using as many keywords as possible. Not all search engines consider these hidden <META> tags, but it will likely help your ranking on some search engines.

- On the visible page itself, you should make sure that every image has a text description attached in the "ALT" part of the <IMAGE> tag. Search engines cannot read the content in images, but they can read the ALT content.

- You should have some regular text on your page that repeats the keywords as often as possible. Some search engines will give more weight to bolded headlines, and others will choose to ignore those headlines completely—it's a bit of a game to decide the best strategy to present your online content so that it will be given the best "placement" marks by a majority of search engines.

3. *Re-registration.* The final step in the process is to submit your optimized Web page to be re-examined by the major search engines. You can choose to visit each search engine yourself and look for a link to manually "Submit a site," or you may use a commercial registration service such as *www.submit-it.com*. You may wish to redo Step 1 Placement Review after four to five weeks to see if you have improved your rankings on your key terms.

A very good resource for learning more about search engines and how to achieve maximum placement can be found at: *http://www.searchengines.com*.

Your Web Site Address

Your Web site address is an important tool for bringing in your online audience. When you chose your Web site address, you should keep in mind that people often find Web sites they are looking for by guessing the address, so try to make your Web site address something that people could guess. For instance, the San Diego Library Association may refer to itself internally as SDLA, but that acronym is not really known to the general public, so *www.sandiegolibraries*.com would probably be better than *www.sdla.com*. It's also important to keep your Web site address short so that it may be remembered easily by someone who might see it in a magazine ad or street poster, and then decide to visit your Web site at a later time.

Registering a new domain is relatively cheap, approximately $40 per year, so it is worth considering the option of registering more than one domain name *alias* if that could help people to guess the correct URL for your Web site. Some organizations register common misspellings or jargon addresses and point them to their correct Web site address. For instance, the Crohn's and Colitis Foundation of Canada has registered some of the common misspellings of that condition's name to point to its primary domain, *www.ccfc.ca*.

You should use your Web site address as widely as possible. It's standard practice now to include your Web site address on business cards, stationery, and in print ads, but some organizations are going even further—using their Web site address as their official logo. For example, no one has to guess at the Web address for Amazon.com or Moveon.org.

Finally, you should consider setting up some *flanker* Web site addresses for special promotional use. These are addresses you would use to promote specific high-profile campaigns, events, or functions that your organization might run on a periodic or recurring schedule. These URLs would be promoted temporarily and help to "brand" the particular event or campaign. For example, the Prostate Cancer Research Foundation of Canada (*http://www.prostatecancer.ca*) runs an annual event called the Father's Day Run, for which they have registered the domain *http://www.fathers dayrun.ca* to use on promotional materials, which will be an easy URL for people to remember. Also Amnesty Canada (*http://www.amnesty.ca*) uses a number of URLs for specific fundraising-related purposes: *http://joinamnesty.ca*, *http://amnesty renew.ca*, and *http://amnestyTV.ca*.

This first set of basic online marketing steps will help to drive more traffic to your Web site, but that's only half of the job. Once your visitors arrive at your site, you want to engage them in the stories and issues that are important to your organization.

Brand Your Organization Effectively Online

The second basic principle of online marketing success is to make sure that your online branding is appropriate and effectively communicates the right message about your organization. Remember that your Web site is a 24/7 public storefront for your organization, so you want that storefront to give people the correct impression. *Look* and *feel* are the first items that affect your online branding. Your Web site visitors should be able to recognize your organization even before they read the first word. That means your logo should be displayed prominently, and the colors used in the overall homepage design should integrate well with the colors in your logo. You should have some images and pictures on your site that are representative of the work you do, and also the beneficiaries of your work, if that's possible to show.

The size and scope of your organization should be accurately reflected in the look of your Web site. If you are the regional chapter of a large national organization, your Web site should have a more official look that includes some visual element on your homepage that indicates this—perhaps a map or recognizable regional symbol. If you are a community-based, local organization, your homepage should include design elements that reflect the local community—local landmarks or symbols and a more friendly, people-oriented look.

A note here—it is almost always money well spent to hire a professional design firm to develop the look and feel of your homepage, rather than relying on in-house nonspecialized staff.

The second consideration in branding your organization online should be looking at the language and choice of content you have on your homepage. How do you want to engage your visitors? If your organization provides primary information and reference services, then your homepage should be organized to facilitate access to your information, and should use a tone and vocabulary that is in line with an information-oriented service (see Exhibit 6.1).

EXHIBIT 6.1 Example of a Research/Information Organized Web Site

On the other extreme, if you are an activist group, or neighborhood association, then you will want to use more active, casual language that speaks to your visitors in a friendly, personable manner. You will want to have items on your Web site that communicate a sense of activity and energy, plus it should be continuously updated and fresh (see Exhibit 6.2).

In reality, your organization is probably somewhere between these two examples, so you will have to find a balance that comfortably represents your organization in the online world.

Exhibit 6.3 depicts a before-and-after example of a rebranding exercise that was undertaken by Oxfam Canada to improve the effectiveness of its homepage. Its original Web site is pictured, and then the redesign.

The original Web site is presented more like a news Web site with the way the main content is organized into a series of articles. In the reorganization, Oxfam created a visual space for the main issue—which has a prominent image and links to several articles. The links below are organized by issue, so they appear less like news stories and more like background articles. Also, the Oxfam logo and colors are not prominently displayed in the original, so they were used more prominently in the redesign. The redesign also increases the use of images to communicate the work of Oxfam— the beneficiaries, as well as the advocacy and education campaigns.

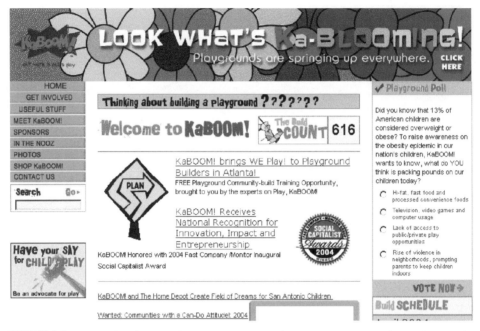

EXHIBIT 6.2 Example of the Well-Branded Web Site for an Organization that Helps Local Community Groups to Build Public Playgrounds

Go to Your Audience—Don't Wait for Them to Come to You

The third basic principle of online marketing is to be an active promoter at all times. Remember the line, "If you build it, they will come"? Well, that's not a good formula for online marketing success. You will achieve much greater marketing results by developing an active outreach and promotion program for your Web site. Later in this chapter we will look at more detailed methods for analyzing your online audience, but in general, you should be actively seeking out your audience rather than waiting for them to "discover" you. Active marketing involves identifying the places on the Internet where your audience goes, and then getting your message into those places so that your audience might encounter it.

Many people who surf the net regularly have a half-dozen or so sites that they visit regularly. This usually includes at least one news Web site, one or two Web sites related to their profession, a couple of Web sites related to hobbies or personal interests, and a site that gives them local information (weather, movies, what's on, etc.). These are all sites that you can target with your messages, using a variety of means:

- Purchasing online banner placements
- Using keyword purchases on search engines
- Posting information about your events in local directories
- Contacting other Webmasters to ask them to set up links to your Web site (particularly if you have a program that is related to their Web site topics)

BEFORE

AFTER

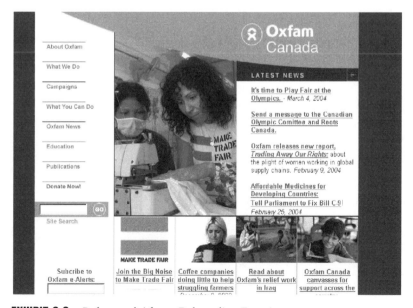

EXHIBIT 6.3 Before and After a Rebranding Exercise

Being proactive in your marketing is a lot easier if you have a budget to spend. The best placements for banner ads are commercial sites that charge for their real estate. These placements can be valuable in terms of bringing in traffic, but you should always be cautious and do as much testing as you can of small placements before you commit a sizable budget to media buys. The result you achieve can vary quite astonishingly between closely related sites, or even between different sections of a large site like Yahoo!.

Here are some banner results from a Mother's Day online banner campaign:

MSN.ca
Impressions: 250,097
Clicks: 545
Click rate: 0.22%

Doubleclick.com
Impressions: 320,012
Clicks: 208
Click rate: 0.06%

Toronto.com
Impressions: 2,035
Clicks: 30
Click rate: 1.47%

Canoe.ca
Impressions: 172,289
Clicks: 1.042
Click rate: 0.60%

A note on results measurement: Although the highest click rate was registered on Toronto.com (the banner was placed on a special Mother's Day page), it actually resulted in only 30 visits to the target Web site, whereas the lower click rates on the other sites ended up bringing in more site visitors (see Exhibit 6.4).

Special Promotions

Your Web site will establish its own regular, reliable audience, but at times you might wish to run a high-profile event or campaign that draws a much larger audience in to your Web site over a limited period of time. Special promotions may take the form of online contests, games, interactive multimedia events, advocacy actions like peti-

EXHIBIT 6.4   Mother's Day Banner

Source: Oxfam Canada

tions or e-mail-a-politician, or a myriad of other possibilities. The special promotion may be linked to a campaign launch or fundraising drive, or to generate some online activity in a lull between other events.

Special promotions provide an easy, direct way for new individuals to come into contact with your organization, and are an excellent way to recruit new contacts for your e-mail and prospecting lists.

Pass-Along Marketing

The key to making a special online promotion a success is being able to spread the word as widely as possible within your potential audiences. An important way to increase your marketing reach is to rely on the energy and assistance of others to pass your work around. *Pass-along methods* may be used to help get the word out about your special promotion. This works best if your special promotion has a "cool" factor that encourages Web surfers to tell their friends to check it out.

The first two screen shots in Exhibit 6.5 are from a World Wildlife Fund online game to raise awareness about over fishing. Note the link to "Recommend a Friend"— that is the pass-along element of this game. And who wouldn't want to enter a contest to win chocolate? The third screen shot in Exhibit 6.5 is an example of an online contest with pass-along appeal—this campaign acquired more than 1,000 new contacts for Save the Children Canada.

Many of us have heard the term *viral marketing,* which was coined to describe extra advertisements that get added at the bottom of some free e-mail services like HotMail. This extra advertisement was viewed as an unwanted *passenger* using a *host* e-mail message to propagate itself throughout the net—hence the similarity to biological virus reproduction. Nowadays, viral marketing is used to describe any form of marketing campaign that relies on individuals to pass messages along to their contact lists—friends, family, colleagues, and so on. I prefer to use the term *pass-along marketing* because that more accurately reflects the intention of the forwarders who are intentionally passing the message along.

Pass-along campaigns can be launched easily by adding a simple line of text at the bottom of an e-mail to "Forward this message to your friends, family and colleagues." There are also quite sophisticated "personal networking" or "eCaptains'" systems that can closely track the forwarding performance of each individual from the first message that was sent out.

Pass-along campaigns are an excellent way for your organization to reach out to new audiences who may be likely to support your work. After all, you are being recommended to them by someone they know and (hopefully) trust.

GIVE YOUR VISITORS WHAT THEY ARE LOOKING FOR

The final basic foundation of online marketing is to make your customers happy. An important success measure of an online marketing campaign is not how many first-time visitors you are able to bring in, but rather, how many second-time visitors you can attract. It's very easy for someone to click on one of your banners or links and arrive at your Web page. Many people will do it just out of curiosity, and once they have glimpsed your page, they take off somewhere else. A better indicator that you have made an impression on a visitor is when they make a return visit. That means you have really made a successful connection.

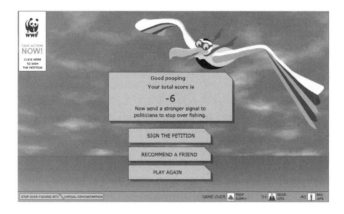

EXHIBIT 6.5   Examples of Special Promotions

It's not easy to measure return-visits to your Web site, so you might never know exact numbers, but you can get some sense of your regularly returning traffic by examining your server stats reports. The key to encouraging your visitors to return to your Web site is very simple—give them what they are looking for.

User-centered Web design is becoming a standard practice for professional web design companies. It reverses the publication equation that most organizations are used to. Instead of starting from the position of having a collection of information that you need to publish, organizations are now approaching their Web site design from the point of view that their visitors are looking for particular kinds of information, and the main function of the Web site is to present it to them as efficiently as possible.

Navigation and architecture of your Web site are important factors in helping visitors to find the information they are looking for. If they have trouble locating the information they are seeking, then they are not likely to come back again, so you should make sure the most-requested information is as easy to access as possible. Your navigation menu should be clear and consistent—the visitors should always be aware where they are in your Web site, and should be able to move easily around your site.

Many of your first-time visitors aren't looking for in-depth, detailed information. They are looking for answers to more general questions. You might consider setting up a Frequently Asked Questions (FAQ) page that makes the answers they are looking for as easy as possible to find. One of the more sought-out pieces of information about your organization is your physical address and phone number. You should have this information—plus your Web site address—at the bottom of every page. That way, when users print a page from your Web site, they can still track down the original source.

Here's a quick exercise: Find someone who is unfamiliar with your organization's Web site and ask that person to visit your Web site and to get answers to four short questions:

1. What kinds of programs does this organization offer?
2. Who is the target group or audience of this organization?
3. What is the mailing address and telephone number of this organization?
4. How can I volunteer or make a donation to this organization?

If your usability tester returns a low score, then you can assume many of your visitors are likely to be disappointed or frustrated after their first visit, and will be less likely to make a return visit. In that case, some revisions are in order.

Once you have successfully established your basic online marketing foundation, you should start to see your online traffic measures begin to improve. In order to realize maximum marketing results for your organization, you should develop a more ambitious and comprehensive marketing strategy.

BUILDING AN ONLINE MARKETING STRATEGY

The next section presents a condensed step-by-step strategy for building an online marketing strategy, from the first steps of understanding your online audience, through to delivering your messages, to building your online community of users. The steps outlined here are for a general, multi-purpose marketing strategy, but this same process may be used to develop more specialized and focused plans to promote particular campaigns or deliver individual key messages. Sample charts are provided as a guide to creating your own marketing matrix and strategic plan.

Step One: Audience Analysis

The first step of any marketing plan is to understand who your target audience is. The online world is no exception. Because of the narrowcasting quality of the Internet, it's even more important to have a clear idea who you are trying to reach with your message, because if it's not delivered right on target, you stand a chance of missing completely.

You probably already have a good idea who your offline audience is, and that is a good place to start. Begin by identifying who these groups are; make notes about their characteristics, how you communicate with them now, and the purpose of that communication. The audience groups you identify could be as broad as "The general public" or as specific as "Our funders from state government." The idea here is to identify the main groups you need to communicate with to pursue your mission and mandate.

Following is a chart showing a sample audience analysis for a local health unit that is promoting smoking-cessation programs in area schools.

Group	Profile	How We Communicate with Them Now	Purpose of That Communication
High school students	Teenagers, some are smokers, others are friends of smokers	Posters in schools, promotion items (bookmarks, highlighters, water bottles)	Getting the message out about stopping smoking and promoting use of the 1-800-BUTT-OUT telephone line
Teachers	Teachers in schools where we have smoking-cessation programs	Materials about how to include nonsmoking content in lesson plans, activities	Getting more classes involved in non-smoking run at local schools
Media	Local paper, radio station	Media releases about upcoming events, such as National No Smoking day	Getting media coverage of nonsmoking events

Step Two: Making the Online Connection

Each of your defined groups likely uses the Internet in a different way, at different times, and for different purposes. That is why it is so hard to reach out to a large audience online. If they do not have some form of Internet behavior in common, then you have to develop specific delivery strategies for each one. Identifying the patterns of Internet use that are typical to each of your main audiences allows you to develop specific approaches to reach them. You don't have to worry about being too detailed or comprehensive—just a general profile of typical internet-related behavior will be enough to guide you at this point.

The exercise then becomes a bit more analytic, and we ask you to start thinking about what online means you have at your disposal to reach out to those groups within the typical-use venues you have identified. Some creative thinking will help out a lot here—try to think of things you have seen yourself, or have heard mentioned in any of the other chapters in this book. Also, try to think practically—there's no use aiming to blanket Yahoo.com with Web banners unless you have tens of thousands of dollars at your disposal. Also, part of this exercise is outlining what kind of response you are looking to generate in your target group when they do receive your message. This is an important step in planning your marketing initiatives; because you want to be able to properly deliver the information they are seeking and encourage them to come back again at a future time.

Again, here is a sample chart with Step Two information filled in for the same youth anti-smoking organization:

Group	How do they use the Internet?	How can we deliver our message to them online?	What kind of response are we looking for?
High school students	For socializing (online chats) and personal interests (music, sports, movies), as well as for school-related research	Send messages in chat rooms • Use word-of-mouse, pass-along invitations (e-postcards) • Post banner ads on popular music, sports, and local cinema Web sites	• Visit our Web site • Do some activity such as send an e-postcard to a friend, or sign up for our cartoon newsletter, Butthead
Teachers	E-mailing communications with colleagues, plus some research for lesson materials	• Have our own e-mail newsletter • Get articles or ads into other teacher-related e-newsletters • Hang posters in staff lounges with our Web site address	• Sign up for our newsletter • Download materials from our Web site • Register a "butt-out" school group in our online group registry
Media	• E-mailing with colleagues, and subjects • Doing Web research on stories, background information • Publishing articles on their own Web site	Build our registry of e-mail media contacts and send press releases and announcements, invitations to events, etc., to encourage them to visit our Web site	• Bookmark our quick facts registry for future reference on smoking-related stories • Contact us directly to discuss a story idea

The information you assemble for this stage of your online marketing strategy is more than enough to get you started with some new online marketing initiatives. The next step in developing your online marketing strategy asks you to take a longer view of the marketing and communications process, and consider how you can build ongoing online connections with your audience groups that encourages their greater participation in your organization's activities.

Step Three: Engaging Your Online Audience

Each of the groups you identified in the earlier steps of this exercise already has an established offline relationship with your organization. It might be nothing more than seeing your advertisements in a local newspaper, but this is the basic ongoing communication that allows you to attract supporters, volunteers, and champions who are vital to keeping your organization working. Of course, the closer the connection, the greater the value, so organizations typically devote considerable expense and resources into building and maintain their relationship with key constituents.

This same process is true online. The Internet might seem at first glance to be a cold, mechanical, and impersonal world, but it is filled with real, flesh and blood people. The Internet offers new ways for people to communicate, to work together, and to form new community connections, and your organization may be able to enhance and deepen existing relationships with your audience groups.

In this last chart, the youth anti-smoking organization describes the existing "offline" relation they have to each group, and then considers the potentials for using the Internet to enhance and maintain that connection.

Group	What kind of ongoing connection do we have now?	What new ways could we engage with them online?	How can we strengthen that online engagement over time?
High school students	Introducing quit-smoking clubs in schools that receive our newsletter and report on their activities	Share success stories, personal affirmations, and challenges in an online support group (bulletin board)	Encourage volunteers to act as group moderators, sending articles, pictures, stories for newsletter and Web site
Teachers	• Reading our regular printed newsletter • Asking questions related to smoking issues to our library and staff	• Offer online discussion group for teachers and health promoters • Share teaching resources on quit-smoking	Offer lesson-plan exchange, building a growing resource of useful teaching materials on this subject
Media	Sending regular press releases and invite to special events	Create media resources center with photos and profiles from programs	Partner with media organizations to get enhanced coverage of our campaigns

The outcomes of this online marketing strategy exercise will likely be a series of short, medium, and long-term objectives that can provide some guidance to the tactical decisions you make in promoting your organization, both online and offline. From this, you can create timelines and plans for resource expenditure to bring your marketing program into action.

CONCLUSION

Online marketing is a core communications activity that can support many of your other online objectives by bringing you into contact with more potential donors, volunteers, allies, and beneficiaries.

Over time, your marketing efforts can build an online constituency that will be a valuable resource for your organization (see the "Community" chapter later in this section). This will only happen if your organization is prepared to make a conscious investment of time and resources into realizing your online marketing strategy.

Remember that online marketing is a continuous process that requires an ongoing investment of human and financial resources throughout the year. You will have times of peak activity, such as around signature special events or campaigns—and these should receive the bulk of your attention—but you also need to keep a low fire burning throughout the rest of the year.

ADDITIONAL SOURCES

Internet Marketing for Dummies. New York: IDG Books Worldwide, 2001.
Radtke, Janel M. *Strategic Communications for Nonprofit Organizations.* New York: John Wiley & Sons, Inc., 1998.

ABOUT THE AUTHOR

Senior Web Strategist with HJC New Media, **George Irish**, ePMT, has designed award-winning Web sites for nonprofit organizations such as Greenpeace Canada, The Body Shop Canada, University of Toronto, Toronto Humane Society, and numerous others. George is currently leading the development of two new Web-based services: http://nonprofitlearning.com, an educational Web site offering online professional development courses to nonprofits, and nonprofit matrix.com, a Web portal providing vital information on new ASP and Portal services for the nonprofit sector. You can e-mail George at irishg@hjcnew media.com.

CHAPTER 7

Building Successful Online Communities

Sheeraz Haji, ePMT
GetActive Software

Greg Neichin
GetActive Software

eBay wasn't a hobby. And it wasn't a business. It was—and is—a community: An organic, evolving, self-organizing web of individual relationships, formed around shared interests.

—Pierre Omidyar, Founder of eBay

MOVING TOWARD A NEW MODEL OF ONLINE COMMUNITY

Most nonprofit organizations have Web sites that provide information to their audiences. Early nonprofit Web sites were *brochureware*—mostly descriptive, static pages that provided information but did not allow for any supportive actions or community interactions. Because of the efficiencies associated with moving core nonprofit business processes online, organizations are rapidly incorporating *actionware* into their Web sites—allowing supporters to subscribe to e-mail publications, engage in financial transactions, participate in advocacy lobbying, and so on. Although many organizational Web sites also offer opportunities for constituent participation via bulletin boards or event calendars, very few have successfully developed engaging, collaborative, online communities—places where constituents can, and do, spend hours interacting with each other, exchanging ideas, and helping the sponsoring organization achieve its mission (see Exhibit 7.1).

Traditionally, organizations have offered online community features in the hope that they would provide a virtual meeting place for their supporters. Much like a classic, bricks-and-mortar town hall, constituents have been expected to visit an organization's Web site to access information, search directories, post comments on bulletin boards, or learn about upcoming events. Such Web sites can provide access to a valuable repository of organizational knowledge and do allow supporters to contribute

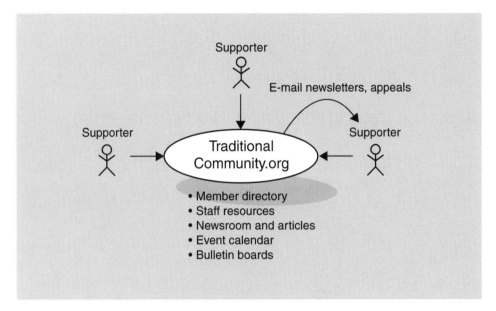

EXHIBIT 7.1 Traditional Online Community

some kinds of content, but most organizations have experienced relatively low participation rates in such communities by their online supporters.

Recent online organizing initiatives by political organizations, such as moveon.org, and commercial ventures, such as friendster.com, are demonstrating that a new set of community-building features can be much more effective at stimulating the growth of vibrant online communities. Rather than offering a virtual meeting place where the content and interaction opportunities are controlled by the sponsoring organization, today's successful Internet communities have turned the idea of top-down organizing upside down. A new model of community is emerging that focuses on providing online tools that stimulate interactions between constituents and enables collaborative participation without the direct supervision of a sponsoring organization (see Exhibit 7.2).

The for-profit world has one excellent example of this type of collaborative community: eBay, the leading online marketplace. At the end of 2003, eBay reported 95 million registered users. Half of these users were active, buying and selling $24 billion of merchandise in 2003. eBay's financial success has been driven by the daily activities of a passionate community of individuals and businesses that depend on the electronic marketplace. eBay is much more than a place to buy and sell all sorts of things, including Pez dispensers (the product that first launched eBay as an online auction site); it's an online community where individuals connect with other members who share common interests. Users rate each other, chat, share stories, debate product specifications, learn selling strategies, share photos, and participate in discussions, polls, and events. eBay has ceded control of its marketplace to its community, resulting in dramatic financial returns for eBay.

Nonprofits also have the opportunity to reap significant rewards by embracing the Internet to build community. A few leading organizations have used the Internet to create passionately engaged communities. Constituents interact with each other online

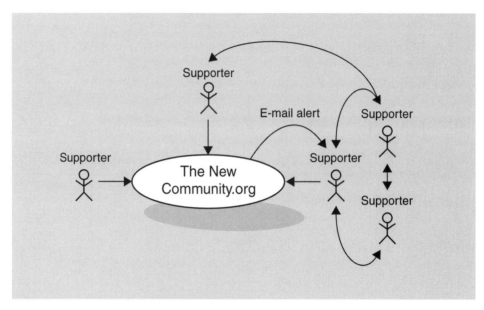

EXHIBIT 7.2 New Online Community Model

and offline. They organize within their social networks of friends and colleagues on behalf of a cause. Sponsoring organizations benefit from community building in numerous ways: increased member loyalty and sense of ownership, membership growth from peer-to-peer recruiting, idea generation, increased fundraising results, expanded participation in public policy and volunteer programs, and a growing network of talent for recruiting new staff.

What have these savvy organizations done to build community? Did they simply build or buy the tools to create interactive Web sites? No. Although building community online does require special tools, the key to success lies in an organization's message and its strategy for strengthening relationships with its constituents. Technology is secondary. As experiences with the first generation of community-building tools have demonstrated, there is no magic "if you build it they will come" solution.

An organization looking to build community should begin by building trust with its constituency and identifying promising opportunities for interaction. Organizations should start with simple tools that allow two-way conversations and then focus on increasing the level of engagement with specific offerings aligned with the online community's interests. This chapter outlines strategies for using the Internet to build community, highlighting successful case studies, identifying challenges, and providing best-practice recommendations.

STRATEGIES FOR BUILDING COMMUNITY

Community Identification: Articulate a Compelling Reason for Individuals to Join Your Community

Communities naturally form around shared interests, whether they are defined by ethical or political values, geographic region, or type of activity (see Exhibit 7.3). In today's online world, there is extensive competition for audience attention in both

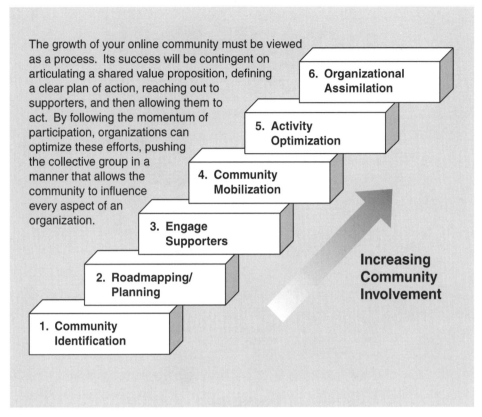

The growth of your online community must be viewed as a process. Its success will be contingent on articulating a shared value proposition, defining a clear plan of action, reaching out to supporters, and then allowing them to act. By following the momentum of participation, organizations can optimize these efforts, pushing the collective group in a manner that allows the community to influence every aspect of an organization.

6. Organizational Assimilation

5. Activity Optimization

4. Community Mobilization

3. Engage Supporters

2. Roadmapping/ Planning

1. Community Identification

Increasing Community Involvement

EXHIBIT 7.3 Building Blocks of Community

the commercial and nonprofit arenas. To succeed, organizations must clearly differentiate their focal interests from competitors and offer an engaging involvement path to individuals. Technology can provide little benefit in the absence of a strong, consistent, and clearly articulated message. A clear identity and engaging content represent the first stepping stones of the community-building process.

Examples of successful community identification exist in virtually every corner of the Internet, from slashdot.org, which provides an open forum for the news, views, and thoughts of the so-called nerd community, to Care2.com, which provides services to consumers interested in living a healthier lifestyle and engaging with social and environmental causes (see Exhibit 7.4).

Since its founding in 1998, Care2.com has maintained a distinct and unique mission to become a leading online destination for the progressive community, bringing together more than 2.3 million consumers, nonprofit organizations, and socially responsible businesses. Community features with a progressive twist, such as free greeting cards, free e-mail, photo albums, discussion boards, and Care2 Connect (a new online networking tool) instill a sense that it's possible to do things one would normally do on the Internet, while helping the environment and social causes.

Tools on Care2, such as GetLocal and Green Thumbs Up, aggregate personalized and localized environmental information to demonstrate to members how they can help the environment in a specific location or when they are shopping online. Through educational newsletters, timely action alerts, and a variety of community applications,

"Our mission at Care2 is to build a community of people who want to lead a healthier and more sustainable lifestyle while using innovative online tools to advance progressive causes."

—Andy Stocking, Vice President, Care2.com

EXHIBIT 7.4   Community Profile: Care2.com

Care2 creates an atmosphere where progressive activism has become part of the social norm. By partnering with leading advocacy groups and nonprofits, Care2 is also able to play an important community aggregation role by organizing petition drives, cross-promoting activist lists (resulting in 1 million new contacts for nonprofit partners), and driving traffic to partner sites (about 100,000 unique daily visitors frequently divert to partner sites).

Much like a commercial business in a competitive market, nonprofit organizations must define and articulate a value proposition that can attract online audiences as loyal supporters. Community identification is a prerequisite to any form of online community-building. If your audience remains unaware of what they have in common with others, they will have little motivation to tap into their network to recruit for your organization, to interact with one another, or to offer other forms of assistance.

Planning: Formulate a Path to Success

Communities are not created; they evolve. The growth of an online community takes time and effort. Relationships must be initiated based on trust, and then carefully cultivated. Develop a plan that articulates specific steps you will take over time to engage your general audience and convert a significant segment into active supporters. Organizations must identify a sequence of steps to increase a constituent's level of involvement and offer a variety of participation options that work to engage different components of their audience. To build a vibrant online community, organizations need more than an individual's donation or membership application—they need ongoing interaction opportunities that will keep a constituent engaged and developing into a lifelong supporter.

In addition to defining a set of interactions, goals must be clearly articulated. Organizations must ask themselves fundamental questions about the nature of the online community that they are building. Communities should be given room to grow in unique and evolutionary directions, but managers must keep focused on deriving and measuring value from the group. List growth, fundraising dollars, advocacy actions, legislative influence, and community feedback are often cited as examples of tangible goals, but every organization must find its own path and metrics of success.

A variety of member-based organizations have perfected the art of lifelong relationships. Major health and welfare charities such as the American Red Cross, the Salvation Army, CARE, and the American Lung Association strive to forge lasting bonds with donors; colleges and universities carefully cultivate alumni from the time that they have a diploma in their hands through retirement and estate planning; and the world of public television and radio broadcasting prides itself on bringing lifelong programming into the country's living room. All of these groups are actively engaged in utilizing technology to further these relationships, and all of them are applying tried and true methods of donor cultivation to the online world. By programming and planning a series of interactions with donors, these groups succeed in building lasting relationships.

Established in 1959, KVIE, Inc. strives "to educate, enrich, enlighten and inspire diverse audiences and individuals through high-quality television programming and related services that enhance the quality of life for people in the communities that it serves. Viewer donations constitute approximately 50 percent of KVIE's annual budget. As a public television station, many donors are motivated to give because of particular programs and lifetime experiences. As a result, fundraising is most effective when communication is thoughtfully planned and personal (see Exhibit 7.5).

KVIE launched a weekly Viewer's Club publication in 2001. Subscribers receive a personalized HTML newsletter with program highlights for the upcoming week. In addition, members receive personalized communications based on stated preferences

Dear David,

My records indicate that you supported KVIE public television in the past by supporting the Drum Corps International Championships program. I thought you would like to know, if you didn't already, that this year's program is on Saturday at 1:30 PM.

If you are interested in learning more about the program, I built a Web page that you can visit. Or if you would like to support this year's program, visit our secure online donation form.

If you know others who would like to watch this program, you can forward this message with Tell-A-Friend.

I hope you enjoy the program!

Regards,

David Lowe

David Lowe
KVIE Vice President, Marketing

Visit the web address below to tell your friends about this.
Tell-a-friend!

If you received this message from a friend, you can sign up for KVIE E-mail Alerts.

If you would like to unsubscribe from KVIE E-mail Alerts, or update your account settings, please click here or respond to this email with "REMOVE" as the subject line.

"Powerful personalization and message targeting ensure that we can integrate our online marketing efforts with the strong demographic marketing strategies we use on air and in print!"

—David Lower, Vice President of Marketing & Development, KVIE

EXHIBIT 7.5   Community Profile: KVIE

and observed activities. Fundraising campaigns are often built around specific programming with a personal and targeted appeal, a unique online donation form, and relevant thank-you messages. KVIE members are encouraged to complete and update personal profiles—information then used to send targeted and relevant messages. Follow-up e-mail campaigns target known program supporters, resulting in outstanding click-through rates topping 30 percent for targeted campaigns. Just two years into a comprehensive effort to improve online relationship building, KVIE has seen its online membership grow by 68 percent and has turned just $2,000 in online gifts in 2001 into nearly $200,000 in 2003.

The art of planning, however, is not reserved solely for lasting institutional relationships. Political campaigns have proven adept at being the speediest online suitors of constituents. Examples of involvement paths containing multiple action opportunities are easy to spot in the political arena, where the entire process of recruiting the unaffiliated and converting them into active supporters is compressed into one election cycle. In an attempt to quickly and effectively build a sense of community, the 2004 Democratic presidential primary saw candidates aggressively offering multiple options for online action. From Howard Dean's high-profile Internet operation, to the online efforts of John Edwards and eventual nominee John Kerry, technology was employed to offer voters multiple opportunities to support a campaign and move them along a path toward increased involvement.

Laying out involvement paths, organizations should not simply replicate the full set of possible engagement tools and offer these to their audience buffet-style. Involvement paths need to be tailored to the characteristics of an organization's audience, as well as its mission and operating style. Although organizations typically possess a good understanding of how different versions of their content stimulate supportive action (from their experience in direct-mail fundraising), they often have limited visibility into the appeal of common online engagement opportunities to their audience (e.g., do my supporters blog?). Deciding on a viable roadmap for building an online community typically requires an organization to revisit strategic plans and test the appeal of different community-building features.

Engage Supporters: Establish Targeted and Personal Communications via E-mail

Once a value proposition and potential involvement paths have been identified, organizations must participate in two-way interactive communications with their audience. Of course every organization should collect e-mail addresses via its Web site and offline sign-up activities in order to communicate with constituents via e-mail. However, it is not enough to simply operate as a publisher, distributing content to e-mail lists. Each organization needs a two-way channel that enables it to learn how constituents interact with the organization's message and engagement offers. In its simplest form, this feedback loop may be implemented via e-mail replies. However, much more sophisticated tools for engagement tracking are now available, and any organization that publishes a regular e-mail newsletter should also be collecting detailed information on how each recipient interacts with its communications efforts (by monitoring the open and unsubscribe rates of its newsletters, tracking the links that recipients click through, and recording the actions constituents take in response to messaging campaigns).

This interaction information is essential for fine-tuning future communications efforts to the interests of specific constituents. In contrast to a broadcast publication, personalized messaging enables an organization to customize its pitch and appeal to different audience segments, increasing participation rates. By making these messages personal and relevant, an organization can create an immediate and powerful sense of community.

MoveOn.org has experimenting with opening its decision making up to participation by supporters (see Exhibit 7.6). An online forum system is used to solicit nominations of issues the group should work on and to rank the overall importance of the issues to the community. In addition, many important decisions are determined by the direct vote of its members (e.g., MoveOn's online primary for the 2004 presidential election).

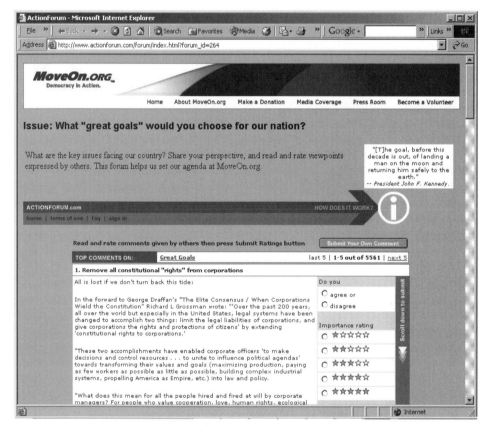

"The hardest thing to get across to the political establishment is that this is not just another set of tools you use to manipulate constituencies and tap them for money. . . . This has to be seen as a way to engage constituencies and engage in a two-way conversation."

—Wes Boyd, Founder of MoveOn.org

EXHIBIT 7.6   Community Profile: MoveOn.org

Engagement is an iterative process, involving the use of a variety of communication tools to distribute action opportunities and obtain feedback on their appeal. Experience demonstrates that it is possible to build a strong sense of community quickly if audiences are made aware that their opinion matters and that their participation counts. Which specific tools are used is less important than an organization's willingness to listen to constituent feedback. Listservs, for example, are a traditional community-building tool that can be as effective as newer tools such as blogs in enabling two-way interactive communication.

The Humane Society of the United States (HSUS), the nation's largest animal protection organization, taps into the power of feedback by reporting the success of its eCommunity efforts to list members.

In a particularly powerful example, the HSUS was able to mobilize its community to respond to Hurricane Charley in 2004. Hours after the hurricane struck, HSUS created an online campaign for its relief fund, soliciting donations from supporters through both e-mails and a fundraising Web page (see Exhibit 7.7). In the ten days that followed the hurricane striking Florida, HSUS was able to raise over $128,000 online for the organization's Disaster Relief Fund. Personalized thank-you messages

DISASTER UPDATE

From the pet experts at...

THE HUMANE SOCIETY
OF THE UNITED STATES

A Thank You Message and Report from our Disaster Animal Response Team

Dear Greg,

The devastation of Hurricane Charley is all around me. It's now Friday, and the situation for animals here in southwestern Florida remains dire.

Thanks to your generous donation to our Disaster Relief Fund, we at The Humane Society of the United States (HSUS) have been working around the clock to save as many animals as we can. I want to give you a personal update about what's been happening this week:

At our disaster relief center here in Punta Gorda, one of the hardest hit areas, we first began accepting animals on Monday. This facility is taking in rescued, displaced, and injured animals, and caring for them until they can be transferred to local shelters.

Even as you read this, fresh HSUS Disaster Animal Response Teams (DART) have stepped up operations in nearby counties. Our highly trained teams have been on site since Saturday, conducting damage assessments from the hurricane and coordinating rescues daily with county animal control officers.

Thankfully, we've had some heartwarming successes amid the tragedy all around us: There was the lab mix, found pinned under a collapsed house, whose injured leg was treated at our Center and who is expected to make a full recovery...the bear found wandering the streets of a subdivision, miles away from the nearest forest, who was tranquilized and transported safely to a

This dog found safety at HSUS's Disaster Relief Center in Punta Gorda, Florida.

Thanks to your generous support of our Disaster Relief Fund, our Disaster Animal Response Teams have been working nonstop in Florida since Saturday.

On behalf of the animals affected by Hurricane Charley, the staff of The Humane Society of the United States says a huge and heartfelt "Thank you."

EXHIBIT 7.7 Community Profile: Humane Society of the United States

with updates on how money was spent and results of the relief effort, kept donors involved and engaged. The results of the Hurricane Charley relief effort dwarfed the several thousand dollars raised the previous year in response to Hurricane Isabel. It is believed that ongoing efforts to develop personalized communications with donors will continue to improve results in the future.

Community Mobilization: What Now? Calls to Action and Increased Participation

Converting an *engaged* constituency into a *mobilized* constituency is perhaps the most challenging aspect of the community building process. At this stage of development, an organization

- Has convinced unaffiliated individuals to join (indicating an initial interest in the community value proposition)
- Has established a trusted connection with a constituent through personalized two-way communications

Now the challenge is to stimulate participation in a sequence of supportive actions along an involvement path. E-mail communications should direct supporters back to Web site tools that allow for participation in actions relevant to an individual's profile, with specific actions varying for different organizations. Politically active groups often use Web-based petitions and advocacy campaigns to enable their supporters to easily participate in the public policy process. Shared-value groups often use listservs or blogs to enable members to contribute their opinions to an ongoing community conversation. Charitable organizations typically focus on facilitating donations. Among your membership base exist ardent supporters willing to commit multiple hours per week (or per day) to your cause. There are others who may scan personal e-mail only on the weekends, but may provide intelligent feedback in a regular manner. Large numbers may open e-mails, but may never actively participate in your calls to action. Tracking these different segments of your membership and tailoring your interactions accordingly is essential to effective community building.

Once an action (or a series of actions) has been initiated, make certain to solicit ideas and respond to feedback. The best way to find out what is interesting to constituents is to ask. Solicit preference information from individuals as they opt-in to your newsletters, give money, complete a survey, or network using your tools. In addition to information supplied by members, pay close attention to behavioral activity as measured by page views, click-through rates, participation rates, and other easily measured characteristics. Combine these statistics with demographics and preferences to build a complete profile of each member and your constituent segments. Constantly look for opportunities to better understand your membership and their motivations for action.

Structure your action offers so that they proceed along an involvement path, allowing for initial, low-barrier to participation actions that lead to the next step up in engagement.

As an example, CARE USA, one of the largest international relief organizations, uses a sophisticated subscription management page (see Exhibit 7.8) allowing community members to supply updated profile information, view activity records and edit newsletter preferences.

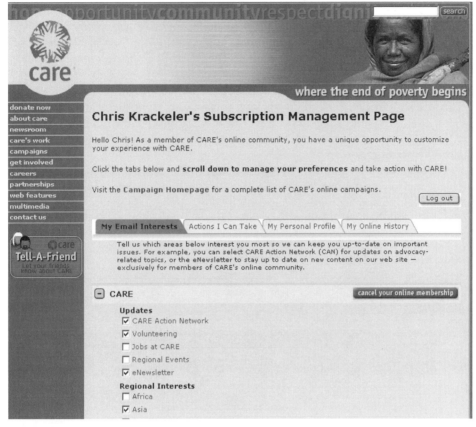

EXHIBIT 7.8   Community Profile: CARE USA

Activity Optimization: Finding the Right Jobs for the Right Supporters

> *These people who link us up with the world . . . who introduce us to our*
> *social circles—these people on whom we rely more heavily than we realize—*
> *are Connectors, people with a special gift for bringing the world together.*

> —Malcolm Gladwell, The Tipping Point

Malcolm Gladwell's frequently cited work on social networking and community building, *The Tipping Point*, refers to distinct types of individuals involved in creating social trends. He uses terms like *connectors, mavens,* and *salesmen* to describe the individuals who take on unique roles in marketing an idea and encouraging the adoption of new behaviors that become social trends. Individuals with these skills exist within the community surrounding your organization. The key to optimizing the value of your membership is to ensure that these people have access to tools that help them be effective in their roles. Ideally, you want the activities that are most supportive of your organizational mission to become the next social trend.

The challenge is to mobilize supporters to use their social networks for the benefit of your organization. In essence, an organization needs to convert a portion of its engaged base into active recruiters and organizers, thereby significantly expanding the reach and impact of its own personnel. Many organizations have already experienced the importance of social networking online as a result of their use of "tell-a-friend" tools. These networking tools have demonstrated that if you provide supporters with an easy way to help spread the word about your organization's activities, many will reach out to their social network and encourage participation.

More sophisticated social networking tools allow supporters to build personal Web pages to communicate their involvement with an organization to their friends and colleagues, and recruit new members or solicit other supportive actions on behalf of an organization.

For example, within hours of President Bush's February 24, 2004, announcement of his intent to seek a constitutional amendment prohibiting same-sex marriage, The Human Rights Campaign (HRC) had mobilized an online community nearly 350,000 strong (see Exhibit 7.9). Having built this community through tireless effort, count-

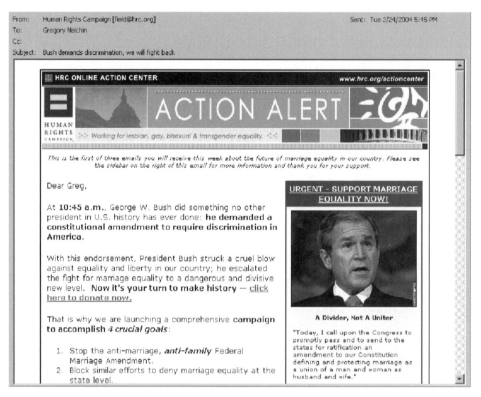

"With this endorsement, President Bush struck a cruel blow against equality and liberty in our country; he escalated the fight for marriage equality to a dangerous and divisive new level. Now it's your turn to make history."

—Cheryl Jacques, President, Human Rights Campaign

(from e-mail appeal—02/24/04)

EXHIBIT 7.9   Community Profile: Human Rights Campaign

less e-mail campaigns, advocacy efforts, petition drives, and correspondence, the HRC staff had an engaged and mobilized constituency ready to act. In a series of e-mail appeals, HRC offered members a variety of ways to support the organizations and its mission. Fundraising was a key element of the campaign, and an ambitious goal of $500,000 within the week was set and surpassed. Advocacy campaigns allowed members to send letters to Congress and the president voicing their opposition. HRC gave activists the ability to build their own pages on behalf of the organization, to tell their stories, post pictures, and to engage their friends and families. By having a community ready to act and by giving them the mechanisms to reach out in their own, individual way, HRC produced a stunningly successful campaign.

The downside of optimizing member activity is that content may need to be carefully monitored. The same tools that give activists an unprecedented ability to voice their opinion and contribute to your cause can often be accessed by those with opposing viewpoints or those simply seeking to post inappropriate content. Organizations must strike a careful balance between giving members the autonomy to develop content, with the desire (and often the legal necessity) of ensuring that content is both appropriate and contributing to the mission of the organization.

Community Integration: Connecting Communities across Your Organization

Online communities can complement the networks that your organization already possesses as a result of your offline constituency development activities. Depending on your organizational mission, you may have cultivated networks of donors, event attendees, volunteers, coalition partners, and so on. Internet-based relationship management and communication tools provide a cost-effective means for managing your offline communities, as well as new opportunities for connecting and optimizing these existing networks. As organizations begin to successfully mobilize online communities, the opportunity to leverage these relationships to support offline activities will quickly become apparent (see Exhibit 7.10). Successful organizations will assimilate the ideas of community building into everything they do, connecting various constituencies into an integrated community network.

Establishing connections between the different communities that support your organization presents both challenges and opportunities. While many charities possess engaged constituencies, they may not have a management culture that welcomes extensive community participation in the decision-making process.

Traditional forms of broadcast publication are now being challenged by a variety of Web-based, interactive communication strategies (e.g., blogs or discussion forums) that allow constituents to weigh in on virtually any aspect of organizational policy. Unless an organization develops an openness to these new forms of participation, it risks discouraging the development of supportive communities.

The opportunities available from integrating community-building considerations into an organization's operations are compelling. Offline constituents can be more effectively managed online, increasing the support they can provide. Online supporters constitute an already-engaged audience of potential participants in real-world activities that are important to a nonprofit, whether the request involves financial support, physical participation in activities, and so on. When an organization pursues consistent messaging both offline and online, based on an integrated view of constituent

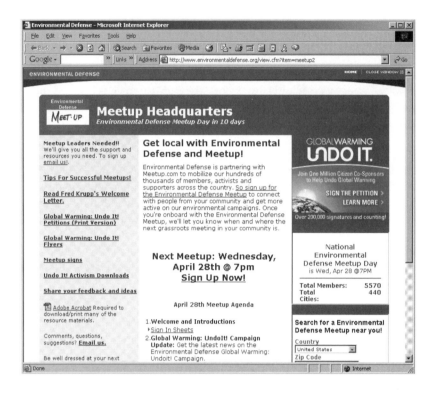

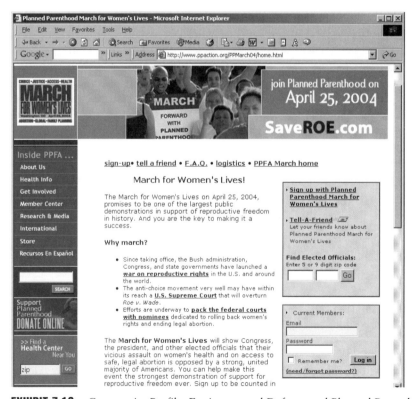

EXHIBIT 7.10   Community Profile: Environmental Defense and Planned Parenthood

activities, they can be more effectively converted into life-long supporters. Connecting communities is the key to success.

ABOUT THE AUTHOR

As the CEO and co-founder of GetActive Software, **Sheeraz Haji**, ePMT, has driven the company to become the leading provider of member relationship management software for membership organizations. His management of GetActive's organizational and development efforts has resulted in the acquisition of over 300 clients and the achievement of profitability in 2002 and 2003. Sheeraz is an active member of the board of directors for Nonprofit Technology Enterprise Network (N-TEN), an associate for Independent Sector, and a trustee of the ePhilanthropy Foundation. Sheeraz has been selected as an expert presenter at multiple industry events sponsored by numerous organizations, including N-TEN, Independent Sector, PBS, NPR, National Council for Nonprofit Associations, and Association of Fundraising Professionals. Before GetActive, Sheeraz led a product management team at Digital Impact, the leading provider of online direct marketing solutions for enterprises. He has also worked as a strategy consultant for McKinsey & Company, where he served both nonprofit and for-profit organizations and focused on corporate strategy, market entry, and operational effectiveness. Sheeraz has a BS from Brown University and a MS from Stanford University. You can e-mail Sheeraz at Sheeraz@getactive.com.

As Vice President of Corporate Development at GetActive Software, **Greg Neichin** has helped shape a variety of new practice areas for the company and has worked closely with some of the country's largest political campaigns, advocacy groups, and educational institutions. Prior to joining GetActive, Greg led a broad range of partner and corporate initiatives for Redback Networks as a member of the Strategy and Business Development team. He has written and lectured on behalf of the Stanford Research Institute's Business Intelligence program throughout North America and Asia. He began his career as a Consultant for Mercer Management Consulting where he worked for a number of Fortune 500 clients. Greg holds a B.A. in Economics and Government from Dartmouth College. You can e-mail Greg at greg@getactive.com.

CHAPTER 8

Building Your Brand Online

Jason Mogus, ePMT
President, Communicopia.net

Pattie LaCroix, ePMT
Vice President, Communicopia.net

Even if you don't think you have a brand as a non-profit organization, you actually do!

The promise of a brand is the idea that it can be trusted and will make your life better. Everyone from banks to your sneaker to your morning orange juice maker want to develop a long-term relationship with you. Brands promise you value. They work to develop an impression that will lodge so powerfully in your mind that you unconsciously turn to them, engage in their story, and adopt the set of values upon which pivots their relationship with you. Building a long-term relationship is the goal of all brands. Put simply, a brand is an organization's story. It promises value to you for the purpose of building a relationship.

Because people can interact with your organization online, nonprofits have tremendous potential to create relationships that will sustain your work. The key to building this relationship is an emotional engagement with your audience. In order to mobilize the audience into becoming involved as either a donor, a volunteer or member, a nonprofit must first understand that the audience they are trying to reach and engage receives many hundred messages a day asking them in one way or another to buy into a relationship. This is because building relationships that deliver value is the very lifeblood that pumps through the heart of the branding exercise.

Virtually all keepers of brands have recognized the power that the Internet holds in building relationships with their different audiences. It is a noisy landscape to be sure, but nonprofit organizations have a story to tell that sets them apart from consumer-product–driven brands. (i.e. Ivory Snow, Levis, and Ford). Consumer-driven brands must create a story that has some value to you for the sole purpose of building a relationship that is predicated on you purchasing their product. Nonprofits, by contrast, have embedded in their very culture, articulated with their mission statements, and delivered through their programs, brands that are saturated with values that can serve to build relationships that are instead based on you as a member of your community—not just as a consumer. In short, product-driven brands focus far more on individual needs while nonprofit or cause-related brands focus far more on the needs of the community. The value-based brands that are held by nonprofits resonate closely with the very core of branding, and as such, the nonprofit sector is incredibly well positioned to use the power of branding to its advantage.

We hear a lot about branding these days. It seems like all products, services, and even people—everyone from sports figures to politicians to industry leaders are conscious of developing their own personal brand. It is key to remember that branding is about creating a relationship of trust and emotional attachment. Even if you don't think you have a brand as a nonprofit organization, you actually do! When you are out in the community, delivering services, working with volunteers and raising support, you are constantly creating an impression of your nonprofit. This impression is associated with a certain value set within the minds of your audience. Values, trust, relationships, benefits, and promises are all associated experiences of your brand. Whether you are deliberate about your brand or not, you are by the very fact of engaging with the community creating a brand for your organization and that brand comes across in everything you do.

It seems natural to explore the possibility that thoughtful branding offline and online of nonprofits holds immense potential in building authentic trusting relationships and emotional attachment with audiences. Before we delve into what edge, if any, the nature of branding gives nonprofits in jostling for brand space in the public's mind, let's take a look at the basics of branding and the impact that online branding in particular has on building relationships.

THE BASIC BRANDING BUILDING BLOCKS

There has been a great deal written about the power of branding and its goal to very deliberately and consciously create a presence, an image, or a memory in our unconscious. This brand positioning within our psyches plays a key factor in our decision-making process. When we reach for a Diet Coke and snack of Lays potato chips we are not randomly choosing these options, we are responding in large part to their "brand promise," which has been lodged somewhere in our mind. The story of these brands focuses on creating and then addressing our individual needs, wants, and desires:

- Diet Coke–Do What Feels Good
- Lays Potato Chips–Bet You Can't Just Eat One

A brand is one of an organization's or a company's greatest assets. Your brand is what people think of you, what they attribute to you, and their expectations of you—essentially, it is your reputation. When managed well, it holds the potential to successfully support your organization and create new opportunities for engagement. Managing your brand, then, needs to rest at the very center of your organization and be integrated into your delivery of services. The story that your organization sends out to the public and the values upon which these messages rest should be key drivers of the strategy and the culture of your nonprofit. Brands for nonprofits are value-based and at the heart of such brands are organic relationships that require nurturing to grow and to sustain an organization. Value-based brands rotate on the experience of the relationship.

This is where the Internet has a particularly powerful role to play in value-based nonprofit brands. The Web is all about people interacting with your organization. Moving your brand online is moving beyond images, tag lines, and graphics and into the space of experiencing of your brand. This is where the greatest challenge is for non-profits and the greatest opportunity as well.

Brands have both tangible and intangible attributes. We are all most familiar with a brand's tangible characteristics. An organization's slogan, colors, or logo are tangible brand reference points. But these tangible attributes of a brand are merely the visible byproducts of its intangible elements—the values, personality, and functional benefits it promises. Delivering on these intangible aspects of your brand means that you are fulfilling your brand promise. Combined, the attributes of a brand help create a market position by differentiating it from the other brands within any given market segment.

It is not unusual for product-driven brands to differentiate them by comparing themselves with their competition. This is not a branding strategy that should be played out within the nonprofit sector; here, differentiation needs to be communicated through a meaningful, attractive, and compelling manner. This is because your values-based brand needs to rest on your own set of values and benefits that are unique to you and that will engage individuals to support your work in the community.

The values of a brand are the values that you want your target audiences to associate with you when they think about you. These values necessarily are aligned with your mission statement. The benefits of your brand need to clarify for your target group what exactly is the benefit of supporting your brand and how will this engagement with your brand make your audience feel. By delivering on your brand promise you create differentiation for your organization within the minds of your target audience (see Exhibit 8.1).

TAKING YOUR BRAND ONLINE

The vitality and strength of any brand is its ability to engage people, to tell its story in a consistent and compelling manner in a fashion that clearly articulates the benefit for the audience. Nonprofits do, in fact, have engaging stories to tell that are of great benefit to both individuals and the community, the best part is these stories do not have to be manufactured—they are authentically present in the very genetic code of non-profit organizations. So why aren't people lining up to volunteer or donate for non-profits? Why aren't nonprofits overwhelmed by public support?

Simply stated, there are three broad reasons. To begin with, nonprofits traditionally have not viewed branding as an integral or even important element of their operations or strategic direction. Secondly, nonprofits do not have large marketing budgets and human resources at their disposal to create and implement effective brand strategies. Donors and funders do not generally support such communication initiatives. Finally, because of the first two reasons cited, nonprofits have not actively engaged with the most powerful communications tool available today, the Internet. In general, the Web has been vastly underutilized to grow the brands of nonprofits and to increase their base of support. What this means is that there is enormous potential for

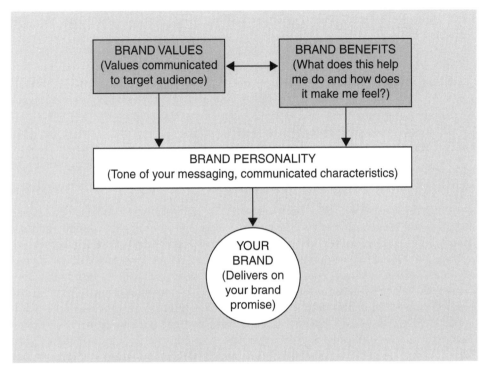

EXHIBIT 8.1 Basic Brand Building Blocks

nonprofits to engage the public in their work, to broaden their base of support and ultimately deliver greater impact within their communities.

When taking your nonprofit brand online, you will mostly likely be seeking to increase your support base and/or enlist volunteers in your organization. Before you do this, take a few moments to review the ePhilanthropy Code of Ethical Online Philanthropic Practices (see Appendix A). When you take your brand online, you are expanding your potential to service relationships and build new ones. Successful relationships are built on trust. When gathering data about your online audience, it is imperative that this data be used for clearly expressed and stated purposes only, that all communication be permission based, and that your online audience's security and privacy are at all times protected. These basic principles should be at the center of any online branding exercise.

Branding your organization online means that your audience has the opportunity to experience your story and interact with your brand promise. This experience is of paramount importance and will, in fact, determine in the mind of the end user whether or not your organization's story is credible and memorable—two key elements of any relationship building activity. So it is fundamental that your branding online be consistent with your offline branding. Your branding strategy will be most powerful when it is integrated with your offline initiatives. If developing a branding strategy seems very much like developing a strategic vision for your nonprofit that is good, both must be inextricably linked because this will create genuine relationships with your audience. When you develop your branding strategy, you need to explore the following questions with staff, volunteers, board members, and other key stakeholders in your organization:

- What is it that we *do* as an organization? (Identity statement)
- What are our *values*? (Core values)
- *Who* are we serving, and what *benefits* can our target audience expect? (Audience and brand promise)
- What makes us *different*? (Key messages)
- What is the *tone* of our message? (Personality)
- How do we *integrate* our brand throughout our organization? (Commitment to consistency)

Once these questions have been answered within your organization, there is one more step before you can get into the tangible aspects of branding like design, taglines, colors, logos, and so on. Before you begin to bring your brand online, it is important to develop an online development process that is driven by key stakeholders in your organization such as staff, volunteers, board members, and donors. Just as this consultation informed the branding strategy it will be instrumental in informing the development of your branding for public consumption. It is a process that—if followed through the development of the design, content, and build of your online communications—can provide you with a wealth of information that can charge your Web site with impact, engagement, and responsiveness culminating in impressive results. The look and feel of your site, the visuals used, the colors, fonts, and typography all go a long way toward establishing credibility online.

A recent study conducted by the Persuasive Technology Lab at Stanford University said that visual cues are ranked as the most important element in establishing credibility in the mind of the end user. People are relying on effective design to gauge the credibility of a site; in fact, 39.4 percent felt this when accessing nonprofit Web sites. Once you have a user-centered process in place, let's look at why the Web is so powerful for developing your brand.

The Web is a powerful medium for developing relationships, and as such, is central to developing a successful brand. The Web, when used to its highest potential, can be the centerpiece of your organization's brand-building exercises. It can play this role because your online communications—whether they be e-mail campaigns or your Web site—can be relevant, responsive, and interactive. It provides a platform where people actually engage with your brand and interact with your organization's values. For example, respecting your end users' privacy, employing only permission-based e-mails, ensuring that your audience is receiving only relevant information that is of real value to them, thanking your supporters for their involvement in your latest campaign and letting them know about a special event in their community, all can serve to underscore the values of your brand. Online is where the integration of your brand throughout your organization can come to life. Your fundraising, donor relations, special events, volunteer recruitment, and member management, which are all key ways that your stakeholders experience your brand, can be integrated and supported through the online medium.

Online you create an impression of your organization within the first five to ten seconds—in general, people do not spend more than five minutes on a Web site.

This might seem daunting, but in fact it is a call for online communicators to have their brand strategy well articulated before setting down the path of execution. The power of online branding rests in three broad areas: relevancy, responsiveness, and interactivity.

The Web is where your branding relationship comes to life as two-way communications. The audience is not merely a passive recipient of your brand but can participate in actually shaping it! For example, when hospital patients are encouraged to go online to the hospital's foundation site and share their experience of their own hospital care, this shared experience provides other potential patients with immensely relevant content and offers donors a first-hand understanding of the impact of their contributions. Your Web site can be exceptionally relevant to your audience and can in fact be the primary experience of your organization's brand, particularly if your organization covers a wide geographical area.

The Web is also remarkably responsive from a fundraising and operational efficiency perspective. Your online communications can support major fundraising campaigns through e-mail action alerts, regular e-newsletter stories, or by simply highlighting your latest campaign on the homepage of your site. Your site can also provide a unique donor recognition experience for relatively very low cost. The effectiveness of your organization's board and volunteers can be greatly enhanced with a password-protected area where internal communications, policies, and documents can be easily accessed. This is particularly relevant for organizations with only one office but servicing a national or regional constituency.

The experience of your brand online can be wonderfully personalized. You can demonstrate that you have truly listened to your audience and respond to them in a myriad of individualized ways. As we know, active listening is the cornerstone of any good relationship. Online technologies can "listen" exceptionally well. They can deliver customized communications and reach out to your audience in a powerful, personalized way. For example, a member of an environmental group can choose how often and when they would like to donate, if they would like to receive an e-newsletter about forests, water pollution, or any number of specific issues in addition to being informed of special events being held in their own community. This member can customize the desired level of involvement online. That is great relationship building!

Now as much as relevancy and responsiveness are important, the interactivity of your online communications can hold remarkable opportunities for your organization to build and engage your audiences. Your Web site, e-mail campaigns, and e-newsletters can, in fact act as your brand hub. It is here in this online space where your organization can integrate its fundraising, volunteer management, staff recruitment, donor communications, and, in varying degrees, even service delivery.

Let's remember before we go any further into this line of thinking that the Internet is merely a platform, albeit a powerful and pervasive one—but a platform just the same. Internet technologies in and of themselves will not sustain or grow your organization; they are tools that people can use to have a greater impact in their community, increase your fundraising reach, personalize your service delivery, increase your educational reach, and build broader bases of support for your work. The Internet holds unique potential for nonprofits to develop relationships with people through providing them with opportunities to interact with the values, benefits, and personality of your organization, in short, experience your brand. Ultimately, what the

Internet does best when used well is engage people, and it is this engagement that will sustain your organization over the long run.

The degree to which your online communications can be relevant, responsive, and interactive is connected with your organization's support of your Web site specifically and in general to your overall online strategy. Keep this in mind when developing your online communications plans. For example, if you create a Web site that cannot be easily updated internally, this may result in stale content and provide no incentive for your audience to engage with your brand online. If you are able to collect data on your audience through your Web site but have no internal database reporting capabilities, your potential to build your brand both offline and online will be dramatically limited. This means that you are missing a key element in building a relationship with your audience and this in turn has a direct impact on your ability to raise funds, recruit volunteers, and build a base of support within your community. Your Web site is not a standalone communications piece that resides in the "Web guy's" cubicle in a dark corner of your organization. It is an integral part of your brand, and consequently, of your organization's health. Your online communications, marketing, IT, fundraising, and executive director need to all be engaged in building relationships online. The values that your nonprofit holds and articulates through the benefits of its work could have limited impact on the lives of those in your community if your online communications is not an integrated part of your operations and your branding. This challenge of developing integrated organizational and branding strategies is greatly mitigated by the very culture of the nonprofit sector itself, which can be summed up as one of innovation, creativity, resourcefulness, determination, humanity, and passion. More and more nonprofits are engaging online consultants and Internet marketing firms to assist them in developing Internet strategies and tactics that will communicate their brand and develop sustaining relationships. The most successful of these engagements will be with firms that approach this relationship not from a solely technology point of view, but from a deep understanding of this unique nonprofit culture.

WHAT MAKES A SUCCESSFUL BRAND ONLINE?

The experience of your brand online is, in fact, your online brand. This cannot be underscored enough. In the online space, every capillary of interactivity carries with it a lasting impression of your brand. For example, if your Web site's navigation is not intuitive and consistent and your links don't work, people will leave your site and not return—and a relationship may be eliminated. This may seem a bit harsh, but if you think about how crowded the landscape is for people's attention and support, you really only have one chance to make a good impression, and nowhere is that more evident than in the world of the Web. Our expectations online are of speed, quick and relevant information, dependable functionality, and intuitive design that doesn't overpower or distract from the content. If users have to wait, think about where they are on your site, or not be able to complete a task, then they are gone. These are the basics of any online communication and are central to a successful, smart online brand:

- *Authenticity.* Tell compelling stories.
- *Accessible.* Don't make them wait

- *Intuitive.* Don't make them think
- *Functional.* Let them complete key tasks

Beyond these interactive branding basics rests the real opportunity to differentiate your nonprofit within the overpopulated online world. It is in this terrain where interactivity, the very nature of the Web, can reach out and create relationships for your organization. But before one gets carried away with the bells and whistles of Internet technologies, a deep understanding of the brand, its personality, and its messages must be present and consistent with offline branding initiatives. Now let's take a look at how interactivity can build relationships for your nonprofit.

INTERACTIVITY IS KEY

Interactivity has the potential to engage people, draw them deeper and deeper into your story, and indeed give them a flavor of the very essence of your organization. As they flow from one experience to the next online they are uncovering your personality, receiving and responding to your messages, and immersing themselves in your values. Let's look at how the Positive Women's Network, a Canadian organization that offers programs, supports and advocates for women living with HIV, took their brand online with the launch of the new program site, Women and AIDS Virtual Education Project (WAVE).

One out of every four people diagnosed with HIV in Canada is a woman, and many women living with HIV experience isolation, lack of support, and no way of connecting with other HIV positive women or skilled health care providers. The Positive Women's Network (PWN) works to care for these women, and key to their core values is that all their community access points show deep levels of support, safety, and connection for women living with HIV. Equally important to PWN and its members is a sense of confidentiality and privacy, due to the stigma still attached to the disease. This brand would best be described as welcoming, supportive, confidential, and informative. The organization audiences are HIV+ women, health care providers, volunteers, and donors.

Keeping PWN's values at the core of our work, Communicopia, through a process of consultation with PWN and its members, developed the WAVE program site and worked to ensure that this Web site was fully integrated with offline communications. PWN's office space centers around a drop in space that looks very much like a big family kitchen, so when designing their new Web site they wanted to keep that same strong and consistent sense of connectedness, welcoming, and intimacy. Through the use of color, visuals, and tone of messaging, PWN's core values come through equally on all major components of its communications collateral—indeed, they work in tandem to deliver a consistent brand promise.

Interactivity was woven into the experience of the PWN brand online by respecting the needs of PWN's audience. On *www.pwn-wave.ca*, privacy policies are prominent on every page, and end users are shown how they can turn off their cookies and eliminate their Internet tracks to ensure privacy. As well, a special low-tech "Hide Site" button allows users to instantly bring up the Google homepage to further ensure privacy and safety. In order to break down the sense of isolation that many women feel when they become HIV positive, WAVE has a bulletin board available to provide a safe space where these women can connect. The site also provides an "Ask An Expert" feature to assist women in getting the information they need to make informed decisions around their care options. All of this works to ensure that its online brand mirrors the brand promise of their real world drop-in center and overall organization.

We discussed earlier that integration not only happens at the strategic and executional level, but also at the operational level to ensure that the relationships developed through a well-planned and executed brand can be supported by the organization.

IT'S ALL ABOUT TRUST

Throughout this chapter you have come across words like lifeblood, circulatory system, organic, nucleus, and capillaries. What does this have to do with online branding? Everything! Branding is the stuff of life for nonprofit organizations. The branding process is a living, breathing part of your organization. It is an integrated endeavor that puts out into the public domain your mission statement and core value set. It exudes your personality and seeks to reach out and build trust with your audience so that long-term relationships can grow and be sustained. If the people are the heart of nonprofit organizations then surely branding is the major aorta. Taking your story online in no way changes your story—it does, however, allow more people to experience your story and be engaged by it. If branding is to have a positive impact on your nonprofit, it necessarily needs to be an integrated activity involving all key stakeholders. When you review the following checklist, don't be surprised if you notice that it goes way beyond "the IT department" and even communications to deal with all manner of fundraising, operational, and strategic planning areas.

Your Quick Checklist to Developing a Successful Online Brand

- Ensure that a consultative process of end user engagement is in place.
- Formulate a clear understanding of your organization's strategic plan.
- Reach a consensus on your values, audience, key messages, and personality.
- Articulate your brand promise.
- Scope out the impact of online branding with other operational elements of your organization (database management, donor recognition, volunteer support, etc.).
- Put in place mechanisms and capacity that will ensure a responsive, relevant, and interactive brand experience online.
- Ensure that your communication is accessible, intuitive, and functional.
- Integrate. Integrate. Integrate. (Offline and online work together to support the organization and work in tandem for its sustainability.)

So as you can see online branding goes far beyond just building a Web site.

THE BRANDING EDGE FOR THE NONPROFIT SECTOR

Earlier it was pondered if nonprofits, because of their value-based branding, have an edge in the marketplace over consumer-based brands such as Coke or Nike. Well, if this edge is defined by market penetration, only then the answer is surely no, because nonprofits do not have at their disposal the multimillion dollar marketing budgets of large multinational brands. But if we agree that branding is about building long-term sustainable relationships, then perhaps the answer may be yes.

There are a handful of entry points to the brand experience, where both consumer-based and value-based brands overlap. Both kinds of brands can engage us emotionally with promises of a better life—both can engage people socially by somehow elevating our status either by wearing a GAP sweater or being recognized on a donor plaque in a hospital. Finally, both can engage us on a functional level by delivering what they said they would deliver, whether that is a great pair of basketball shoes or a T-shirt, we are proud to wear for participating in a fundraising run. But both kinds of brands *cannot* deliver on the spiritual touch point of their brands.

The spiritual aspect of a brand is a place of authenticity, a place of individual connected to community and a place where the human spirit can be rejuvenated through this connection. Although this might sound a tad lofty in connection to the over-used and corporately tainted notion of branding, let's just deconstruct what we mean by this. The spiritual aspect is the people-centered aspect of the branding exercise that nonprofits can corner the market on. It is aligned with the nonprofit culture of passion and humanity and it is at its very essence about caring, about doing something about caring and about connecting with others who care. This is not the purview of Coke and Nike, but rather of organizations working in human rights, in the environmental movement, working to improve our schools or our health care, working to protect biodiversity, working to find a cure for cancer, working against prejudice and intolerance and working for peace.

But let's be clear: Uncovering this edge will be quite limited if we use it only to point the finger at corporations who brand consumer products. Some products have great value in our life and have improved our life immensely. Also, let's not forget that corporations are made up of people who, at some level, may also be seeking out the unique branding experience offered by nonprofits. The branding edge is not about defining the nonprofit brand in relation to a consumer-based brand—it is about creating trusting relationships that are uniquely possible because of the stories the nonprofits have to tell. The ability for these stories and values to have impact on our communities necessitates thoughtful, integrated planning and a complete embracing of the power and potential of online branding. Employing the best practices of off- and online brand building can give your nonprofit the edge it needs.

ABOUT THE AUTHORS

Jason Mogus is the president of Communicopia, Canada's leading online communications and Web-site development company. A serial technology entrepreneur, Jason has in-depth knowledge of the nonprofit and socially responsible business sectors and is the senior client strategist on many key accounts.

Jason is passionate about supporting social change through technology, volunteerism, and philanthropy. A sought after advisor, public speaker, and media source, he is a thought leader in the fields of nonprofit technology, youth entrepreneurism, venture philanthropy, and multiple bottom line business. He is a partner and board member of BC Technology Social Venture Partners, and maintains a "Technology Fund" at the Tides Canada Foundation. He is the convener of the annual Web of Change conference at Hollyhock Retreat Centre and an "ePhilanthropy Master Trainer" certified by the Washington, D.C., based ePhilanthropy Foundation. You can e-mail Jason at Jason@communicopia.net.

Pattie LaCroix is the vice president of Communicopia, Canada's leading online communications and Web-site development company. Pattie has more than a decade of communications and marketing experience, with special emphasis on developing high impact and results-driven Internet marketing strategies. She is passionate about helping NGOs and social mission-based business meet with success. She spent many years in the NGO community in Canada, Africa, and South Asia directing communications, fundraising and marketing programs. She managed the Interactive Production Division at Palmer Jarvis DDB, Canada's award-winning advertising agency. She has worked in film, print, radio, and the Internet and has a strong understanding of how to effectively create engaging brands that develop long-term relationships with target audiences. Pattie is a member of AFP and speaks regularly at conferences about branding for non-profits. You can e-mail Pattie at pattie@communicopia.net.

CHAPTER 9

Inspiring Donors Online: How Your Message Can Make People Feel Extraordinary

Todd Baker
Champions of Philanthropy

Yesterday, the most successful nonprofits were those that donors knew best. Today, the most successful nonprofits are those that know their donors best.

THE AWAKENING

With a determined wiggle to the left and a hasty waggle to the right, our family's adopted caterpillar twirls its way forward. Her face pressed worryingly against the aquarium glass wall, my daughter Emily asks, "Daddy, what's wrong with Fuzzy?" My assurance that Fuzzy and his actions are by all means natural is met with Emily's, "Then why does he look sick?"

For the next several minutes, I told Emily the enchanting story of how Fuzzy's earthbound life of crawling and climbing is just the first step to the sky—that he will eventually be transformed into a butterfly who will soar far above the foliage he now consumes. Emily's eyes brightened with every word as her young mind began to conceive of how life ascends to greater heights.

The magic I recognized in my daughter's eyes is like what I see when I share the mystical story of the sleeping giant cocooned along the Information Superhighway with nonprofit staff.

So, here's the story. You have heard about the Information Superhighway. It's a transnational conglomeration of computer networks—a relentlessly expanding infrastructure that's revolutionizing communications and methods of commerce. Also referred to as the *Internet,* it offers access to information and supports written communication through e-mail and various forms of electronic conferencing. And unless you're a computer programmer this last paragraph has done little to spark enthusiasm in your heart. Simply telling people what the Internet is will not win the hearts of men and women.

111

Perhaps it's the disconcerting lack of spirit in the maze of information that makes many people feel there's little coherence or purpose to the Internet. It often seems as if it's nearly impossible to join others who share fundamental values. That's because the Internet's origin was powered by scientists and technologists consumed with a different passion—to achieve the seamless distribution of messages across a vast planet—not to connect people at the deepest level.

That means an awakening must take place in order to unlock the Internet's true purpose of not merely delivering rudimentary communication, but rather, to shape messages to elicit emotion, engender trust, and persuade people to take action. The Internet is still in its caterpillar form, only waiting to transform itself into the soaring butterfly of a more meaningful electronic community.

THE DONOR

Yesterday, the most successful nonprofits were those that *donors knew best*. Today, the most successful nonprofits are those that *know their donors best*. And not simply as statistics, but as real people. That's because donors are not ATMs! They act on a set of principles that dictates their giving behavior:

- Donors are driven by needs and wants, and they give based on an exchange of values (between donor and nonprofit), which allows them to:
  - Enhance their self-worth
  - Do the right thing
  - Create a return on investment

- People give to people who:
  - Are in need
  - Are in crisis
  - Are in despair

- Donors are loyal to charities that:
  - Are perceived to be leaders
  - Connect with them emotionally
  - Provide relevance and meaning
  - Offer significance and fulfillment
  - Help them make a statement about what they value
  - Help them to meet their vision for the world
  - Help them change the world now and for the future
  - Provide them with a sense of belonging to something greater than themselves

- People best respond to communication that:
  - Seeks first to listen and understand its constituencies
  - Has a vision for relationship building
  - Is responsive to donor inquires and requests
  - Is relevant to the donor's life
  - Allows itself to be driven by the donor

It's clear that today's donors are looking for relationships with charities that provide a sense of true partnership. A donor's personal vision and passion for making a difference is no different than the nonprofit's own motivation. And like all of us, donors want to seek out others with whom to share that experience.

Understanding the motivation of donors leads me to a new fundraising paradigm: View marketing as something you do *for* donors and not *to* donors. Your fundraising has to be something that serves donors. That mission is to match the impact that the donor makes with the donor's feelings for having given. Since marketing plans and strategies are vital to success, let me encourage you to write your next plan with the purpose of building donor loyalty. This is a strategy that leverages all of your organization's marketing communication efforts in order to find, develop, and strengthen relationships. An *in-your-face* marketing strategy is shortsighted. An *in-your-life* approach endures. It ensures that what is communicated connects to the donor and fulfills their desire to help make positive change. Of course, to allow this to happen, you must have an organizational culture that integrates all communication mediums in order to be responsive and relevant. Northwest Medical Teams of Portland, Oregon, is a great example of an organization that understands how to be relevant in the lives of donors. They provide medical relief and doctors in times of disaster throughout the world.

Your nonprofit must inspire donors to be loyal. This is accomplished when donors truly feel a part of the effort—when they can envision themselves standing side-by-side with you to assist a worthwhile cause. Let donors in. Your mission and their mission must become one. Then listen to them refer to the charity as *we* and not *you*. The only way to do this is to see donors as champions, just as you are a champion of philanthropy.

As I walk down the streets of Portland, Oregon, with a Northwest Medical Teams jacket on, I begin to lose count of the number of people who approach me with a spirit of thankfulness and honor. Without a doubt, the pride of Portland is Northwest Medical Teams. When a disaster strikes anywhere in the world, Portland's finest medical personnel board a plane. After decades of these kinds of consistent imagery and outstanding relief efforts, northwest folks have a special pride for the charity like I've never seen anywhere else.

THE MESSAGE

Nonprofits, which some people would call slumbering giants when it comes to realizing the potential of the Internet, possess powerful messages that can capture countless hearts and minds. However, most organizations utilize their 15 megabytes of fame to present tedious corporate-speak taken straight from annual reports. These nonprofit Web sites are often cluttered with facts and figures; very few sparkle with impact and personality.

The good news for charities is that online, the possibilities to inspire are endless. And so it will be the nonprofit leaders who will transform the Information Superhighway to the Inspiration Superhighway. Just like the caterpillar, our quest is to have nonprofits' online presences soar high above where they began in the 1990s.

Adopting solid storytelling techniques is the way forward for nonprofits on the Internet. And we can see good storytelling applied to the nonprofit Web sites we hold up as case studies. A great story will grab hold of your heart and not let go. Its powerful imagery and carefully presented narrative captures your attention and changes your perspective.

My own personal transformation came during a business trip. The view of New York's Central Park from 17 stories high is incredible. For a brief moment the scenery calms my nerves as I dress for the most important appointment of my career. All of us have attended meetings where it seems the world's fate will be determined. Well, my little world is up for discussion this morning.

Pressing the last wrinkle out of my blue oxford shirt, I relentlessly switch from one television station to another, searching for anything to pull my thoughts back from anxiety.

On the screen appears a little dishwater-blonde girl. In a small voice, she describes how she eats just once a day, often receiving that single meal because her parents have gone without to ensure she has at least something in her tummy.

Her mother holds a stunted, palm-sized watermelon and explains that the family's only recourse is to survive on the sickly fruits and vegetables gleaned from their dreary garden—or to have no food at all. Their weather-beaten trailer is located in the backwoods of Kentucky.

Larry Jones, president of Feed the Children, directs the organization's cameras into the family's home. Their life is encapsulated in a few camera angles, appraised in mere seconds. This artful presentation concentrates on the little girl as she opens a kitchen cupboard door attached to its frame by a single screw. Countless cockroaches scatter from the light, leaving the cabinet bare except for a sole bag of flour.

Overwhelmed with compassion, I sit down on a lavish leather chair inside my $350-a-night hotel room. My eyes begin to swell with tears. Next, Larry's wife, Frances, introduces me to a shirtless boy who opens his lips wide to show his blackened, cavity-riddled mouth. He points to each pain-stricken area, saying, "It hurts here and it hurts here, and here." My heart seems to double in size within my chest as I weep uncontrollably. Even now, writing this to you, I cannot restrain my emotions.

Have you ever been truly hungry, uncertain of your next meal? Hunger consumes the mind and pierces through you as sharp as knives. It challenges the best of souls. Imagine being a hungry child, wondering when your next meal will be, while plagued by fear for your parents' well being. Now imagine what it's like to travel just a few minutes away and see enormous wealth, other children laughing and playing with full stomachs and nice clothing. This is reality. It's not the Third World; it's our world, our country, our state, our community, and our neighborhood.

Compelled, I reach for the phone to dial the number on the television screen. My mind quickly calculates the cost of my clothing; redirected, that money could feed four children for six months. Humbly, I dial. The woman on the line senses my emotional turmoil and gently poses a few questions. Reciting my credit card number, my voice cracks with every single digit. Gasping for air, it's difficult to breathe. Compassion has knocked the wind out of me. "Thank you," were the only words I could muster as the call ended.

As I hang up the phone my mind's eye is still focused on the hungry little girl and the cavity-plagued boy. Tears stream down my face and I realize how incredibly fortunate I am. In a New York minute my little world has collided with reality, and today's "important" meeting suddenly, unexpectedly, warrants a new perspective.

Something profound is happening inside of me. It's the arrival of peace, and it comes to transform my spirit—to capture my thoughts with a vision of great purpose.

The prize of peace is a life view more spectacular than the one from my balcony, and its reward comes each time our focus turns outward. Suddenly, I notice the paralyzing sting of anxiety from a few minutes ago is gone.

My "most important" day concluded as one of my best days. Events like these are gifts. Embrace and cherish them as new opportunities to make positive change in your life. The next time anxiety invades your spirit, embrace this truth: The room in your heart always provides the best view.

Open minds to your organization's stories and help, such as the case in offline media, the online audience to imagine what they must do to help. Is it to cheer a Special Olympics athlete, comfort a fallen firefighter's family, provide a safe place for a child after school? Through compelling narratives and accompanying pictures, your mission is to bring us to the heart of your mandate. Let me encourage you to read the wonderful stories found at *www.wish.org*; your soul will be moved mightily.

So, let me give your organization a gentle nudge and whisper in its ear, "Wake up and begin your metamorphosis. Present your message so it will win the hearts of people. For if you win their hearts, the rest of them will follow."

CAREFULLY DESIGN THE MESSAGE

Perhaps now you aspire to inspire—to effectively translate your organization's story to this medium. If you are willing to lead by sharing your passion online, then my Baker's Dozen of stirring ideas might help you get your desired result. Let me provide you, in my humble opinion, the best nonprofit Web site I've ever experienced is Special Olympics' *www.investinalife.org* (see Exhibit 9.1). It beautifully incorporates many of the following ideas:

- *Establish an over-arching goal for your organization's Web site.* Although I have an open mind, I cannot imagine the ultimate goal to be anything other than to raise money. You may have other objectives for individual Web pages, but they should support the achievement of the primary goal. Most charities do not solely exist to produce informative Web sites on a particular subject matter. Therefore, ensure that this media is working to raise money so you may go out and fulfill your mission.
- *Make an impression.* People will often forget the details of a particular encounter, words that were spoken or one's attire, but they will never forget how you made them feel. Therefore, present your message in such a way that people will feel extraordinary about themselves if they support your mandate.
- *Write to connect on an emotional level.* Your visitors have a passion to do something significant, so make sure your message speaks directly to their hearts. Philanthropically, people are looking for a place to belong; so be true to your cause so they can find you. Here are three secrets to writing emotionally effective copy:

  1. *Embrace clarity.* Use concise, straightforward communication to help the reader grasp the gravity of your message.

2. *Engage the reader by bringing them into the story.* Explain their critical role so they feel a part of something greater than what they can do on their own.
3. *Encounter the heart with picturesque phrases.* Write like a painter, so the reader can visualize and feel the power of the story.

- *Select the most interesting perspective from which to tell your story.* Each story can be told from various points of view. Captivate readers by letting them see the most fascinating angle.
- *Find your organization's voice: a unique blend of charisma, courage, and concern.* This will help differentiate your charity from the next in the minds of prospects and donors.
- *Be persuasive by first making clear the specific action you want the reader to take.* Then, through images and words, direct the readers to see themselves taking that action.
- *Be human; don't be an organization.* Show the donor that you're people who support a worthy cause, and that you're searching for more folks just like you. Allow donors and prospects to connect and join real people from your organization. As P.T. Barnum once said, "Nothing draws a crowd like a crowd."
- *Illustrate your mission through images and pictures.* Allow people to become inspired by your visual presentation. It has been said that the eyes are the window to the soul. Keep that in mind when you choose the photos or moving pictures for your Web site.
- *Present a virtual tour of your mission.* Not everyone will have the firsthand opportunity to see your organization in action, and a virtual tour is the next best way to give people an idea of what you do. Let Web site visitors meet the constituency you serve or "what the alley looks like for a person who calls it home." Furthermore, your e-mail gift acknowledgment might include a link to a virtual tour of their gift in action; perhaps a warm smiling face that appears to say, "Thank you for saving me."
- *Write in an active and conversational style.* The Internet is the most powerful marketing medium because you can have a conversation with your potential supporters. Don't communicate with people as if they are reading your corporate brochure, but rather, as though they were sitting across your desk from you.
- *Stop spending 90 percent of your organization's resources on technology and only 10 percent on the message.* Let others chase the latest technology solution for you: it's always changing and they will find the latest solutions for you. It's the words, imagery, and personality you present that will stand out in the hearts and minds of people, not the flexing of your proverbial "Flash" muscle.
- *Give your headlines soul.* Many people read in scan mode, skimming for relevant information before deciding to read on. They may only read one headline, so you should approach this text as the ultimate short story. Headlines that work have these qualities:
  - They seize the reader's attention.
  - They affect the reader on an emotional level.
  - They spark curiosity, which motivates the reader to continue.
- *Understand online human behavior.* People read differently when they peruse a Web site as opposed to a newspaper or a magazine. On the surface, we might per-

form the same functions (absorbing text and pictures to create a narrative), but our expectations of the mediums, patience levels, and cognitive results are very different. Here are three things that will help you present your online message so it is embraced:

1. *Make a good first impression.* In seconds, people will decide whether they should stay or go. Therefore, the words and images on your homepage must communicate the most compelling reasons to motivate people. How many times have you walked out of a fast-food restaurant or kept driving if the line was too long, despite your belief that waiting 20 minutes for a table at a fine restaurant is acceptable? You must not hide your best stories deep within your Web site. Adopt the mindset that you must have instant appeal.

2. *A book-reading atmosphere does not permeate the Internet.* People are not curled up in a big comfortable chair, turning pages underneath soft lighting. Rather, they sit in a chair designed for work, vigorously scanning, clicking, and scrolling. This is how people navigate through information online—so make sure your inspirational message is presented in the most convenient form.

3. *Each page of your Web site should have an objective with the visitor in mind.* Help readers discover their passion for you as quickly and efficiently as possible.

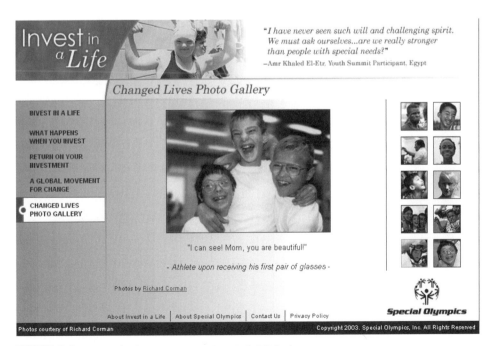

EXHIBIT 9.1   Special Olympics' Invest in a Life Web site

HOPEFUL EMILY

Embrace the possibility that your role is to inspire and cultivate hearts for your cause. Forget the *you* mentality and begin to embrace donors as real friends. While many worthwhile nonprofits focus solely on the donor dollar, you can outmaneuver them by focusing 100 percent on making your donors feel extraordinary.

Emily can't wait for Fuzzy to wake up now that she knows how beautiful he will be. She's excited to see him fly free, to watch him soar as high as he wants to go. My promise to Emily is that Fuzzy will break out of his cocoon at any moment, and this is my vision for your online presence—to help you see what is possible, to give this Information Superhighway a soul. Who better to replace mere information with inspiration than you, another champion of philanthropy?

ABOUT THE AUTHOR

For nearly two decades, **Todd Baker** has helped some of the top charities in North America, assisting them in the development of Mission-Driven Marketing™ strategies. Baker is the author of the free e-book, *Nonprofit Websites*, the first of its kind, which has been downloaded by tens of thousands of charities in more than 50 countries. Baker recently published *Champions of Philanthropy*. He writes the "Baker's Dozen" for *The Nonprofit Times*, a series of fundraising articles. Baker spent more than 13 years with World Vision. You can e-mail Todd at tbaker@mail.championsofphilanthropy.com.

CHAPTER 10

Online Advocacy: How the Internet Is Transforming the Way Nonprofits Reach, Motivate, and Retain Supporters

Vinay Bhagat, ePMT
Convio, Inc.

Online tools have enabled advocacy groups to mobilize constituents quickly and cost-effectively

INTRODUCTION

The Internet is transforming grassroots advocacy. High-profile online campaigns like Moveon.org (a democratic mobilization campaign founded in late 1998 that has grown to 2 million members) and Dean for America (the campaign for Democratic presidential candidate Howard Dean, which grew its online support base to 650,000+ constituents in one year) are poignant illustrations of how quickly organizations can recruit and mobilize large numbers of supporters via the Web. Online advocacy is not just applicable to high profile, politicized campaigns. Nonprofit organizations across issues from health research to animal welfare, and both large and small, can benefit from new Internet tools and strategies.

Online advocacy is not just important for public policy professionals. Too many nonprofit organizations do not fully appreciate the huge impact that a grassroots advocacy program can have on other aspects of their operations, in particular, fundraising. Nonprofit groups can leverage online advocacy programs to cost-effectively develop potential donors. They can use advocacy as a tool to increase donor retention rates. It is also important to consider current trends and what the future is likely to hold for online advocacy.

DEFINING ADVOCACY

*Ad · vo · ca · cy (n.) 1. The act of pleading or arguing in favor of
something, such as a cause or a policy. 2. Active support.*

—Webster's Dictionary

*Advocates give voice to the needs and concerns of those who do not have
access to the people or institutions who have power over their
circumstances.*

—World Vision Office of Public Policy & Advocacy, *www.seekjustice.org*

The primary goal of advocacy is to drive positive change in support of an organization's mission. Positive change may come in the form of influencing government legislation, securing an allocation of government funding or a policy change adopted by
a corporation. In the case of securing government funding, advocacy can create a
highly leveraged effect on an organization's impact. For example, disease research
organizations such as the Alzheimer's Association have achieved government appro-
priations to fund research many multiples of the direct funds they can raise themselves.[1]
Traditionally, there have been two distinct approaches to advocacy—grass-tops and
grassroots. *Grass-tops* advocacy is the act of engaging in one-on-one dialog with key
government or corporate officials through representatives and/or professional lobby-
ists. *Grassroots* advocacy is the approach of influencing the public to agree with an
organization's opinion and getting them to help influence policy makers through personal contact, phone calls, letters, and media. Many groups engage in both grass-tops
and grassroots advocacy as they can be complementary.

HOW INTERNET TECHNOLOGY IS
TRANSFORMING ADVOCACY

The Internet and the introduction of online advocacy and customer relationship
management (eCRM) tools have both had a profound impact on grassroots advocacy.
In 2001, 42 million Americans used the Internet to research public policy issues;[2] 23
million sent comments to public officials about policy choices; 13 million participated
in online lobbying campaigns; and 68 million visited government Web sites. In the
same year, the U.S. Congress received 117 million e-mails, up from 80 million in 2000.
Internet technology is transforming online advocacy by enabling the following:

- Easy, low-cost activist mobilization
- Increased response rates through easy response mechanisms and personalization
- More recruiting of activists
- Much better tracking
- Better relationships and stronger loyalty
- An integrated approach to managing constituent relationships

Let's look at these in more detail.

Easy, Low-Cost Activist Mobilization

Online tools have enabled advocacy groups to mobilize constituents quickly and cost-effectively through e-mail (see Exhibit 10.1), far more so than sending mail. Responding in real-time to urgent and deadline-sensitive issues now is possible. Cost reduction is also significant, particularly important for 501(c)(3) groups that have strict limitations on how much they can spend on advocacy. Organizations such as the American Society for the Prevention of Cruelty to Animals (ASPCA), which used to send letters to advocates, have moved to an e-mail-based mobilization approach. Newer advocacy groups—for example, Tobacco-Free Kids—started their advocacy programs with an online- only approach.[3]

From:	American Humane [info@americanhumane.org]
To:	vinay@convio.com
Cc:	
Subject:	Leave no child behind

Take Action American Humane. donate

Dear Vinay,

Millions of children are left without adequate healthcare each year. Senate 448 -- a Bill to Leave No Child Behind -- and its House companion HR 936 extend health insurance coverage to every child in the nation. And they include several other provisions to help low-income parents educate and care for their children.

Take Action

Help ensure no child is left behind! Contact your Senators now!

Make a difference today.

If this bill is passed, healthcare coverage would be extended at no cost to families that make less than 150% of the poverty level. Families that make more than 150% would have the option to access the program on a sliding scale relative to their income. In addition, other suggested benefits, such as better access to prescription drugs and pediatric services, will greatly enhance cost-savings.

The physical well-being of children is at stake without an affordable means to healthcare.

Click here to learn more about legislation that can help extend needed health coverage to children of needy families. *And click here to Take Action now!*

Help raise awareness about child welfare --
Forward this message to a friend!

EXHIBIT 10.1   Mobilization E-Mail Example

Increased Response Rates through Easy Response Mechanisms and Personalization

New online tools make it much easier for advocates to respond. Online response forms on Web sites recognize returning advocates, pre-fill their information, and map legislative targets to individuals based on their ZIP codes. These forms allow constituents to personalize the messages they send (see Exhibit 10.2), and can automate delivery of messages via e-mail or fax.

A technique utilized by some groups to increase response rates (make it even easier for constituents to respond) is enabling response directly from e-mails. All the recipient needs to do is hit "reply." The conservation group, the National Trust for Historic Preservation, has used this technique. An organization also can increase response rates by targeting issues according to a constituent's interests or profile. Many advocacy groups have yielded higher, more consistent response rates through targeting messages by geography (e.g., sending messages about Texas issues and/or campaigns to people living in Texas). For example, the advocacy group Mothers Against Drunk Driving ran a "split-cell" test, sending a generic e-mail appeal to one sample of constituents and a personalized appeal to another segment. The personalized appeal told people the specific grade their state achieved for drunk driving regulation effectiveness (see Exhibit 10.3). The personalized message achieved a 155 percent higher response rate than the generic message.

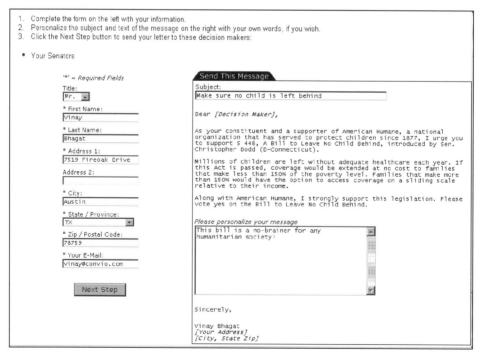

EXHIBIT 10.2   Online Response Form

Source: American Humane

Dear Matthew,

It's report card time and MADD has graded each state and the nation on their efforts to prevent drunk driving and underage drinking. Today, throughout the country, we are unveiling the MADD Rating the States 2002 report. As a supporter, we want you to be among the first to know the national results as well as the results of your own home state.

While alcohol-related deaths have been cut by a third since MADD's founding two decades ago, **the nation's attention has waned and progress in eliminating drunk driving deaths has stalled in recent years**. In fact, the number of alcohol-related traffic deaths increased last year to 17,448 in addition to more than half a million injuries resulting from this crime. We need your help to make our roadways safer and to change the grade in the next Rating the States report card.

Your state's grade is a call to action and away from complacency. **Please visit our site and send your governor a brief note** on the importance of these issues. You can help change the grade of your state and make your roads safer. Here's a brief overview of the report card:

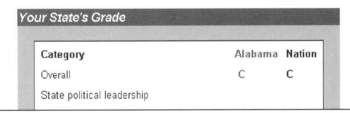

Category	Alabama	Nation
Overall	C	C
State political leadership		

EXHIBIT 10.3   Personalization of Advocacy Appeal by Recipient's State

Source: © 2004, Mothers Against Drunk Driving. All rights reserved.

Increased Message Delivery Rate through Utilizing Multiple Channels

Leading online advocacy tools enable messages to be sent via e-mail, fax, letters, or Web form submissions on a legislator's Web site. Some tools will actually automatically roll over from one delivery channel to another (e.g., from fax to e-mail if the targeted fax number is constantly busy). Enabling such multichannel message delivery options helps increase the message delivery rate. Furthermore, legislative offices have different preferences on methods of contact. Increasingly, legislative offices are moving away from accepting e-mails and mandating submission of information through their Web sites (i.e., Web form submissions). Again, the leading online advocacy tools enable automatic posting of advocate messages on these Web forms, despite the fact that every Web form is different.

More Recruiting of Activists

Advocacy campaigns are by nature *viral*—that is, they spread from person to person (also known as "pass-along"). The Internet has significantly increased the viral effect because it is much easier to forward an e-mail message to a group of friends than mail or shepherd a paper petition. The American Humane Association Advocacy Center, for example, gives people who have taken action the option to send an e-mail message to friends (see Exhibit 10.4). The taxpayer watchdog organization Citizens Against Government Waste regularly experiences a viral effect with its advocacy alerts. In the group's most recent campaign, as many as 11.7 percent of people *taking action* (i.e., contacting their legislators) were tracked as referred by friends either through forwarded campaign e-mails or "tell-a-friend" links on the organization's Web site.

Much Better Tracking

Traditionally, it has been difficult to track the number of people taking action in a grassroots campaign. It also has been almost impossible to know who specifically has taken action to determine who the best activists are. One of the major benefits of moving advocacy efforts online has been much stronger tracking. Tracking both aggregate response and individual response is far easier with new online advocacy tools. With these new capabilities, the American Diabetes Association has been able to develop

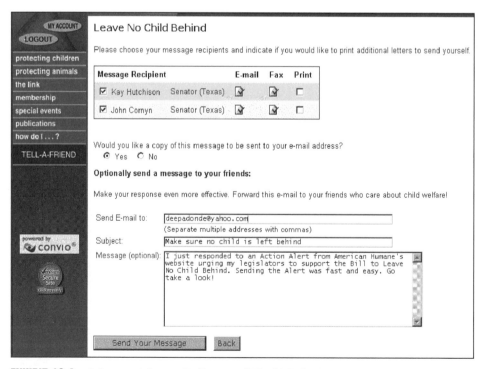

EXHIBIT 10.4   Advocacy Message Delivery and Viral Marketing

Source: American Humane

benchmarks for national versus state appeals. They know that a national alert typically yields a 5 to 6 percent response and a regional alert yields a 20 percent response.

Better Relationships, Stronger Loyalty

The Internet has also made stewardship of advocate relationships easier by keeping advocates informed about the impact of their lobbying efforts. It is quick, simple, and cost effective to send a targeted e-mail to people who take action. The American Diabetes Association (ADA) has not only thanked people for their support of an action, but also encouraged them to write and thank their congressional representatives who supported the legislation. Such strategies keep advocates excited about being involved and build loyalty to the cause and organization (see Exhibit 10.5).

Forward to a Friend

Update on Medicare Prescription Drug Legislation

Dear Diabetes Advocate,

Instructions:
If your member of Congress is listed below, click here to say thanks for his or her support on this issue.

Since the beginning of June, the American Diabetes Association has been working to improve the Medicare prescription drug legislation in the House of Representatives and Senate. Over 4,000 diabetes advocates contacted their members of Congress to urge them to support diabetes amendments to the legislation. These amendments included provisions to cover insulin syringes and reimbursement for diabetes screenings.

Success!
We are happy to report that the efforts of our advocates made an impact! The House and Senate passed legislation that aims to reform the Medicare system and create a prescription drug benefit for senior citizens. Each chamber included provisions to cover insulin syringes in their legislation. In addition, the legislation that passed the House included a provision allowing for Medicare to cover diabetes diagnostic screening tests.

So what happens next?
The House and Senate versions of the legislation are very different and these differences must be worked out and changed in what is known as a "conference committee." At the conclusion of this conference, the legislation will be voted upon again by each body of Congress. We may once again ask you to contact your members of Congress to urge them to keep the diabetes provisions in the legislation.

Advocates made a difference.
Diabetes advocates played a major role in crafting this groundbreaking legislation. If you took the time to contact your members of Congress about the Medicare bill, thank you.

Members of Congress who deserve our thanks...
Several current members of Congress - and one notable former - were instrumental in getting the diabetes provisions in the Medicare bill. If you see your representative or senator listed below, please take a moment to say thanks. They are:

For their efforts to include diabetes screenings and insulin syringes in the House legislation -
- Speaker of the House Dennis Hastert (R-IL-14),
- Rep. Xavier Becerra (D-CA-31),
- Rep. Ernie Fletcher (R-KY-6),
- Rep. Vito Fossella (R-NY-13),
- Rep. Gene Green (D-TX-29),
- Rep. Billy Tauzin (R-LA-3),
- Rep. Bill Thomas (R-CA-22), and
- Rep. Fred Upton (R-MI-6)

For their efforts to include insulin syringes in the Senate legislation -
- Sen. Max Baucus (D-MT),
- Sen. Susan Collins (R-ME),
- Sen. Charles Grassley (R-IA),
- Sen. Blanche Lincoln (D-AR), and
- Sen. Zell Miller (D-GA)

Special thanks must also go to former Speaker of the House Newt Gingrich for communicating with his former colleagues on the importance of the diabetes provisions.

As always, if you have questions about this bill, please contact us at makingnoise@diabetes.org.

Sincerely,

Your Advocacy Team at the American Diabetes Association

EXHIBIT 10.5   Advocacy Relationship Management by American Diabetes Association

Integrated Approach to Managing Constituent Relationships

New, integrated online customer relationship management (eCRM) tools, which combine support for advocacy with fundraising and general communications, make it possible to manage relationships with all external constituents (e.g., news subscribers, volunteers, clients, donors, advocates, media and other groups) in a more congruent fashion than in the past. For example, a constituent might be a donor, but not yet an activist. An organization can use eCRM tools to encourage the constituent to join the activist network or take action for/donate to a specific campaign based on his or her profile (see Exhibit 10.6 for an illustration of this concept in use at the ASPCA). Using this type of strategy, an organization can get each constituent to participate in a variety of ways—financially and nonfinancially. It is a way to maximize constituent relationships and build a strong, loyal support base.

HOW ONLINE ADVOCACY IMPACTS FUNCTIONS IN ADDITION TO PUBLIC POLICY

Advocacy can play an important role in supporting other areas of nonprofit operations—in particular, fundraising. A grassroots advocacy program can help in these ways:

- Develop strong prospects for other areas
- Grow donor/member loyalty
- Reinforce the organization's brand

Let's look at these tactics in more detail.

Develop Strong Prospects for Other Areas

A grassroots advocacy program can be a great source of prospects for fundraising, volunteering, and other forms of participation. The act of advocating is a show of inter-

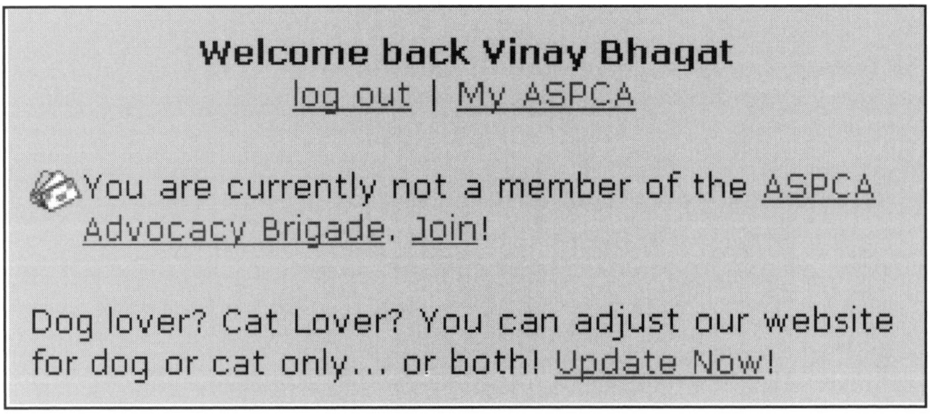

EXHIBIT 10.6   Profile-Based Relationship Management at the ASPCA

Source: ASPCA

est and support. Not surprisingly, we find that advocates frequently are more receptive to additional requests for support (e.g., fundraising appeals) than *cold prospects*. In a recent campaign, the Brady Campaign to End Gun Violence along with the Million Mom March found that e-advocates (people who had signed an online petition) responded to two consecutive e-mail fundraising solicitations at a rate of approximately 3 percent.[4] Contrast this to traditional, direct mail–based acquisition programs using rented lists (cold prospects). A reasonable response rate for a direct mail acquisition campaign is 1 percent. This response rate results in a typical cost per dollar raised (CPDR) for acquisition of $1.15 to $1.50. Using a grassroots advocacy campaign to develop a prospect list, and then converting that list through the mail, would drive the cost per dollar raised down to $0.38 to $0.50. Converting some portion, or all of the prospects via e-mail instead (per the Brady Campaign/Million Mom March) would yield an even greater cost reduction.

An organization can use online grassroots advocacy campaigns to build large prospect lists. By nature, advocacy campaigns are viral because activists commonly forward messages to friends. The Brady/Million Mom March campaign asked people to sign an online petition and then forward a message to 10 friends (see Exhibit 10.7). In just two months, the group grew its e-mail list from 39,000 to 117,000 constituents, nearly a tripling (see Exhibit 10.8).

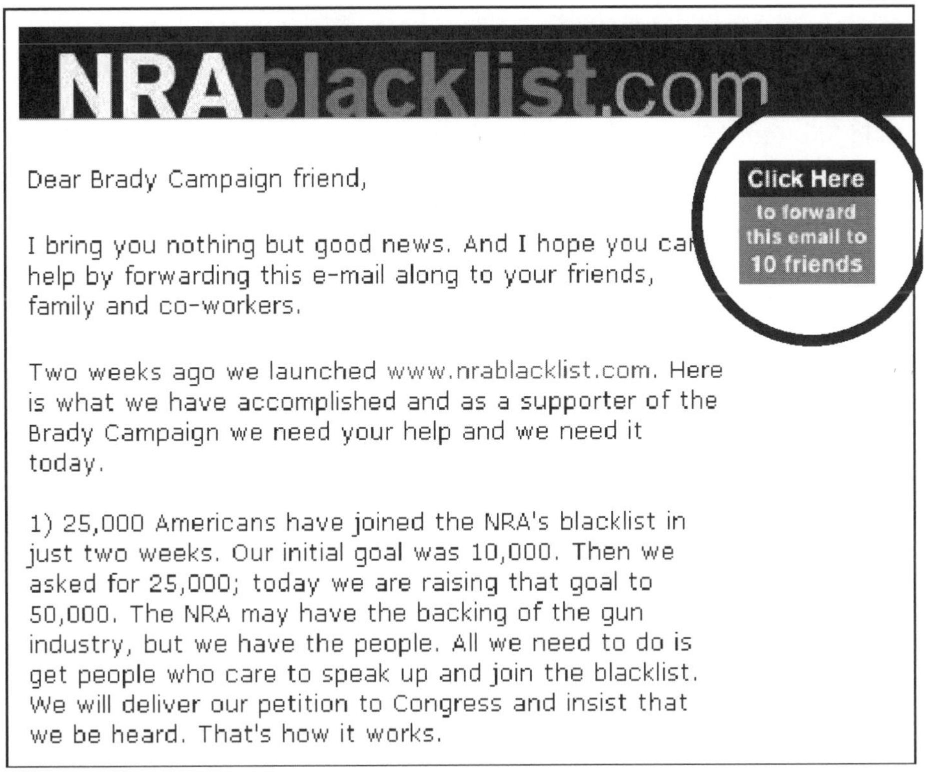

EXHIBIT 10.7 Brady/Million Mom March Petition Campaign

Source: Brady/Million Mom March Campaign

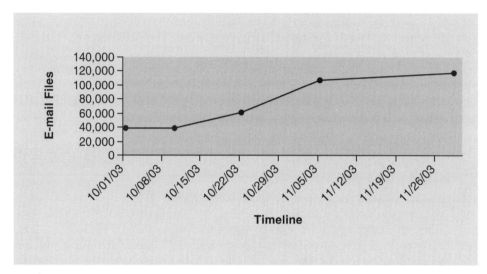

EXHIBIT 10.8   Growth in E-Mail List during Petition Campaign

Source: Brady/Million Mom March Campaign

There are, however, some philosophical barriers to overcome. Fundraising and advocacy functions historically have been hesitant to share lists, fearing that advocates would be turned off if asked for money and donors would be turned off if asked to advocate. Based on Convio's work with advocacy groups, there seldom is any noticeable alienation of advocates when asked to donate, or alienation of donors when offered the opportunity to advocate. When a national women's advocacy group made an e-mail-based fundraising appeal to activists and nonactivists (e-mail newsletter subscribers), activists actually responded at a 15 percent higher rate than nonactivists, and very few activists un-subscribed (a measure of alienation).[5] At a regional social services/advocacy organization, 50 percent of new online donors were initially advocates who converted to donor advocates.[6] Furthermore, many nonprofit groups are keen to reach younger donors. Advocacy inherently attracts younger constituents who, over time, can become good prospects for development, volunteering, and other forms of support.

Grow Donor/Member Loyalty

Every nonprofit organization struggles with donor/member retention. Donors/members have many causes and groups from which to choose and inevitably contribute more to those with whom they have the strongest affinity. Any tactic that helps build involvement or affinity aids donor retention. Advocacy can be an effective method to further involve supporters. Most donors can and will give only one to two times a year, but they can advocate for an organization multiple times annually, keeping the cause or group top-of-mind.

Reinforce the Organization's Brand

Branding is an important factor in driving donor preference.[7] Studies show that older constituents, in particular, are influenced by brand.[8] An organization can use advocacy as a strategy to build its brand. Successful grassroots advocacy campaigns reach and touch many people, including members of the general public (prospective and current donor community) and the media. Such contact helps increase awareness, reinforces the organization's message, and sometimes produces editorial coverage.

CASE STUDY: A STORY ABOUT AN ADVOCATE BECOMING A STRONG FINANCIAL CONTRIBUTOR

Sometimes stories about individual donors can be very illustrative. Recently, I learned about a supporter of the American Diabetes Association (ADA) who initially connected with the organization by signing up for its e-mail newsletter to receive health and dietary tips. ADA's public policy group subsequently contacted this constituent via e-mail to ask him to support a piece of legislation, and he responded by contacting his senator. He continued responding to several other online advocacy "asks." Impressed by the work the group was doing, when ADA invited him to walk in one of its events and raise funds, he responded positively. He made a small contribution himself and went on to raise $1,500 for the organization.

TRENDS AND PREDICTIONS

Online advocacy already is having a profound impact on the grassroots programs of many nonprofit groups. Changes are occurring that will further increase the efficacy of online advocacy. Nonprofit professionals with oversight for public policy, as well as those managing other functions, should keep a watch on the latest trends in order to keep online campaigning effective.

Legislative Offices Will become More E-Responsive

Advocacy professionals are constantly trying to find the most effective way to reach legislators. Common wisdom is that the most effective vehicle is a personal visit by a constituent, followed by a letter, phone call and, lastly, an e-mail or fax. However, electronic contact with legislative offices is becoming increasingly accepted. According to a survey of House Correspondence Management System (CMS) vendors, an estimated 25 percent of House offices now answer e-mail with e-mail, compared to 10 percent in March 2001. For example, Representative Zach Wamp's (R-TN) office heavily promotes use of e-mail with constituents and has seen a dramatic shift in its correspondence. In 1999, e-mail accounted for 13 percent of the office's total mail volume. Now e-mail is almost half of the constituent communication. And, while the average volume of incoming e-mail per week has increased by 52 percent, postal mail volume has decreased by 48 percent. This has reduced the amount of time staff spend processing mail, reduced the mail turnaround time, and saved staff from having to deal with some of the ugly irradiated paper that most House offices encounter! Representative Wamp's experience shows what an office can achieve when it encourages constituents to use a more efficient and faster means of communication.[9]

Increasing Prevalence of Web Forms versus Acceptance of E-mail Submissions

Nonprofits should pay close attention to the shift by legislators to block e-mail and instead force constituents to submit information via Web site forms. More members of Congress are shifting from receiving constituent communications through e-mail to relying on Web-based forms: 66 U.S. senators and 226 representatives are not using public e-mail addresses, and are directing constituents to their Web sites to send messages.[10] The aim is to reduce spam from nonconstituents and automated messages, and reduce the workload for internal staff. The challenge Web forms have created for nonprofit groups is that almost every Web form is different, so automating message delivery is difficult. However, advanced online advocacy tools solve this problem by automatically entering data into a legislator's Web site in the correct format. This capability will become increasingly important to nonprofit organizations to ensure effective message delivery (see Exhibit 10.9 for an example of a legislative Web form used by the White House).

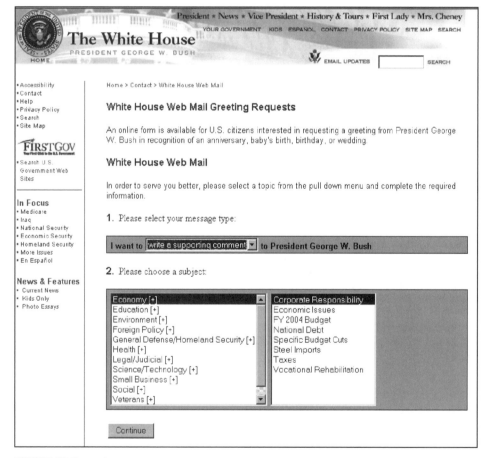

EXHIBIT 10.9   White House Legislative Contact Form

Source: https://sawho14.eop.gov/PERS?verified=1

Measurement of Activist Participation, Segmentation, and Moves Management

Most fundraisers actively measure or estimate the value of donors over their lifetime, based on a calculation of their average gift size, giving frequency, and years of support of the organization. Many fundraisers then group donors according to value segment and target communications accordingly to advance their relationships and increase donor value. Historically, advocacy functions have not measured the participation levels of individual activists *en masse*. Participation levels in a paper world are difficult to measure. Early online tools tracked aggregate response but yielded little to no information about individual constituent response profiles. Consequently, it was not very easy to actively advance advocate relationships through a sophisticated segmentation approach. New online advocacy and constituent relationship management tools make measuring constituent engagement much easier. Such tools allow an administrator to assign different "scores" to advocacy-related activities—such as taking action online, signing a petition or forwarding messages to friends—and correspondingly measure an advocate's value. An organization then can use this information to create segments for differentiated communication. The American Humane Association has recently started an engagement measurement and rewards program for its activists. Every time an activist takes action, he or he accumulates points. This enables the association to track its best activists. Also it's able to create rewards programs to encourage higher response rates or other actions.

Divisions between Fundraising and Advocacy Will Be Eliminated

Some nonprofit organizations are starting to break down the barriers between advocacy and development for list sharing and constituent communications. Although not every advocate wants to become a financial donor and vice versa, coordinating advocacy and fundraising efforts makes inordinate sense, and modern, integrated eCRM tools make that goal much easier to achieve. New approaches to measuring and managing constituent relationships in an integrated fashion greatly aid in *cross-marketing* from advocacy to giving, and vice versa. Leading online constituent relationship management tools allow nonprofits to target messages to constituents based on their profile (e.g., this person is a donor, but not yet an activist). New tools also allow a group to measure constituent engagement in a holistic fashion, ascribing value to both fundraising and advocacy contributions.

Increased Reliance on and Automation of Peer-to-Peer Marketing

Growing adoption of online grassroots advocacy has created a tremendous opportunity to reach new constituents and get them involved in supporting a cause. Viral marketing, which occurs when constituents distribute an organization's messages to their friends and relatives, is already having a big impact. As consumers become inundated with electronic marketing messages and spam, expect to see more emphasis in this area because a message from a friend is more likely to be read. Specialized tools are being built to make it easier for activists to resend messages to their personal networks, and recruit other activists. One of the best illustrations of this concept in action today is actually a political example—the GOP Team Leader Web site by the Republican Party (see Exhibit 10.10). The Democratic National Committee also has developed a similar capability called eCaptains. In both cases, the party rewards loyal activists with points for outreach and actions, and they can redeem the points for party merchandise.

Building Activist Engagement through Community— Online and Offline

Today's progressive organizations are using the Internet to market to activists so they will take action and contact their friends. Increasingly, organizations will create opportunities for activists to interact directly to build communities and more powerful advocate networks. As activists have a chance to interact with each other through online community forums or physical meetings in the offline world, they become more engaged and passionate. Political campaigns and advocacy groups such as Dean for America and For Our Grandchildren, respectively, use online blogs, or online diaries, (see Exhibit 10.11), to build community. Many groups also are encouraging their activists to coalesce in person through services like Meetup.com.

CONCLUSION

The Internet has already transformed online advocacy for many nonprofit organizations. New advancements in online technology are only pushing the potential further. Nonprofit professionals in other functions aside from advocacy should not only be

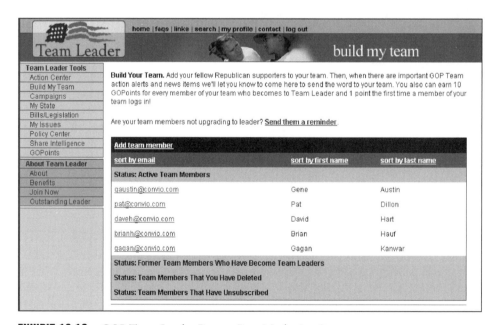

EXHIBIT 10.10   GOP Team Leader Peer-to-Peer Marketing System

Source: http://www.gopteamleader.com/

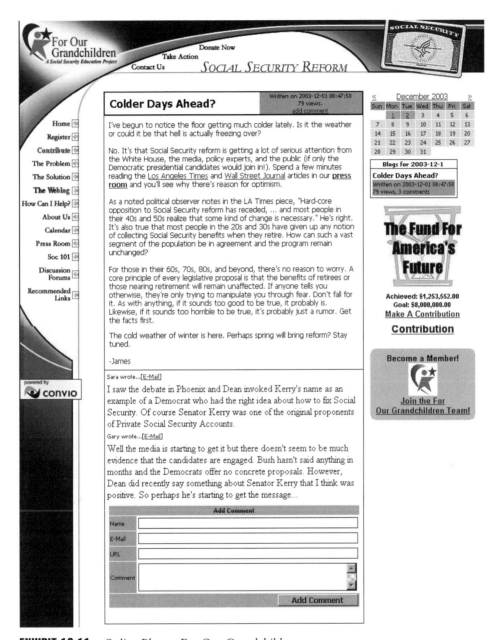

EXHIBIT 10.11   Online Blog at For Our Grandchildren

supportive of the role of online advocacy within the organization, but also should determine how to most effectively integrate efforts—key for maximizing the synergy between functions and, in turn, constituent involvement. New online tools now make the notion of measuring and managing constituent relationships in an integrated fashion (factoring advocacy and fundraising participation, for example) a real possibility.

ABOUT THE AUTHOR

Vinay Bhagat, ePMT, is founder, chairman and chief strategy officer for Convio, Inc. Before founding Convio, Vinay was director of e-commerce at Trilogy Software where he shaped Fortune 500 customers' thinking about developing their Internet strategies, and was the product visionary for customers facing e-commerce applications. Before Trilogy, Vinay was a consultant and team leader at Bain & Company, the leading strategy consulting firm. Vinay graduated from Harvard Business School with high distinction as a Baker Scholar. He holds an MS from Stanford in Engineering-Economic Systems, and MA from Cambridge University in Electrical and Information Sciences with first class honors. Vinay is also a member of the Association of Fundraising Professionals and a frequent speaker on eCommerce panels, and seminars on applying Internet technology to nonprofits. You can e-mail Vinay at vinay@convio.com.

ENDNOTES

1. Interview with Stephen McConnell, senior vice president, Advocacy and Public Policy, Alzheimer's Association (October 7, 2003).
2. Pew Internet and American Life Project, *The Rise of the E-Citizen: How People Use Government Agencies' Web sites*, (April 3, 2002), *http://www.pewinternet.org*.
3. Interview with Carter Headrick, manager of Grassroots, Tobacco-Free Kids (October 2003).
4. Convio client data analysis—Million Mom March united with the Brady Campaign to Prevent Gun Violence.
5. Convio client data analysis.
6. Convio client data analysis—regional advocacy/social services organization.
7. Michael Birkin, "Non-Profit Brands: Friend or Foe?" OnPhilanthropy.com newsletter (February 7, 2003).
8. Sarah Durst, "Target Analysis Group—Benchmarking Trends in Nonprofit Giving," Target Analysis Year 2000 Cross-Industry Study.
9. Pew Internet and American Life Project, *The Rise of the E-Citizen: How People Use Government Agencies' Web sites*.
10. Ibid.

CHAPTER 11

Volunteer Recruitment and Management

Alison Li, ePMT[1]

HJC New Media

The online environment provides a rich range of services and resources to augment the volunteer recruitment and management activities of nonprofit organizations. E-mail and the Web provide many opportunities to recruit, train, support, manage, and recognize volunteers. Online tools are not just supplementing traditional methods of interacting with volunteers, however; they are challenging organizations to expand their conception of volunteers and volunteering activity.

Volunteer managers can now find a wealth of online resources and services to support their work. Leading nonprofit organizations are not only using Internet tools to make existing volunteering programs more effective, but are developing innovative ways of reaching new constituencies and creating new forms of volunteer endeavor.

An organization's Web site is now often its first point of contact with members of the public, and is, therefore, an important means of reaching potential volunteers. A first step many organizations take in using their Web sites to foster volunteering is to provide an online form allowing visitors to offer to volunteer. Prospective volunteers can indicate their skills and interests as well as availability. Organizations can also post descriptions of specific volunteer opportunities.

Nonprofits, however, can use the Web environment to go much further in connecting with prospective volunteers by vividly portraying what the volunteer experience might be like, from the sights and sounds these volunteers might encounter, to the social and emotional challenges they'll face. The Global Citizens for Change Web site (*http://www.citizens4change.org/virtual_tour.htm*) provides personal stories and a virtual tour to help prospective volunteers understand what it might be like to serve overseas in a developing country (see Exhibit 11.1). The virtual tour helps interested visitors explore how they might prepare for their volunteer service and to consider how they might feel coming home after living abroad.

ONLINE VOLUNTEER MATCHING

A very significant development in volunteer recruitment is the growth of online volunteer matching services. These services allow organizations to reach new prospective supporters beyond their usual geographic borders, and open up a wider range of

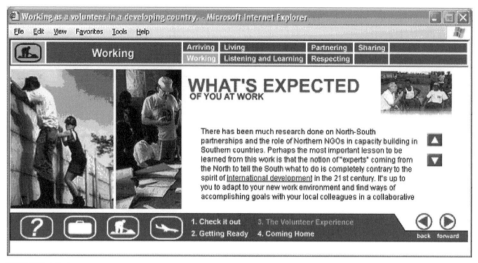

EXHIBIT 11.1   Global Citizens for Change Web Site, Virtual Tour

Source: http://www.citizens4change.org/virtual_tour.htm (March 28, 2004).

possibilities to interested volunteers. Organizations can post information about their missions and volunteer needs. Prospective volunteers can search for opportunities by name of organization, location, mission, or other criteria. For example, in the United States, Youth Service America's SERVEnet program provides a large database of more than 6,000 registered nonprofit organizations, 35,000+ service projects and more than 52 million volunteer opportunities available. At the SERVEnet site, prospective volunteers can enter their ZIP code, city, state, skills, interests, and availability and be matched with organizations needing help (see Exhibit 11.2). Visitors can also search for calendar events, job openings, service news, recommended books, and best practices.[2]

There are several well-established online volunteer matching services at the local, national, and international levels. These services include Action Without Borders, *www.idealist.org* (United States); VolunteerMatch, *www.volunteermatch.org* (United States); the Australian Volunteer Search, *www.volunteersearch.gov.au* (Australia); and Volunteer Opportunities Exchange, *www.voe-reb.org* (Canada). Many volunteer databases also exist at the local level, often as an offering of the local volunteer center. Other specialized databases focus on specific volunteer groups such as youth or seniors, or those with particular characteristics, such as those with technical skills. Others are targeted to specific causes; for example, AidsVolunteers.ca (site to be launched in 2004) will meet the volunteering needs of AIDS service organizations in Canada. The profiles of both the agencies and the volunteers, as well as the associated search function, are more closely tailored to the needs of AIDS volunteering than those found in a general volunteer matching service. Supporting materials include an online "AIDS 101" primer to help volunteers gain a familiarity with critical facts about AIDS and HIV.[3]

These online services allow volunteers interested in a particular cause to home in on the set of organizations that might provide these volunteering opportunities, potentially learning about organizations that they might not have known about or

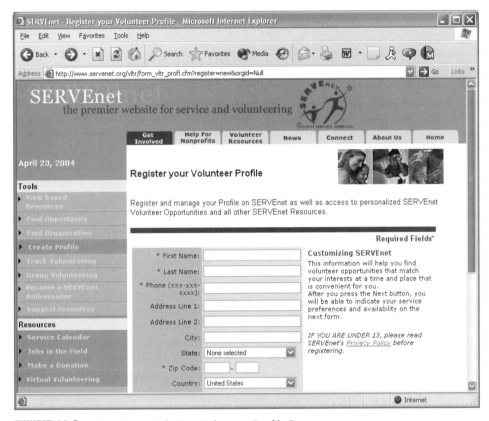

EXHIBIT 11.2   SERVEnet Web Site, Volunteer Profile Page

Source: http://www.servenet.org/vltr/form_vltr_profl.cfm?register=new$orgid=Null

thought of before. Online matching services are especially valuable to small nonprofits, some of which might not able to mount their own Web sites or which may not be sufficiently well known to attract potential volunteers directly to their own sites.

EXPANDING THE BOUNDARIES OF VOLUNTEERING

Nonprofits are looking for ways to reach volunteers who do not fit the traditional molds by virtue of age, disability, race or ethnicity, or availability. A number of Internet resources can help volunteer managers creatively rethink the way volunteers are recruited and managed.

A number of matching services and informational Web sites are targeted to specific groups of volunteers or volunteer activity. The SERVEnet Web site is dedicated to increasing the quality and quantity of volunteer opportunities for young people in the United States, ages 5 to 25, to serve locally, nationally, and globally.[4] In the United Kingdom, RSVP (the Retired and Senior Volunteer Programme of Community Service Volunteers) taps into the wide range of skills and experience of people aged 50 and over and puts them to work for the benefit of their local communities.[5]

Web sites such as Familycares.org provide information and resources for family volunteering.[6] Family volunteering offers an opportunity for organizations not only to increase the volunteer pool exponentially in the short-term, but also to help strengthen families and to cultivate volunteers for the future, since individuals who experience volunteering as part of their upbringing are more likely to volunteer as adults. To prospective volunteers who might not otherwise be able to incorporate volunteering into their lives, family volunteering gives individuals a chance to spend meaningful time with their family members while also giving back to their communities.[7]

Board membership is an area in which new online initiatives are making an important difference in challenging traditional perceptions of volunteering. As Volunteer Consulting Group's Executive Director Brooke Mahoney explains, the public image of a board trustee is of someone who is "old, white, male, and rich." Moreover, there was little awareness of how someone willing to serve on a board might offer their services, since the perception was that membership was based on "whom you know." BoardnetUSA challenges these perceptions and encourages transparency in the process by providing means for nonprofit boards to reach beyond their existing networks. It also encourages talented individuals to assert themselves in seeking board membership and provides them with a broadly accessible channel by which they can connect with interested nonprofits (see Exhibit 11.3). It provides tips to help nonprofits analyze their board needs and court candidates. At the same time, it helps to cultivate board talent by answering the questions of prospective board members and providing information on such issues as the legal responsibilities of board members and a board career strategy.[8]

VIRTUAL VOLUNTEERING

Nonprofits are also beginning to take advantage of the new types of volunteer services that individuals can offer in whole or in part via the Internet. Virtual volunteering offers opportunities to those who might otherwise not be able to contribute. This might include people with disabilities who find it difficult to volunteer in person, or those who, because of work or family responsibilities, are not available to come to an organization's offices during regular hours. A recent study indicates that virtual volunteers are more likely to be people who want to commit a smaller amount of time and also are more likely to be new volunteers.[9]

Virtual volunteering activities can include such valuable contributions as peer counseling, mentoring, editing and translation of documents, Web design and other technical services, professional consulting, online marketing, and advocacy. Volunteers might complete some or all of their work on their home computers and communicate via e-mail and telephone. There are good indications that if a volunteer is matched with an organization through an online database rather than through traditional means, that volunteer, perhaps not surprisingly, is much more likely to undertake a virtual volunteering activity.[10] The Virtual Volunteering Project Web site (*www.serviceleader.org/vv*) provides a rich set of resources for both volunteers and organizations interested in these new possibilities. Articles include information on how to establish a virtual volunteering program and how to make e-mail communications more effective; there is also a detailed guidebook to virtual volunteering by Susan Ellis and Jayne Cravens.[11]

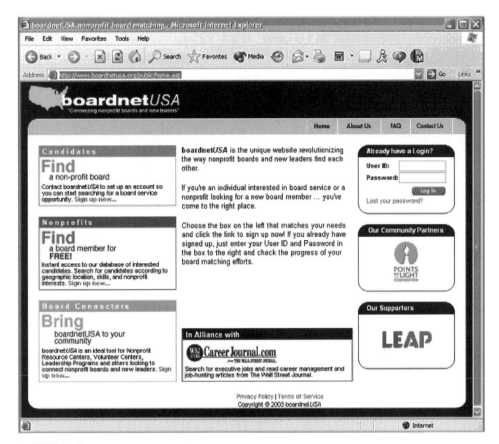

EXHIBIT 11.3   BoardNetUSA Web Site

Source: http://www.boardnetusa.org/

MANAGE AND RETAIN VOLUNTEERS

Internet resources can also be used to improve management and communication between organizations and their volunteers. Online tools can allow volunteers, especially virtual volunteers, to schedule their work and log their hours via e-mail or using a secure online scheduling system.

E-mail, newsletters, and online calendars, can all be put to use to allow volunteer managers to communicate with their volunteers in a convenient and economical fashion. Moreover, simple tools like listservs and bulletin boards allow communications to be more than a two-way discussion between an individual manager and a volunteer: They allow volunteers to communicate with each other, to exchange ideas and concerns and build community with those with whom they share a common cause.

For board members, Intranets can provide spaces for discussion and collaborative work on documents. Intranets for volunteers can also be used to provide orientation manuals, tips, and other useful documents to volunteers.

The online environment also enables interactive learning for those who are not able to attend sessions in person. These courses might combine written manuals with

Web-based chats, bulletin boards, and conferencing. Online courses can either be self-paced or be facilitated in real time. For example, see the e-learnings module provided by Board Match, which provides orientation to both prospective board members and nonprofit boards.[12]

RECOGNIZING VOLUNTEER EFFORTS

The Web is also an excellent place to recognize the accomplishments of volunteers. The stories of individual volunteers can inspire others with their commitment and contributions. For example, the Online Volunteering Service of UN Volunteers features stories of volunteers from around the world, telling in their own words what challenges they've faced and why volunteering is important to them.[13]

Volunteer managers can also find guidelines, toolkits, and best practices to help them with such questions as how to measure the economic value of volunteering at such sites as World Volunteer Web (United Nations), or Volunteer Canada (Canada).[14] The Points of Light Foundation Web site provides an ePractices section of effective practices to strengthen volunteer programs and organizations. This is a searchable database available to members only. Members are also encouraged to submit their own best practices and are eligible for small thank-you gifts when they have their first, fifth, tenth, and twentieth ePractices accepted.[15]

The Giving and Volunteering Web site by Canadian Centre for Philanthropy and Volunteer Canada provides key statistics from the National Survey of Giving and Volunteering and Participating of 2002.[16]

INTEGRATING ONLINE AND OFFLINE METHODS

Despite the rapid growth of online tools such as the volunteer matching databases, it is important to remember that these databases represent only a tiny portion of all volunteer opportunities and volunteer candidates on the Web. Moreover, as convenient and powerful as these online tools might be, it is important not to forget the crucial human element that makes a volunteering experience meaningful and gratifying.

Best practices for integrating online and offline methods hinge on successfully integrating the online and offline methods to take advantage of the best features of each. For example, if an organization uses e-mail and Web-based communications with volunteers, it is critical to make sure the e-mails are responded to promptly, but also to combine e-communications with face-to-face meetings or telephone calls. It is also important to learn the medium well and to develop good e-mail practices and policies, because it can be all too easy to send communications that are inadvertently annoying, embarrassing, or off-putting to your recipients.[17]

Some prospective supporters will find the ease and anonymity of using the online matching services to be a great advantage. Others may, however, feel that the process can be alienating and that finding the right fit can be time consuming. The Framework Foundation in Toronto, Canada, addresses the needs of this latter group who might feel more inclined to making a commitment of time if the process was made easy, fun, and timely (see Exhibit 11.4). The Foundation takes a lead from special-event fundraising and has created an innovative way to meld online and offline methods. It recruits volunteers aged 22 to 35 online but matches them with nonprofit organizations at an innovative real-world *time-raiser* event. Prospective volunteers register on-

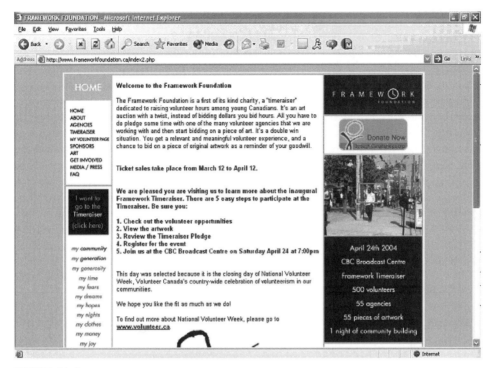

EXHIBIT 11.4   Framework Foundation

Source: http://www.frameworkfoundation.ca/index2.php

line and must pay a $20 fee (or have their companies sponsor them), pledge an initial 20 hours of volunteer work to register for the event, and select up to three organizations with whom they would like to speak at the event. At the event itself, artwork is auctioned, but the bids are not in dollars but in hours of work. Once matches are made, volunteers and their organizations can once again use the online tool to track volunteer hours. When volunteers fulfilled their pledge, they are recognized with a special award.[18]

Nonprofits can also provide online tools to empower their volunteers in their work for the organization. Amnesty International Canada used online tools to help its volunteers organize their own Write-a-thon parties. Prospective hosts could register at the Web site and send e-mail invitations to their friends to a gathering at which they were to write cards and letters in support of prisoners of conscience. At the end of the marathon, the Web site became a reporting tool where each party organizer could report on the number of letters they had written, as well as submit anecdotes and pictures of their event for display in an online public scrapbook.[19]

NEW DIRECTIONS

An important new direction for volunteer recruitment and management is connecting these online tools with corporations. Many corporations are searching for ways to help their employees volunteer and to serve their communities. For example, SERVEnet (USA) and VolunteerMatch (USA) provide corporations with the opportunity to use their databases and online tools via an interface that is branded to the corporation's Web site. VolunteerMatch explains that these co-branded sites can feature the corporation's own values and initiatives. Corporations can also track their employees' volunteer activities through this tool.[20]

Although many of the online resources and databases are local in scope, such as those of local volunteer centers, others we have looked at in this paper are regional and national. Given the nature of the Internet, it isn't surprising that volunteering is going global, as well. Since many corporations are global in reach, SERVEnet is challenged with making these tools work for users worldwide with its corporate strategy.

The Online Volunteering (OV) service,[21] managed by the United Nations Volunteers (UNV) program, provides a service to link up virtual volunteers with nongovernmental organizations (NGOs), UN organizations and academic institutions all over the world. Organizations that serve the developing world can register to recruit virtual volunteers. Virtual volunteering can be used for development work in a variety of projects, such as the following:

- Translations
- Editing and preparation of proposals and press releases
- Research and data collection
- Creation of Web sites, brochures, and newsletters
- Graphic design and database design
- Tutoring and mentoring
- Offering of professional expertise and advice (in everything from business and marketing to organic farming)
- Managing other virtual volunteers

The WorldVolunteerWeb .org [22] uses the Internet as a cost-effective way to connect individuals, groups, civil society organizations, and governments. The WorldVolunteerWeb Web site provides information and resources about volunteering worldwide, including research, statistics, a library of legislation and policy, case studies and real-life examples of volunteer projects and initiatives. The service also connects visitors to technical and programming support. The service aims to represent the diversity of volunteerism in all of its cultural forms, and to bring global ideals to local voluntary actions. The lives and work of individual volunteers are beautifully portrayed through personal anecdotes, examples of best practices, and artistic expressions.

CONCLUSION

All of these virtual tools amount to nothing if they cannot motivate individuals in the real world. The most important lessons we can learn involve reminding ourselves of old truths. George Irish, senior consultant with Hewitt & Johnston Consultants, recounts:

My mother tells the story of how in the 1960s and '70s she was an active part of a vast volunteer network across Ontario that supported the annual March of Dimes fundraising drive. As one of the hundreds of Mothers who March in towns across our province, my mother took on the task each year to walk all around the neighborhoods of our small country town, going door-to-door to raise money for the March of Dimes. Once she had completed her rounds, which took several weeks, she would sit down at the kitchen table, carefully total up all the donations and send them, together with her report, off to March of Dimes headquarters. A few weeks later, she would receive a package back containing the tax receipts for all of her donors, so she would put her walking shoes on once again, and go door-to-door to deliver the receipts, and maybe have a cup of tea and a chat with each one of her donors.

This was a ritual that she repeated year after year up until the 1980s, when the Ontario March of Dimes decided for efficiency reasons to centralize the whole fundraising process. My mother, along with the hundreds of other Mothers who March, *sent all of her carefully updated donor cards in to the central office, from which the annual direct mail fundraising program has been directed ever since.*

When it disbanded the Mothers who March, *the Ontario March of Dimes gave up a vast network of volunteers (which today we would call a grassroots, community-based network), but it also lost something else, possibly something just as important: it lost the personal fundraising power of my mother. Most of the doors my mother knocked at were the homes of our friends, neighbors, fellow parents, and members of the local church congregation—people with whom she already had a personal relationships. And when she asked for money for the March of Dimes, she was presenting more than just the very worthwhile cause of the March of Dimes, she was also making a personal pitch that was rooted in her standing in our little town and in the years of history she had with each of her donors. And that is a very powerful combination.*

Irish argues that the Internet provides us with an exciting new way to counter the "mass appeal" fundraising methods that have occupied nonprofits since the 1960s.

But now, in the age of the Internet, we are presented with an opportunity to break the mass media mode. Not only does the Internet allow for broadcast of public information from the nonprofit to the individual, but it is also increasingly used for private and personalized communications such as e-mail, instant messages, and Web logs. Irish argues, "The growth of these new forms of personal communications has inspired a number of new online tools for nonprofits that support the creating and development of grassroots volunteer networks—both virtual and real—and seek to revive the old tradition that spawned the *Mothers who March.* He cites online event registration and pledging tools in which participants send e-mail sponsorship requests to their friends, family, and coworkers (see Chapter 15). The sponsorship system recreates what an individual would do with a pledge book in the real world, but by allowing the participant to tap into their e-mail contact list rather than depend on the people they see in their daily activities, it opens up the potential of contacting many times more people, including those from around the world. Now, when so many people have e-mail accounts flooded with unsolicited e-mail, individuals may think twice about opening an e-mail from an organization, but they are far more likely to open one from a friend. These volunteer fundraisers become champions for these organizations, lending their legitimacy and personal interpretation and passion to the message of the organization. [23]

It is clear that online services and resources have the potential to be of great value to a nonprofit organization's volunteering activities, making volunteer recruitment and management more effective and efficient, and reaching broader audiences. These tools also challenge organizations to rethink their traditional image of the volunteer and volunteering activity opening up the possibility of volunteer service to those who might not have been able to offer their services because of distance, disability, or time constraints. However, the key to using these tools successfully is to retain a sensitivity to the motivations and volunteering experiences of the individuals who will be using them.

ABOUT THE AUTHOR

Alison Li, PhD, ePMT, is director for Design and Production Services, for HJC New Media. Drawing on her experience as consultant and project leader for HJC's nonprofit clients, she authored a chapter on "Raising Money for Multi-Level Organizations" in *Fundraising on the Internet: The ePhilanthropy Foundation.Org's Guide to Success Online.* Alison is co-author of a study on Internet regulation in *The Nonprofit Sector in Interesting Times* (2003), author of *J.B Collip and the Development of Medical Research in Canada* (2003), and co-editor and contributor to *Women, Health and Nation* (2003). Alison received her Ph.D. from the University of Toronto and was Assistant Professor, Science and Technology Studies, at York University before joining HJC. You can e-mail Alison at alisonli@hjcnewmedia.com.

ENDNOTES

1. The author gratefully acknowledges the contributions of Steve Culbertson, Volunteer Recruitment and Management, and Brooke Mahoney, executive director, Volunteer Consulting Group, to the writing of this chapter.
2. SERVENet Web site, *http://www.servenet.org/*.
3. AIDSvolunteers.ca Web site (to be launched).
4. SERVEnet Web site, *http://www.servenet.org/* (March 28, 2004).
5. *http://www.csv-rsvp.org.uk/*.
6. Familycares.org Web site, *http://www.1-800-volunteer.org/learn/family.jsp* (March 28, 2004).
7. Points of Light Foundation and Volunteer Centre National Network, Family Volunteering Primer, *http://www.pointsoflight.org/organizations/primer_family_wel.cfm* (March 28, 2004).
8. BoardNetUSA Web site, *http://www.boardnetusa.org/* (March 28, 2004).
9. Vic Murray and Yvonne Harrison, "Virtual Volunteering: Current Status and Future Prospects," Canadian Centre for Philanthropy (2002), *http://www.worldvolunteerweb.org/dynamic/infobase/pdf/2003/030101_CAN_virtual.pdf*.
10. Ibid.
11. Susan Ellis and Jayne Cravens, "The Virtual Volunteering Guidebook: How to Apply the Principles of Real-World Volunteer Management to Online Service," Service Leader Web site, *http://www.serviceleader.org/new/documents/vvguide.pdf*.
12. Board Match Web site, *www.boardmatch.org*.
13. Online Volunteering Service Web site, Stories, *http://www.onlinevolunteering.org/stories/stories.php*.

14. World Volunteer Web, *http://www.worldvolunteerWeb .org/research/toolkits/index.htm;* *Volunteer Canada, http://www.volunteer.ca/.*

15. Points of Light Foundation and Volunteer Center National Network, *http://www.pointso flight.org/epractice/.*

16. GivingandVolunteering.ca Web site, *http://www.givingandvolunteering.ca/home.asp.*

17. For tips, see Susan Ellis, "Making E-mail Communications More Effective," Service Leader Web site, *http://www.serviceleader.org/new/virtual/2003/04/000104.php.*

18. Framework Foundation Web site, *http://www.frameworkfoundation.ca/.*

19. Amnesty International Canada, Write-a-thon Web site, *http://www.amnesty.ca/write athon/.*

20. Volunteer Match, *http://www.volunteermatch.org/about/corporate/index.jsp.*

21. Online Volunteering Service, *http://www.onlinevolunteering.org.*

22. World Volunteer Web , *http://www.worldvolunteerweb.org*

22. George Irish, "Rediscovering the Power of Volunteer-Based Fundraising," unpublished manuscript.

e-Stewardship or e-VRM: Building and Managing Lasting and Profitable Relationships Online

Jason Potts, ePMT
THINK Consulting Solutions

The lesson for the nonprofit sector is clear: We need to manage holistic relationships with our constituents.

INTRODUCTION

New media, like it or not, are changing our world in the most profound manner. For fundraisers, new media are changing forever the environment in which donors and potential donors work and communicate together. Don't look any further than the fact that in 1992, 1 in 778 people across the planet had access to the Internet and 1 in 10 owned a mobile phone; yet, by 2004, 1 in 237 people in the world have access to the Internet and 1 in 5 a mobile phone. It is also estimated that 625 million[1] people will be able to interact with information via their television by 2006.

The Internet, wireless technology, and interactive TV are changing the communications and entertainment landscape on a daily basis. How we harness the reach and power of new media for nonprofits to develop relationships with their constituents is the objective of this chapter.

Although the Internet and e-mail are the key tools now, it is advisable to consider SMS (text messaging), MMS (picture messaging), and interactive TV in planning nonprofit projects over the next few years. In more developed economies, all these channels will be converging over the next five years, enabling consumers to use the display devices they have around their home in a variety of roles, whether as computers, TVs or communications tools (for e-mail, SMS, or MMS).

Although this might sound like science fiction, it is likely to be the new face of communicating with donors in the not too distant future. Thus, it is important to remember that many of the rules nonprofits apply to offline communications with donors will still apply. Nonprofits have been communicating with constituents through phone, mail, or face-to-face meetings for years. And throughout it all, one of the main guiding principles still applies—that you will get 80 percent of your income from 20 percent of your donors. This principle makes us all focus on doing a good job of looking after the people who give us money—no matter what medium we use to communicate with them.

Several factors have conspired over the past few years to make this commitment an even more important area for fundraisers:

- The increasing costs of donor recruitment, particularly in more mature fundraising markets
- The growing importance of planned (committed) giving for most nonprofit organizations
- The expanding public usage of new communications channels, such as the Internet, e-mail, and SMS that have made individuated mass communications possible (forgive the tautology, but you know what I mean!)
- Companies who have adopted new technologies, (most notably banks and airlines) have raised expectations of the kind of service customers expect.

As fundraisers, we have to accept that things have changed, and use that change as intelligently and efficiently as possible.

In an ideal world, organizations would look to seamlessly integrate the Internet, e-mail and SMS into existing donor communications cycles. However, there has to be a learning period when we begin to understand how these new technologies can best be used in harmony with more traditional communications channels.

Commercial Learning

It is estimated that the commercial sector will invest $11.8 billion[2] in electronic customer relationship management (eCRM) in 2004. Commercial organizations are investing heavily in order to have complete views of their customers, however they choose to interact with them. The terminology they apply to the relationship is *customer touch points*, which means they want as much information as possible about every interaction an individual has with their business. This information is then used to inform future interactions (for example, if a customer calls with a query about a product or their account), to improve customer service and to inform subsequent marketing communications. The lesson for the nonprofit sector is clear: We need to manage holistic relationships with our constituents. Gone are the days when it was satisfactory to have pictures of donors from only single transactions. Individuals are just as likely to campaign or volunteer or buy a product as they are to make a committed gift or leave you a legacy. Therefore, we need to use all this data to inform our service, fundraising, and overall marketing intelligence.

We all know that if a company or organization treats us well, and has some sense of our history with that company, then we will be more kindly predisposed to future communications from it.

NEW TECHNOLOGIES ARE CHANGING THE ART OF THE POSSIBLE

The Internet and e-mail, and increasingly SMS, are allowing us to manage relationships in ways that we have not been able to do in the past. Improvements in database technology, linked with e-mail advances, have made it more affordable and possible to have segments of one. It is now possible to manage very complex segmentation in an automated way, based both on what individuals have told you about themselves, and what they actually do when they are sent communications.

Where we have the most to learn is in understanding the business metrics associated with these new media. Logic and experience indicate that the perfect combination of channels would most likely be a mix of offline and online. Therefore, our job as fundraisers is to learn the combinations that are most effective in creating loyalty and keeping costs down.

How these channels will most effectively combine is just starting to be discernible, but we still have a long way to go to know more. The case studies that follow examine a few disparate organizations that have had distinct experiences; their variety is valuable for a broad understanding and to see the patterns that are emerging.

CASE STUDY: GREENPEACE INTERNATIONAL

Managing Online Relationships, a Twelve-Month Test by Greenpeace International

Greenpeace International (*www.greenpeace.org*) has one of the most visited nonprofit sites on the planet; it has been attracting donors for many years. As an international organization based in Amsterdam, with online supporters from more than 170 countries, the cost efficiencies of online acquisition and service make perfect sense for this organization. However, the significant challenge that faced the organization was to learn how to keep acquired online supporters loyal and how to develop online activists (cyberactivists) and subscribers to e-mail communications into financial supporters.

In November 2002, Greenpeace began a test with a subset of its online donors and cyberactivists, to learn whether a more personalized, one-of-a-kind electronic relationship (through e-mail/Web/e-newsletters) would create a more satisfied, loyal, and more generous supporter for the organization. It also wanted to engender greater loyalty from those who take online action in support of the organization. The test concluded in August 2003.

Aims

The test had these aims:

- To learn about managing online relationships
- To maximize value and minimize cost
- To learn about the benefits of allowing visitors choices with the information and services they receive
- To learn about enhanced communications and customer service online and see how this affects value (financial and action-related)

- To learn about the most effective types and frequency of e-mail communications
- To learn how different types of supporters interact with the organization and the relative value of each of these groups
- To reduce attrition

There were approximately 20,000 individuals in the test, and these were divided into six test cells (with approximate numbers given):

1. Monthly givers—individuals who gave a regular monthly gift: 2,000
2. Single givers—individuals who had donated in the last 18 months
3. Lapsed givers: 4,000
4. Cyberactivist supporters: 2,500
5. Cyberactivists who told a previous survey they did not mind being asked for a donation: 9,000
6. New recruits that were added to this cell as they joined via Web site

Test Activities and Results

The Initial E-mail

An initial e-mail was sent to begin the test cycle. It invited the individuals, segmented into their test cells, to visit a Web page, choose a password and fill in a simple form (see Exhibit 12.1). This information told Greenpeace which components of their work interested the respondents, and what kind of e-mail communications they wanted in future. The e-mail copy asked how Greenpeace could be more efficient in sending the supporters the information they wanted, and wondered when they wanted it. Approximately 20 percent signed up to preferences.

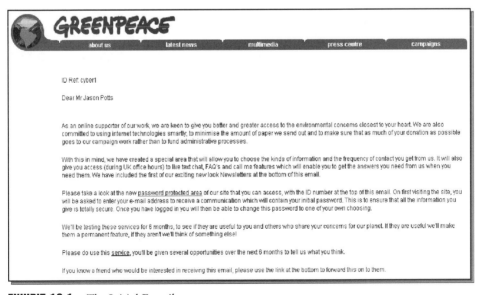

EXHIBIT 12.1   The Initial E-mail

The Preference Center

The page the respondents arrived at by clicking through the initial e-mail was called the Preference Center (see Exhibit 12.2). Throughout the test period this was available for individuals to change their communication preferences at any time (every e-mail that was sent had a link to the preference page). On this page an individual could let Greenpeace know which of the organization's six key campaign areas most interested them (A): genetic engineering; ancient forests; oceans; climate change; nuclear threats, or toxic chemicals.

They could also select the type and frequency of e-mail communication they wanted, (B). The majority of people who signed up wanted more e-mail communication; 80 percent wanted action alerts (which would be sent whenever an important action occurred); 78 percent wanted the monthly e-newsletter; and only 8 percent selected the quarterly newsletter.

In the left-hand menu of the Preference Center, individuals were able to manage their account with Greenpeace by changing preferences they had previously set up, (C), by changing their password; letting the organization know about e-mail address changes (this is important with acquired online supporters as one does not often have a full postal address); and finally, by using the unsubscribe facility (widely considered best practice for e-mail communications).

Also provided was a "Contact us" section, (D), where supporters could access various other ways of communicating with the organization. These included:

- A *Call Me* button, where someone could choose a time for Greenpeace to call them to answer questions. This was available during Amsterdam office hours, so a time zone converter was supplied to enable supporters to select an appropriate time to be called.

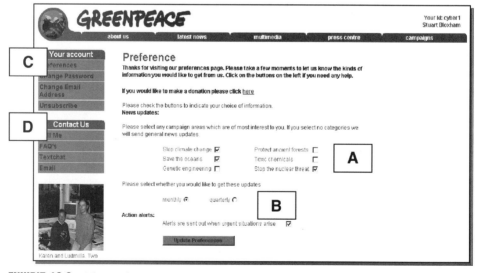

EXHIBIT 12.2   The Preference Page

- An *FAQ* section, where there was a growing resource of the questions that had been asked of the Greenpeace Supporter Services team—anything from questions about donation payments to, "are whales fish?" (It is worth a visit to the site just to check out the FAQs.)
- *Textchat,* which is similar to Microsoft's Instant Messenger or AOL's AIM. It provides functionality for supporters to have a live text chat with the Supporter Services Team, during Amsterdam office hours.
- *E-mail,* so users can ask specific questions or make comments. Queries would be answered within 48 hours.

The e-mail and the textchat were by far the most used of the options. Typical subject areas over the test period included the following:

How can I participate?	34%
How can I donate?	15%
Spanish Oil spill	12%
Where are your offices?	12%
Forest interest	3%
Genetic engineering	3%

At the end of the test period, the Preference Center was modified as Greenpeace began to learn about what the users wanted, and how they were using the tools provided. The latest version of this area shows that much more cross-selling of other areas is being done, and slightly more sophisticated and weighted information is being requested (see Exhibit 12.3).

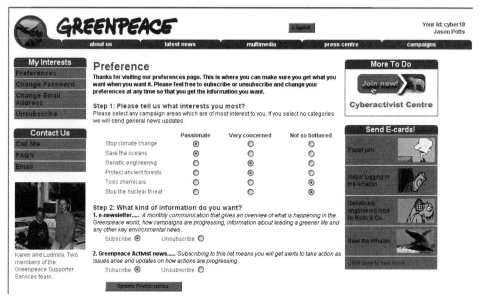

EXHIBIT 12.3 Preferences Revised

Survey

As the supporter entered the Preference Center for the first time, they were asked to fill in a simple survey so that a base level of visitor satisfaction could be ascertained (see Exhibit 12.4).

The E-Communications Cycle

Once the test parameters were established, a regular cycle of e-mail communication was delivered, based on the test cells and individual preferences. These fell into four main categories:

1. The monthly e-newsletter
2. Service e-mails, including renewal e-mails and credit card expiry reminders
3. Specific appeals
4. Action alerts

All e-mails were sent in a text or an HTML version, depending on what each recipient was able to read. (This is rapidly becoming less of an issue as more and more people around the world can receive HTML e-mail). From a fundraising perspective, the ability to use images and to have greater control over the look and feel of e-mail communication allows for far better response rates across a wide variety of organizations.

The Monthly E-Newsletter

The e-newsletter went through a few iterations during the test period. Refinements were made based on regular reviews of response rates. The main areas where changes were made were the subject line and form fields of the e-mail (these have the most im-

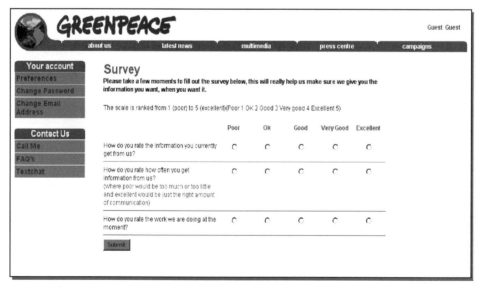

EXHIBIT 12.4 Survey Form

pact on open rates), and the content and formatting of the e-mails (which can impact on click through and subsequent action rates).

The first e-newsletter in this test campaign was sent in August 2003. This was a very brief announcement e-mail with a link to click through to read the main e-newsletter (see Exhibit 12.5). The metrics for this e-mail were

Mailed to: 16,432
From: Greenpeace
Subject: Greenpeace Supporter update
Open rate: 32% of delivered
Click rate: 7% of delivered

The refined e-newsletter had far more content and images, as well as regular features of things that people can do to help Greenpeace (see Exhibit 12.6). The metrics for this e-mail were

Mailed to: 16,432
From: Greenpeace
Subject: Greenpeace Supporter update
Open rate: 33% of delivered
Click rate: 19% of delivered

The lesson here is that while open rates have remained pretty constant, the impact on the click-through rate has been significant. After several e-newsletters had been sent out, Greenpeace was able to establish the best time of day to send e-mails to its global audience to achieve the best overall open rate (see Exhibit 12.7).

EXHIBIT 12.5 The First E-Newsletter

February 2004   Tell a friend about Greenpeace   Make a donation

Dear Jason

In a generation the orang-utan, Asia's only great ape will be extinct in the wild at the current rate of logging. Find out what the Rainbow Warrior is doing in Indonesia to try and combat illegal logging and how you can send a chilling message to government representatives trying to tackle climate change.

In this month's Newsletter:

1. Rainbow Warrior on Forest Patrol in Indonesia
2. Dolphins Die in Trawler Nets
3. Diane vs. Dow
4. First Steps to European Ban on Genetically Modified Crop
5. Terrorists Aren't Targeting Windmills or Solar Panels
6. Postcard From Patagonia

Rainbow Warrior on Forest Patrol in Indonesia

 Greenpeace's flagship is visiting the diverse tropical forests of Indonesia, Malaysia, Papua New Guinea and the nearby archipelagos. We will document what is being lost, support the people working to protect it, and hold accountable those responsible for the destruction.

Read the crew's weblog and join us in protecting the world's ancient forests. **more >**

Dolphins Die in Trawler Nets

 Our ship Esperanza has been monitoring U.K. fisheries for evidence of dolphin

3 THINGS
YOU CAN DO RIGHT NOW TO SUPPORT A GREENER PLANET!

1). Join Greenpeace or make a donation

Since we don't accept money from businesses, governments, political parties, or other pressure groups, we really depend on the help of people like you to keep protecting the Planet. Click here to make a secure online donation.

2). Become an online activist. With just a few clicks you can add your voice to those of others from around the world. Click here to visit the **Greenpeace Cyberactivist community.**

3). Help us spread the word. When there are more of us we can accomplish more. Forward this newsletter to friends, family

EXHIBIT 12.6   The Refined E-Newsletter

Renewals and Reminders

Often it is the systematic supporter service communications that have the greatest impact on your organization's overall revenue. Unsurprisingly, the online environment is no different. By taking the information Greenpeace gathered from its donors at the point of transaction, (i.e., when they joined), it allowed the nonprofit to know the dates when the supporter would be due for renewal, or their credit card would expire. With this information, Greenpeace set up an automated reminder process to make sure these supporters were not lapsing because of administrative oversights.

These simple but timely messages most likely did a lot to improve the renewal rate over the test period (see Exhibits 12.8, 12.9, and 12.10).

Specific Appeals

Within the regular e-newsletter and renewals communications cycles, various appeals were sent over the test period (see Exhibit 12.11). The first was an upgrade appeal to protest against the impending War in Iraq. It encouraged regular monthly givers to increase their donation amount.

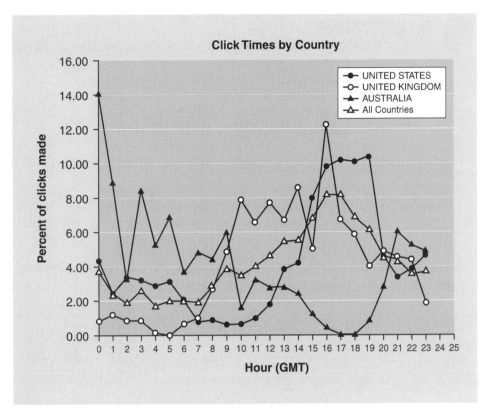

EXHIBIT 12.7   Best Time of Day to Achieve Best Overall Open Rate

EXHIBIT 12.8   Renewal E-Mail, Sent a Month Prior to the Renewal Date

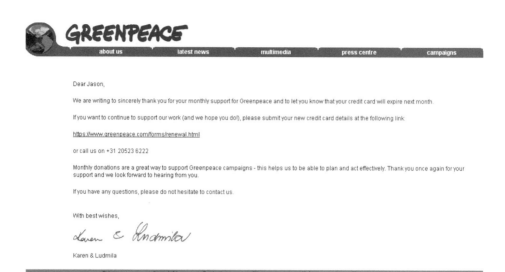

EXHIBIT 12.9   Credit Card Expiry Reminder

This e-mail appeal achieved an open rate of 43 percent. Of this, 17 percent clicked through and 8 percent of those who clicked made a transaction. The appeal achieved a return on investment of approximately 40 to 1, including the cost of the creative and the e-mail "mailing" costs.

An appeal was also tested in the June 2003 e-newsletter. It was related to the Iraq War, which was, by then, full blown. The appeal had an incentive that offered individuals a set of mock "most wanted" playing cards. (The U.S. government had issued a set of playing cards identifying senior Baath party members and military personnel whom they most wanted to capture). Greenpeace used the same printers and print-

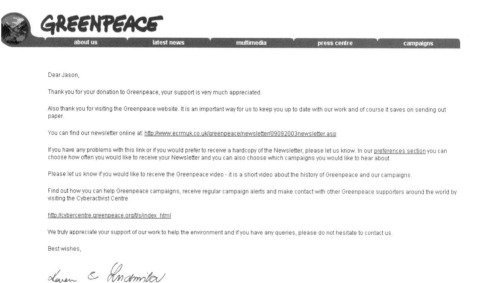

EXHIBIT 12.10   Thank You

Dear Chop,

War in Iraq looks increasingly inevitable. We must act to stop this impending conflict. Because of the urgency of the situation we are asking you to consider making a regular monthly donation, to help us mount actions to expose the real reasons behind this impending conflict. Please click on the link to make a regular gift.
https://www.greenpeace.com/forms/gpiconw.html

The Rainbow Warrior recently blockaded a UK port to prevent a military ship leaving for the Gulf. We then set up a peace camp on board a military supply ship. We need your help to take further actions to stop this war before it's too late!

Behind all the talk of weapons of mass destruction and 'war on terror' lurks the hands of the oil barons, manipulating events to get their hands on Iraq's oil. So, not only will this war lead to inevitable short-term environmental destruction, we also face the prospect of the longer-term impacts of shipping Iraqi oil all over the planet...

Are all these things coincidences?

- George Bush is a former oil man.
- Vice President Dick Cheney is a former head of the world's largest oil service contractor.
- National Security Advisor Condoleezza Rice sat on the board of Chevron and recently had a tanker named after her.
- Iraq happens to have the world's second largest proven oil reserves.

We need to expose this hypocrisy. We need to stop this war! Please make a regular gift. Please go to our donations page.

https://www.greenpeace.com/forms/gpiconw.html

Thank you

Gerd Leipold
Executive Director

EXHIBIT 12.11   Upgraded Appeal

ing plate to produce their spoof set, which featured the likenesses of President George Bush and UK Prime Minister Tony Blair, among other Allied leaders (see Exhibit 12.12).

The appeal was segmented to existing lapsed and new donors, as well as to cells of potential donors and cyberactivists. These different groups received slightly different versions, reflecting their current status and asking whether this would be a first gift, a conversion from a single gift, a change to more committed giving, or finally, an upgrade from an existing monthly gift. The playing cards were used as an incentive for making a gift.

The test cells of existing, lapsed, and new donors had a 35 percent open rate, with a 20 percent click through, of which 50 percent clicked on the give link and 24 percent made a transaction. Test cells of potential donors and activists had a 28 percent open rate, 20 percent click through, 56 percent clicked on the give link, and around 10 percent made a transaction.

Action Alerts
The alerts were sent whenever an issue hit the news. They had a more urgent feel than the regular e-newsletters, and urged individuals to take action by signing a petition or e-mailing a politician. Of all the communications sent during the test period, the action alerts achieved the highest open and click through rates. The February 2003 action alert had a 65 percent open rate, of which 30 percent clicked. Of that 30 percent, 75 percent went on to complete the action. This is an amazing statistic, and important to see when organizations are looking at the effectiveness of the communications they send.

Dear Jason

If you had the power to change the world, to stop climate change, to protect our ancient forests, to save our oceans, wouldn't you use it?

Of course you would.

Well, you have that power.

That's why we're asking you to <u>join Greenpeace today.</u> By joining Greenpeace you'll be giving our fragile earth a voice. You'll be helping us to continue winning global campaigns to safeguard our environment and our future.

Join with a regular monthly gift of $10 or more, or a single gift of $40 or more, and <u>we'll send you a complimentary pack of our most sought-after nuclear playing cards.</u>

These limited edition playing cards are hot! Back by popular demand, they're a spoof of the 'Iraq most wanted' deck. The Greenpeace cards name and shame world leaders who are sitting on the true weapons of mass destruction - nuclear weapons. They also contain easy-to-understand nuclear facts, one per card. You can't buy these cards in the shops, or anywhere else on the Internet.

<u>Click here to join and claim your playing cards.</u>

Remember, your gift will truly make a difference. We hope you'll support us and accept these cards as our thanks.

EXHIBIT 12.12   Incentive-Based Appeal

Test Results and Conclusions

Overall, Greenpeace learned that it could begin, manage, and develop online relationships in a cost-effective way for a global audience.

Over the course of the test period, Greenpeace became increasingly sophisticated in its e-marketing. By tracking each e-mail communication in detail, and by asking supporters what types and frequency of information they wanted, Greenpeace began to understand how its supporters and activists interact with the organization. It used the Preference Center to identify the interests of their supporters with regards to the organization's six key global campaign areas. It did that by e-mailing newsletters with stories from each of these key areas to see which were clicked on. In this way, every newsletter became an informal market research tool as the organization began to see which of these campaigns was of most interest to its supporters at different times.

Overall the test aimed for the following information and got the italicized results:

- Greenpeace would learn about the benefits of allowing visitors choices about the information and services they get.

  - *Those who signed up for preferences were four times more likely to respond to a communication than those who hadn't.*
  - Over the initial 12-month test period, those who signed up for preferences were worth $93 versus those who hadn't signed up were worth $72.

- Greenpeace would learn about enhanced communications and customer service online and see how this impacts on value and reduces attrition.

- Attrition amongst those who signed up to preferences was reduced by 10 percent; and as shown above, their value was increased 21 percent, for a total of 31 percent more revenue, from this group during the test period.
- Activist alert e-mails had a 61 percent open rate, and two thirds of those who clicked went through to the action page.

OTHER CASE STUDIES FROM AROUND THE WORLD

As organizations look to understand the economics of online communications with their supporter base, testing becomes a more useful tool. Through iterative testing, one North American organization has found that sending e-mail communications to its supporters increases their likelihood to donate, on- or offline. Other nonprofits are running comprehensive testing programs.

Greenpeace Brazil

One of the most cost-effective uses of online communications I've found has been accomplished by Greenpeace in Brazil. Not only does it acquire almost 50 percent of its new supporters online, it also uses low-cost online channels to renew as many supporters as possible before moving to more expensive options such as phone and snail mail. Greenpeace Brazil achieved this in the following way. The initial goal was to create an e-mail members list. In the space of two years, several strategies increased the members list by 72 percent:

- A huge telemarketing operation to update data, including e-mail
- Putting the request for e-mail addresses in the telemarketing script
- Asking for e-mail addresses in all printed forms
- Requesting e-mail addresses on adverts in the supporter magazine
- Launching an intranet for members, and advertising this in the quarterly magazine
- Aggressively asking the e-mail supporters to communicate more frequently
- Giving members the option to choose how many times per month they wanted to receive news from Greenpeace

The results of these activities speak for themselves (accurate for the 2002 year-end):

- 10% of Greenpeace Brazil members now visit the intranet.
- Attrition rates of members who joined online were reduced by 50 percent.
- Feedback from members about supporter services and current campaigns increased, improving supporter relations.
- Costs were significantly reduced, since Greenpeace Brazil sent e-mails instead of regular letters in many cases.

Cultivating its e-mail program and Web site have now become important parts of Greenpeace Brazil's donor and prospect cultivation. Key tactics in that strategy include the following:

- Sending, according to the member's choice (weekly, every 15 days or monthly), an e-newsletter, including appeals to take action, which increases overall supporter involvement

- Hosting an intranet for members where they can debate with other members on environmental issues, vastly improving interaction between the organization and its members
- Sending online invitations for events, which generates a 30 percent response rate

Greenpeace integrated its online and offline appeal for donors to upgrade. The campaign was launched in the quarterly magazine, and was supported by e-mail and a button banner on the members' extranet. As a result:

- 42 percent of responses (before outbound telemarketing commenced) were made online via e-mail or Internet form.
- The average online upgrade was 36 percent higher than the average of the overall results for the program.

Easter Seals

One of the largest nonprofits in the United States has been taking online activities seriously for some time, and has multiple Web sub-sites, powered by one central system, for all its local chapters across North America. It is referred to as the *Online Network*. Easter Seals uses the power of automated local messaging; driven by centralized tools, to deliver tailored communications to its constituents.

The Easter Seals Online Network e-newsletter is personalized for users, including each supporter's name and information provided by their local affiliate. Each month, tens of thousands of constituents receive local news from their affiliate. Open rates and click-through rates for Online Network newsletters are more than twice the industry average of 1.5 percent.

- Since the launch of the Online Network, Easter Seals' e-mail contact and prospect base has grown from 500 names to more than 16,000.
- The online interface for the national site and local affiliate sites provides a seamless and consistent user experience.
- Obtaining information about local affiliate services and online resources is quick and easy.

This tailored e-mail communication is helping Easter Seals meet some of its key organizational objectives—most importantly, that of engaging a younger audience.

The average age of the online donor is 50; the average age offline is 73.

CONCLUSION

Understanding the value and importance of managing online relationships is still in its infancy. Clearly, a great deal of time and effort is being expended in the commercial sector, and increasingly, in the nonprofit sector. Organizations like Greenpeace and Easter Seals are demonstrating how these technologies can add value to our fundraising and the way we interact with our constituents.

As more organizations begin this journey, I believe the next few years will prove that the online environment will be an important facet of how nonprofits manage relationships. This is not something to be feared: far from it, it's exciting! Anyone who gets a buzz out of direct marketing can't fail to appreciate the depth of information being garnered online, which, in turn, allows nonprofits to ask questions of their constituents that will improve fundraising and relationship building.

Enjoy the ride. I have.

ABOUT THE AUTHOR

Jason Potts, ePMT, director, THINK Consulting Solutions, began working in digital media nine years ago at a time when the market was just beginning truly to develop in Europe. He has worked with many leading International nonprofits, including Amnesty, Greenpeace, The Red Cross, UNICEF, and UNHCR. He has also experience of working in North America, Africa, Australasia, and Latin America.

He is widely recognized within the global not-for-profit community as an innovative and pioneering contributor to the development of the e-commerce and e-business marketplace. He speaks regularly at conferences around the world about the future of digital media for the sector. He writes articles for several industry journals and is regularly quoted in the press. He has recently been featured in several books: Wiley's *New Trends in Direct Response Fundraising*, Jim Greenfield's anthology of fundraising best practice, for the North American market, and *The Worldwide Fundraiser's Handbook*, published by The Directory of Social Change.

Jason is a board member of the ePhilanthropy Foundation and an ePhilanthropy Master Trainer. You can e-mail Jason at Jason@thinkcs.org.

ENDNOTES

1. GartnerG2, 2003.
2. *The Economist* (October 2003).

CHAPTER 13

Introduction to Building an Integrated Fundraising Strategy

Stephen Love, ePMT
Vervos

Shelby Reardon
Craver, Mathews, Smith & Company

Fundraising is a delicate fabric of tightly woven threads, each of which is endowed with a distinct integrity, each of which contributes a vitality to the total strength, and each of which confers a dignity upon the whole.

—Henry Rosso, Achieving Excellence in Fund Raising

INTRODUCTION

Henry Rosso's description of fundraising from his 1991 book resonates even more strongly today. Imagine all that has happened since the author penned his description, one of the most significant being the rise of the Internet.

Although many technophiles lined up to proclaim the death of traditional media and how the Web would supplant other channels in the commercial world, this also happened in the world of nonprofit organizations. Many of the evangelists claimed that the power of the Internet would allow organizations to *do more with less* financial and human resources *in real time*. It was about building communities, attracting audience, and hoping, just hoping, that the technique would raise more money.

Now back to reality—the Internet is not the silver bullet. Stripping the hype and looking at the realities, yes, it is true that the Internet can and must play a substantial role in your communications and fundraising strategy, but it must be tightly woven with the various other threads to create a strong program. Whether your goal is fundraising, advocacy, or even basic awareness and education, the Internet can help to achieve these goals, but only through a disciplined approach and effective strategy that ties all of your communication channels together. Direct mail, telemarketing, public service announcements (PSAs), PR events, and now the Internet must all build off each other to garner the maximum impact. Not one of these methods alone can truly succeed in a standalone way.

Although the crux of this chapter and book focuses on fundraising on the Internet specifically, the conversation must be broader and look at all of the threads and how this woven fabric can effectively communicate an organization's mission to move individuals from passive to active, engaged constituents.

THE CHALLENGES AND OPPORTUNITIES OF MODERN FUNDRAISING

Rising costs, increased competition, technological innovation, and the unrelenting pressure of ever increasing financial need demand that we once again re-examine our current fundraising efforts and cast an eye on those efforts that are likely to prove most productive for the future.

Today that means focusing on members who have the greatest capacity to make substantial contributions to an organization and establishing a regular communications track—an information partnership—with them that provides a clear sense of the organization's work plan for the future.

Upgrade premiums, therefore, must be largely informational in nature—to draw the best members closer to the organization's program, increase their understanding, foster their commitment, and encourage their desire to give more.

Committed giving is the way to think about direct response fundraising today. These are high-dollar direct mail and monthly giving programs modeled on the traditional principles of organized fundraising.

It is the well-known Pareto Principle—80 percent of an organization's income should be derived from 20 percent of its membership—applied to highly targeted direct response techniques that will define winners in today's highly competitive marketplace.

This approach is the antithesis of traditional direct mail, which was a volume-based numbers game in which the goal was to mail high quantities of low-cost packages in a shotgun fashion. This might have worked in the days of limited or no computer power, but today's donors expect and deserve more from the organizations they support.

This new world of fundraising also means that organizations must fully integrate all media in support of its committed giving programs. Today, alerting, mobilizing, and informing and soliciting members must be done using the communications channels preferred by the member or potential member. Integration is the new watchword for today's nonprofit organizations.

A fundraising program that retains the silo approach (e.g., direct-mail acquired donors get only direct mail, Internet-acquired donors receive only e-mail, etc.) are missing a golden opportunity to integrate multiple channels of communication and identify the channel(s) a particular member prefers at any given moment in time.

With our clients, we have found that many Internet acquired donors respond better to subsequent solicitations through postal mail than e-mail. Outbound telefundraising has also proven highly effective with Internet and direct-mail acquired donors. The key is to identify the channel most preferred by a member and apply that channel at the appropriate moment in the member's relationship with the organization.

It is the marriage of information rich communications with the proper communications channel that is defining cutting-edge fundraising in twenty-first century America.

MESSAGING FUNDAMENTALS

At the heart of any organization lies a purpose. It is just that simple. Whether your mission is to eradicate a disease, provide shelter to the homeless, defend human rights, or protect endangered species, it must be something that can be easily communicated. For many, but not all, this does not create too much difficulty. The real challenge comes when needing to illustrate to donors and prospects how your organization is best equipped to tackle these societal concerns.

It is in this notion of *results* that many organizations fall short. That is not because they are unable to illustrate how funds are utilized, it seems to be more as a result of the internal looking approach of many organizations. For insiders, it is assumed that they are using the funds of donors to address their mission. This assumption can often negatively impact the ability to cultivate potential donors in a pretty severe way.

From Rosso's *Achieving Excellence in Fund Raising*, we borrow a core principle that is universal and time tested. He called it the *L-A-I (Linkage, Ability, Interest) principle*. It is a simple concept and serves as a good quick test to apply to your online and offline fundraising initiatives. Essentially, the concept can be applied with these simple questions:

- *Linkage.* Do you have access, or have you had prior connection to the prospect? For example: school alumni, ticket buyers at your theater, activists for your organization, or even peers of current donors. This is very relevant to online viral campaigns, which we will cover later.
- *Ability.* How might the prospect help the organization, and at what donation level? For example, identify the right dollar amount or even alternative asks such as activist/volunteer involvement.
- *Interest.* Is this prospect informed about your organization, and does it move them?

If your organization cannot answer yes to each question, you must refine your efforts to help meet these core requirements. The Internet offers an abundance of opportunity to address these particular issues. We will examine some of these more tactical approaches later in the chapter.

Rosso continues on this concept by investigating how to cultivate existing relationships for greater involvement and commitment. For this, L-A-I becomes *L-I-A (Linkage, Involvement, Advocacy)*. Many successful online programs utilize this approach to turn existing constituents into *evangelists* for their organization through the use of viral fundraising campaigns (also referred to as *friendraising*).

In the L-I-A model, the questions to ask are:

- *Linkage.* What audiences are currently engaged that can communicate, inform, and engage the new prospects?
- *Involvement.* What opportunities for participation are appropriate and will motivate the prospect?

■ *Advocacy.* What activities are available for the prospect to become proactive for our cause?

With many of our clients, we present this concept simply as *educate, motivate, and activate.* Applying this to all campaigns allows us to pull from the case statement and create an engaging campaign. First, an organization must define who you are and why you are best suited to address an issue. Second, you must explain the need for urgency and provide the context of this reality. Lastly, you must define succinctly and clearly what it is you want the prospect to do.

Although many organizations are very good at the first two, the last becomes problematic. This occurs when the goals are not clearly stated. For example: Is the goal of the campaign to acquire e-mail addresses? Are you trying to immediately raise money online? Do you want to have people sign a petition or take another action? If your organization cannot prioritize, the site visitor will become confused and often do nothing when presented with too many options on the homepage.

THE ONLINE ENVIRONMENT

Now that we have set forth some basic principles and issues relevant to fundraising today, let's examine some of the unique aspects of the online environment and how this applies to the overall challenge. First, it is key that when we talk about the Internet, this involves much more than a Web site. Organizations that think in those terms are missing out on the real benefit that e-mail, peer-to-peer, and other multi-directional communications approaches can provide.

Second, the idea that by just having a Web site, people will show up in droves from all over is not a very realistic notion. In reality, the Web should be leveraged in ways that allow for laser-sharp targeted communications. It is about a dialogue—as you learn more about your donors, visitors, and prospects, you can more effectively target the messaging to their unique attributes. One challenge you face in this area is the need to integrate and synch up varying data sources. This will be discussed in detail later.

In a broader sense, who is online? The number of Americans online continues to rise. See Exhibit 13.1 for an example of just one month of growth between November and December 2003. The purpose of pointing this out is simple—*the Internet is not going away.* You *must* address how it is integrated into your efforts.

One other important observation about the online audience is that the fastest-growing segment of new users are 65 and older. For many nonprofits, this is a vital audience. A reality that faces many nonprofits has to do with the age of their file. Although there are certainly exceptions, many donor files consist of people with an average age of more than 70.

EXHIBIT 13.1 American Users Online

Country	November 2003	December 2003	Growth	Change
United States	131,052,267	132,151,758	.84%	1,099,491

Source: Nielson//NetRatings

EXHIBIT 13.2   Growth Rate in Users over 65

Age Group	October 2002	October 2003	Growth
65+	7,642,000	9,554,000	25%

Source: Nielson//NetRatings

The purpose of examining this 65+ audience is again to reinforce that the Internet is not going away. Users of all types are online and the numbers are growing. From the youngest child to the seniors, the use of the Internet is more and more pervasive every month.

The growth in this audience is good news. Although this doesn't ensure that your aging donor file is rushing online, it signals an evolution that will continue to play a role in what effect online initiatives can have for your whole file. Exhibit 13.2 shows the increase in usage, just in the years 2002 to 2003.

THE ONLINE EXPERIENCE

For many organizations, there are a variety of ways individuals interact or are involved. Volunteers, activists, and donors all play a vital role in helping organizations achieve their mission. They are not all the same in age, mindset, financial status, and other key areas, so it would be a mistake to try and treat them in a one-size-fits-all approach.

Too often, nonprofits fall into the trap that any organization could—that is, the inability to understand your audience's needs or leveraging what you already know about them. By projecting the internal bias of the internally focused perspective, it becomes difficult to provide communications and infrastructure based on the needs of the site visitor, donor, or prospect.

Exhibit 13.3 illustrates how this reality can manifest itself and therefore cause missed opportunities for connecting your donors and visitors to the site. This should not be viewed in only the terms of the Internet, but all communications. Although all organizations are different, the mindset of why people give to particular organizations is becoming increasingly competitive. Therefore, nothing should be taken for granted. The most significant disconnect in this chart falls in the area of fundraising. Essentially, how can I become a member, and if I do, what will you do with my funds?

Both NPO and user data was obtained through a series of surveys. NPO survey was sent to a sample of 1,100 from their newsletter file. The User data were collected through two surveys of samples consisting of 4,300 and 8,900 individuals.

PREVENTING THE INTERNET FROM BEING A LOOSE THREAD

Top-Level Organizational Issues

The biggest hindrance to successful fundraising, especially when it comes to the Internet, revolves around the inability to break down departmental barriers. Although it is true in all initiatives, the need for interdepartmental collaboration is even more apparent online.

EXHIBIT 13.3 Ranking of Various Web Site Characteristics by Nonprofits and Online Visitors Shows Different Priorities for Each Group

Characteristics	NPO	User
Easy to use	1	3
Significant content about cause	2	1
Visually pleasing	3	8
Memorable URL	4	10
Info about how to get futher involved	5	4
Donate online	6	9
Info about how donations are spent	7	2
Volunteer opportunities	8	7
Become member	9	5
Advocate for cause	10	6
Forum for discussion	11	11

Source: Network for Good, The BridgeSpan Group, GuideStar

Having worked with a variety of organizations, we have seen many ways that this factor creates inefficiencies and redundancies, and impacts the bottom line directly. In some cases, organizations have invested in toolsets that would not be needed if membership could work with communications. In others, advocacy initiatives are not as effective due to the inability to leverage other department's e-mail addresses.

There are two primary realities that must be understood and addressed:

1. Users do not care about how your organization is structured, so your site's structure should not directly mirror your organizational structure. Architect the online experience to the user, not to your organizational issues.
2. Your donors, activists, and other individuals have a relationship with the organization, not your department. Provide a clear communication plan for all of your segments that intelligently reinforces the organizational mission; don't "protect" them for just the use for individual departmental needs.

Setting Combined Goals

As you look at yearly goals or even special campaign initiatives, it is important that there is an understanding and support of these across departments. Whether you are fundraising, developing advocacy programs, creating general awareness, or all of the above, it is vital to have the whole organization understand how these goals interact. Removing the barriers inherent to the organization will allow you to better communicate with your audience and get the most out of them. If you cannot commit to clearly defined goals, it will be readily apparent to the user and make it unclear for them, causing fewer conversions.

There are many challenges from a technology and organizational perspective to this, but they can be overcome. Many organizations that we have worked with run into issues when trying to organize a campaign that cuts across advocacy and membership. The issues stem from the lack of data integration, multiple records, and even the lack of sharing of data—meaning, it's "my" activist, and I don't want you soliciting them for a fundraising campaign or vice versa. Specific to fundraising, organizations struggle with the notion of online numbers versus traditional fundraising goals. In our experience it is best to have a single goal since much of what we are doing cuts across media. When we discuss tactics on pre-e-mail appeals and other similar methods, it becomes clearer that without a single goal, there is difficulty in really defining what is a Web gift or a response to a traditional solicitation. After all, when push comes to shove, once the credit card clears, it is all the same kind of money.

THE TRUTH ABOUT DONORS

Simply put, donors are donors. As we continue to test different methods of solicitation, we find interesting trends. One of the most important successes that we have seen is the conversion of Web-acquired names performing in the mail. Conventional wisdom would say that if an individual came into the organization via a Web-based initiative, they would prefer Web-based communications and solicitations. The numbers show otherwise and continue to reinforce the idea that it is the message, not the medium.

Although this is an ongoing examination and test that we are doing, it demonstrates that integration is key. It is about communicating to the prospect and donor through a variety of channels that can best get the message across, not retrofitting messaging to certain channels—essentially force-fitting something to work online or in the mail, because that is what you have done in the past.

As you plan your prospecting and appeal strategies with your house lists, it is important to utilize regular communications so that the only thing an individual sees is a blatant solicitation. By creating an ongoing dialogue with your audience, you create a natural flow of communications that can be turned up or down in volume and tone. The donors of today are more demanding, want to learn more about what their money is doing, and want to be regularly informed of the issues. In this Information Age, the sophistication of the audience necessitates an equally intelligent and informed approach from the organization. The rest of the chapter will explore ways to increase integration through a variety of approaches and technologies.

ONLINE DONATION TOOLS

As technology advances and more people than ever before use the Internet as a source of information, it is vital that every nonprofit, no matter how big or small, has a Web site to advertise their organization. Allowing people to donate online is a necessary step for any nonprofit to integrate into their fundraising strategies.

Five Things to Look for in Online Donation Tools

1. *Is the online transaction processing occurring on a secure server?* No one will give his or her credit card information online if it's not on an identifiable *secure server*.
2. *Is it easy for the potential donor to use?* A donor is more likely to not give online if the process is confusing and takes too long.
3. *Compare the upfront costs and the transaction fees.* Often, a tool that has a low implementation cost can have excessively high *per-transaction fees*. Expect to pay to develop and implement an online donation processing system, but monthly costs and transaction fees do vary by service provider. Compare the ways each

service provider breaks down costs on a monthly and per-transaction basis. There are often thresholds established that are broken down either by the number of e-mails sent each month or the number of active records that are stored in the online database system that determine the level of monthly fees. It is important to compare these thresholds to make sure you find the best option for your organization.

4. *How quickly does your organization receive the online donations?* The most time-effective service providers have online donation tools that will automatically deposit donations into your organization's merchant account.

5. *If the donation tool is from a different vendor than your Web site tools, how seamlessly can they integrate?* You do not want two different looking sites—one for information and one for donating. Ideally, you want both sections of your site to look and feel the same to the donor.

Impact of Successful Data Integration on Messaging

The key to success of any integrated fundraising program is successful data integration between all sources of data. Just as a traditional direct-mail program has sophisticated database requirements in order to successfully track and monitor revenue, online donation systems are based on complex database systems. The task of integrating the data from these two systems can seem like a daunting task to anyone. Fortunately the leading service providers for online donation tools have experience dealing with the major nonprofit fundraising database systems, such as Team Approach®, Raisers Edge®, and others.

All database systems in your organization should have fields to accommodate the vital information that will be used to match data back and forth between them. This is extremely important for analytical purposes when determining the donation rate for integrated appeals and stand-alone fundraising e-mails.

The ability to effectively integrate data between a traditional fundraising database and an online fundraising system is essential in order to integrate a new medium into the complete life cycle of a donor. *Web-acquired donors,* or online donors, are stored in both database systems, and not only do they need to be tracked as part of the overall donor system, but their online activity needs to tracked in both systems. Developing a seamless transfer of data on a regular basis will allow for sophisticated cultivation and retention planning for all donors that can reach beyond traditional direct-mail and telemarketing methods.

A large environmental nonprofit organization is currently implementing protocols for a sophisticated system of data integration in order to launch an integrated (direct mail, telemarketing, and online) fundraising campaign that will run for eight weeks. This is a team effort of internal membership, activism and development staff, along with several consultants, to coordinate multiple data transfers, develop cross-platform content for segmented audiences, manage multiple delivery mediums, and ultimately track the entire campaign revenue and expenses to determine the return on investment (ROI) of an integrated campaign. The expectation is that by utilizing traditional mediums for fundraising with the less expensive online options, the ROI will be higher overall.

Several methods for sophisticated targeting and effective use of online database and e-mail tools for fundraising are described in the following section.

WEAVING THE FABRIC TO RECRUIT, CULTIVATE, AND RETAIN DONORS

A successfully integrated fundraising plan must look at all phases of acquiring donors—recruiting, cultivating, and retaining—through all mediums.

Prospecting: Search Engines and Paid Placement

The basic requirement for all online initiatives is to ensure that the site can be found. Since people become aware of you through a variety of means, they often need to use Google or Yahoo!. If you are working with an outside firm for your Web initiatives, it should be able to provide detailed information. There is also a good guide on Microsoft's site (*http://www.submit-it.com/subopt.htm*).

When it comes to paid placement, there are a variety of different flavors, and the costs vary. One cost-effective method is through keyword buys on Google and the Overture network. The fees are priced per click, and for many of our clients, the costs are around $0.25 to $0.50 per click. The key when using this method of acquiring prospects is to have the ad link directly to a focused campaign page, either immediately soliciting them for a donation or tied to another acquisition device such as a petition or newsletter sign-up. Many ads that I have reviewed drop users to the main homepage. However, this often does not provide the visitor any value because there is not a clear actionable item. (See *https://adwords.google.com/select/* and *http://www.overture.com.*)

Another more costly method is paid banner placement. Even more than keywords, this should be explored for larger initiatives that have a clear goal. Issue-based campaigns that are timely and need a large splash often get a good bump from these. In particular, we have had large success on political campaigns quickly building e-mail lists for future solicitation. Again, this may be a costly route to go, but should be explored when planning campaign strategies.

Prospecting: E-Mail

E-mail communication is an inexpensive way to raise awareness and money for your organization. Building an e-mail list of your friends, donors, and volunteers builds on your house direct-mail list as an invaluable prospecting tool.

There are several ways nonprofit organizations can capitalize on using e-mail to build your list to recruit and cultivate donors. A few of the most effective follow:

- *A monthly e-newsletter.* Aggregate important battles, accomplishments, and other key stories while also including calls to action.
- *Action alerts.* Use special appeals that focus on a current battle. Alerts are a call to arms.
- *Tell-A-Friend campaigns.* Campaigns that ask current supporters to forward information to family, friends and colleagues they feel might also be interested in the cause.
- *Viral Campaigns, often utilizing Flash animations.* Campaigns that ask anyone who might receive the information to send to as many people as possible. Also known as "pass along" campaigns.

One important rule to remember when building an in-house e-mail list to use for prospecting purposes—a rule that is often hard for offline fundraisers to accept—is that it's more important to grab that e-mail address first, and then ask for the street address during follow-up communications. The less you ask of someone online, especially when asking for personal information, the more inclined the visitor is to sign up for your e-newsletter or action alerts. Once you have that e-mail address, a strategic plan of follow-up cultivating communications can successfully convert subscribers to donors.

Tip: When developing an online prospect list, ask only for name and e-mail with online campaigns. The follow-up e-mails requesting action will be the key to gathering more personal information and converting prospects to donors.

The Integrated Appeal

A new approach to integrating traditional fundraising mediums and online donations is weaving e-mail communications into the direct-mail process. Don't just start throwing your direct-mail appeals into an e-mail! You will want to develop a strategic plan to fully tap into the potential of online fundraising—one that focuses not only on a specific appeal but draws back to your case statement and explains why someone would want to donate to your organization.

It is important to remember that an integrated appeal will show results across the board. So while you might not see a significant increase with online donations from your pre e-mail, you might see an increase in the response rate from the group of donors who received that e-mail through your direct-mail returns.

This type of integration is a perfect example of why data integration is *key* for the successful continuing of message throughout the various communication channels (direct mail, e-appeals, Web site). In order to successfully carry out integrated appeals, your data need to be as up to date as possible and should be routinely updated with e-mails collected from various sources. A clean direct-mail file with good addresses and out-of-date e-mails will not perform well in an integrated appeal campaign.

There are a few paths to take when planning an integrated direct mail/e-appeal campaign. Take a look at your house file and determine the number of valid donor e-mails you have—this can determine the best path for your organization to take. If you are unsure which path your organization should take concerning integrated appeals—*test, test, test!* The best way to determine the optimal levels of communication with your organization's donors is to test each path to see how well they respond. The list size for a valid test varies—it really depends on the size of your own organization's list. If you have limited time and resources, you can plan a test series for your organization's donor list using one appeal. Create an e-mail list from all donors receiving the appeal and divide the list into three subsets to test each path described as follows. Compare the response rates between each subset, making sure to include both online and offline revenue. Choose the path that works best for your donor list.

Paths for Integrated Appeals
- Pre and post e-mails
- Pre e-mail only
- Post e-mail only

These paths focus on the timing of your communications with your donors. The *pre e-mail* is an e-mail message letting your donors know they will be receiving a very important letter from your organization soon, but they can give online. A *post e-mail* reminds your donors they received a very important letter from your organization, and if they haven't given already, they can give easily online. As just stated, the best way to determine what path works best for your organization will be to perform a series of integrated appeal tests. What works best for one group's donors can be the complete opposite for another.

Example: A national nonprofit with a large online donor base implemented a pre-e-mail program for each direct-mail package that went to both prospects and current donors. After a period of testing pre-e-mails with post-e-mails, it decided to use only the pre-e-mail path. The pre-e-mail online response rate remains around 1 percent, but the overall response rate per package has increased. While it may not drive significant online donations, people know the direct-mail piece is arriving in the mail soon, and they respond through the mail. It is an inexpensive exercise worth testing for your organization's donor base.

Regardless of which path your organization decides upon for integrated appeals, the important things to remember are correlating the data between offline and online systems and messaging. The importance of proper messaging cannot be stressed enough when developing integrated appeals. Direct-mail letters do not work well as fundraising e-mails—the messaging is not conducive to the e-mail format. E-mails fight for attention in your donors' e-mail inboxes, and you want to capture their attention with your core message in a few seconds.

Online Renewals

An online e-renewal program is similar to the e-appeals described earlier, yet to be effective it should rise to a higher level of sophistication. The keys to successful e-renewal programs are messaging, timing, personalization, and ease of use.

Many online donation service providers do not yet have the capability to provide custom giving pages, or are reluctant to do so for privacy concerns. If you can utilize this function, it will increase the likelihood of a repeat donation. This feature allows for a unique identifier to pass through a donation link in an e-renewal e-mail, which takes the donor to a giving form with, at the very least, their contact information already filled in. The more sophisticated tools can include custom giving strings on the forms dependent on what amounts the donor has given before or what amounts were added to the database. All that is left is for the donor to input personal credit card information to renew his or her commitment to your organization. If your online donation tools are not equipped to do this, do not worry—you can still develop an e-renewal program, focused more on messaging then personalization.

If your organization wants to set up an e-renewal program, there are a few critical steps to keep in mind:

- *Data integration with offline database system is critical.* E-renewals programs can be used for all donors (online and offline)—essentially any donor who has provided an e-mail address. Ideally, your organization's offline donor database is the most up to date, with both online and offline donor information, so plan to pull the most recent file of all donors up for renewal each month, with valid e-mail addresses and upload them into the online donation system (see Exhibit 13.4).

- *Integrated messaging.* The best way to get the most bang out of an e-renewal program is in the messaging. Do not simply copy and paste your direct-mail renewal letter into an e-mail and send it! Start the message reminding donors that they will receive a letter in the mail reminding them their membership will expire soon. Then let them know they can simply renew now with a secure online donation.
- *Test, test, test!* There are several ways to set up an e-renewal program, so it's best to take a look at your organization's current renewal process and pick the best way to integrate an online option. Whether your organization uses a calendar-based or expire-date renewal system will affect the structure of an e-renewal program. Set up a test series of e-renewal e-mails with a select subset of donors over a few months and test the response rate.
- *Develop a structured e-renewal program for maximum results.* Don't just send a few e-mails and hope for the best! Before you even start your test series, develop a strategic plan based on appropriate mailing dates for mail and e-mail, how to define the subset of expiring donors each month, and how long the e-mail series will run. Doing this up front, testing it, and finalizing the plan will make analysis easier and save headaches with data-integration issues.

One large national nonprofit sends an average of 7,000 e-renewals each month, based on a series timed with its members' expiration date. It is a four-month e-mail series that nets an average donation rate of 10 percent.

CONCLUSION

Since the beginning of modern fundraising, new technologies and techniques have and will continue to evolve. The growth of the Internet audience and increased sophistication of donors makes it very necessary for organizations to embrace this reality and harness its power. While it is not the silver bullet, it needs to be integrated into the

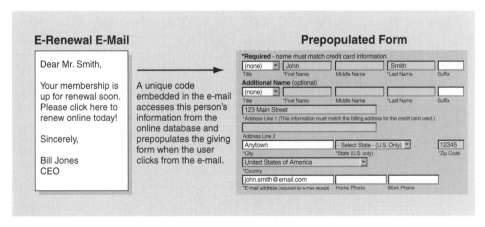

EXHIBIT 13.4 E-Renewal Program

larger strategy. Just like a woven fabric, the strength of fabric is often greater than the individual thread.

By knocking down the organizational and data integration barriers, the mission of your organization will be clearer to your audience and therefore more effective. At this point, the focus turns back to how you can effectively communicate and solicit individuals as opposed to struggling with internal barriers to true integration.

Finally, *test, test, test* (both online and off)!

TECHNOLOGY PROVIDERS AND RESOURCES

Blackbaud	*http://www.blackbaud.com*
Convio	*http://www.convio.com*
ePhilanthropy Foundation	*http://www.ephilanthropy.org*
GetActive	*http://www.getactive.com*
Kintera	*http://www.kintera.com*
Network for Good	*http://www.networkforgood.com*
The Nonprofit Matrix	*http://www.nonprofitmatrix.com/*
TechSoup	*http://www.techsoup.org*

ABOUT THE AUTHORS

In March of 2001, **Stephen Love,** ePMT, president and founder of Vervos, brought a team of seasoned communication strategists, designers, and technologists to create Vervos with a focus on integrating traditional and Web-based media to educate, motivate, and activate organizations' key constituents. Representative clients include America Coming Together, the Christopher and Dana Reeve Paralysis Resource Center, Conservation International, Emily's List (Campaign Corps), Hull for Senate (D-IL), the International Association of Firefighters, Network for Good, and the Women Sports Foundation.

Prior to founding Vervos, Stephen served as executive creative director of the Commerce One Design Center (previously AppNet and NMP, Inc.). In his six years with the company, he built and managed a team of 40 brand consultants, designers, copywriters, and interface engineers. Stephen was responsible for representing the Design Center in sales engagements, as well as ensuring the successful delivery of projects. He also served as interactive marketing consultant and Creative Lead on several client engagements, including the Association of Fundraising Professionals, Cancer Care, CARE International, Common Cause, Discovery Channel, Doctors Without Borders, GreenpeaceUSA, International Red Cross, NARAL, Nature Conservancy, Project HOPE, The Wilderness Society, UN Foundation, and World Wildlife Fund.

Stephen began his career at Craver, Mathews, Smith & Company, the renowned fundraising agency, as a marketing and production specialist working with clients such as the Susan G. Komen Breast Cancer Foundation, Planned Parenthood Federation of America, and Families USA.

Earlier this year, he was certified as an ePhilanthropy Master Trainer (ePMT) by the ePhilanthropy Foundation, speaking at many of their eTour stops. Stephen was also contributing author to Fundraising on the Internet, the ePhilanthropy Foundation's Guide to Success Online and writes ongoing updates delivered via e-mail to buyers of the book. He was also a featured speaker at this year's Catholic Charities USA national conference.

Stephen holds a bachelor's degree from Brown University in American Civilization, focusing on cultural trends and how they impact society. You can e-mail Stephen at slove@vervos.com.

Shelby Reardon is the senior project director with Craver, Mathews, Smith & Company's Interactive division, where she works with organizations to increase their online fundraising opportunities and enhance the organization's Web presence. Shelby manages the operations of the Interactive division while coordinating online strategies for CMS clients, including Covenant House, Environmental Defense, Habitat for Humanity International, Democratic Congressional Campaign Committee, and the American Civil Liberties Union.

Shelby has almost a decade of experience working with nonprofit organizations to develop technological tools to enhance activist, fundraising, and campaign strategies. Before joining CMS, Shelby worked with the Carol Trevelyan Strategy Group (CTSG) as an Internet project manager and client services manager. There she developed customer service protocols to help clients utilize their custom Internet applications, while managing several custom Internet application and site design projects. A sampling of projects she managed include an online pro-choice voter guide for the Planned Parenthood Affiliates of California, the development of Online Action Centers for American Rivers, NARAL, The Wilderness Society, and the Electronic Frontier Foundation.

Prior to her work with consulting firms, Shelby worked at a variety of nonprofit organizations in the Washington, D.C., area, including the Women's Research and Education Institute, NOW Legal Defense and Education Fund, and the American University. At these organizations, she managed an internship program, special event programs, and publication development and distribution programs, and assisted with fundraising and marketing efforts. Her long history of activism is enhanced with stints as a government relations intern at the National Organization for Women, a community organizer with ACORN, and as a Union Summer organizer in the AFL-CIO's Union Summer program.

Shelby holds a BA in Sociology, Social Services from the University of California, Davis, and a Master of Public Administration, Urban Affairs, from American University in Washington, D.C. You can e-mail Shelby at shelbyr@cms1.com.

CHAPTER 14

Annual Giving: Acquiring, Cultivating, Soliciting, and Retaining Online Donors

Michael Johnston, ePMT
HJC New Media

When nonprofit organizations first think about raising funds online, they tend to see this new money through the lens of what fundraisers call the annual fund campaign.

To the layperson, the term *annual fund* draws blank stares—most people don't know what this fundraising jargon means. To professional fundraisers, annual fund campaigning has these characteristics:

- Repeats itself on an annual basis and is therefore predictable—relying on repetition for success
- Seeks immediate cash gifts from individuals
- Seeks gifts that are for unrestricted use by the nonprofit
- Addresses short-term needs (one year or less)
- Builds on campaigns from one year to the next
- Builds an expectation with the donors that they'll be asked every year for a similar, renewable gift

Perhaps most importantly, an annual plan is created that tries to leverage repetition, loyalty, and precision to be as efficient as possible in raising money in a mass marketing exercise.

Annual fund theory could be further distilled into three central tenets:

1. The annual fund plan to *renew* as many donors as possible.
2. Use the annual fund plan to *acquire* as many donors as possible.
3. Use the annual fund plan to harness an organization's limited human resource, financial, and organizational resources increasing the *annual fund's ability to renew and acquire donors.*

Annual fund theory has traditionally tried to renew as many repeat donors as possible while simultaneously trying to find a maximum number of new donors. How can we apply this model to online fundraising?

Online fundraising shares an affinity with annual fund theory: in most cases it garners immediate, unrestricted cash gifts from individuals to address an organization's short-term needs. In many nonprofits raising money online for the first time, the responsibility often falls to annual fund staff to run the ePhilanthropy campaign.

There is no doubt that online giving is a good match with the objectives of annual fund giving. This chapter will outline how good annual fund practice can be successfully applied to online fundraising. Still, there is much more to online giving than simply asking for modest, yearly donations.

The Children's Hospital of Los Angeles has decided to jump into ePhilanthropy with both feet. It currently makes very little from online giving, but sees great potential. Not surprisingly, it has assigned its director of Annual Giving, Stephanie Eversfield to kick-start the program.

Stephanie is focused on creating an online giving plan that is related to the traditional annual campaign structure for raising money. She is also creating a monthly schedule of solicitations and e-newsletters that ask for money.

Stephanie understands that to fully leverage the tools and techniques of ePhilanthropy, she'll have to focus on how the online environment can reinforce all areas of fundraising for the CHLA Foundation. Exhibit 14.1 captures the holistic approach that CHLA is taking with online giving.

EXHIBIT 14.1   Holistic Approach to Online Giving

GOAL SETTING IN ANNUAL FUND GIVING

One of the challenges in understanding online giving is the lack of comparative data on results that would help inform projections. To get around this lack of data, Stephanie Eversfield initiated a survey of other children's hospitals and their ePhilanthropy results.[1]

That survey of 10 children's hospitals yielded information that helped Stephanie to do the following:

- *Project the average online gift amount.* $109.33 was the average among seven participating organizations.
- *Project the number of monthly, EFT donors in relation to single gift donors.* An average of 5 percent of online donors made an EFT gift when it was available as an option. These gifts averaged $14 a month.
- *Project the gross revenue* by knowing the average number of donors times the average gift size.

With this data in hand, Stephanie was able to set reasonable ePhilanthropy annual giving goals for CHLA's fiscal year:

- Twelve e-newsletter appeals yielding 10 donors per newsletter at an average gift of $109.33, for a total of $13,119
- Six e-mail appeals during the year yielding 30 donors per appeal at an average of $109.33, for a total of $19,679

As recommended earlier, Stephanie and CHLA have projected additional online income (above the money raised through the annual campaign) through these avenues:

- Creation of a prominent in-memoriam gift opportunity on the home page, increased online media traffic, and a search-engine optimization strategy—all geared toward yielding an additional 200 donors, and giving an average of $109.33 for a total of $21,866
- Promotion of a third-party peer-to-peer solicitation tool by volunteers, affiliates, and so on, to yield another 200 donors, at an average of $89.00 for a total of $17,800
- Internal online workplace tool allowing employees to give a total of $30,000

The annual fund planning, in conjunction with other ePhilanthropy goals, has given Stephanie an achievable projection of $102,464. The goal is supported by market research, takes into account a schedule of monthly solicitations, and includes not only annual fund initiatives but also all potential areas of online giving.

THE BASICS—YOUR HOME PAGE, GIVING FORM, AND CATCHING EYEBALLS

In annual fund campaigns, direct mail is often the centerpiece of a repeating system of solicitations. Many fundraisers start every appeal by creating the response coupon for the campaigns. In that spirit, here is a critique of two online reply forms for Mothers Against Drunk Driving and Children's Hospital of Los Angeles, along with recommendations for improving online giving forms like these. Both organizations currently have online forms that are unevocative.

Compare the current MADD online giving form with the recommended improvements to the form (see Exhibit 14.2). The reader will notice that the improved form includes the following:

- An affirmative statement to motivate the prospective donor
- The use of color and font size to make giving easier
- Pictures to create a more emotional impact than the current neutral form

When prospective online donors to Children's Hospital of Los Angeles are driven to the giving form, they see an effective picture of a child on the left-hand side and the

CURRENT FORM

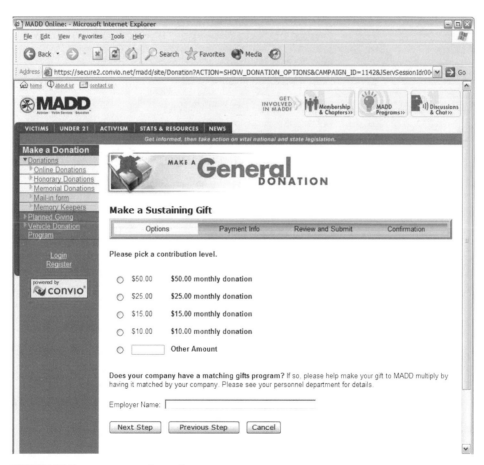

EXHIBIT 14.2   Improving the Online Giving Form: MADD

(continues)

RECOMMENDED IMPROVEMENTS TO THE FORM

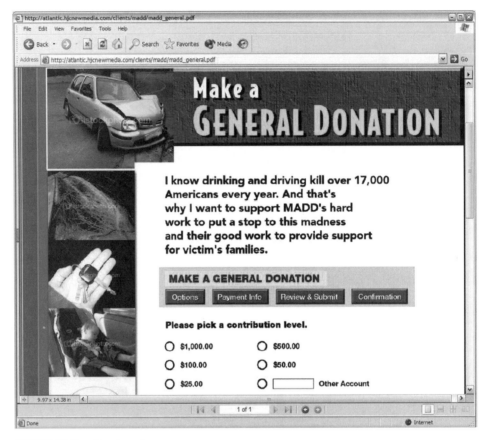

EXHIBIT 14.2   Continued

colorful logo of the organization above the child's picture. However, after a prospective donor's eyes pass over those elements, they come to rest on a form that is missing the helpful elements in the improved MADD giving form. Exhibit 14.3 compares the hospital's current online giving form with a second form showing what the hospital might do to improve it.

THE HOME PAGE

Every organization can improve its fundraising results—including support for the annual campaign by making sure that online giving is emphasized on the home page. It's the place where more individuals land—and in most cases needs to provide giving opportunities in a larger space than most organizations have given it in the past.

In 1999, Greenpeace International had millions of visitors to its home page, but very few donors. It had a standard giving link much like the two organizations already discussed. Greenpeace was advised to place a more prominent, colorful JOIN button on the front page.

Daryl Upsall, the international fundraising director at the time, recounted what happened: "Overnight there was an increase in giving—and when we decided to animate the 'o' in join there was an immediate rise in donations again. We were literally catching eyeballs with the animated give button."

It will be a difficult political battle to win, but by placing a more prominent giving button on the home page, any nonprofit organization will increase its online giving—as Greenpeace did—and you'll be leaping past other children's hospitals with a more effective fundraising home page.

Not only do organizations need to win a more prominent place for a generic giving button, they also need to win space for online giving opportunities that are unique to their mission and supporter constituencies. For one major health charity in North America, simply putting a more prominent banner/button for in-memorial giving on the home page raised online memorial donations by more than 400 percent.

Exhibit 14.4 is an example of a banner prominently displayed on the home page of the American Lung Association, directly soliciting for memorial gifts.

CURRENT FORM

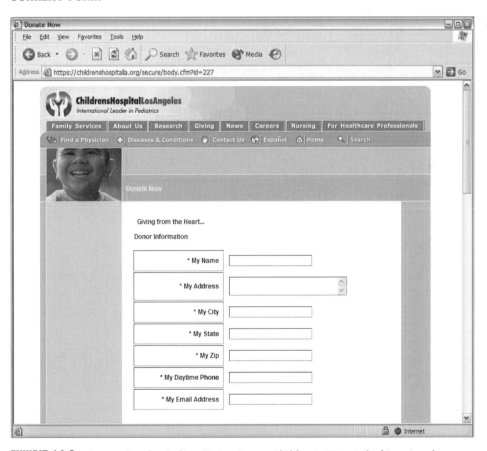

EXHIBIT 14.3   Improving the Online Giving Form: Children's Hospital of Los Angeles

(continues)

RECOMMENDED IMPROVEMENTS TO THE FORM

General Donation

File Edit View Favorites Tools Help

Back Search Favorites Media

ChildrensHospitalLosAngeles
International Leader in Pediatrics

Family Services | About Us | Research | Giving | News | Careers | Nursing | For Healthcare Professionals

Find a Physician | Diseases & Conditions | Contact Us | Español | Home | Search

Make a

GENERAL DONATION

Yes, I want to offer hope and healing to sick children, youth, and their families. Here's my tax deductible gift to the Children's Hospital of Los Angeles for:

$1,000.00 $150.00 $100.00

$75.00 Other

DONOR INFORMATION

My Name

My Address

My City My State My Zip

My Daytime Phone

My Email Address

PAYMENT INFORMATION

Credit Card Type Month Year AMEX Month 01 Year 2004

Credit Card Number

Card Holder's First Name

Card Holder's Last Name

Zip Code

Phone Ext

Gift Amount

DESIGNATION OPTIONS

I would like my contribution to benefit the following area in the hospital

HONOR/MEMORIAL GIVING

I would like to dedicate my gift:

In memory of:

In honor of:

to commemorate a special occasion:

to acknowledge an achievement or special event:

Please send acknowledgement to (amount of gift will not be disclosed):

Name

Address

City State Zip

SUBMIT

Check your information then click, "Submit".
Contributions to Children's Hospital Los Angeles are tax deductible.

You may mail this form to:

Children's Hospital Los Angeles Foundation, Attn: Donor Services
4650 Sunset Blvd., MS29, Los Angeles, CA 90027

PRINT THIS PAGE RESET

Children's Hospital Los Angeles • 4650 Sunset Boulevard • Los Angeles • CA 90027 • (323) 660-2450 • webmaster@chla.usc.edu
© Copyright 2003 | Disclaimer

Internet

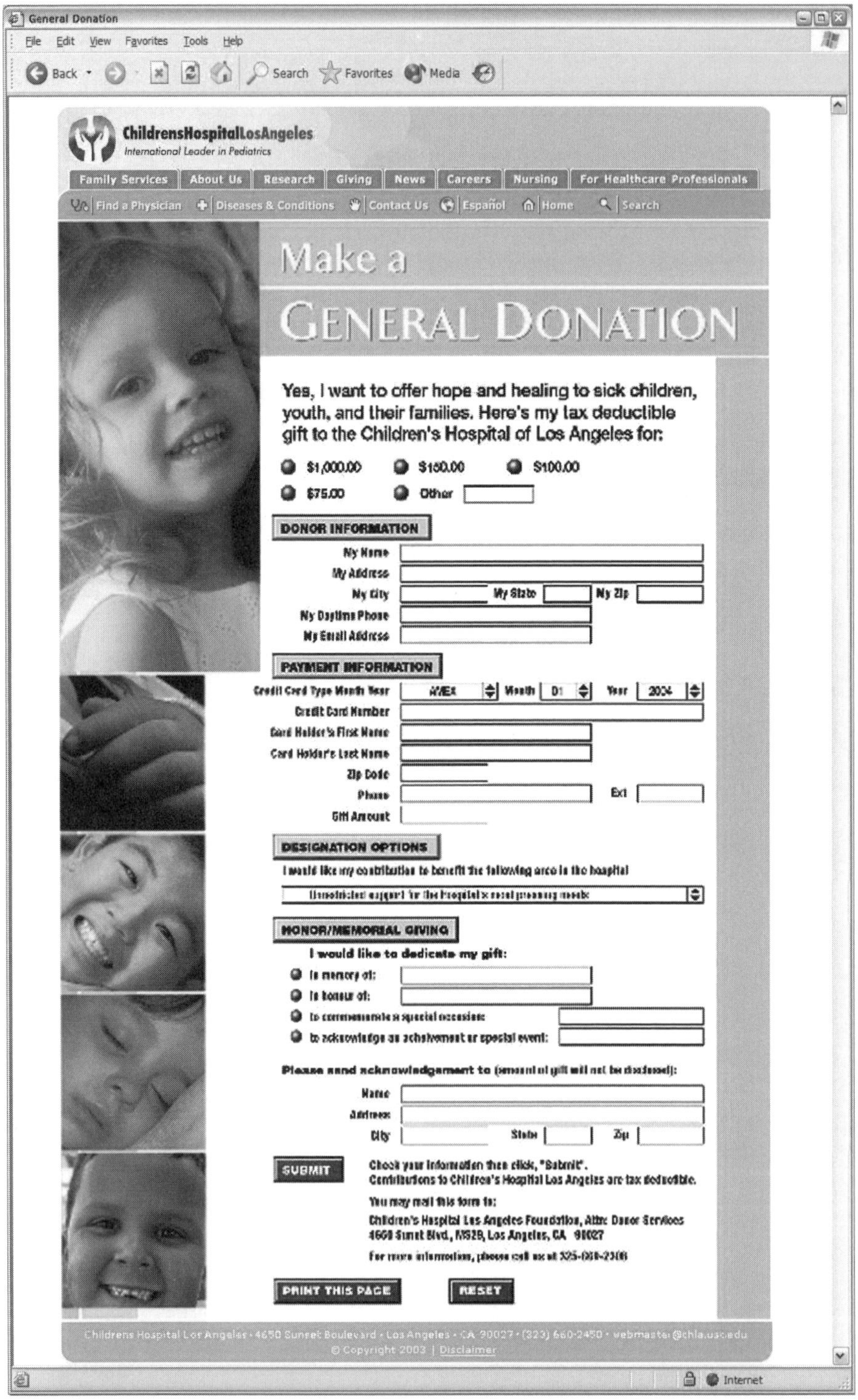

EXHIBIT 14.3 Continued

> Memorialize a loved one by donating online.

EXHIBIT 14.4 American Lung Association Home Page: Prominently-Displayed Banner for In-Memorial Giving

Every organization needs to have its home page present more than a small text link—it needs more noticeable, animated spots to help increase online giving—whether for an annual fund gift or special giving in memorial.

E-MAIL RENEWAL RATES—THE MISSING PILLAR OF ANNUAL FUND CAMPAIGNING ONLINE

Almost all nonprofit organizations raising money online are relying on gifts that come in through a number of methods *except* sending an e-mail to past donors to ask for another donation.

Remember one of the three principles of successful annual fund campaigning is to renew past donors. Generally this strategy is missing from most online fundraising strategies. Most organizations are relying on prospective supporters to come to the site and make a gift for the first time. This new source of fundraising is seen as pennies from heaven, and if a lot of online donors are coming to the site on their own accord, the money seems like it's freely acquired.

E-mail is just starting to be used for renewal purposes. In a 2003 study of 30 multilevel nonprofit health charities across North America, the average response rate for an e-mail sent to a past online donor list was between 3 and 5 percent.[2]

And that's it. At the time of publication that is the only study we've got, but it is a start for constructing accurate annual campaign fundraising.

On the cost side of sending out renewal e-mails, there is a bit more information. There are a wide variety of technical solutions being used to deliver e-mail renewal solicitations. eFundraisers should take note of a study conducted by Vinay Bhagat of Convio, Inc. that found the cost of delivering e-mail for fundraising (versus other mediums) is cheaper, with e-mails costing between 0.03 to 0.13 per e-mail versus $1.50 per direct-mail piece.[3]

AN E-MAIL SOLICITATION PRIMER

There are very few books you can take off the shelf to help you create an e-mail solicitation. Facing a dearth of information, the following list should help you with some of the basics of creating and sending out annual fund e-mail appeals:

- *Subject line.* Urgent, immediate, with a piece of the solicitation approach embedded: organization and goal. While the potential list of words that may cause unwanted scrutiny by spam filters is quite long, common examples that legitimate senders might also use include: free, available, chance, convenient, excellent, information, new, opportunity, simple, super, unique, and so on.

- *To line.* Personalize if possible.
- *From line.* Personalize if possible, and if your brand is recognizable and respected, include it.
- *Top one third.* Many e-mail readers will give the recipient a window (above the scroll) to look at the top of the e-mail. Make sure the organization, solicitation, and hypertext link are made to fit the approximate window size.
- *Opt out.* In compliance with the ePhilanthropy Code of Ethics (see Appendix A), there should be reference to how someone can avoid future appeals (opting out of further correspondence).
- *Privacy policy.* There could be a link to a privacy policy.
- *List control.* Make sure that the e-mail is sent to a test group before being sent out to your e-mail list, and if using an outside firm to send your email, make sure that you sign off on the final tested version, before it is sent.
- *Getting personal.* Personalization of the main text area: (Dear <name>, thank you for your gift of <gift>)

You should address two additional challenges when you're trying to get your e-mail appeal out to your donor or prospective donor.[4]

1. *Special instructions for communicating with AOL e-mail users.* Tens of millions of potential and current donors use AOL as their e-mail software. Every non-profit organization needs to know that the default setting for AOL 9.0 strips all graphics from HTML messages and renders URLs unclickable. AOL 9.0 also assigns anything it even suspects to be spam to a black hole called "Spam Folder." Here are some ways to work around this:

   - Select all AOL addresses from your database and send a plain-text message.
   - Place a line of copy at the beginning of your e-mail that asks AOL recipients to click a link, "Show images & enable links," that AOL puts at the top of each message.
   - Suggest that recipients make a global change to their default settings so that they can see all messages as they were designed (and therefore be able to interact with all embedded links).
   - Perhaps the best solution is to ask recipients to click the "Add Address" icon to the right of your message. This will allow future e-mails to pass through AOL filters and be rendered properly.

2. *Special instructions for communicating with Outlook 2003 users.* Outlook 2003 allows users to block receipt of all e-mailed HTML content. Blocking HTML disables Web bugs—tiny graphics containing code that can be inserted into e-mail allowing advertisers to collect personal data when recipients read bugged messages.

   In previous versions of Outlook, graphics and links were delivered to the computer and appeared in Outlook's preview pane (in default mode). Now, HTML, images, and rich media are cached on the server and downloaded only when the message is actually opened. Users must either manually click to load a message's images and links or turn off the image-caching feature in the preferences. Because many e-mail tracking programs use invisible graphics files to indicate if an e-mail has been opened, open rates will inevitably drop as Outlook 2003 is more widely adopted.

WHY MONTHLY GIVING HAS TO BE EMPHASIZED WITH ONLINE ANNUAL CAMPAIGN FUNDRAISING

With renewal rates as low as 3 percent per e-mail solicitation to past online donors, the overall yearly retention rate is perilously low. This may change—it may not. These renewal rates are certainly lower than standard response rates for most direct mail programs.

Let's conduct a quick test for a hypothetical online renewal program. The make-believe animal rights group, Protecting Puppies and Kitties (or PPK), has found 1,000 online single gift donors in 2002. In 2003, it decides to send out 10 e-mail appeals throughout the year to try and renew those past online donors.

Based on the average rate of renewal found in the study mentioned earlier, those 10 appeals multiplied by 4 percent (the average rate) would give the organization a simplified 40 percent renewal rate. Of course, multiple gifts by a small percentage of very loyal donors would lower that overall renewal rate, but let's keep this simple for now.

So, a 40 percent renewal rate would leave 600 of those 1,000 online donors in a newly lapsed category. The author believes that even that 40 percent is anecdotally an optimistic projection in comparison to the renewal rates rumored to be associated with other organizations.

With a 40 percent renewal rate for past online donors, what would the lifetime value be for those donors? A study conducted by the Canadian Direct Marketing Association in 2002 looked at the life expectancy of a new donor who appears on a nonprofit organization's database, based on the average renewal rate for all donors.

Please refer to Exhibit 14.5, taken from that study. To calculate the lifetime value of online donors at a renewal rate of 40 percent, you would calculate the average gift to be $75. If Protecting Puppies and Kitties found 1,000 new online donors and can renew 40 percent of them, then the lifetime value of the donor's gift would be $112.50, or the $75 gift multiplied by their time spent on the database (1.5 years).

Now, let's compare the lifetime value of a single gift online donor with a monthly deduction via Electronic Funds Transfer from a bank account or via a credit card. For Amnesty International Canada's Andrew Bales, Internet fundraising director, the value of his online monthly donors is many, many times higher than his single gift donors.

A comparative review of online single gifts and monthly donors from January 2000 to February 2004 shows a renewal rate of 82 percent for monthly deduction donors versus a renewal rate of 40 percent for single gift donors.

If the life expectancy chart in Exhibit 14.5 is used to calculate the lifetime value of each online donor group, it shows:

- The single gift donors have an average gift value of $75 over four years and a renewal rate average of 40 percent—meaning the $75 is multiplied by 1.5 for a lifetime value of approximately $112.50.
- The monthly gift donors have an average gift value of $20 a month, with an annualized value of $240 and a renewal rate of 82 percent—meaning the $240 is multiplied by 9.5 for a lifetime value of approximately $2,280.

The difference in the lifetime value is staggering, but there's a catch—it's incredibly difficult growing your committed monthly online donor. Is it worth it? A

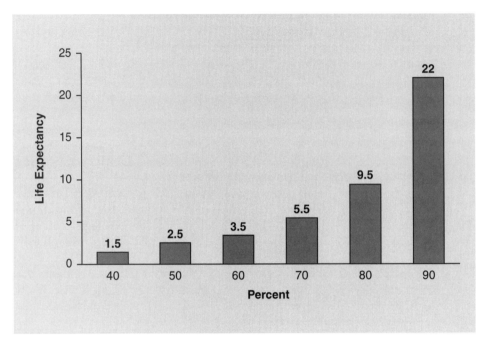

EXHIBIT 14.5   Lifetime Value of Online Donors

Source: Canadian Direct Marketing Association

comparison of those two disparate lifetime values should be enough incentive for any organization to try to capture as many monthly committed online donors as possible.

But how does an organization do that? The first place to start is with the online giving form.

In 1999, Greenpeace International, *www.greenpeace.org,* was receiving millions of visitors to its Web site, but getting very few gifts—and absolutely no online monthly gifts. That situation changed as soon as it altered its giving form to emphasize monthly donating. The number of single gift donors increased from 111 single gifts in 1999 to 883 in 2000—an impressive 795 percent increase, but it's the number of monthly donors that is the most exciting finding—increasing from 30 in 1999 to 613 in 2000— an increase of 2,043 percent.

If the reader remembers that the lifetime value of an online monthly donor is many times higher than a single gift donor, then this 2,043 percent increase for Greenpeace would raise a lot more money than concentrating on single gift donors. What did the new form look like? See Exhibit 14.6.

At the start of 2000, every prospective Greenpeace donor arriving at their new giving form at *www.greenpeace.com/forms/gpicontr.html* saw monthly giving emphasized on the first screen, and then would scroll down to see how to leave a single gift— as already described. This form has been very successful in capturing monthly donors—so successful that this same form has been up and running since the start of 2000 through 2004. If this form works for Greenpeace for that many years, then let's adopt it for other organizations.

For a comparison, the reader should take a look at the giving form for Amnesty International Canada at *www.amnesty.ca/response.html,* which also emphasizes

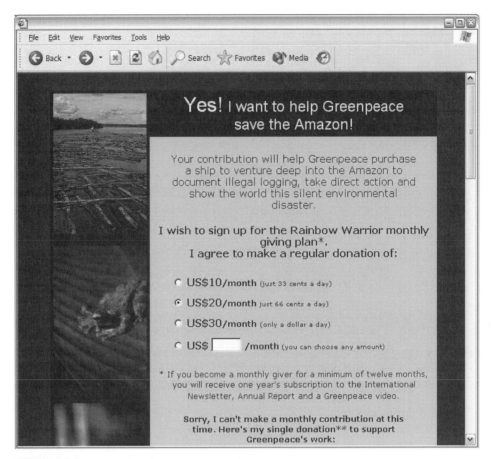

EXHIBIT 14.6 Revised Online Donation Form

Source: Greenpeace International

monthly gifts and adds a wonderful layer of persuasion and detail by outlining what different monthly gift levels deliver to those in need. For example, $30 a month can pay for a doctor's visit to a tortured victim or $50 a month can help pay for a human rights researcher to travel and investigate human rights abuses.

But does a more overt monthly emphasis make a difference? Amnesty International Canada would say it does. Amnesty made changes to its form to emphasize monthly giving and launched the new form. Exhibit 14.7 shows the point at which they launched the new form and saw an immediate increase in monthly committed fundraising results.

An organization might want to do even more to emphasize monthly giving online:

- Rebrand your online monthly giving to become a club that someone would want to join. For example, Children's Hospital Los Angeles has created a derivation of their major giving club, the Red Wagon Society, and launched an online derivation—the Red Wagon Club.
- If possible, offer a premium for joining the monthly giving club. Send them a special monthly giving T-shirt, or pin, or some other paraphernalia if they join at $10 or more a month.

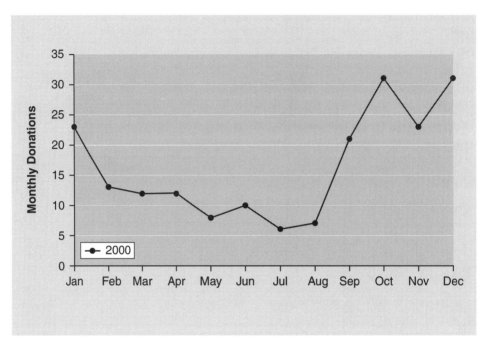

EXHIBIT 14.7   Introduction of New Monthly Giving Form in August 2000

- Investigate the possibility of matching gifts from corporations or associations who already support the organization.

IMPROVING THE FUNDRAISING SIDE OF YOUR E-NEWSLETTER

An important component of online stewardship comes from a regular electronic communication vehicle—an e-newsletter. A nonprofit's e-newsletter should be a regular (monthly) communication (test more or less frequent distribution) avenue with various online constituencies (e.g., supporters, families, volunteers).

Studies have shown that e-mail newsletters work. Seventy percent of e-consumers conduct e-commerce as a result of getting, and reviewing, permission-based e-newsletters. The e-newsletter should primarily be a communications vehicle, but each issue should have a strong fundraising element.

Best Practice Example

The Salvation Army of California (Golden State Division) has been running a successful e-newsletter for a few years. Listen to a few words of wisdom from their Golden State Internet fundraiser, Nicci Noble. She outlines the basics:[5]

- *E-mail regularly* (at least once a month and maybe a few special alerts throughout the year). In the case of a health charity, an alert might be a very important breakthrough or campaign announcement. If you're a food bank it could be a special issue (and appeal) during a food drive. Being regular means donors will remember they are subscribed—which is a good thing!

- Mail in HTML, text, and AOL formats
- *Always ask for a gift in the e-newsletter, and make the request prominent.* Exhibit 14.8 shows an example of making the gift prominent in the Salvation Army's e-newsletter. Position online and offline contact information in a prominent place.
- *Set realistic goals.* If it's a fundraising goal, make it modest and overdeliver.
- *Develop a schedule of publications and appeals.* Plan a year in advance.
- *Park the institutional ego.* Make sure the e-newsletter is about the reader and the children and families you help, not about your institution.
- *Be prepared to deal with responses.* Every nonprofit organization needs to assign someone to deal with the responses and inquiries that a regular e-newsletter will create. Remember, it's easy and quick to shoot off an e-mail compared to composing and mailing a letter. The volume will be larger than you might expect.

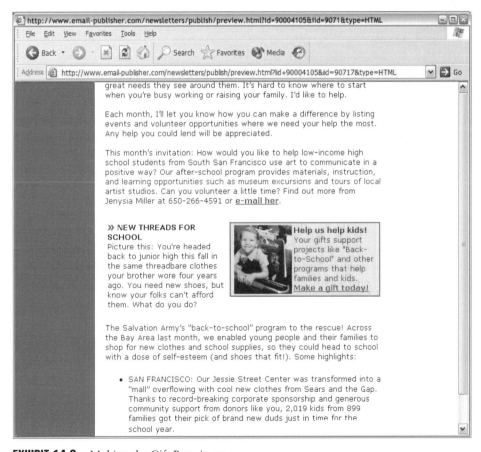

EXHIBIT 14.8   Making the Gift Prominent

When reviewing the e-newsletter in Exhibit 14.8, the reader should notice the following:

■ Every month should have a straight ask box in a prominent place, like the Salvation Army example. It would be separate from a full story link and would go directly to an improved donation form. The box should have a strong lead, a description of what the online gift would accomplish, and a prominent link to the giving form.

■ Every month should have a full fundraising story that presents a paragraph or two to hook the reader and lead to a full-page description (ideally only one or two full screens at the most) with a link to the giving form.

■ Every month should have a story that emphasizes one particular kind of giving. Following is a draft sample of how an organization could schedule over a number of months:

  ■ *Month one.* A story on why making an EFT gift is the most cost-effective way to support the nonprofit organization—with a link to the new monthly emphasis on the giving form, and the story should be from a current EFT donor (if you have one!).

  ■ *Month two.* A story on bequest giving—from someone living who's made a bequest—with the story linking to a bequest section of the Web site explaining why leaving a bequest is an important way to support the nonprofit organization.

  ■ *Month three.* A story from a volunteer supporter on how and why they support the nonprofit organization and why others should both give and volunteer—with a chance for people to join a volunteer group or to volunteer themselves.

  ■ *Month four.* A story from a corporate supporter, explaining why their company supports the nonprofit organization and how it improves staff *esprit de corps* and helps fulfill the nonprofit's mission at the same time. The story would link to information about how companies can support the nonprofit organization.

  ■ *Month five.* A story from someone who's raised money in honor or in memory of a friend, family member, or colleague. The link would go to an online area where others similarly inspired could raise money in honor or in memoriam—or make a direct gift online for the same reasons.

  ■ *Month six.* A story from someone who has made a major gift. The link would go to an area that detailed how someone could make a major gift and what it could accomplish. Notice the giving bar that the Salvation Army put into one of its e-newsletters. It clearly solicits for a major gift and explains what $125,000 could accomplish.

When crafting appropriate content for the e-newsletter, make sure you take three important steps:

1. Ask yourself, "What's in it for the reader?' when you create content.
2. Make sure you create a summary style for many stories instead of what can best be described as a complete text format. In any medium, heavy editing can often turn a longer story or article into one that's both shorter and more effective. Mark Twain said, "If I'd had more time, I would have written a shorter letter." This is

more important online than offline. Every nonprofit organization should remember that individuals subscribe to a maximum of three to four e-newsletters. You want to be one of those three or four and keep them reading.

3. Make it easy for subscribers to unsubscribe or subscribe, as well as be able to reach a human being. An anecdotal review of nonprofit organizations reveals that if your opt-out rate begins to climb above 1 percent, you should think about scaling back on the frequency. Similarly, if the open rates drop below 25 percent, you should also think about scaling back the frequency of newsletters.

ONLINE ACQUISITION STRATEGIES

In the online environment, like the offline world, a nonprofit organization can't build a Web site and expect people to find it on their own. Sure, some people will—but only the very committed, the incredibly motivated. However, the vast majority of prospective supporters need some help to find you online and to make a donation.

That's why every organization has to be proactive with online acquisition approaches. This section will briefly outline the possibilities. But why even try to find new donors online when they could very well be old donors from traditional mediums that you're cannibalizing?

Quite simply, online acquisition makes the fundraising pie bigger. A 2002 study for a well-known human rights organization found that 54.8 percent of the online donors acquired that year were not on the existing database—they were brand new donors.[6] That study showed that they are younger, more affluent, and better educated than any other fundraising source of donors. In addition, the average donation is roughly double the size of a gift through traditional media.

The reader might want to flip to George Irish's chapter (see Chapter 6). He provides more helpful information for organizations contemplating acquiring new donors online.

Acquisition Basics

At a minimum, *e-mail signatures* at the bottom of every e-mail sent by staff, volunteers, and other affiliated supporters should have a fundraising message. That message could change according to the time of year. It makes sense to link the fundraising stories created for each newsletter and put them at the bottom of e-mail signatures from time to time.

Recent studies have shown that roughly 30 percent of online donors find an organization through search engines.[7] A Forester study found that the three key ways for surfers to find a Web site, were in ascending order of importance:

1. Guess the Web site address
2. See reference in offline media
3. Use search engine (75% of visitors in this study)

For some organizations, the order can be slightly different, but search engines remain a core acquisition tool. Regardless, giving is impulsive, and many individuals will hear a compelling story of need from an organization and subsequently feel the impulse to give right away. They might guess your Web site address, but many will use a search engine.

You must *optimize your search engine ranking*. Your Internet service provider or internal technical staff can help you do this. It is essential that the optimization, if done for fundraising purposes, allow for keywords related to fundraising to be passed on to the search engines. To help someone make best use of search engines to drive new donors to a nonprofit organization's site, please visit www.searchengines.com to understand the world of search engines. Also, for tips on submitting a nonprofit site to search engines, the reader should visit *www.howtointernet.com/tips.html*.

Contests, quizzes and advocacy are a great way to build your warm e-mail list (acquired e-mails) and then convert them into donors. You should be integrating contests and quizzes into your e-newsletter.

Save the Children Canada conducted an online acquisition campaign in 2002 to build its e-mail list of interested citizens by running a mission-related contest. The organization wanted to build awareness in Canada around the issue of child slave labor used to harvest the cocoa found in much of the chocolate eaten around the world. The campaign was called "Positive Chocolate," and had both terrestrial marketing, advertising, and fundraising educating Canadians on the issue. The campaign directed consumers to chocolate that was from nonchild slave labor sources.

To support the offline campaign, Save the Children created an online contest. Anyone driven by interactive banners to a landing page (seen in Exhibit 14.9) had the

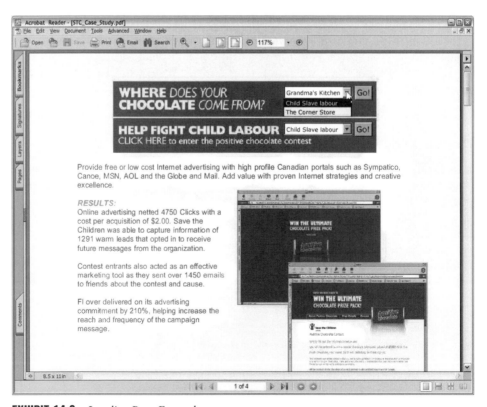

EXHIBIT 14.9 Landing Page Example

opportunity to leave their e-mail address in a contest to win $500 worth of child-labor-free chocolate.

The commercial vendor who ran the campaign delivered on its advertising commitment and found the organization 1,291 warm leads for a cost of $2.00 a lead.

Measuring the Success of the Plan

Was it an online fundraising success or failure? The answer lies in the missing link in Save the Children's online acquisition equation: the conversion of a prospect list into real donors. It never happened in this acquisition campaign. Once we know what the donor conversion rate was, then we can begin to make sense of how this quiz/contest acquisition campaign worked. Save the Children has yet to e-mail these warm names to convert them into donors. Once they've done that, they'll be able to judge their potential success or failure.

Seeing an acquisition campaign as an opportunity to build a warm list to be converted into donors is admirably outlined in a case study from Amnesty International Spain.

In the spring of 2003, two Nigerian women in the north of that country were to be executed under the Muslim *sharia* law. There was global outrage at the thought of two women who had children out of wedlock being put to death, while the men involved in the relationships were not to be punished.

In response to the human rights debacle, Amnesty Spain created a campaign Web page that asked Spanish citizens to leave their e-mails as signatures on an online petition protesting the abuse of the rights of these two young women.

The Spanish citizenry responded, and in a matter of weeks, more than 240,000 e-mails were collected. After 20,000 e-mails were rejected through purging, 220,000 e-mails were sent out from the original 240,000 that were collected via the online petition.

The results were better than Amnesty Spain had expected. A subsequent e-mail solicitation, seeking to convert petition signers, yielded 1,022 (0.46% response) committed monthly donors giving 13 euros a month (approximately US$14 a month) for a yearly total of approximately $159,000. There were also 688 (0.31% response) single gift donors who gave an average of 50 euros (approximately US$55) each for a total of $37,840. With a total of approximately $10,000 for all expenses, the return on investment (ROI) was very impressive for an acquisition campaign.

An important test was conducted during this acquisition/conversion campaign. Half of the warm list was sent a text-only appeal while the other half received an HTML version that added a picture of one of the Nigerian women holding her child. The Amnesty International logo was also added as a stylized graphic. The HTML version received a 50 percent higher response rate and was clearly the winning solicitation.

Two months after the first acquisition solicitation, Amnesty Spain ran the petition campaign again. It gathered another 200,000 e-mails and subsequently e-mailed another conversion e-mail to the 180,000 e-mails that survived a purging.

This time out, an HTML only version was sent out (since it had outperformed the text only version by 50 percent). The results were even better than the first appeal:

■ 1,478 committed monthly donors giving 14 euros a month for a yearly total of approximately $250,000.

■ 977 single gift donors giving 44 euros for a total of approximately $45,000.

Not every organization can expect these kinds of acquisition results, but it does show that when there is a high-profile event connected to an organization's core mission, online acquisition techniques like contests, quizzes, and petitions can gather significantly larger warm lists—which then can be subsequently converted to online donors. Every organization should take inspiration from this example and try to duplicate its ROI success—perhaps hoping for the same kind of 20:1 return.

Amnesty Spain's challenge is to now show discipline in creating a plan not only to execute more acquisition campaigns in the future, but also to renew the monthly and single gift donors it has found in these acquisition successes.

CASE STUDY: AMNESTY SPAIN'S eANNUAL FUND PLAN

The recent acquisition of a large group of online donors made Amnesty Spain focus on how to take care of this Internet-based constituency, ensuring that their contributions are renewed and maintained on an annual cycle, as well as encouraging them to increase their donation levels over time, either at the point of renewal or with a special appeal.

The eAnnual Fund Plan aims to help Amnesty Spain establish an ongoing and increasingly rewarding relationship with every online donor. This is accomplished by establishing a year-long plan that addresses the main types and timing of communications from Amnesty Spain with the eDonors, offering them content that further engages their interest, and occasionally encouraging their participation in some form of special online or offline action.

For many donors, the act of making a donation is a part of their ongoing relationship with an organization. It may be just one way in which they express their support, since they may also be involved in other activities with the organization. These donors have a broad understanding of the organization they support. For other donors, the act of donating is a solitary action on their part, made in response to a particular campaign or appeal that struck a chord with them. These donors have only a narrow understanding of the organization's full mandate, and are not necessarily aware of or interested in other aspects of the organization's activities. The eAnnual Fund strategy recognizes these two categories of donors, and sets out a plan for increasing the engagement of both kinds.

The eAnnual Fund strategy also considers the concept of sustained engagement for an organization's supporters. Recognizing that it is not possible to sustain a high level of engagement over a long period of time with most supporters, the eAnnual Fund strategy focuses on a limited number of high-engagement opportunities, where the primary renewal, upgrade, and/or special gift appeals would be forwarded, along with other communications such as petitions, viral marketing campaigns, and other promotions.

Amnesty Spain's eAnnual Fund strategy had six goals:

1. Ensure that monthly/regular donors continue to support Amnesty Spain, and do not cancel their ongoing gift.
2. Encourage monthly/regular donors to upgrade their donation amount, or increase the frequency if not already a monthly donor.

3. Encourage monthly/regular donors to make a special one-time gift in support of a high-profile campaign.
4. Ensure that single donors will renew their gift within 12 months of their last gift.
5. Encourage single donors to make a larger renewal gift.
6. Encourage single donors to make a special one-time gift in support of a high-profile campaign.

Let's look at one more case study—the case of the Daily Bread Food Bank of Toronto.

CASE STUDY: THE DAILY BREAD FOOD BANK

The Daily Bread Food Bank of Toronto is a food bank that primarily provides food services to more than 170 social service agencies in Toronto. In April of 2001, the food bank created its first Web site for $1,000. The Web site integrated a free donation service through *www.canadahelps.org* that allowed the organization to process online credit card gifts.

During the 14 days of the Easter food drive in 2001, the organization told the city about its new Web site only through Executive Director Sue Cox mentioning the new Web site to news reporters who were covering the food drive. The only way for a citizen to know that they could give online was through a series of newspaper articles like this one, and the initial results were encouraging:

- In 14 days in April, 2001, $8,000 in online donations with investment of $1,000 to build the Web site with an overall ROI of 8:1
- 73 donations were made, with an average gift of approximately $120.

In the fall of 2001, during the Thanksgiving food drive, the Daily Bread Food Bank decided to add incremental improvements to its online fundraising. It created a single advertising banner and asked a number of high-volume local sites, like *www.toronto.com*, to run a simple banner.

The organization continued to have the executive director make reference to online giving in media coverage during the Thanksgiving campaign, but it benefited from broader online coverage through the banner advertising. The 14-day online Thanksgiving campaign raised $31,000.

Now things were getting interesting and profitable for the food bank's online fundraising. In 2002, the food bank continued to integrate online giving into their high profile food drives. Online donations continued to grow.

In 2002, the organization experienced another interesting development. Media and food companies who supported the food bank presented the nonprofit with an original online giving idea—a new Web site that would heighten awareness about online giving in support of the food bank. The new site, *www.givegroceries.com*, was soon created. The site allowed corporate supporters to make a more cobranded Web site that was singularly focused on fundraising.

The new site, in marketing terms, is called a *flanker brand*. A flanker brand is a product created to support the central brand, in this case *www.dailybread.ca*, by bringing more attention to the issues of hunger in the city of Toronto and the good work of the food bank.

The companies who created this site—at their own cost—ensured that Daily Bread did not have to put money into this online endeavour. In addition, the food companies promised to match every dollar raised through the site with a matching gift.

Since April 2001, *www.dailybread.ca* has raised more than $250,000, while *www.givegroceries.com* has raised more than $200,000. The food bank has received online donations from more than 2,000 citizens.

If we go back to our initial definition of annual fund giving, the food bank has done a wonderful job of fulfilling the acquisition side of the equation. But how have they done with the renewal side of the online annual fund campaigning?

The reader is invited to guess at the renewal rate for the 2,000 online donors who've given from April 2001 to the start of 2004:

0%
10%
40%
60%
90%

The answer is ZERO! Did you guess correctly? The answer might be a bit surprising, but there is a simple answer for it: the food bank hasn't addressed the full definition of an annual fundraising campaign, which is to not only acquire new donors, but also to renew donors. Unfortunately, it has not asked for a second gift from any of the past donors.

Now, there are a few good reasons for this. The first is the fact that *www.canada helps.org* is a free donation service that doesn't provide the e-mail addresses to the charity so that it might build a relationship. The second reason is that the medium is still very young, and it just isn't thinking of the potential yet. The Daily Bread Food Bank does have a direct-mail program that follows a traditional annual repeating structure: (1) a renewal mailing during Easter, (2) a renewal mailing during the summer time, (3) a renewal mailing during the Thanksgiving food drive, and, finally, (4) a year-end holiday mailing.

The good news is that The Daily Food Bank is about to address this issue in its online annual fund giving. It is planning to send out renewal e-mail solicitations at the same time as the direct-mail program. After it has added this component to its online program, it will have an online fundraising endeavour that may raise hundreds of thousands of dollars a year at a cost of only a few thousand dollars. The final addition of an online renewal schedule will make the food bank's online giving even more efficient.

CONCLUSION

In annual fund campaigns, the little things count.

When an organization is asking for money repetitively, incremental improvements can yield important results. This chapter has outlined how small improvements and best practice on the home page, in the giving form, in e-mail solicitations, and with e-newsletters can make more money online.

It's also about making a plan and sticking to it. Planning and executing a schedule of appeals is the key to online annual fund giving. The beginning of this chapter outlined three basic tenets to annual fund theory: to acquire donors; to renew donors; and to make a plan that maximizes the first two points.

The experience of Amnesty Spain highlights the opportunities of conducting effective and cost-effective acquisition of online donors. But the lifetime value of those newly acquired donors will be lost unless they plan and execute a yearly schedule to maintain and foster the relationships.

The experience of The Daily Bread Food Bank is another example of how the Internet can help acquire donors at a cost that is much lower than through traditional mediums like direct mail. However, the organization has slipped up on the renewal side of online fundraising. If it can find a commitment to create and execute an online renewal schedule, the organization will retain many of its online donors and make the online giving program more profitable.

Finally, any practitioner of ePhilanthropy has not only to master the planning and tactical implementation of an annual fund to acquire and retain donors, but it must also understand that online annual fund campaigning has to complement a more holistic approach to online giving that this chapter hinted at in its beginning.

ABOUT THE AUTHOR

Michael Johnston, president of HJC, is an expert in fundraising and the use of the Internet by nonprofit agencies. Mike has worked with more than 100 nonprofit organizations, ranging from third-world development organizations, to hospitals, to peace and disarmament groups, in Canada, the United States, and the United Kingdom. He gained considerable experience as a senior consultant and director with Stephen Thomas Associates, one of the first fundraising firms in Canada, to work exclusively with NGOs. He has been a past member of the Ethics Committee of the Canadian Society of Fund-Raising Executives (CSFRE) and was a volunteer fundraising leader with the United Way in its Management Assistance Program. Mike is also a past board member and current member of the Association of Fundraising Professionals (AFP) and sits on the AFP's Volunteer Online Council in Alexandria, Virginia. He has recently joined the board of directors of the U.S.-based ePhilanthropy Foundation. Mike sits on the executive committee and is the chairman of the product development and education committee.

Mike is a skilled communicator and his skills are known throughout the nonprofit community. He is the author of *The Fund Raiser's Guide to the Internet* and *The Nonprofit Guide to the Internet,* and the editor of *Direct Response Fund Raising,* all published by John Wiley & Sons. He has worked with a range of educational institutions, lecturing on the Internet and the nonprofit sector and has spoken at five AFP International Conferences, teaching both full day seminars and short workshops. From his seminars to television appearances to his published articles, Mike has been able to analyze the implications of the Internet for thousands of people in the nonprofit sector. Michael Johnston is committed to the nonprofit sector and dedicated to helping organizations reach their charitable goals. You can e-mail Mike at mjohnston@hjcnewmedia.com.

ENDNOTES

1. A survey of ten North American children's hospitals conducted in March 2004.
2. A Hewitt and Johnston online survey polled 32 North American multilevel health-related charities for Cancer Research UK.
3. Vinay Bhagat, "The Internet—A Powerful Relationship Management Tool for Fundraisers," in James M. Greenfield, ed., 2002 Supplement to *The Nonprofit Handbook: Fund Raising*, 3rd ed., The AFP/Wiley Fund Development Series (New York: John Wiley & Sons, Inc., 2002), p. 19.
4. Special thanks for Nicci Noble, Salvation Army, Golden State Division for these points.
5. Nicci's eight-point primer comes from her wonderful presentation at the 41st International AFP Conference, titled, "How Do You Replace the Kettle with the Wireless Credit Card Machine?"
6. Amnesty International Canada surveyed its 406 monthly donors and 614 single gift donors who came on board in 2002.
7. A study of 2002 of visitors to *www.greenpeace.org* showed that search engines were a key way for new donors to find, and give, to an organization online.

CHAPTER **15**

Special Events and Sponsorships

Philip King, ePMT
Artez Interactive

Dianne Sheridan
Artez Interactive

Online special events and campaigns are exciting new options for many organizations.

POWER OF THE FEW

Janet Davis was turning 30, and on this important birthday she was going to do something different. Janet had long been interested in environmental issues, so when she saw the subway ad that World Wildlife Fund Canada was hosting an event to raise money, she was intrigued. The concept: Climb the CN Tower in Toronto, Canada (the world's tallest free-standing structure) and ask friends and family for donations (see Exhibit 15.1).

Janet went to WWF Canada's Web site to learn more, where she found a link to an online event and campaign management system. There she was able to sign up online, choose her language of preference (English or French), and promise to raise $75 in pledges in lieu of paying a $25 registration fee (see Exhibit 15.2).

But more important to Janet than the efficient transaction processing was the ability for her to personalize (see Exhibit 15.3). She uploaded an image of her with her pet dog, Snow, and created content for her personal "climb page," where she urged her friends to donate in multiples of 30 to recognize her birthday: $30 or $300 or $3,000.

She then e-mailed her friends and family telling them of her plan to climb the tower (see Exhibit 15.4). Since each e-mail was from Janet (not WWF Canada), the chance of her message breaking through too-full inboxes was much better. When interested recipients clicked the link in Janet's e-mail, they were automatically taken to her personal donation page, where they viewed the photo with Snow and Janet's fundraising goal.

When they made a donation on Janet's behalf using a secure credit-card facility provided by the system, the funds were immediately deposited into WWF Canada's bank account. And to top it off, each donor received a thank-you e-mail from the

EXHIBIT 15.1 World Wildlife Canada Fundraiser

foundation's president with attached e-receipt (an Adobe Acrobat document) within seconds! (See Exhibit 15.5.)

Janet's results: she raised $3,200 from 37 friends and family members!

According to Janet: "It was amazing to me how easy it was to raise money for a great cause. When I've done this type of event in the past, I tended to just pay the registration fee since I hate asking people for money. In a strange way, the ability to hide behind my e-mail was all I needed!"

Janet and many others like her made the WWF Canada event a success. When compared to the prior year's registration statistics, it was clear that their participant base quickly embraced the online registration (close to 70 percent of participants registered online). But the system also attracted more registrants earlier in the event schedule—an important target when registrants are encouraged to fundraise (see Exhibit 15.6).

CANADA LIFE CN TOWER CLIMB FOR WWF

Create a new user

Please create your account with us by providing your contact information and specifying a username and password.

*denotes required information

Personal Information

Title:

First Name: Janet *

Last Name: Davis *

⦿ Home ○ Business

Address: 35 Wells Hill Ave *

City: Toronto *

Province: Ontario *

Postal Code: M5V1V1 *

Country: CANADA

Phone Number: (416) 815 8777

Email Address: pking@artez.com *

Account Information

Username: janetdavis *

Password: ********* *

Retype Password: ********* *

EXHIBIT 15.2   WWF Canada Registration Form

In fact, WWF Canada was so confident that the online tool improved results and lowered costs that in the following year the organization actively drove registrants to use this channel with a page titled, "Ten Reasons Why You Should Sign up Online" (see Exhibit 15.7).

To round out the WWF Canada example, we must look at its strategic use of HTML e-mail to encourage, thank, and motivate participants for the next year.

The day after the event a personalized e-mail from the organization's president thanked participants "on behalf of wildlife and wild places" for their collective efforts (see Exhibit 15.8).

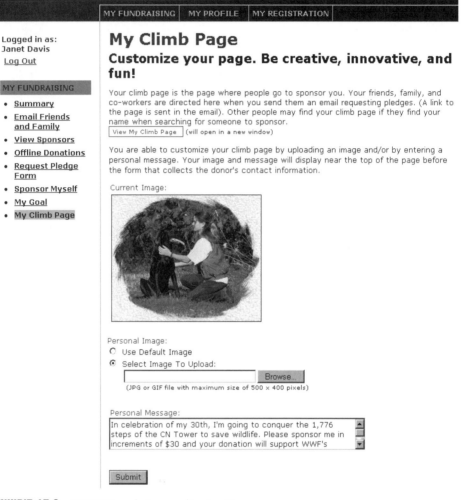

| MY FUNDRAISING | MY PROFILE | MY REGISTRATION |

Logged in as:
Janet Davis
Log Out

MY FUNDRAISING

- Summary
- Email Friends and Family
- View Sponsors
- Offline Donations
- Request Pledge Form
- Sponsor Myself
- My Goal
- My Climb Page

My Climb Page
Customize your page. Be creative, innovative, and fun!

Your climb page is the page where people go to sponsor you. Your friends, family, and co-workers are directed here when you send them an email requesting pledges. (A link to the page is sent in the email). Other people may find your climb page if they find your name when searching for someone to sponsor.

[View My Climb Page] (will open in a new window)

You are able to customize your climb page by uploading an image and/or by entering a personal message. Your image and message will display near the top of the page before the form that collects the donor's contact information.

Current Image:

Personal Image:
○ Use Default Image
◉ Select Image To Upload:
[   ] [Browse...]
(JPG or GIF file with maximum size of 500 x 400 pixels)

Personal Message:
In celebration of my 30th, I'm going to conquer the 1,776 steps of the CN Tower to save wildlife. Please sponsor me in increments of $30 and your donation will support WWF's

[Submit]

EXHIBIT 15.3   WWF Canada Personalization Form

As the following e-mail analysis shows, participants opened the e-mail at a very high rate: 78 percent.

Thank You E-mail Analysis

	Total	% of Total Received
Recipients	1212	N/A
Recipients who opened e-mail	942	78%
Recipients who clicked any link	39	3%
Click-throughs	51	4%
Recipients who replied to e-mail	4	0%
Recipients who unsubscribed	1	0%

A month later, the president sent another personalized e-mail, this time giving participants a sense of the impact that their fundraising was having on wildlife (see Exhibit 15.9).

| MY FUNDRAISING | MY PROFILE | MY REGISTRATION |

Acquire Sponsors

Enter one or more email addresses below to send a message to your friends and family requesting pledges of support. The recipients are directed to your personal climb page by which they can securely donate online. Donors will receive their tax receipt by email.

See who I have invited to sponsor me online >

To: (one email address per line)

pking@artez.com

Subject:

Climbing the CN Tower for my 30th!

Optional Personal Introduction:

The following information will automatically be appended to your message:

You have been invited to pledge for Janet Davis in the Canada Life CN Tower Climb for WWF.

On Saturday, April 24, I am heading to the CN Tower and taking on its 1,776 steps for World Wildlife Fund Canada. Please sponsor me as I reach my personal and fundraising goals.

WWF and I would really appreciate your donation.

Secure online donations can be made with VISA, MasterCard and American Express. An electronic tax receipt will be sent to you by email. You can make an online donation now.

link goes here

Thank you for your generous support.

EXHIBIT 15.4 Sponsor Acquisition Form

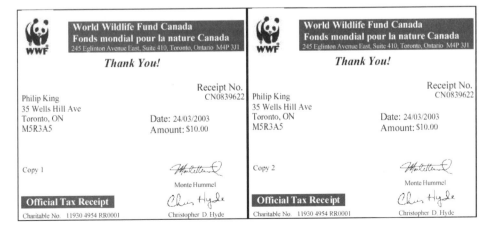

EXHIBIT 15.5 Donor E-Receipt

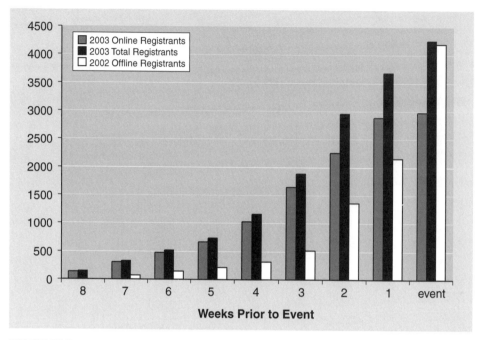

EXHIBIT 15.6   Registrants by Week

Although the open rates were less for this e-mail (67 percent), it still demonstrated that the vast majority of participants would open e-mail from this organization: a privilege WWF Canada is careful not to overuse.

Impact E-mail Analysis

	Total	% of Total Received
Recipients	1192	N/A
Recipients who opened e-mail	803	67%
Recipients who clicked any link	129	11%
Click-throughs	211	18%
Recipients who replied to e-mail	1	0%
Recipients who unsubscribed	5	0%

DEFINING THE DIGITAL DONOR ELITE

The story of Janet and her thirtieth birthday is exceptional, but it isn't unique. All around the world, the Internet is amplifying the impact that passionate people can have on a fundraising campaign.

When we looked at our data we found many examples of the *digital donor elite:*

- One volunteer raised $9,010 from 139 donations.
- Another volunteer raised $15,059 from 98 donations.
- Still another raised $25,974 from 944 e-mails.

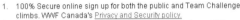

CANADA LIFE CN TOWER CLIMB FOR WWF

Ten Reasons Why You Should Sign up Online

Online sign up and personalized fundraising for the Canada Life CN Tower Climb for WWF.

1. 100% Secure online sign up for both the public and Team Challenge climbs. WWF Canada's Privacy and Security policy.
2. Create your own personalized fundraising page to help you raise pledges.
3. Send emails to friends and family linking them to your page.
4. You do not need to collect any cash. Secure pledges can be made on our site.
5. Set a fundraising goal and track your progress.
6. You can also enter pledges you collect offline to track your overall progress.
7. After you sign up online you can still call or email us any time for assistance.
8. Your supporters instantly receive their tax receipt when they pledge you online.
9. Saves you lots of time.

10. Sign up **online** before Mar. 15 and receive free this 16 month Wildlife of the World calendar, courtesy of Toronto Star! While quantities last.

TORONTO STAR

Here's what a few WWF supporters had to say about our online system.

"The online sponsoring this year was fantastic. Usually I dislike asking people to sponsor me, so I simply make a single contribution from myself. This year it was convenient and I found it easier to draw in some sponsors."
B. Roach

"The on-line pledging really helped me raise more money than last year. I certainly did not have difficulty raising $805.00 and plan on trying to top $1000 next year."
J. Kirner

"I just want to comment on how extremely easy to use and slick your registration process and website are. Nicely done!"
N. Folliott

PUBLIC CLIMB
Sign Up

TEAM CHALLENGE
Sign Up

EXHIBIT 15.7 Online Measurement Tool

Clearly these are exceptional individuals who have passion for their causes. The online tools allowed them to share their passion in numbers and geographies that otherwise would have been unthinkable with paper pledge forms.

When we studied online campaigns we found that the aggregate data told a striking story: on average, the top 10 percent of online fundraisers accounted for more than 50 percent of all online dollars collected. When we shared these statistics with experienced offline fundraisers, the reaction we received was "Of course—we've known for a long time that it only takes a small percentage of people to account for most of our fundraising."

But this message hasn't played a central role in online fundraising discussions. Too often, we find organizations with no plan, or insufficient plans, to follow up and communicate with this digital donor elite in a way that could be distinguished from plans for their general online donors.

Think of how your organization would steward someone who wrote a check for $25,000. How about someone who e-mailed friends, family, and colleagues to collectively raise $25,000 online?

EXHIBIT 15.8   Personalized Thank You

PEOPLE GIVE TO PEOPLE

High Tech and High Touch

For years we've heard how the Internet will radically change the operations of non-profit organizations in the future. But bear in mind that *high tech* without *high touch* won't go very far.

EXHIBIT 15.9 Follow-Up E-Mail

Recall the last time you made a contribution to a charity. Did you wake up one morning with the desire to give and then seek out a worthy organization to accept your generosity? Or were you prompted to give? If you're like most of us, the reason you didn't give to a cause is because you were never asked to give. If you were asked to give but didn't give, then the wrong person is asking you.

The Internet gives us the ability to take this simple concept—getting the right person to ask you to give—to tremendous scale. Imagine a charity that you care for deeply. Now imagine that charity asking you to ask two friends for a gift. You'd likely call them, or mention it to them the next time you met. But what if the charity needed you to ask 50 friends? At that point, you'd have to turn to e-mail.

Getting Your E-Mails Read: The Power of "From"

We've been fretting over e-mail newsletters for some time now. At first we were dazzled by the ability to personalize the e-mail "Dear Philip." If we knew something about Philip (such as my past year's gift), we could go even further: "Dear Philip, thank you so much for your gift last year of $100. . . ."

We would also play with the subject line, trying to measure which phrase would increase the open rate of the e-mail. Some of us would apply good direct-mail logic and create test cells to understand if the subject line "You can help today," or "Today, you can help," would be better.

I'm sorry to break this news, but in e-mail much of this doesn't matter! The real magic is in the "From" field.

Your inbox likely resembles the image in Exhibit 15.10. We all have *too much* e-mail. As you read this chapter, you might experience a slight sense of stress that you've spent too much time away from your e-mail inbox, and that as the minutes tick by, it's becoming more and more congested.

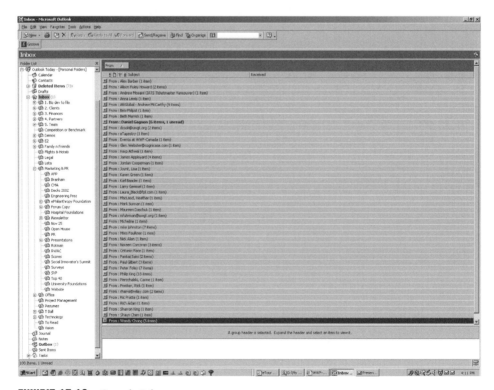

EXHIBIT 15.10   Sample Inbox

How do we sort through too much information in our inboxes? We look to see who sent it. If it's from our boss, our friend, an important client or donor, we'll open it first. If it's from someone we don't know, we might delete it without opening it for fear of a virus. In fact, I've found that there is a certain satisfaction in rapidly deleting any message that doesn't appear at first glance to be important, thus pruning my overflowing inbox.

This trend of deleting messages that aren't "From" the right person will only increase in the future. If you've upgraded your Microsoft Outlook lately, you'll notice that much effort has been put into the Junk E-mail and Trusted E-mail filters. With the click of a mouse, I can label someone—or some organization—as junk. As a nonprofit organization, you *never* want to be labeled as *junk*. And in the future, we might only be able to reach some people who have labeled us as "trusted."

People with the Right "From" Field Can Raise the Money You Need

Given this situation online, organizations should rely on their connected supporters. Let's say I am a supporter of Charity A, and Charity A wishes to find new donors and dollars.

There are several big benefits for Charity A to ask me to leverage my online network. First, I know many people that Charity A does not. I also have abundant information about my personal network that Charity A does not (e.g., who would consider giving to Charity A, who just received a raise, etc.). Finally, I have the power of "from" that Charity A does not—my e-mail will be opened by my peers.

If Charity A provides me with an easy way to help find donors (and possibly fun incentives for doing so), I'll help (see Exhibit 15.11). This is not rocket science. We're simply finding new ways to more efficiently execute old ideas.

MANY THINGS CAN BE AN ONLINE SPECIAL EVENT

When we refer to special events, nonprofits typically envision some type of *-thon* activity: a walk-a-thon, a bowl-a-thon, and so on. They tend to imagine large-scale activities that involve street-closures, T-shirts, and waiver forms. While these types of special events will continue to do well and will continue to generate a tremendous number of online donations for charities, the Internet has allowed many groups to reframe the online special events discussion.

Brainstorming activity: Sit down on the floor, take off your shoes, and take a deep breath. Exhale slowly. Now, think of programs or activities that you currently manage, and write them down on a set of Post-Its. Use a different color of Post-Its and write *online* on each of them. Simply match up one of your activities with *online* and consider the result.

BAKE SALE + ONLINE = ?

DOOR-TO-DOOR CANVASSING + ONLINE = ?

ETC.

The following are just a few examples of how forward-thinking charities have begun to redefine online special events.

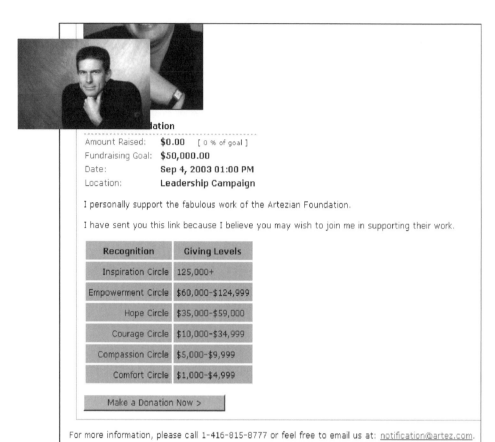

EXHIBIT 15.11   Leveraging on Online Network

Golf Tournaments

A nonprofit named *Kids Help Phone (http:// kidshelp.sympatico.ca)* is dedicated to providing online and telephone counseling to teens in distress. It has become a leader in online campaigning. Its flagship special event is the Bell Walk for Kids, a national event in two languages that has been online for three years.

In the spring of 2003, the nonprofit was interested to know if it could take some of its lessons learned in the Bell Walk for Kids and apply them to smaller-scale activities. Its focus was an annual golf tournament that attracted many of the city's financial services community.

The plan: Utilize its Internet-based event management technology and ask golfers to register and solicit pledges online. Although many doubted that an activity such as playing golf could generate pledge dollars (the common wisdom being that someone had to at least sweat a little to ask for a donation), Kids Help Phone proved them wrong. Golfers were asked to create a personal page explaining why they felt Kids Help Phone was a worthy cause, and e-mail personalized solicitations to their coworkers, suppliers, and clients (see Exhibit 15.12).

Pledge Michael Beckerman

Help raise money for Kids Help Phone.

BMO is hosting a ten hour golf a thon to raise money for Kids Help Phone. All the funds raised will go directly to Kids Help Phone, as many generous corporate sponsors are underwriting the operational costs of putting on the event. Kids Help Phone is Canada's only 24 hour, toll-free, bilingual and anonymous phone counselling service for children, and receives approximately 1,000 calls every day from kids across the country.

Michael Beckerman

Amount Raised:	**$8,005.00** [80 % of goal]
Fundraising Goal:	**$10,000.00**
Event Date:	**Jul 3, 2003 07:30 AM**
Location:	**Angus Glen Golf Club**

I will do my best to stay on the course, but anticipate spending much of the ten hours in woods and pastures. I am asking you or your company to sponsor me a lump sum pledge for completing the ten hours. A tax receipt will be sent to you. Thank you in advance for any support you can offer for this important cause.

EXHIBIT 15.12   Online Golf

The results: an incredible $95,000 was generated through online pledges. "We were extremely happy with the results and plan to expand this next year," notes Development Director Mary Proulx. "It taught us once again that what matters most is who is doing the asking, not whether that person is walking 5K or playing golf."

Virtual Events

Across the continent in San Francisco, another organization is stretching the definition of online special events. Nicci Noble, Internet Development Director and National Project Consultant for Salvation Army USA, describes the Salvation Army's approach: "We felt we had to aggressively use the Internet to broaden our base of support, and special events seemed like a natural place to start." Nicci led a team that developed a Web site called "Angel Giving Tree." The idea was simple: Focus online fundraising efforts around a very special event—Christmas. Individuals could go to the Web site, select from the wish list of a child in need, and then shop for that child online, thanks to a partnership with a large online retailer. The results: $144,000 was raised from 1,582 donors with little or no marketing.

Moving forward? Nicci observes: "Now that we've proven the technology works and individuals *do* want to contribute in this way, our focus turns to marketing and building awareness online to leverage the strong brand equity of The Salvation Army that exists offline. We understand that we must surround our technology with an integrated marketing and communications strategy in order to continue our success."

Engaging the Thirty-Somethings

Street Kids' International wanted to grow a specific segment of its donor base: young professionals between the ages of 25 and 35. It had tried golf tournaments and wine-tasting events, and these had been mildly successful, but it didn't feel that it was speaking the same language as prospective thirty-somethings.

"We found that many young professionals didn't want us to determine the type of event to attend . . . they wanted more control. They were willing to raise funds for us from their social network, but it had to be on their terms," notes board member Robert Barnard.

Club de Cent was the response. The goal of *Club de Cent* ("Club of 100" in French) is to recruit 100 young professionals who each agree to raise $1,000—any way they see fit (see Exhibit 15.13). They may hold a dinner in their home, organize a pool tournament, invite their friends to watch the Oscars—they are in control to determine what's appropriate based on their peer network.

"I started my fundraising with what I called a 'Lame E-mail Campaign,'" says Robert. "I have an extensive contact list of associates who have plenty of money, but very little time. I explained in my e-mail that I wasn't asking them to buy tickets, or attend a gala . . . and that I wasn't going to run 5K. All I was going to do was e-mail them; all they had to do was pull out their credit card and give and we'd all save time and support a terrific cause. I raised over $500 in the first day."

These creative organizations are but a few examples of groups thinking outside the box when they consider the possibilities of online special events.

Are there existing events or campaigns you run to which you could apply online solicitation?

Register

If you have any questions about Club De Cent, or require assistance, please contact us by phone (416) 504-8994 xt. 26 or by email: mpusey@streetkids.org

This is the registration page to join Club De Cent. Club De Cent is an exclusive club of 100 individuals, each raising $1,000 for Street Kids International in their own unique ways, over a one year period. Street Kids International is a Canadian-based not-for-profit that is a global leader in enhancing the impact and capacity of local organizations that provide direct services to street involved youth. We strive to give street involved youth around the world the choices, skills, and opportunities to make better lives for themselves.

Register for Club De Cent

Register

Already Registered?

Username:

Password:

Login

Forgot your password? Click here.

Make a Donation

Make an online donation directly or by sponsoring a participant.

EXHIBIT 15.13   Entry Page to Club de Cent

Are there groups of your supporters who would happily solicit their influential network if given a good excuse? Are there opportunities for you to create a "non-event event" that would save everyone time but allow them to express support for your terrific cause?

WHAT ABOUT SMALLER ORGANIZATIONS?

Many of the online fundraising success stories have come from large organizations with household names, robust technology budgets, and multisite special events. But what about smaller organizations?

The National Colon Cancer Campaign does not have any full-time staff. Amy Lerman-Elmaleh created it, in memory of her mother who succumbed to the disease in 1998. To help fund research to find a cure to this type of cancer, Amy established the foundation and manages it as a part-time volunteer in addition to her full-time job.

"I wanted to create a special event that could jump-start our fundraising, but didn't have the staff or time to do it in a traditional, offline manner. The data input and receipting would have taken more hours than I had," Amy said. She turned to the Web (see Exhibit 15.14).

Amy explains, "In some ways I feel small groups are better suited to gaining the advantages from online event management than big groups. For one, we didn't have a large offline process that we had to re-engineer to fit the Web; we were pretty much starting from scratch. We didn't have any staff, so we had to look for ways that would allow participants and donors to perform their own data input. And given our abilities

EXHIBIT 15.14   From Amy's Personal Donation Page: Photo of Amy and Her Mother

to receipt online, we saw this as a natural fit." Her results: More than $40,000 was raised online in the first year.

BUT WE DON'T HAVE ANY E-MAILS

A classic reason for many charities to defer the leap into the online fundraising world: "We don't have many e-mail addresses." That might be true, but it's not a good excuse for delay. Online special events and campaigns will be a tremendous source of new e-mail addresses, and need only begin with a few excited supporters.

Your organization may not have many e-mail addresses, but it's likely that each of your board members, in their own Outlook contacts file, have many e-mail addresses. It's *those* e-mails that you need to leverage in an appropriate manner. Or how about a "Friends and Family" campaign that begins with the e-mail addresses that your staff have in their own personal contact files?

IF YOU CAN'T AFFORD IT, GET SOMEONE ELSE TO PAY: THE ROLE OF SPONSORSHIP

The costs of online fundraising technology often deter organizations. But two important trends are helping charities get online: (1) the costs of online fundraising solutions are dropping, and (2) many sponsors are eager to defray the start-up costs in exchange for some tasteful recognition. Online special events and campaigns are natural ways to engage an existing or new corporate sponsor or supportive philanthropist.

Online special events and campaigns appeal to sponsors for a variety of reasons, but four reasons stand out in particular:

1. It's a great naming or branding opportunity to put a logo in the header or footer of each Web page since the online special event or campaign site will be "touched" by hundreds or thousands of people.
2. It appeals to many sponsors' desire to help the charity become more efficient in fundraising.
3. It has a unique ability to provide back to the sponsor deep statistics and reports regarding the adoption of the technology (how many visits, when, how long, etc.), which sponsors love!
4. It still has a sizzle factor.

For many corporate sponsors their interest goes beyond doing the right thing for their community and presenting a positive public image for their customers: It is their employee base that is their focus. Corporations are searching for ways to motivate and retain talented staff, and have long realized that philanthropy is an important activity for this.

Online special events and campaign tools provide greater ability for a corporation to engage and measure the activity of an employee base. (See Exhibit 15.15.) Today's online applications can allow teams of employees from HR to challenge those in finance. Some corporations have a separate point of entry to the online application for "employees only." And the reporting produced from the applications can allow senior management to see which employees took on leadership roles within the charitable activity.

BEYOND THE BASICS

So you've selected an online provider whose tools, pricing, and culture fits your organization. You've incorporated online registration and solicitation in your first special event or campaign. Now what?

If you're like most of our clients, your statistics will look something like this for a first year-effort:

- Percentage of your registrant population who registered online: 15–30
- Percentage of online registrants who solicited gifts from others (in other words, went beyond paying the registration fee online and asked their friends and family for a pledge): 25
- The ratio of average gift online to average gift offline: Double
- Average gift online: $60

We also know that, on average, your total online dollars will double from year 1 to year 2. So how do you improve your results? How do you perform better than "average"?

EXHIBIT 15.15 Example of Online Fundraising Appeal to Employees: Support Kids Help Phone

According to Brian Pendleton, president of CauseForce Inc., whose company organizes "Weekend to End Breast Cancer" (see Exhibit 15.16) events, strategic and timely communication makes a big difference:

> *The event starts the day the person registers. . . . In our events each participant is required to raise $2,000 to participate, so from the very start we wanted to promote the quick and convenient benefits of online fundraising. . . . We knew that our participants would be watching their fundraising results very closely and would want real time fundraising totals so we promoted online as the preferred method of fundraising.*

Attention All Walkers!

The Weekend To End Breast Cancer is approaching quickly and we need the help of your friends, family, neighbors, and co-workers. Let them know that they can join the fight against breast cancer by becoming a Weekend to End Breast Cancer Crew member.

Crew members are essential to the success of the event. The Crew is composed of dedicated and remarkable people who move gear, set up camp, serve nutritious meals, and do much, much more, encouraging the walkers at every step of the way.

The Crew commits to helping out for the whole weekend, testing their physical abilities and mental endurance. Each member of the Crew will experience cooperation, happiness, and compassion for humankind like they have never experienced before.

If you know anyone who might be interested in becoming a Crew member, tell them to register online at www.endcancer.ca or call 416.815.WALK.

Please contact Todd Merrill, Crew Coordinator at todd@endcancer.ca with any questions or concerns.

Thank you for your brave and noble commitment to ending breast cancer.

Sincerely,
The Staff of The Weekend To End Breast Cancer

ONE WEEKEND | 60 KM | SEPT. 19-21, 2003 | TORONTO, ONTARIO

B E N E F I T I N G

Princess Margaret Hospital
University Health Network

www.endcancer.ca
(416) 815 WALK

> Visit Our
Website

EXHIBIT 15.16 Example Weekend to End Breast Cancer E-Mail

*We took them through step-by-step training for the online tool during partic-
ipant orientations sessions, using event information guides and e-mail communication. And we maintained frequent, creative, and direct e-mail contact with
participants once they registered."*

Brian's tips and tricks are:

- Get sophisticated online fundraising technology.
- Make sure your communication differentiates you from the pack.
- Speak to your participants specifically and directly.

For an event Brian coordinated for Princess Margaret Hospital Foundation in
2003, he feels the results speak for themselves:

- More than 60 percent of participants registered online.
- More than 50 percent of all donations were processed online.
- 70 percent of registrants conducted fundraising.
- Average online gift was $78.00.

There are many ways to improve your online special event or campaign results.
If you haven't already, you can join other organizations that are experimenting with
the following:

- Reduced registration fee payments for online participants
- Special coupons from sponsors for online registrants only
- "Fast-track" lines at event day sign-in for online registrants (similar to e-ticket lines
  at airports)
- Gold-club membership for top online fundraisers
- Incentive prizes available only to online fundraisers
- E-mail newsletter featuring top online fundraisers throughout the campaign

NEW DONORS, NEW DOLLARS

Online special events and campaigns are exciting new options for many organizations,
and can provide a powerful channel for participants and donors to interact with their
charity of choice. Depending on the prices paid for online technology, there is a compelling cost-saving argument to be made for saving printing, mailing, data input, and
other hard costs.

But very quickly, champions of these tools will be challenged by fundraisers and
board members to prove that they are, *in fact,* bringing in new donors and new dollars
to the organization. Review of data from the Canadian Breast Cancer Foundation
shows how this works (see Exhibit 15.17).

The Canadian Breast Cancer Foundation manages the largest single-day fundraising event in Canada (The CIBC Run for the Cure *www.cibcrunforthecure.com*) and
has been allowing participants to register and solicit sponsors online since 1999. And
as Exhibit 15.17 demonstrates, each year it has become more and more successful with
its online fundraising.

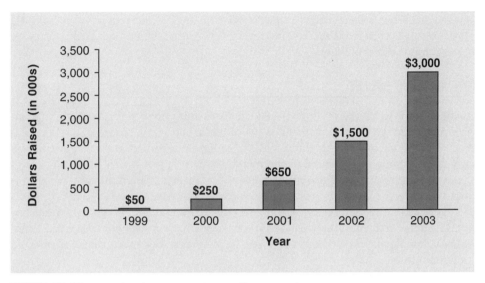

EXHIBIT 15.17 Run for the Cure: Online Dollars Raised

In 2003 alone, CBCF managed 41,131 registrations and 46,626 donations through its online system, which links automatically to their Blackbaud Raiser's Edge backend system. This represented an increase in online registrations of 44 percent from 2002, and an increase of 115 percent in online donations.

For the past two years the board has asked staff to calculate what percentage of dollars was new to the organization due to the online tool, and what percentage of dollars may have come to CBCF offline had they not used online tools (albeit through a less-efficient channel).

The first part of the calculation involved isolating donations that came from out of country. Since CBCF had given its supporters easy-to-use online tools to solicit its friends and family, and since supporters have friends and family residing outside of Canada, CBCF noted that in 2003 donations arrived from 47 countries outside of Canada—up from 35 countries in 2002. These out-of-country donations totaled 5.5 percent of all donation dollars.

CBCF then looked at the relationship of the postal (or ZIP) code between an average solicitor and their donor. They determined that in their offline population 13 percent of all donations came from *distant relationships* (which was defined as a difference in the first letter of the postal code between a solicitor and their donor).

When compared to the distant relationships in the online population, which represented 31 percent of the total dollars, they determined that the incremental difference was 18 percent (or 31 percent, less 13 percent).

When this 18 percent of distant dollars was added to the 5.5 percent of out-of-country dollars, staff argued that 23.5 percent of all online donations were new to CBCF, and the donations would not have occurred had not the online tools been used.

Board accepted this calculation, and noted that likely it was a conservative estimate given that the average donation online ($44.27) was more than double the average offline donation ($21.33).

Furthermore, 54 percent of online registrants and 37 percent of online donors *opted in* to a permission-based e-mail relationship with CBCF, interested in learning more about the organization.

NOT A SILVER BULLET

In conclusion, we'd like to emphasize to readers that online special event and campaign technologies are a powerful new set of tools that organizations can leverage to find new donors, new dollars, and make existing fundraising more efficient and exciting. The examples presented in this chapter are but a few stories of organizations that are creatively applying these tools to their fundraising mission. But these solutions are not a silver bullet. These tools will not run themselves.

A theme that spans all of our examples is that of *integration*. Teams from fundraising, IT, marketing, and donor services must work collaboratively to create successful online campaigns. Just because the tools are new does not mean that old rules no longer apply.

The best advice we can give is launch and learn. Select a series of campaigns or events to which you apply one (or more) online solutions. There is nothing like direct experience to learn if your team, your selected solution provider, and your campaign mix is the proper fit for your organization. Set realistic goals for your campaigns and measure against those goals to determine their effectiveness.

But don't be afraid to start; there are many organizations that have already begun to cultivate your donors online. And if you've already started, don't be afraid to innovate for better results.

ABOUT THE AUTHORS

Philip King, ePMT, expresses his passion to empower nonprofit organizations through his role as president and CEO of Artez Interactive (*www.artez.com*).

Artez has managed over $ 100 million in online donations over the past three years. Prior to Artez Philip was the vice president of e-Business at the United Way of Greater Toronto, where he developed an online workplace fundraising application for United Ways across North America. When not working, Philip has advised multiple levels of government on issues surrounding nonprofits' use of technology, and has taught a technology strategy course at the Joseph L. Rotman School of Management at the University of Toronto, where Philip earned his MBA. He serves on the board of directors for the ePhilanthropy Foundation in Washington, D.C. You can e-mail Philip at: pking@artez.com

Born in Tennessee, he says he endures the Canadian winters to enjoy the civil society of Toronto, where he lives with his wife, Leta, and two sons, Adam (7 years old) and Sam (3 years old).

Seeking new and more effective ways to bring community passion and fundraising strategies together online is **Dianne Sheridan's** role with Artez Interactive.

Dianne joined Artez in January 2003, after more than 12 years of national and local experience in the nonprofit sector. Prior to Artez Dianne worked at Kids Help Phone, Juvenile Diabetes Research Foundation, and United Ways in Peel and Peterborough. Dianne also has experience working with several non-profits in a volunteer and board member capacity. You can e-mail Dianne at dsheridan@artez.com.

CHAPTER 16

Seeking Big Gifts Online: Planned Giving and Major Gifts

Michael Johnston, ePMT
HJC New Media

INTRODUCTION

Many nonprofit professionals don't believe that the *Internet, planned giving,* and *major gifts* deserve to be spoken in the same sentence. The prevailing attitude in fundraising is that larger gifts need personal, intimate contact to be consummated.

Who would ever make a charitable annuity online? Or indicate they wanted to leave a bequest? Aren't these kinds of gifts best secured over banana bread and tea?

Without a doubt, larger charitable gifts can be secured through a more personal, face-to-face approach, but not every donor is the same. The online request doesn't necessarily have to secure the gift—it might just inspire a prospective planned gift or major donor to seek the banana bread and tea experience. Or there could be major gift and planned gift donors who do not want to spend time with earnest (and perhaps tedious?) gift officers in any circumstance and will enjoy the online major gift/planned gift experience from beginning to end.

EPhilanthropy in support of major and planned gifts is already happening. This chapter will review the opportunities—and real results—available to organizations that embrace a definition of ePhilanthropy that encompasses larger and planned gifts.

WHY BUILD A PLANNED GIVING SECTION ON A WEB SITE?

First and foremost, older individuals (those 55 and older) constitute the fastest-growing demographic group online.[1] They are the late adopters. Young and middle-aged people were the early and middle adopters of the technology, respectively. The last group to go online are older individuals, and it makes sense that they would take advantage of maturing technology to become the fastest-growing group of users.

The same study showed that one-fifth of North Americans are between 45 and 64 years old. This user group accesses the Web more often, stays online longer, and visits more Web sites than younger Internet users.

In addition, the study revealed that the oldest surfers (those 65 and older) have these characteristics:

- Surfed an average of 14.7 days per month
- Visited more than 75 unique sites per month
- Viewed more than 500 Web pages
- Clicked on an average of 1.8 banners per month

These numbers indicate more use of the Internet than those aged 35 to 64. Therefore, it appears that older online (65 and older) users are spending a great deal of time online. These users are an organization's best-planned giving prospects (especially for bequests).

For all of these reasons, older individuals are increasingly online, and that means some of them will be looking for planned giving material on the Web sites of their favorite charities.

But even if older people make up a larger share of the online user demographic, will they visit planned giving Web sites? The anecdotal evidence is encouraging.

In a 2002 interview with Liz Gibbs, the marketing manager for Save the Children New Zealand, she outlined

> *We've had a Web site for the last eight years, and over the last year or two we've had more and more visitors to the planned giving section of our Web site—to the point where it's the second most visited part next to the child sponsorship pages. We don't market those pages, but they continue to get increasing numbers of visitors (see Exhibit 16.1). I can only guess that with a donor base over seventy years old that we're getting more and more late adopters online and coming right to our planned giving pages.*[2]

Christian Children's Fund USA has had a similar experience to Save the Children New Zealand—the planned giving area of their Web site has been an often-visited page.[3]

The demographic *and* anecdotal evidence about visitors to planned giving sites shows the potential of online planned giving content for an organization. If a nonprofit goes without a planned giving site, then they're likely missing out on the 72-year-old donor who's decided to support a few charities in their will, and are surfing nonprofit Web sites to learn about leaving a bequest.

ELECTRONIC MEDIA AND THEIR EFFECT ON ALLIED PROFESSIONALS IN PLANNED GIVING AND MAJOR GIFTS—ESPECIALLY WITH BEQUESTS

Estate lawyers are reporting that more of their older clients are using e-mail to correspond with them when planning changes to their wills. The planned giving director of a hospital foundation recently said that the foundation has had to implement a policy to create PDF (portable document format) documents, which are unalterable, for clients' wills because of the many changes being made in files being e-mailed back and forth. Final versions were becoming difficult to agree upon.

Nonprofits should offer advice to estate lawyers and Web visitors, reminding them to track changes in all word documents (by providing simple explanations about how to create PDFs).

This is also true of allied professionals of the financial advisor nature. Online tools that allow financial advisors to quickly calculate the value of more sophisticated major gifts (outlined in more detail later) will bring these advisors closer to the nonprofit organization and hopefully help influence and direct major gifts from the prospective major gift donor, through the online-connected financial advisor, and to the nonprofit organization.

EXHIBIT 16.1   Save the Children New Zealand's Bequest Page—Second Most Visited Page

STILL DOUBTFUL ABOUT GETTING MAJOR GIFTS OR BEQUESTS ONLINE?

Oregon Public Broadcasting has had significant results with a site it created a year ago with the help of online planned giving practitioner, Dick Kellogg. Oregon Public Broadcasting set up the site at *www.endowopb.org*, with a URL separate from the main site, *www.opb.org*. This made it possible to make televised references to send people directly to the giving site. Dick commented,

> *When the site first went live, I believe they ran two months of on-air spots. That was about a year ago. They then stopped the spots but the traffic has remained fairly constant. Basically, the stats show they have eleven people a day, seven days a week, reading their "brochure" on planned giving and Oregon Public Broad-*

casting. It received a call in the first several weeks from a young dot-com-type ex-ecutive who was in possession of appreciated stock and therefore faced a tax problem. He had heard the ads, went to the Web site, read the material we have on the site concerning giving appreciated assets. That led to a $175,000 gift. The neat thing is that it came not only from someone the organization had no previous contact with, but also from someone "way outside the target market."

Oregon Public Broadcasting has proven the effectiveness of acquiring major gifts online. If the reader can imagine that they have even more constituents who might be like the young, caring, wealthy somewhere in their database, they should be building major gift opportunities online. Since that major gift online, Oregon Public Broadcasting has had notification from four people of an intention to include OPB in their wills. All four were also previously unknown to the nonprofit.

WHAT SHOULD GO INTO AN ONLINE PLANNED GIVING AREA?

Perhaps the best guidance comes from Jerold Panas and his book, *Mega Gifts: Who Gives Them, Who Gets Them.* [4] In that seminal work, Jerold outlined the main reasons individuals make large gifts to charity:

- Belief in mission
- Community responsibility, civic pride
- Fiscal stability of organization
- Regard for staff leadership
- Respect for the institution locally
- Regard for volunteer leadership
- Service on the board of directors, a major committee, or other body with the organization
- Respect for the institution in a wider circle—region, nation, and so on
- A history of being involved with institution

With that list in mind, a nonprofit can craft its planned giving area online to offer the following:

- A focus on mission
- A message from respected leadership addressing the issue of planned giving
- Stories of like-minded supporters making a planned gift (This could take the form of a video.)

The Juvenile Diabetes Foundation of Canada created a video message from Board of Directors President Cam Jackson about why he had made a bequest (and why others should, too). It's an inspiring piece of digitized storytelling that every organization can emulate. The video is effective online for the following reasons:

- It shows a close-up of Cam's face, so you can see the whites of his eyes. The on-line video window is often very small, and you want the person's face taking up most of the screen. Any object too much in the background will be lost.

- The video's script allows him to tell the very personal reason he or she made a bequest. In this case, Cam's daughter was diagnosed at an early age with juvenile diabetes.
- The script allows Cam to explain why planned gifts are important while also emphasizing why immediate cash gifts are important, too. These online video clips must allow the video storyteller to explain the long-term, strategic value of leaving a planned gift.

A nonprofit online video like this needs to provide the following information to visitors:

- Contact information of the planned giving officer
- A way to display the value of each kind of planned gift, and what it means to them and to the organization

The archdiocese of Baltimore (*www.archbalt.org*) provides an excellent chart that provides the information succinctly (see Exhibit 16.2).

By providing a chart like the one in Exhibit 16.2, an organization is giving every prospective donor some help to understand the wide range of major gift and planned gifts that the donor could make. Such a list can act as an empirical reminder that a donor can give both immediate gifts of cash as well as planned gifts of assets for the future. There's a basic tenet that *a knowledgeable donor is a more generous donor.* In the case of planned gifts and major gifts, explanation of these kinds of gifts can only help the donors understand they can give more than they thought possible.

In Exhibit 16.2 there are two forms of Charitable Remainder Trusts that are missing: the Pooled Income Fund and the Life Estate Agreement. It's a reminder that every organization should only list the planned gifts and major gifts that they will accept. An organization should offer the following information:

- Information to help financial advisors get the support and information they need to help their clients
- A description of programs that the planned gift would help deliver
- A response form that is easy to use, which also makes it easy for the organization to know if someone has left a planned gift

Please take a look at the planned giving response form for Darlington School (see Exhibit 16.3), a private college preparatory school at *http://www.darlington.rome.ga. us/development/giftresponse.asp*. The form gives the prospective donor a wide range of disclosure options—from agreeing to be publicly recognized for the bequest, to remain anonymous, or to request more information. It's a simple form that aims to make the donor comfortable in filling it in and e-mailing it back.

Molly Avery, vice president for development at Darlington School, tells us that the form "has been well received by alumni. And wonderfully, we've received a few expectancies online which was unexpected but a fantastic return on the investment in our online planned giving area."

EXHIBIT 16.2   A Clear Outline of Planned Giving Choices and Benefits to the Donor

Type of Gift	Benefit to Church	Benefit to You
Bequest	Bequest could be a help in perpetuity and invested to fund church needs.	Possible estate tax deduction; opportunity to make a perpetual gift
Charitable Gift Annuity	Assets not used to pay annuity to the donor or others benefit the church.	Guaranteed fixed income for life; portion of income is taxfree; deferred income possible if desired; possible income and estate tax deductions
Insurance Policy	Church receives full face value of policy upon death of the donor, or may receive current surrender value prior to donor's death.	Income tax deduction for value of the policy when transferred; premium payments may be deducted as gifts; possible income and estate tax deductions
Charitable Remainder Trust	Upon the death of donor or last surviving income beneficiary, remaining assets benefit the church.	Variable or fixed income; deferred income possible if desired; possible income and estate tax deductions
Charitable Lead Gift	Income for duration of trust; helps church meet spiritual and human needs that exceed the capabilities of most parishes or schools.	At the end of trust period, principal returns to donor or other beneficiaries; principal can pass to others with little or no shrinkage from taxes; possible income and estate tax deductions
Retirement/IRA	Significant gift upon death of donor	Estate and income tax savings may cover a substantial portion of the gift.

Live Chat

A number of nonprofit organizations have been investigating the use of a live text chat function in their online planned giving area. The Juvenile Diabetes Research Foundation has introduced a chat button in its planned giving area (see Exhibit 16.4).

When a visitor clicks on the box, a small window pops up that allows someone to type in a question for Christina Decaprio, planned giving officer for the Juvenile Diabetes Research Foundation (see Exhibit 16.5).

Christina hears a ring from her computer when someone wants to talk. Other nonprofits might like to investigate the cost, and then test a live chat button in your online giving area. Go to *www.livehelper.com* and see what it can offer your organization.

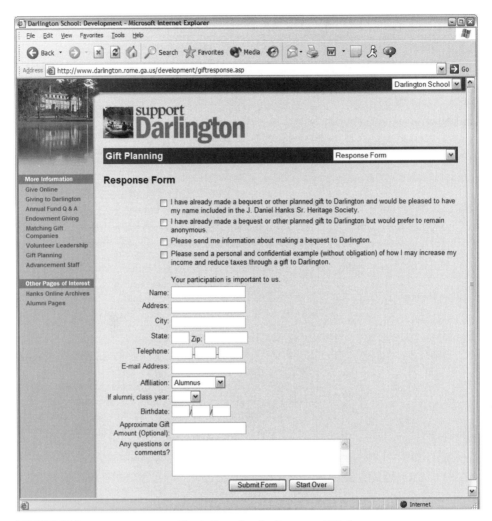

EXHIBIT 16.3   A Bequest Form That's Easy for the Donor to Fill Out

Interactivity

The planned giving area should allow for an easy connection to a planned giving officer. It should also present a story about the archetypal bequest donor through text, photo, and video storytelling. And finally, the Web site should also implement tools that allow a visitor to calculate the value of a gift of life insurance and other planned gift vehicles. A nonprofit could benefit from a visit to the following Web sites:

- *GiftCalcs, www.pgcalc.com.* This organization provides online programs that can be slotted into a planned giving Web site. The software allows for prospective donors to calculate the value of a wide range of financial planned gifts, including gift annuities.

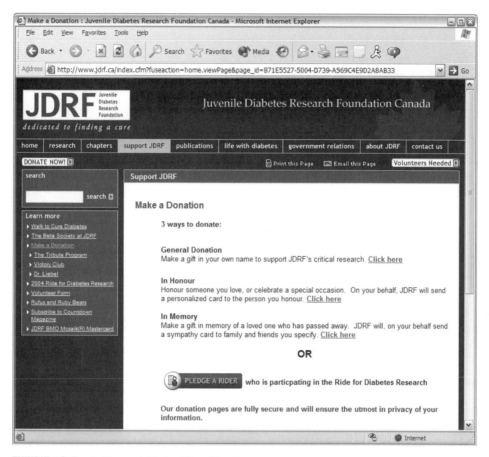

EXHIBIT 16.4   A Planned Giving Live Chat Button

- *Philanthrotec, www.ptec.com.* This organization provides online software, much like the other company just listed, that allows organizations to place easy-to-use calculators on their planned giving Web site—allowing someone to play with the possibilities of making more esoteric, but very valuable planned gifts that includes:
  - Charitable gift annuity
  - Charitable remainder annuity trust
  - Charitable remainder unitrust
  - Pooled income fund
  - Charitable lead annuity trust
  - Charitable lead unitrust
  - Life estate agreement
  - Bequest by will or living trust

But how do these calculators work? Let's pretend that a Web site visitor is a 66-year-old recent retiree. In the past month, the visitor's 69-year-old brother died and

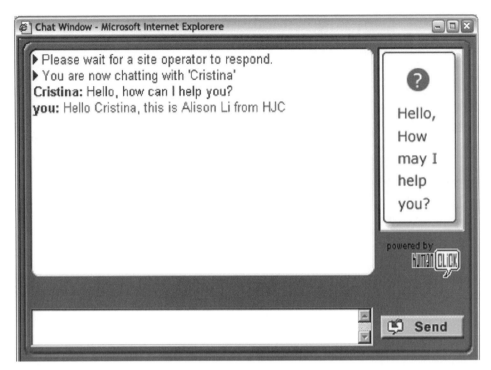

EXHIBIT 16.5   Live Chat Box Pops Up for the Donor

left him a six-figure amount of cash in their will. The visitor, recently retired, is living on a fixed income that is relatively small. What if this person donated the cash gift to a favorite charity, Save the Puppies and Kitties (SPK), and asked for a charitable annuity from SPK to improve that retiree's yearly cash flow?

Imagine the retiree went to the SPK planned giving Web site and saw a gift calculator that would allow exploration of the possibilities of giving the cash gift to the charity in exchange for a guaranteed yearly income until he or she died.

The retiree would enter age and size of the cash gift, and the magic of an online planned gift calculator would provide returns depicted in Exhibit 16.6.

The visitor would get a significant tax deduction of $95,713.44, and an income of $18,300.00 a year until death. Each of the person's next 19.1 years' payments of $18,300.00 will contain $10,695.63 of tax-free income and $7,604.37 of ordinary income. All income will be ordinary after 19.1 years.

Suddenly, online planned gift calculators give everyone—not just financial planners—the ability to explore the possibilities of leaving planned gifts. And as older donors demand more autonomy, and conduct more of their own financial research, these calculators will be used by more and more prospective planned gift donors. Every nonprofit should investigate whether they can offer these kinds of additional services on their online planned giving Web site, but only once they've covered the basics listed earlier in this chapter.

The situation is no different for major gifts. The calculators can provide assistance to both the donor and financial advisors to go to a nonprofit's major gift calculator to

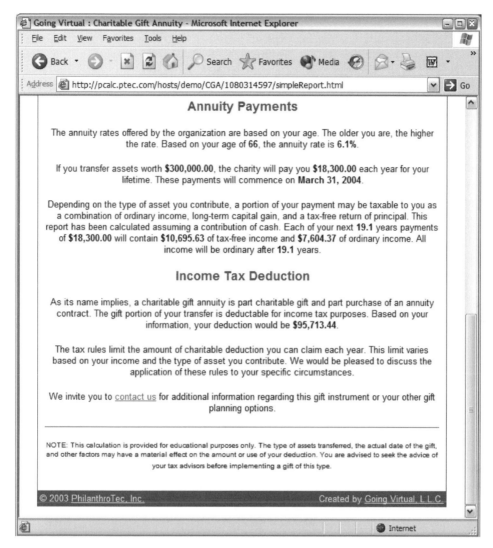

EXHIBIT 16.6   The Magic of a Planned Gift Calculator Online

see how immediate gifts can help reduce taxes over a five-year carryover, for example. Planned gifts need calculators to show the benefit to the donor and the nonprofit organization—in the distant future. That distance demands calculations that can prove the value of these kinds of gifts.

For major gifts, handing over financial assets immediately can have immediate tax implications—that's part of the attraction of giving a major gift. And even though the gift calculations might not extend far into the future, a calculator that can help outline the tax benefits of that major gift in the short term can be extremely helpful and persuasive to the prospective major gift donor. Therefore, it should be a part of any major gift giving area online.

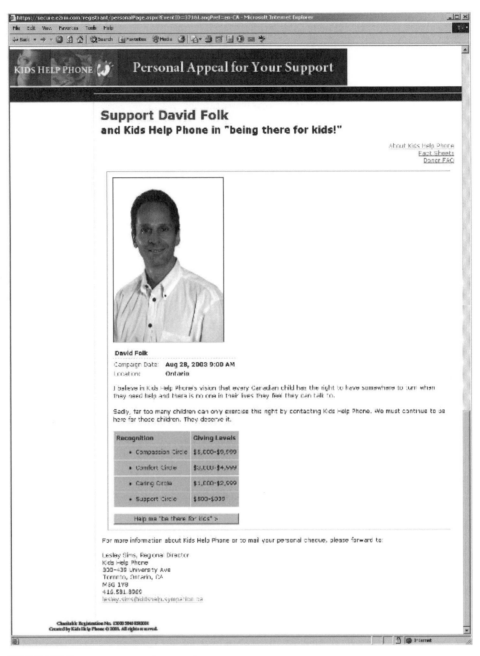

EXHIBIT 16.7 A 50,000 Online Goal

MAJOR GIFTS ONLINE: HELPING BOARD MEMBERS MEET THEIR PERSONAL GOALS

Many nonprofit organizations have board members who have not reached their minimum fundraising responsibilities—whether through giving or asking. The online peer-to-peer fundraising tool may help these board members meet their responsibilities. The board members could get instruction from a teleconference, teaching them how to create their own personal page. They could then efficiently solicit colleagues, family, and friends—and even set their goal on a personal Web page.

Kids Help Phone is a charitable organization in Canada that provides telephone support and help to children anytime, day or night. The past board chairman, David Folk, decided that he'd like to use an online peer-to-peer tool to solicit his colleagues online. He set a $50,000 goal. As a venture capitalist who often works in the technology field, David knows that many of his peers use the online environment as a primary pathway for communication.

David asked Kids Help Phone to help him set up his online fundraising area. Exhibit 16.7 shows his home page, which allows prospective supporters to learn more about Kids Help Phone and to make a quick, easy credit card donation.

IT'S MORE THAN JUST MONEY—HOW ePHILANTHROPY SHOULD SUPPORT YOUR CAPITAL CAMPAIGN

Many nonprofits get involved in capital campaigns. The Web site for most organizations could better support their capital campaigns.

West Park Healthcare Centre altered its home page (*www.westpark.org*) to highlight the look and feel of its Raising the Bar capital campaign. The organization made a strategic decision to have the capital campaign dominate the first page that visitors see. The most prominent link is to information about the campaign.

That link leads visitors to information at *http://www.westpark.org/Raising TheBar/main.html* that includes the following:

- A list of donors who've made a difference to the capital campaign
- A running total at the top of the dollars raised
- Information on how the campaign is spending the donor dollars
- Volunteer information

How could West Park improve its online capital campaign/major gift area? It could begin with recognition. With the low-cost publishing ability of the Web, any organization can put up great detail on the recognition opportunities with larger gifts. For example, West Park could outline gift prices for the naming of buildings, floors, rooms, scholarships, and so on. This could be connected to images and virtual tours of the plans so the prospective major gift/capital campaign donors could see, and imagine, what their names would look like on the front of a new building. And if an organization wanted to go as far as possible, they could allow someone to enter his or her name on the front of an image of the new building and see an online version of the final building—with his or her name on it. Or someone could take a virtual tour through a lobby—or emergency care area—that would be named with his or her major gift. The online environment allows the prospective donors to step into the finished product and use their imagination with images and interactivity.

GETTING PLANNED GIFTS ONLINE: A QUICK CASE STUDY

Millikin University was founded in 1901 by James Millikin, a prominent Decatur businessman, and affiliated with the Presbyterian Church (U.S.A.). It is located in Decatur, Illinois. Millikin University is a coed, independent university with a four-year program, offering studies in Arts & Sciences, Business, Fine Arts, and Nursing.

Millikin University has an active alumni office that tracks graduates and stays in touch with alumni and friends. Recently, the university added comprehensive information about planned giving to its Web site through the use of a content provider in California, Future Focus (*www.futurefocus.net*). Anne-Marie Berk, director of Major Gifts at Millikin, wanted donor-oriented content to begin building the relationship fundamental with potential planned giving donors.

Anne-Marie was pleasantly surprised when she received a phone call from an alumnus inquiring about a charitable gift annuity. Subsequent conversations revealed that this alumnus had found the Investment Giving section of the MU Web site and the information regarding planned giving and gift annuities. After reading the information and a donor story about a charitable gift annuity, the alumnus realized that he would benefit from writing a gift annuity with the university.

The alumnus had been a contributor to the annual fund at about the $250 level, but he had not been approached by the Alumni Office to make a planned gift. It was the *available to all* Investment Giving section on the MU Website that prompted a $25,000 gift.

CONCLUSION

The demographic studies, the anecdotal evidence, and available case studies, indicate that donors are using the Web and e-mail to research making larger gifts—whether they are major gifts or planned gifts. Older and younger donors are finding the Web a place to educate themselves about more significant ways to support the organizations they believe in. Therefore, nonprofits need to plan and execute thoughtful, interactive areas online that can inspire online donors to make planned and major gifts.

The future of planned and major gifts will still include tea and banana bread, but it's also going to embrace Web sites with online gift calculators, video stories, capital campaign support, major gift campaigns, and other uses of technology we haven't imagined yet. It's an exciting future, and one the author urges the nonprofit reader to explore.

ABOUT THE AUTHOR

Michael Johnston, president of HJC, is an expert in fundraising and the use of the Internet by nonprofit agencies. Mike has worked with more than 100 nonprofit organizations ranging from third-world development organizations, to hospitals, to peace and disarmament groups, in Canada, the United States, and the United Kingdom. He gained considerable experience as a senior consultant and director with Stephen Thomas Associates, one of the first fundraising firms in Canada to work exclusively with NGOs. He has been a past member of the ethics committee of the Canadian Society of Fund-Raising Executives (CSFRE) and was a volunteer fundraising leader with the United Way in its Management Assistance Program. Mike is also a past board member and current member of the Association of Fundraising Professionals (AFP) and sits on the AFP's Volunteer Online Council in Alexandria, Virginia. He has recently joined the board of directors of the U.S.-based ePhilanthropy Foundation. Mike sits on the executive committee and is the chairman of the product development and education committee.

Mike is a skilled communicator and his skills are known throughout the nonprofit community. He is the author of *The Fund Raiser's Guide to the Internet* and *The Nonprofit Guide to the Internet* and the editor of *Direct Response Fund Raising,* all published by John Wiley & Sons. He has worked with a range of educational institutions, lecturing on the Internet and the nonprofit sector, and has spoken at five AFP International Conferences, teaching both full day seminars and short workshops. From his seminars to television appearances to his published articles, Mike has been able to analyze the implications of the Internet for thousands of people in the nonprofit sector. Michael Johnston is committed to the nonprofit sector and dedicated to helping organizations reach their charitable goals. You can e-mail Mike at mjohnston@hjcnewmedia.com.

ENDNOTES

1. MediaMetrix Study, 2002.
2. Interview with Liz Gibbs, May 05, 2002, at the FINZ Conference, Auckland, New Zealand.
3. It is in fact the second most requested page in its fundraising area—as heard in an interview with officials at Christian Children's Fund.
4. Jerold Panas, *Mega Gifts: Who Gives Them, Who Gets Them* (Chicago: Pluribus Press, 1984).

CHAPTER 17

Institutional Support: Foundation and Corporate Giving

Bob Carter
Ketchum

Kristina Carlson, CFRE, ePMT
FundraisingINFO.com

The secret is to discover a method to quickly access relevant information to create successful solicitation strategies.

Fundraising has been a field defined by slow evolution, low-level technological advances, labor-intensive practices, and relatively expensive time and resource requirements. At the very end of the last century, the Internet arrived, bringing dramatic changes. Suddenly, almost any organization could increase the use of technology, streamline the use of labor, and reduce expenses in ways that were once available only to larger, older institutions with significant budgets and expertise. Foundation and corporate fundraising was once thought of as tiresome, mysterious, and even downright scary to the small institution or novice in the fundraising profession. Only a decade ago, researching a foundation or corporation often required getting in a car, driving to a local library, and reading through books and microfilm—or subscribing to a number of different expensive publications that often contained outdated information. As recent as the early 1990s, gaining access to public companies' most recent annual reports required having a good relationship with a stockbroker or waiting months to receive copies via the mail.

Access to this information was not enough. Researchers often took days, weeks, and months locating, analyzing, and recording data to be used in the effective solicitation of prospects.

Now more and more companies are putting their annual reports on their Web sites, philanthropic foundations have started providing funding applications online, and Web sites such as *www.sec.gov* and *www.guidestar.org* offer free financial information on companies and foundations. Professional fundraisers have wisely realized that the Internet has the potential to dramatically affect their corporate and foundation fundraising efforts.

The Internet now provides charities around the world with these advantages:

- Access to data
- Retrieval on demand
- Speed of retrieval
- Breadth of data
- Depth of data

Still, information alone does not raise money. Much more data are available, but it is still important to place an emphasis on the utilization of available information.

Information should help guide successful strategy between funding sources and charities. This chapter discusses how to both effectively gather information about funding sources as well as how to use information to engage volunteers and create successful solicitation strategies.

THE INTERNET'S RELATIONSHIP TO INSTITUTIONAL SUPPORT

To fully appreciate and understand how to use the Internet's great assets, one must understand a bit about the culture of institutional support.

Finding Corporate Prospects

In 2003, U.S. corporations contributed $12.19 billion to charitable institutions. With literally billions of dollars at stake, every nonprofit organization should take seriously the development of a comprehensive strategy.

Today, nonprofits can log on to the Internet, click on a few screens, and develop a small list of "suspects" from the corporate sector who might be interested in making a gift to the organization.

Finding a prospective funder online does not guarantee success. The corporate sector wants relationships, partnerships, and strategic alliances—not more solicitations. Many businesses and larger corporations are seeking opportunities to align themselves with the nonprofit community for one obvious reason: Such alliances are good for business and viewed as the right thing to do. Studies of customer attitudes reinforce the notion that the more alignments a business has with *do-good* organizations, the more the public will trust and embrace the business.

How does the Internet impact such activities?

The use of corporate data available on the Internet enables an organization to discover—as well as to rule out—corporations likely to listen to its case. No longer does a small institutional fundraising program need to resort to the costly and ineffective *shotgun* approach to fundraising. Corporate information available in the public arena through Internet sources is changing corporate gift programs, sponsorship efforts, and, in some cases, leadership enlistment in ways that will continue to affect the discipline for years to come.

Plan for Stewardship before Solicitation

The Internet plays an even greater added-value role concerning stewardship. A corporation generous enough to make an investment in an institution deserves a stewardship program equal to the aggressiveness and effectiveness the organization displayed while soliciting and realizing the gift. Fortunately, the capacity to provide comprehensive stewardship reports to donors is unparalleled in fundraising history. For example, an organization can efficiently provide corporate funders with monthly summaries of campaign progress, program successes, and other reinforcing documentation.

Ongoing personalized and customized communication allows the corporate donor to be engaged in a dialogue that can lead to the next funding opportunity.

While the Internet's access and communication tools allow for effective, quick, and easy exchanges of ideas and an opportunity for an institution to set itself apart from the competition, stewardship is a strategy yet untilled by many funded charities.

Finding Foundation Information

Although the 1990s represents the strongest period of foundation support in history, more and more foundations are narrowing the focus of their funding and looking for ways to create greater impact with their dollars, therefore increasing challenges to charities. The Internet creates an illusion that readily available information about a foundation's guidelines and application procedures are all that you need to secure a grant. It is important to note that the fastest growing sector of foundations is family foundations and charitable gift funds. In many ways these types of foundations require a strategy more aligned to personal, individual giving than large grant guidelines and applications. More information about foundations is available online today than ever before.

RESEARCHING CORPORATIONS

It represents just 5 percent of all charitable giving, but corporate giving is easier to research on the Internet than any other funding source. Why? The Internet is replete with sites for researching corporations. Most public companies now consider it essential to include vital financial and stock information on a public Web site. Since companies desire to receive the most bang for the buck concerning publicity for contributions, many funders post press releases and other details of corporate giving.

The secret is to discover a method to quickly access relevant information to create successful corporate solicitation strategies. And, as with individual and foundation fundraising, successful corporate fundraising boils down to finding a personal connection between an organization and a decision maker at a company.

Create a Corporate Profile

A good initial step toward establishing this connection is to prepare a complete company profile. Such a profile can help volunteer leaders more readily see a connection between their organization and the company, build their confidence, and help with scheduling face-to-face meetings with decision makers. Exhibit 17.1 is a profile outline

EXHIBIT 17.1   Profile Outline

Name of Company
Confidential

Name of Company

Street Address
City, State ZIP code

P: xxx-xxx-xxxx
F: xxx-xxx-xxxx
http://www.

[Typically, the company address, phone number and fax number can be found on its corporate Web site. If you have difficulty locating this information, use a phone number search engine such as *www.anywho.com* or *www.theultimates.com*. If you are having trouble locating information about a company on the Internet, *http://www.corporateinformation.com* allows you to do a free search to find all the Web sites that cover a particular public company.]

OVERVIEW AND RELATIONSHIP TO YOUR ORGANIZATION

[Get a good description of the company, its products and services, and the communities where it has locations by visiting the company's Web site. Be sure to put the connection to your organization up front for the volunteers to see. Include the company's support to your organization by listing things such as past giving, gifts made by the company's employees, any sponsorships, and any volunteers that are employed by the company.]

Total employees: [When soliciting a company, it can be helpful to have information on the size of its employee base. This information is often listed on the company's Web site in the section usually titled "Investors" or "Investor Relations." It may also be found in the company's annual report.]

FINANCES

Total annual revenue ending 12/31/03:
Total annual net income ending 12/31/03:

[You will want to know the most current financial status of the company. Remember, most companies are making gifts out of budgets or profits. If times are tight, budgets may be getting cut and profits may not exist. It is very hard for a company to justify giving money away if it is laying off employees or cutting shareholder dividends. Financial information is often posted on the company's Web site or can be found on Web sites such as *www.sec.gov*, *www.hoovers.com*, and *www.fool.com*.]

(*continues*)

EXHIBIT 17.1   Continued

OFFICERS/DIRECTORS

[Getting a face-to-face meeting with a decision maker is key to getting a significant gift from a corporation. Officers and directors and brief bios on them are often listed in the company's proxy statement or DEF14a. This form, DEF14a, will also contain current stock holdings of officers and board members, insider stock holdings, details of stock options, and key bits of information that do not appear in the annual report. To find the most recently filed proxy statement for a public company, go to *http://www.sec.gov/edgar/searchedgar/company search.html* and search using the company name. Use this information to identify decision makers that have a connection to your organization. In preparing a research report, it is helpful to organize the officer and director information in a table such as the one that follows:]

Name	Title	Dates of Service	Other Affiliations

GIVING OVERVIEW

[There is a saying that the hardest gift to get is the first gift, and that is true for corporations and individuals alike. If the company has never made a donation, there is probably no system in place for who makes such decisions, how they are paid, and so on. If a company has no history, you might find yourself selling the virtues of giving, rather than your cause. Look for the general types of projects and programs that a company funds. This information might be listed on the company's Web site or its foundation's Web site. Look for areas on the company's Web site titled "Community Involvement," "Foundation," or "Corporate Giving." If these areas are not readily found, look for the "About us" section or similar section.

You especially want to list any funding priorities that match your organization's programs, projects, and mission.]

provided by FundraisingINFO.com, Inc. that shows the type of information that is necessary for creating a successful solicitation. The profile also addresses sources for finding needed information. A completed sample corporate profile appears at the end of this chapter.

Philanthropic Information

Try to find specific gifts the company has made. This will give you a good sense of the size of gifts it generally makes and the kinds of programs it likes to fund. If the company has a foundation, get the foundation's 990-form from *www.guidestar.org* to view a list of past gifts made by the foundation. If the company does not have a foundation, use your favorite search engine and do the following searches:

"name of company" + gift
"name of company" + contribution
"name of company" + sponsor
"name of company" + donor

Fortunately, many companies issue press releases when they make large gifts. Therefore, be sure to check on news sites such as *www.bizjournals.com*; *www.news library.com*; and *www.forbes.com*.

Organize the gifts that you do find in a table with the following column heads:

- Amount
- Recipient
- Date
- Grant guidelines and application instructions—be sure to check if the company makes gifts through a matching gift program.
- Political contributions—a company's political contributions can help you continue to find a connection to your organization. Political contributions can be found on sites such as *www.opensecrets.org*.

Finally, keep in mind that if you are unable to produce a report like this yourself, there are a few companies that will produce them for you. Three include the following:

1. FundraisingINFO.com
2. InfoRich Group, Inc.
3. ResearchProspects.com

CLASSIFYING FOUNDATIONS

To formulate appropriate strategies for approaching specific types of foundations, a development officer must understand the classification of foundations. The following provides the specific functions of each type as a guide through the various foundation entities.

Operating Foundations

Operating foundations accept donations but fund only one organization. Foundations operated by state universities are the most common type of operating foundations. Virtually all state colleges and universities accept donations; however, the universities themselves are programs of the state government rather than 501(c)3 organizations that can receive donations. The universities establish operating foundations that become registered charities and, therefore, can receive tax-deductible donations. Such operating foundations are also common in hospital settings. To determine if a foundation is an operating foundation, look to Part III of its 990 form for its "Statement of Program Accomplishments." An operating foundation will explain its purpose with a phrase such as, "The University of State Foundation was chartered in 1947 to establish and maintain endowments for the support of academic programs at the University of State."

Community Foundations

Community foundations typically pool donors' money for management and oversight and allow donors some input into how the donations are made. Typically, this is attractive to philanthropic individuals who do not possess sufficient resources or time to set up and administer their own private foundations. Most community foundations deal primarily in donor-advised funds. In these arrangements, donors direct the foundation to the areas or organizations they wish to fund. In some cases, the responsibility falls on the foundation to find organizations and projects in the community that fit the donors' criteria and suggest them to the donors. In other cases, donors suggest organizations to the foundation. In all of these cases, two separate groups are involved in the decision-making process: the donor and the community foundation staff. However, the ultimate decision as to the funding amounts and the recipients remains the responsibility of the community foundation.

Charitable Trusts

Charitable trusts are organizations that make donations but are typically set up as part of an estate plan. These may be permanent or temporary trusts. Typically, the decision makers for trust donations are the donors' lawyers, bankers, and so on. Although some trusts are created with very specific directions as to how and to whom donations can be made, others leave such decisions to the discretion of the trustees. Charitable trusts operate much like charitable foundations but require less reporting. Thus, charitable trusts are often more difficult to research online.

Charitable Foundations

Charitable foundations are public charities established for the explicit purpose of making donations to 501(c)3 organizations. While not legally distinct, the two types of charitable foundations differ functionally.

Family Foundations

Family foundations enable the donors (and/or family, friends, heirs) to serve as trustees and managers of the foundation. Since such foundations typically do not have staff, the duties of the foundation are distributed among the trustees. Trustees are, therefore, very involved in the decision-making process and the administration of grants. Soliciting a gift from a family foundation is often similar to soliciting a gift from an individual trustee. Family foundations, which come in all shapes and sizes, generally do not have application forms or complex processes.

Professional Foundations

Professional foundations employ professional staff to administer grants and operate the foundation. Professional foundations are typically larger than family foundations, as the foundation must incur the expenses of employing staff members, office space, and so on. These foundations also tend to involve more complex application procedures, decision-making processes, and reporting requirements.

Although technically they are the same type of corporation, family foundations and professionally managed foundations offer unique opportunities. Professionally managed foundations tend to have more structure and more clearly defined application procedures. Family foundations, by contrast, tend to give to organizations that have a connection to the family members.

SECURING GRANTS FROM CHARITABLE FOUNDATIONS

Writing and sending unsolicited *boilerplate* proposals to foundations without the benefit of prior conversations is one of the most unproductive activities a fundraising professional can perform. Development professionals can greatly increase the likelihood of receiving a grant from either type of charitable foundation by establishing a personal connection with the decision maker(s) before ever sending something in writing.

Success in securing grants from charitable foundations involve nine key steps:

Step 1: Identify Potential Funders

The first thing to keep in mind when researching foundations is that foundations do not make decisions about grants. People do. Therefore, the more a researcher learns about the people making the decisions—and the more established a personal relationship with these decision makers becomes—the greater the chance a proposal will receive funding.

Narrow the search process when identifying potential funders.

Geography

Start by securing a list of foundations located in the community or possessing a specific interest in the community. Nearby foundations are much easier to personally contact than foundations located hundreds of miles away. GuideStar, *http://www.guidestar.org*, provides users an opportunity to search its database of 990 forms for free. Researchers can narrow the search to a certain city and state. When looking for a charitable foundation, insert "Private Nonoperating Foundation" in the Nonprofit Type field (see Exhibit 17.2).

Keywords

Keywords can match a mission and programs. By searching for foundations that fund specific types of programs or organizations, a researcher can develop an initial list of prospects. For example, if a nonprofit organization aids children, search for keywords such as youth, children, and adolescents. The following fee-based services also allow users to search foundation databases by keyword:

BIG Online	*www.bigdatabase.com*
Foundation Center	*www.fdncenter.org*
FundraisingINFO.com	*www.fundraisinginfo.com*
Grantstation	*www.grantstation.com*
Grants Direct	*www.grantsdirect.com*

Current Supporters

Current supporters often lead to new foundation prospects. Research the connections of current supporters. A number of companies offer services to quickly screen entire

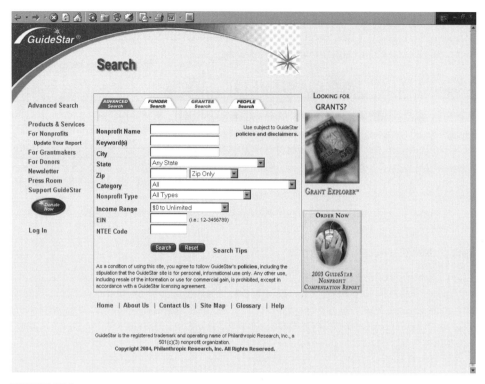

EXHIBIT 17.2   GuideStar Search

databases of supporters to identify which individuals also serve on corporate and foundation boards. Some of these services include

MaGIC, Inc.	*www.majorgifts.net*
P!N	*www.prospectinfo.com*
Target America	*www.tgtam.com*
Wealth Engine	*www.wealthengine.com*

Step 2: Focus Research

After identifying potential foundation prospects, the next step is to focus on programs and needs and determine if a fit exists between the foundation and the organization. An easy first step, using a search engine, is to determine if the foundation has a Web site. For example, visit *www.google.com* and perform the search illustrated in Exhibit 17.3 to locate the Web site for the Kresge Foundation.

After locating a foundation's Web site, check to see if it provides the following information:

- Who are the key decision makers?
- When are the deadlines?
- Is an application form available?

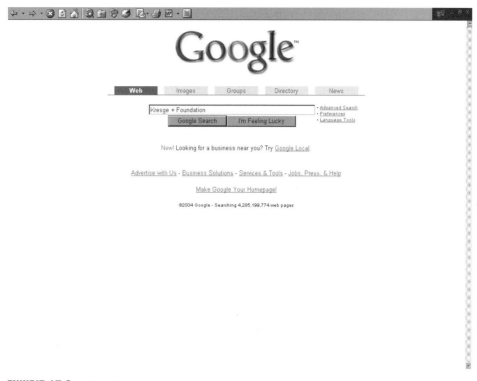

EXHIBIT 17.3   Google Search

- What types of projects does the foundation fund? Are these similar to the non-profit organization's projects?
- What size grants are typically given?
- If seeking building funds, learn if the foundation gives to capital projects. Locate similar information concerning endowment, programs, seed money, and so on. This is the one area where the guidelines are black and white. No matter how compelling a case statement may appear, a foundation will not provide money for bricks and mortar if it doesn't support capital projects. This is also the one area where deciding to make a request, disregarding information that a foundation clearly won't fund such a request, can make a development program appear naïve and unprofessional.
- Does the foundation support organizations with specific programs and services? If guidelines state a foundation only gives to botanical gardens, it is unlikely that a prep school can craft a presentation that fits the criteria.
- Does the foundation only fund pre-selected organizations? If so, the first essential step is to find a personal connection to a decision maker before sending materials to the foundation.
- Does the foundation state geographic limitations? Most foundations specify a geographic limitation, and qualifying organizations must meet the requirement. A facility might not need to be located in the specified geographic area if, perhaps, it serves a great number of people living in that area.

Finally, evaluate the organization's needs, the size of the project, the status of fundraising efforts and how these elements relate to a foundation's giving pattern. For example, consider an organization in the very early stages of a $1 million capital campaign. If the organization discovers a foundation prospect whose largest gifts are $25,000, it would not be appropriate to include the foundation as one of the campaign's first calls.

Likewise, if a foundation prefers to give very large grants to relatively large projects (e.g., its average gift size is $250,000 to campaigns in the millions of dollars), it would not be appropriate to approach such a foundation for a gift of $10,000 to refurbish a playground.

Lastly, before making any contact with a foundation, be sure to understand the application process and time line—essentially, how and when the foundation prefers to be approached.

Step 3: Find a Connection

Next, the development professional must identify someone within a sphere of influence who has a connection to the foundation. A board member, former board member, or volunteer might know the foundation executive or one or more board members. One approach is to share the list of targeted foundations and their board members with the development committee and ask for their help in identifying the connections between the organization and the foundation's leadership. Another approach is to research the foundation board members to identify their nonprofit, corporate, and associated connections. By matching these connections with the connections of board members and volunteers, the campaign director can specifically ask a board member or volunteer to help approach a foundation.

Step 4: Schedule a Meeting

After identifying an individual with a connection, ask for help regarding how to approach the foundation. Ask for specific assistance, such as attending a meeting with the foundation to talk about the organization and project before asking to submit a proposal for a grant.

This step is critical. Foundations get hundreds, even thousands, of requests every year. Most do not perform in-depth research concerning every organization that submits a request. A foundation may look for signals to indicate that it can trust an organization. Past experience is one indicator; good reputation is another. Another indicator is that a known individual is involved with the organization and endorses it. Volunteer leadership can play an invaluable role at this point.

Step 5: Prepare a Presentation

Research serves as a vital factor when deciding which programs and projects to discuss. During an organization's first contact with a foundation, representatives may need to share details of the organization's history. Remember the importance of a good first impression, so be prepared. Script the ideal meeting, including introductions, speakers, and answers to specific questions.

Be sure to determine up front who will have the responsibility of asking the foundation specific questions related to a gift amount.

Step 6: Ask Questions and Listen

A meeting can be worthless if the organization's representatives do not know how to proceed with a grant request, the appropriate size grant to request, and when to request it. Once background has been covered, the appointed person should say, "We were hoping to submit a proposal to the foundation for $_____ toward this project."

Immediately following that statement, is it time to remain quiet and listen. The request has been made. Be prepared to listen carefully to the response. The next words spoken will indicate if such a grant is likely and how to proceed in order to secure a grant. Appoint someone attending the meeting to take notes, especially notes related to any instruction that is given about how to approach the foundation, as well as comments made along the way concerning the foundation's likes and dislikes.

Step 7: Prepare and Submit Proposal

Once the meeting is over, make sure that all attendees send a thank-you letter. And, if the contact was made through a foundation board member connection, make sure the board member also receives a thank-you letter and update that the meeting occurred and the status of submitting a proposal.

Finally, it is now time to put pencil to paper and write a winning proposal. Make sure that written information conforms to foundation's guidelines. Some foundations require information to be presented in a particular order. If so, follow the order.

Some foundations have limitations on length. Stick to it. Be sure to follow any advice given during the meeting to adhere to a predetermined outline. Incorporate suggestions concerning information to include, exclude, or highlight.

The proposal must address the following three subjects:

1. The foundation will accomplish one or more of its stated objectives or goals by funding the project.
2. The organization is capable of performing what it promises to accomplish with the funding.
3. The organization realizes how much the program will cost and how it will fund it (especially if asking the foundation for a portion of the costs).

Some foundations require numerous facts, figures, and information concerning reporting procedures. Others, typically smaller family foundations, may just want to know that they will be doing something good.

Whether or not a proposal should include an emotional appeal depends on the foundation. A staff-run foundation may prefer facts and figures, which can still be very heartfelt (i.e., if another organization is helping more people for fewer dollars and can prove it with facts and figures, that proposal will probably win out over an emotional appeal by an organization that does not reach nearly as many people for the same money).

In general, the proposal should include a mission statement, the requested dollar amount, a description of how the money will be spent, information on reporting procedures, and evaluation techniques. Other helpful information could include a board of directors list, previous years' financial statements, and a listing of other major donors. Again, the most important things to include in any proposal are the elements the foundation requested during the meeting.

Step 8: Receive the Gift

One of the biggest mistakes fundraising professionals make is contacting foundations solely when they need money. Keep foundations appraised of progress in the fundraising effort and concerning programs in general. The more a foundation is aware of an organization's accomplishments, the less time it takes staff to bring them up to speed when returning for the next grant.

Step 9: Follow Up

Be sure to honor all terms of the grant. If a foundation requests quarterly updates, make sure the reports arrive on time. If a naming opportunity was part of the grant, make sure the obligation is met to the foundation's satisfaction. If the gift included the condition of anonymity, make sure the act remains anonymous. Set up a system to track when the foundation meets, when grants are made and which volunteers have been involved in securing grants in the past. Finally, don't let the relationship fade. At the least, send a very personal letter each year to the foundation explaining progress and the impact of the grant. Better still; request a face-to-face meeting once a year to convey that message. Try to make them feel as if they are one of the family.

LOOKING TO THE FUTURE

In corporate and foundation development work, the Internet has rapidly changed the face of research—resulting in better proposals receiving funding at higher levels, a more cost-effective use of energy, staff and resources, and an opportunity to engage funding sources in the routine lives of institutions. Use of such technological advances now results in better, more cost-effective fundraising efforts, along with improved proposals and strategies.

Although most would quickly agree that easy access to limitless research data is the paramount advantage of this new technology, many development professionals continue to overlook the Internet's vital role in improving communications. The ability to connect quickly and effectively with corporate and foundation officers allows new and exciting opportunities for stewardship of major gifts. The introduction of e-mail and other tools has enabled the institutional family to become much more inclusive than in days past.

The Internet allows development officers to efficiently compile lists of funding prospects, research corporations' giving histories with the click of a mouse, and quickly disseminate information as e-mail attachments. For centuries, fundraising practices changed little, but the advent of the Internet guarantees that this is no longer the case, as technological advances in the future will continue to significantly impact the ease and effectiveness of research and communications efforts.

With that said, the methodologies in developing strategies and targeting prospects are not likely to change. The Internet's advantages are simply enhancements to the personal relationships that result in major gifts and grants to institutions. The fact remains that trust in leadership and program competence are the fundamental driving forces behind fruitful fundraising results.

EXHIBIT 17.4   Sample Corporate Profile: ProspectINFO[(c)]: Citigroup

Citigroup
Confidential

Citigroup

Sanford I. Weill, Chairman
399 Park Avenue
New York, NY 10043
P: 212-559-1000
http://www.citigroup.com

Overview

Citigroup Inc. (Citigroup and, together with its subsidiaries, the Company) is a diversified global financial services holding company whose businesses provide a broad range of financial services to consumer and corporate customers with some 200 million customer accounts doing business in more than 100 countries. Citigroup was incorporated in 1988 under the laws of the State of Delaware. The Company's activities are conducted through the Global Consumer, Global Corporate and Investment Bank (GCIB), Private Client Services, Global Investment Management (GIM) and Proprietary Investment Activities business segments. Citigroup International serves 54 million customer accounts in approximately 100 countries, working in partnership with the Company's product organizations.

Total employees: approximately 140,000 in the United States and 119,000 outside the United States.

Finances

Total annual revenue ending 12/31/03:	$77.4 billion
Total annual net income ending 12/31/03:	$17.85 billion

Officers/Directors

Name	Title	Dates of Service	Other Affiliations
C. Michael Armstrong	Director		Chairman, Comcast Inc.
Alain J.P. Belda	Director		Chairman and Chief Executive Officer, Alcoa Inc.
George David	Director		Chairman and Chief Executive Officer, United Technologies Corporation
Kenneth T. Derr	Director		Chairman, Retired, ChevronTexaco Corporation

(continues)

EXHIBIT 17.4   Continued

Name	Title	Dates of Service	Other Affiliations
John M. Deutch	Director		Institute Professor, Massachusetts Institute of Technology
Roberto Hernández Ramírez	Director		Chairman, Banco Nacional de Mexico
Ann Dibble Jordan	Director		Consultant
Dudley C. Mecum	Director		Managing Director, Capricorn Holdings LLC
Richard D. Parsons	Director		Chairman and CEO, AOL Time Warner
Andrall E. Pearson	Director		Founding Chairman, Yum!Brands, Inc.
Charles Prince	Director		Chief Executive Officer, Citigroup Inc. Chairman and CEO, Global Corporate and Investment Banking Group
Robert E. Rubin	Director, Chairman of the Executive Committee	1999	Chairman of the Executive Committee and Member of the Office of the Chairman, Citigroup Inc. Former Secretary of the Treasury under Clinton. Director of the Ford Motor Company; Trustee of Mount Sinai-NYU Health
Franklin A. Thomas	Director		Consultant, TFF Study Group
Sanford I. Weill	Chairman		Chairman, Citigroup Inc.
Robert B. Willumstad	President and COO		President & Chief Operating Officer, Citigroup Inc.
Arthur Zankel	Director		Senior Managing Member, High Rise Capital Management, L.P.
The Honorable Gerald R. Ford	Honorary Director		Former President of the United States

Giving Overview

In 2002, Citigroup surpassed $100 billion toward meeting the $115 billion, 10-year commitment made in 1998 to lend and invest in U.S. LMI communities and small businesses, putting it on track to meet its goal four years ahead of schedule.

EXHIBIT 17.4 Continued

Citigroup has pioneered and funded microlending programs around the world for close to 40 years. Over the past four years, the Citigroup Foundation has awarded $11 million in grants to 145 microfinance organizations in more than 50 countries.

On June 2, 2003, Citigroup joined with nine other banks to adopt the Equator Principles, a voluntary set of guidelines developed by the banks for managing social and environmental issues related to the project financing of development projects in all industries. The Equator Principles are based on World Bank and IFC policies and guidelines.

Numerous steps have been taken to strengthen employee volunteer efforts at Citigroup. These include launching an internal employee volunteer Web site, holding a U.S. national day of volunteering with 1,400 employees in 26 states participating in 45 different projects, and providing volunteer opportunities by funding Habitat for Humanity building projects in 44 U.S. cities and dozens of countries around the world.

Of Citigroup's $77.7 million in philanthropic giving in 2002, foundation and corporate grants totaled $58.8 million to organizations in 83 countries and territories.

In fact, over the last three years, the foundation's international grant making increased steadily, from $8.09 million in 2000 to $14.3 million in 2002. In addition to the foundation's support, Citigroup businesses made contributions of nearly $19 million, more than half of which were outside the United States.

Citigroup Foundation
850 3rd Ave., 13th Fl.
New York, NY 10043
Telephone: (212) 793-8451
Contact: Charles V. Raymond, C.E.O. and Pres.
FAX: (212) 793-5944
E-mail: *citigroupfoundation@citigroup.com*
URL: *http://www.citigroup.com/citigroup/corporate/foundation/index.htm*

Purpose and activities: Funding priorities are economic and community development and education. Second-tier interests are arts and culture, and health and human services. *Interest area(s)*. Building communities and entrepreneurs; educating the next generation; employee matching gifts program; financial education; volunteer incentive program.

Geographic focus: National; international.

Types of support: Employee matching gifts, general/operating support.

Limitations: Giving on a national and international basis. No support for political causes or religious, veterans' or fraternal organizations, unless they are engaged in a significant project benefiting the entire community. No grants to individuals, or for fundraising events, telethons, marathons, races, benefits, or courtesy advertising.

Application information: The foundation solicits proposals from preselected organizations; relatively few unsolicited proposals are considered.

(continues)

EXHIBIT 17.4   Continued

Philanthropic information:

Amount	Recipient	Date
$1,150,000	National Academy Foundation	2002
$1,000,000	Raza Development Fund	2002
$800,000	Asia Society, NYC	2002
$60,000	Kenan Flagler Business School	1998
$600,000	Grameen Foundation USA, DC, For Microcredit in China program.	2002
$550,000	Enterprise Foundation, New York, NY, For Risk Capital Fund for Housing and Child Care Initiative	2002
$500,000	Alvin Ailey American Dance Theater	2002
$500,000	National Community Reinvestment Coalition, DC, For Citigroup Financial Literacy Leadership Initiative.	2002

Political contributions: Citigroup Inc. Political Action Committee-Federal has contributed $176,493 to federal candidates in the 2004 election cycle: 73 percent to Republicans and 27 percent to Democrats. It contributed $463,000 in the 2002 election cycle, with 45 percent going to Democrats and 55 percent to Republicans.

Chairman and/or Chief Executive Information

Sanford I. Weill is chairman of Citigroup Inc., the diversified global financial services company formed in 1998 by the merger of Citicorp and Travelers Group. Mr. Weill retired as CEO of Citigroup on October 1, 2003, and will serve as chairman until April 2006. Mr. Weill became a director of the Federal Reserve Bank of New York in 2001.

He also served as a director on the boards of United Technologies Corp. from 1999 to 2003, AT&T Corp. from 1998 until 2002, and E. I. Du Pont Nemours and Company from 1998 until 2001.

Mr. Weill has been chairman of the board of trustees of Carnegie Hall since 1991, and previously served as co-chairman of the steering committee for the campaign that raised $60 million for the Hall's restoration.

Mr. Weill was director of the Baltimore Symphony Orchestra; chairman of the board of overseers for The Joan and Sanford I. Weill Medical College and Graduate School of Medical Sciences of Cornell University, having joined the board in 1982 and become chair in 1996 (Cornell named the medical college after the Weills in April 1998 in recognition of its gifts totaling $150 million.); trustee of New York Presbyterian Hospital; overseer of Memorial Sloan-Kettering Cancer Center; member of The Business Council and The Business Roundtable.

Long a proponent of education, Mr. Weill instituted a joint program with the New York City Board of Education in 1980 that created the Academy of Finance, which trains high school students for careers in financial services.

He serves as chairman of the National Academy Foundation, which oversees more than 394 academies that operate across the country, and is the principal sponsor of New York City's High School of Economics and Finance.

Mr. Weill, who was born on March 16, 1933, is a graduate of Cornell University.

ABOUT THE AUTHORS

As president of Ketchum, **Bob Carter** leads the firm's sales team and provides senior-level development and campaign counsel to a broad cross-section of gift-supported organizations throughout the United States.

Prior to joining Ketchum in 1981, Mr. Carter served as vice president for University Relations at The Catholic University of America; director of Development for Arts and Sciences and Engineering and Associate Director of Annual Giving at The Johns Hopkins University; assistant to the Headmaster at the Gilman School in Baltimore; and both taught and organized the development office at The Boys' Latin School in Baltimore. He has 35 years of experience in development and capital/endowment campaigning.

He is a resident of Pittsburgh, where his wife, Carol, serves as vice president of University Relations at Duquesne University. You can e-mail Bob at bcarter@viscern.com.

Kristina Carlson, CFRE, ePMT, is president of FundraisingINFO.com, an Internet-based company that provides more than 3,000 nonprofit organizations with affordable solutions to their fundraising challenges. In this capacity, Ms. Carlson oversees FundraisingINFO.com's operations, sales, and marketing including its fundraising information services, seminars, workshops, and prospect research services.

With more than 17 years of fundraising experience, Ms. Carlson is a Certified Fund Raising Executive and has directed successful capital campaigns, with goals ranging from $1 million to $200 million, for international organizations as well as smaller grassroots groups. Her experience includes the direction of collaborative capital campaigns for public/private ventures in Charlotte, North Carolina, and Portland, Maine. Ms. Carlson has also established resource development programs for two health-care organizations and the negotiated philanthropic gifts ranging up to $16 million. You can e-mail Kristina at Kristina@fundraisinginfo.com.

Ms. Carlson is a trustee of the ePhilanthropy Foundation and author of the nationally known workshops "How to Use the Internet to Improve Fundraising" and "The Internet's Secrets to Finding Donors." She has authored numerous articles and fundraising guides and is a frequent speaker for Association of Fundraising Professionals, nonprofit resource centers, and other organizations around the country.

Carlson holds a master's degree in community economic development from the University of Southern New Hampshire and a bachelor's degree from Oral Roberts University, with a major in marketing and studies in computer science and mathematics.

ePhilanthropy Regulation and the Law

Bruce R. Hopkins
Polsinelli Shalton Welte Suelthaus P.C.

One of the most difficult of contemporary issues is whether fundraising by charitable organizations by means of the Internet constitutes fundraising in every state—or, for that matter, in every locality.

The law rarely keeps pace with sociological and technological change. Almost always, the rules are written considerably after the controversy, crisis, or like development that prompted them. In this regard, legislatures and regulatory bodies are usually slow, and the courts understandably are even slower.

ePhilanthropy exists and is expanding, yet the law regulating it barely exists.[1] Although this state of affairs is changing (which is to say that specific regulation is on the way), in the meantime regulators and lawyers must largely extrapolate from current law principles.[2] For philanthropic organizations, the principal areas of concern as to the law are the unrelated business income rules, federal and state regulation of fundraising, and the administration of charitable giving programs. There are, not surprisingly, many other areas of the law that help compose the universe of ePhilanthropy regulation.

The chief regulator in this regard at the federal level is the Internal Revenue Service (IRS). In one of its few, albeit salient, observations on the point, the agency noted that the "use of the Internet to accomplish a particular task does not change the way the tax laws apply to that task." The IRS continued: "[F]undraising is still fundraising."[3]

TWO HOT ISSUES

The U.S. federal tax law constantly attempts to quantify various activities of philanthropic organizations and occasionally attempts to impute the functions of one or more other entities to philanthropic organizations.

Quantifying Activities

The federal tax law requires philanthropic organizations to measure the extent of a variety of activities—principally, program, management, fundraising, attempts to influence legislation, and unrelated business. Usually, these activities are assessed in terms of the amount of money expended in the conduct of them; sometimes, the amount of time involved is a factor.

This approach does not work very well, or not at all, in the context of activities conducted by philanthropic organizations by means of the Internet. These undertakings can be transacted at a small fraction of the expense that would have been incurred were traditional forms of communication used.

Current law does not contain a basis by which these activities can be quantified. A likely outcome is use of an ephemeral facts-and-circumstances test, which will take into account the nebulous factor of *influence*. This aspect of the ePhilanthropy regulation permeates all aspects of the subject.

Import of Links

The Web site of a philanthropic organization often contains one or more links to other Web sites. These other sites may be maintained by other nonprofit organizations, government agencies, or for-profit organizations. In assessing the presence of a link for law purposes, the most serious aspect of the matter is the prospect of *attribution* of Web site content of a linked organization to a philanthropic organization.

In one of the few instances of IRS guidance in this field, a set of tax regulations issued by the IRS in early 2002,[4] accompanying legislation enacted in 1997[5], offers some important insights. The mere presence of a link by a tax-exempt organization to the site of another entity generally has no adverse affect. In some circumstances, however, a message on another organization's Web site can be attributed to an exempt organization for tax law purposes. The implications of this type of attribution are enormous.

UNRELATED BUSINESS ACTIVITY

Business activity by philanthropic organizations is being conducted on the Internet. Products and goods are being advertised and sold, in business activities, by this means. The Internet, being a medium of communication, offers to these organizations (and others) a magnificent opportunity to create business, market goods and services, and sell these goods and services to the general public. As is the case in other contexts, however, the federal tax law does not provide any unique treatment to transactions or activities of philanthropic organizations involving related or unrelated business activity simply because the Internet is the medium of communication.

Much of this business activity is couched by the philanthropic community, in terms such as *social entrepreneurialism, social enterprise, marketing* (including advertising, branding, and research surveys), and *communications* (including promotions, public information dissemination, publications, and media relations). From a federal tax law standpoint, however, one of the core issues is whether the activity conducted by a tax-exempt organization rises to the level of a *business*. If it does, then the law quickly focuses on determining whether the activity is *related* or *unrelated* to the organization's exempt purposes.

Internet Unrelated Business Activity in General

The IRS stated, in a pioneering exploration of the unrelated business rules and tax-exempt organizations' use of the Internet, that "it is reasonable to assume that as the

Service position [on philanthropic organization Web merchandising, advertising, and publishing] develops it will remain consistent with our position with respect to advertising and merchandising and publishing in the off-line world."[6] Thus, the rules as to unrelated business activity by exempt organizations embrace this type of activity by means of the Internet.

There are four forms of Internet communications in this setting:

1. A communication published on a publicly accessible Web page
2. A communication posted on a password-protected portion of a Web site
3. A communication on a listserv (or by means of other methods such as a newsgroup, chat room, and/or forum)
4. A communication by means of e-mail

The IRS observed that "[m]any tax-exempt organizations now have a Web page that describes their purpose, discusses their activities, provides lists of upcoming events, lists local affiliates, provides contact information, and more." The IRS also noted that, "[b]y publishing a Web page on the Internet, an exempt organization can provide the general public with information about the organization, its activities, and issues of concern to the organization, as well as immediate access to Web sites of other organizations."[7]

Business Activities

The federal tax law defines—by application of the fragmentation rule——a tax-exempt organization as a cluster of businesses, with each discrete activity evaluated independently from the others. The fundamental statutory definition of the term, in the unrelated business setting, is that a business includes "any activity which is carried on for the production of income from the sale of goods or the performance of services."[8] Thus, nearly everything that an exempt organization engages in by means of the Internet is a business. Indeed, utilization of the Internet by a tax-exempt organization entails either the operation of one or more businesses or is a component of one or more businesses.

The Web site of a typical tax-exempt organization primarily, if not exclusively, contains information concerning the organization's programs. Its operations and purposes are described, often in some detail. In some instances, substantive information is provided pertaining to its area or areas of interest. Some collateral information may be on the site; photographs, maps, membership lists, and staff directories are common. Many charitable organizations include information about giving opportunities. Some tax-exempt organizations discuss their advocacy activities. Rarely, however, are unrelated business endeavors openly reflected on an exempt organization's Web site.

It is not common for a Web site to function wholly as one or more discrete businesses. Rather, these various postings are extensions of offline programs and other activities. A university's site, for example, summarizes its undergraduate and graduate programs, describes its various schools, and offers information as to how and when to apply for admission. A scientific research institution's site inventories the research projects in process and perhaps highlights the work of a particular scientist. An association's site enumerates its various programs, perhaps contains information about its advocacy efforts, and includes information about its other efforts, such as certification and enforcement of its code of ethics. Usually all of this information is also available elsewhere.

One of the major difficulties in this regard is the allocation of time and expenditures to these Web site offerings. There are, of course, expenses of building and maintaining a site. The costs of posting the information, however, are negligible. Thus, an unanswered question is: How are Web site establishment and maintenance costs allocated to a tax-exempt organization's various programs and other activities?

Perhaps the fragmentation rule should be applied in such a way that Web site establishment and maintenance itself is a business, or perhaps two or more businesses. Certainly the matter of determination and allocation of expenses would be simplified. For most tax-exempt organizations, this approach would mean that Web site creation and maintenance is wholly a related business. For other exempt organizations, even with this approach, however, the expenses of activities such as fundraising, advocacy, and unrelated business would have to be factored out for reporting and other purposes.

Regularly Carried On

For the most part, activities reflected on a philanthropic organization's Web site are regularly carried on. Organizations, from time to time, change the content of the site, of course, but usually the categories of information (programs, directories, fundraising, advocacy, certification, ethics enforcement, and the like) remain the same.

Substantially Related

As noted, nearly everything on a philanthropic organization's Web site—often, everything—consists of information and material that is related to the organization's exempt purposes. The biggest exception is fundraising activities. Many organizations that are involved in unrelated business do not, as noted, openly reflect that fact on their Web site. Likewise, the participation by an exempt organization in a joint venture (such as a partnership or limited liability company) usually is not mentioned on the site; the same is true with the use of a for-profit subsidiary.

Advertising in General

One of the major uses by philanthropic organizations of the Internet is for advertising of themselves. Today one of the principal purposes of an exempt organization's Web site is advertising of its programs—services, products, and facilities. Visits to Web sites lead to invitations to apply to a college, join an association, explore a museum, tour a scientific research facility, and much more. Some sites are entirely bastions of advertising, with headings such as "Who we are," "What we do," "FAQs about us," and so forth.

Usually, advertising by philanthropic organizations of the products or services of other persons is considered to be an unrelated activity. Pre-Internet, rare was the situation where advertising was considered a related function.

The advent of the Internet has not changed the rules as to commercial advertising, however. From this perspective, three categories of information dissemination are in the realm of advertising: related advertising, commercial (unrelated) advertising, and acknowledgments in the context of corporate sponsorships. As between related and unrelated advertising, the Supreme Court instructed that a tax-exempt organization can "control its publication of advertisements in such a way as to reflect an intention to contribute importantly to its . . . [exempt] functions."[9] This can be done, wrote the Court, by "coordinating the content of the advertisements with the editorial content of the issue, or by publishing only advertisements reflecting new developments."[10]

One of the issues of the day in this regard is whether a communication that would otherwise be an acknowledgment is transmuted into advertising because of a link between the exempt organization and its corporate sponsor. An IRS private letter ruling suggests that a link causes conversion of the communication to advertising.[11]

Compensation for Advertising

The IRS observed that the advertising rates charged by a tax-exempt organization "will vary considerably based on its area of concern, the quality of its Web site and the user traffic it generates."[12] The IRS includes as advertising the display of a "banner, graphic, or statement of sponsorship." The agency noted that exempt organizations generally favor the "less obtrusive" sponsorship statements rather than the banner advertisement, in that the latter is "perceived as more appropriate to commercial sites and potentially more offensive to potential donors." Also, a moving banner is "probably more likely" to be considered taxable advertising than other approaches.

One way for an exempt organization to be compensated for Web site advertising is by means of a flat fee. An organization may offer pay-per-view advertisements, where it earns a credit each time a site visitor views the advertisement. A related form of compensation is the click-through charge, where the advertiser pays only when an individual clicks through the banner or corporate logo and visits the advertiser's site.

The IRS addressed the fact that many exempt organization Web sites include links to related, affiliated, or similarly recommended sites. Some organizations exchange banners or links. The IRS wrote that it is currently unclear whether it will treat link or banner exchanges as "similar to a mailing list exchange or whether an organization that participates in such a program may incur liability for unrelated business income." The agency added that, in analyzing these exchange mechanisms, their purpose is critical, in that it must be determined "whether the link [or banner] exchange is an exchange of advertising or rather merely an attempt to refer the site visitor to additional information in furtherance of the organization's exempt purposes and activities."

Online Corporate Sponsorship

The IRS recognized that the "differences between an advertisement and corporate sponsorship is [sic] further complicated in the Internet environment." The agency noted that it is "not uncommon" for a tax-exempt organization to have all or part of its Web site corporately sponsored. This financial support may be acknowledged through display of a corporate logo, notation of the sponsor's Web site address and/or 800 number, a moving banner, or hypertext link.

In an understatement, the IRS stated that, "[g]enerally, exempt organizations prefer to view payments as corporate sponsorship rather than advertising income, which is more likely to be subject to unrelated business income tax." The agency wrote that the "use of promotional logos or slogans that are an established part of a sponsor's identity" is not, alone, advertising. It was also noted that display or sale of a sponsor's product by an exempt organization as a sponsored event is an acknowledgment, not advertising.

A payment cannot be a qualified sponsorship payment if the amount is contingent, by contract or otherwise, on the level of attendance at one or more events, broadcast ratings, or other factors indicating the degree of public exposure to an activity. Although the IRS did not say so, this rule seems to preclude pay-per-view or click-through arrangements from constituting qualified corporate sponsorship arrangements.

It is because of the evolution of this aspect of the law that nonprofit organizations now have their first inkling as to the position of the IRS as to the tax law import of links. It came in the final regulations concerning corporate sponsorships, where the agency considered whether the use of a link in what would otherwise be an acknowledgment changes the character of a payment from a qualified (nontaxable) corporate sponsorship to taxable advertising. The essence of the IRS position is that the mere presence of a link by a tax-exempt organization to the site of a corporate sponsor does not defeat characterization of the payment as a nontaxable sponsorship. If, however, the sponsor's Web site contains advertising in the nature of an endorsement of a product or service by an exempt organization, the protections of the qualified corporate sponsorship rules may fall away, at least in part.

Online Storefronts

The IRS has mused about the proper tax treatment of "[o]nline storefronts complete with virtual shopping carts." Not surprisingly, the agency is relying on its "traditional" assessment of sales activities by tax-exempt organizations, particularly museum shop sales.[13]

Once again, the determination of ultimate causal relationship and its importance is based on the facts and circumstances of each case. As with museums, the IRS will determine relatedness of sales based on the nonprofit organization's primary purpose for selling the item. If the purpose underlying the production and/or sale of the item is furtherance of the organization's exempt purposes, the sale will be considered a related one. Where, however, the primary purpose for a sale is utilitarian, ornamental, or only generally educational in nature, or amounts to the sale of a souvenir, it is not likely to be regarded as related. Various factors are considered by the IRS in analyzing this primary purpose, as the agency probes the "nature, scope, and motivation" for these sales. The factors include the degree of connection between the item being sold and the purpose of the exempt organization and the "overall impression" conveyed by the article; if the "dominant impression" leads to the conclusion that "non-charitable use or function predominates," the sale would be an unrelated one. The fact that an item could, in a different context, be held related to the exempt purpose of another tax-exempt organization does not make the sale by the organization under review a related activity.

Thus, the IRS is comparing Internet merchandising to sales made in stores and through catalogs and similar vehicles. Merchandise will be evaluated on an item-by-item basis—the fragmentation rule again—to determine whether the sales activity furthers the accomplishment of an organization's exempt purposes or is "simply a way to increase revenues."

Online Auctions

The IRS is looking at online auctions in part from the standpoint as to how they are conducted. Some tax-exempt organizations conduct their own; others use outside service providers. Some online auction Web sites provide services for exempt organizations only; some sites and search engines also operate auctions for individuals and for-profit organizations. The advantages to utilization of an outside auction service provider include provision of a larger auction audience than might be available if the exempt organization conducted it itself and avoidance of credit card fraud problems. Yet, as the IRS delicately phrased the matter, "entering into an agreement with an outside service provider might have tax implications."

One of the factors considered by the IRS is the degree of control (if any) the tax-exempt organization will exercise over the marketing and conduct of the auction. The IRS wants the event to be "sufficiently segregated from other, particularly non-charitable auction activities" (whatever that may mean) and the exempt organization to retain "primary responsibility" for publicity and marketing. Otherwise, the agency "may be more likely to view income from such auction activities as income from classified advertising rather than as income derived from the conduct of a fundraising event."

Also, the IRS has characterized these service providers as "essentially professional fundraisers." It is not clear what the point of that analogy is, but nonetheless the IRS will scrutinize their functions and fees "using traditional [private] inurement and private benefit principles." The agency might have mentioned that the intermediate sanctions rules also are applicable in this setting.

Online Charity Malls

Internet sites may permit online member shoppers to shop at affiliated vendors through links on the site. For each purchase, the vendor agrees to remit, through a charity mall operator, an agreed-on percentage of the purchase price to a designated charity. A few of the charity mall operators represent that they use volunteers and pass on all of the funds raised to the designated charities. Others retain a percentage of the proceeds for site maintenance and development. Some malls solicit paid advertisements. The mall operator credits the charity with the contribution upon receipt of the rebate from the vendor.

A nonprofit organization that operates one of these malls as its primary purpose probably cannot qualify as a tax-exempt charitable organization "since the marketing and operation of the virtual mall is a trade or business ordinarily [regularly] carried on for profit." Among the concerns the IRS has about virtual charity mall operations are (1) that the beneficiary organizations "do not appear to have any agreement with the virtual mall operators and do not appear to be entitled to any record of member designations or transactions" and (2) the exempt organization "has little recourse if it finds its name used in association with such mall operators, who may or may not prove reputable."

Merchant Affiliate Programs

Affiliate and other co-venture programs are growing in popularity—online and off—with many variations. Probably the most ubiquitous of these programs on the Internet

involve co-ventures with large, online booksellers, although art galleries, toy mer-
chants, and event credit report providers have these programs. Organizations are offered the option of making book recommendations that may be "displayed" or listed
on the organization's Web site or simply using a logo or other link to the bookseller.
The exempt organization earns a percentage of sales of recommended materials as well
as a commission on other purchases sold as the result of the referring link. The exempt
organization receives a periodic report detailing link activity.

The controversy over the tax treatment of income received by tax-exempt organizations from affinity card programs may have an impact on the taxation of income
generated by these ventures.

The IRS noted that a "distinct advantage that these programs have over the virtual
mall type operations from the point of view of the charity is that the exempt organization itself enters into an agreement with the merchant and is provided an activity
report in order to ensure that it [is] credited with the appropriate royalty."

In this context, then, the IRS seems to have conceded that these payments qualify
as a tax-excludible royalty (see following section). Indeed, the payments discussed in
some of the preceding sections constitute excludible royalties.

Professional and Trade Associations

Many professional and trade associations[14] have Web sites accessible by the general
public, along with material that is restricted to members. Many of these member-only
sections "provide access to research services, continuing education opportunities,
employment listings, membership directories, links to various organization benefit programs, legislative alerts, publications, etc."

The IRS issued this caution: "Organizations and Web designers must be aware that
the traditional rules with respect to prohibitions on providing particular services, treatment of advertising income, [and] sales activity, as well as lobbying restrictions [,]
still apply to Web site activities."

Web Sites and Rules as to Periodicals

The corporate sponsorship rules intertwine with the general unrelated business rules
as applicable in the Internet communications context in several instances. Again, the
fundamental issue is whether the communication by the sponsored organization, in
response to receipt of the corporate support, is merely an acknowledgment of the
support or is a communication that amounts to advertising.

This dichotomy between acknowledgments and advertising becomes irrelevant if
the communication involved appears in a periodical. That is, in this circumstance, the
exception for corporate sponsorship payments is not available. Technically, the exception for the qualified corporate sponsorship does not apply to a payment that en-
titles the payor (sponsor) to the use or acknowledgment of the name or logo (or
product line) of the payor's business in a periodical of a tax-exempt organization.[15]

A periodical is regularly scheduled and printed material published by or on behalf of the payee (sponsored) organization that is not related to and primarily distributed in connection with a specific event conducted by the payee organization.[16] Thus,
the exception does not apply to payments that lead to acknowledgments in a monthly
journal but applies if a sponsor received an acknowledgment in a program or brochure

distributed at a sponsored event. Read literally, this rule denying the exception cannot apply in the Internet communications context because of the reference to printed material, which presumably is confined to hard copy. Yet it is difficult to believe that this is, or will be, the state of the law. Surely, at least under certain circumstances, a Web site will be regarded as a periodical. (In a comparable situation, where the statutory law makes reference to printed material,[17] the IRS promulgated a regulation providing that the term includes material that is published electronically.[18])

Moreover, should a Web site be considered a periodical, the rules for determining unrelated business taxable income from the publishing of advertising in periodicals would apply.

The IRS continued in this analysis, however, to say that, in considering how to treat potential income from Web site materials for unrelated business income tax purposes, the agency "will look closely at the methodology used in the preparation of" Web site materials. It added that the IRS "will be unwilling to allow the exempt organization to take advantage of the specialized rules available to compute unrelated business income from periodical advertising income unless the exempt organization can clearly establish that the on-line materials are prepared and distributed in substantially the same manner as a traditional periodical." That means that, if there is advertising, the special rules for calculating unrelated business taxable income in the case of periodicals would not be available.

Unrelated business taxable income that is earned from advertising on a Web site that is not a periodical is determined by the general rules, namely, by adding the gross income from the advertising to the gross income generated from any other unrelated business activity (other than advertising in periodicals) and subtracting the expenses that are directly connected with carrying on the unrelated business or businesses.[19] The reference to an expense that is *directly connected* to the conduct of unrelated business means an expense (to be deductible) that is an item of deduction that has a "proximate and primary relationship" to the carrying on of an unrelated business.[20]

If the "facility" is used both to carry on exempt activities and to conduct unrelated activities, the expenses attributable to these activities (as, for example, items of overhead) are to be allocated between the two uses on a basis that is reasonable.[21] The same rule applies with respect to the expenses associated with personnel (as, for example, salaries). It is common to make these allocations on the basis of time expended on the various activities.[22]

If the unrelated activity involved constitutes an exploitation of an exempt activity, the allocation rule is different. For expenses to be deductible, the unrelated business activity must have a "proximate and primary relationship" with the exempt purpose activity.[23]

The third of the IRS questions inquired as to the proper methodology to use when allocating expenses for a Web site. Again, simply by referencing the subject of allocation, the IRS must be thinking that a Web site comprises, if not more than one publication, then certainly more than one communication. Before allocating expenses of a Web site, however, the expenses themselves must be determined. There are the costs of establishing the site and the costs of maintaining the site. Much of the material on a Web site was previously created for online use, such as articles, directories, and information about charitable giving, certification, and ethics. Thus, it appears that there must be allocation of expenses as between offline and online material and information. There may not be that much left over to allocate in the context of Internet communications.

The question presupposes that allocation is required. That, however, may not always be the case. A tax-exempt organization that uses its Web site for related purposes (i.e., there is nothing on the site pertaining to fundraising or unrelated business) and not for advocacy purposes may see no reason to allocate expenses among programs. In that case, the organization may simply have a line item for Web site expenses.

When allocation is required or desired, the simplest of approaches is to separate a Web site into discrete communications on the basis of the amount of space each communication occupies on the site. As the IRS noted, expense allocation could be based on Web pages. This is often the approach taken in the case of print publications. In some instances, however, a primary purpose test is applied (or at least advocated), so that if the primary purpose of a publication is to communicate a particular message, the entire publication is deemed to have communication of that message as its purpose.

Summary

The law as to unrelated business activities will prove to be one of the most difficult of the components of the law of tax-exempt organizations to apply in the Internet communications context. Fragmentation of Web site activities into discrete businesses will often be difficult, as will the allocation of costs to them. These activities will usually be regularly carried on. Saving this area from even worse catastrophes is the fact that most of this activity will consist of related endeavors. The commerciality doctrine may be a problem, however, in that nonprofit Web sites are being operated in essentially the same fashion as for-profit sites.

The rules as to advertising will cause difficulties for many tax-exempt organizations, for this is an area where the IRS is likely to concentrate its efforts. Directly tied to this will be application of the corporate sponsorship rules, where line-drawing as between qualified and non-qualified payments will be exacerbated by Internet communications. Creative uses of the royalty exception may be anticipated in this setting. Related tax-exempt organizations will, however, be able to provide Web site-based services to each other without fear of unrelated business income taxation.

FUNDRAISING REGULATION

Another area of the law concerning philanthropic organizations where Internet communications are involved is the blend of increasing Internet use and fundraising. This mix of fundraising and Internet use will be generating new law, and new interpretations of preexisting law, at the federal, state, and local levels.

Confusion reigns in this realm. The universe of state law regulation of charitable fundraising, with its panoply of differing charitable solicitation acts and regulations, is a shameful mess. There are vagaries inherent in the state law concept of charitable *solicitation*. Inevitably, charitable fundraising and gift receiving by means of the Internet is increasing.

Introduction

There is a common perception that there is a single type of activity called *fundraising* and that all contributions are made in cash. (Fundraising by means of the Internet is likely to exacerbate and perpetuate that belief.) Certainly the federal, state, and local approaches to regulation in this area are founded on this view. Likewise, public attitudes of charitable fundraising—both positive and negative—are largely rested on this belief.

Charitable gifts can be made with property as well as money. The contribution may be of tangible personal property, intangible personal property, and real property. A contribution may be of the donor's entire interest in the property or of a portion of the donor's interest in the property. The latter is technically termed *partial interest giving*, meaning gifts to charity by means of techniques such as charitable remainder trusts and charitable gift annuities. Gifts of money and all types of property may be solicited by means of the Internet. Although gifts of money can be facilitated and received by means of the Internet, gifts of property, at least for the most part, must be formally executed and received offline.

A gift *solicitation* can be made in one or a combination of five ways: in person, by telephone, by regular mail, by facsimile, or by means of the Internet. As to the last of these, the asking for a gift can be done by e-mail or Web site communication.

Just as there are a number of ways to solicit a gift, there are a number of types of fundraising. One category—the one most suitable for the Internet—is annual giving programs. The other two overarching categories are special-purpose fundraising and the fundraising done in the context of planned giving and financial and estate planning. As to the category of annual giving fundraising, these solicitations are done by direct mail (donor acquisition or donor renewal), telephone, radio, television, advertisements in publications, door-to-door solicitations, on-street solicitations, and, of course, by use of the Internet. Special events, commemorative giving, donor clubs, and sweepstakes and lotteries can be utilized in this setting. Gifts can be solicited and received, and tickets sold, by means of the Internet.

Special-purpose programs are not likely to be enhanced much by Internet communication. This type of fundraising entails major gifts from individuals, grants from private foundations and government agencies, and capital campaigns. Certainly research in support of these undertakings can be done on the Internet, but the "ask" is not likely to be done that way and the gift acquisition is not likely to be accomplished that way either (although some elements of a capital campaign might involve Internet-made gifts).

Fundraising is not (or almost always is not) *program*. Many individuals, including some in law and fundraising, regard fundraising as part of an organization's program activities because its purpose is to promote the organization's purposes in some fashion. This misunderstanding is fueled in part by the distinctions in law simply between exempt functions and nonexempt functions, or more technically between related businesses and unrelated businesses. Because it is inconceivable that fundraising is a nonexempt function, it must be an exempt function—so the logic goes. From that position, it is an easy jump in logic to the conclusion that fundraising is the same as program (inasmuch as neither is a nonexempt function), but such a conclusion is erroneous. (Indeed, some fundraising activities are unrelated businesses.)

These distinctions are mirrored in the concept of *functional accounting*, an exercise imposed by the IRS on charitable and other tax-exempt organizations as part of the annual information return preparation and filing process. This method of accounting separates a tax-exempt organization's functions into three categories: program, administration, and fundraising.[24]

This aspect of fundraising has only been lightly treated in law. Indeed, the first attempt by a court to squarely face and analyze the difference, for tax purposes, between fundraising activity and business activity engaged in by a nonprofit organization resulted in a reversal by the Supreme Court.[25] Yet the reasoning of the lower court has continuing merit. This court wrote that, where the tax-exempt organization involved in an unrelated business case is a charitable one, the "court must distinguish between those activities that constitute a trade or business and those that are merely fundraising."[26] Admittedly, said the court, this distinction is not always readily apparent, as charitable activities are "sometimes so similar to commercial transactions that it becomes very difficult to determine whether the organization is raising money 'from the sale of goods or the performance of services' [the statutory definition of a business activity] or whether the goods or services are provided merely as an incident to a fundraising activity."[27] Nonetheless, the court held that the test is whether the activity in question is "operated in a competitive, commercial manner," which is a "question of fact and turns upon the circumstances of each case." "At bottom," the court wrote, the "inquiry is whether the actions of the participants conform with normal assumptions about how people behave in a commercial context" and "[i]f they do not, it may be because the participants are engaged in a charitable fundraising activity."[28]

State Fundraising Regulation in General

Nearly every state regulates fundraising for charitable purposes—although the extent and intensity of enforcement varies greatly. This regulation is accomplished principally by means of statutes termed *charitable solicitation acts*. There are more than 40 of these laws.

Overview of State Law

These laws are often intricate. In addition to their complexity, there is a considerable absence of uniformity, although the states are making some progress toward a uniform registration process. This combination of intricacy and nonconformity makes this a body of law with which it is difficult to comply—a problem aggravated by a disparity in regulations, rules, and forms.

More than 30 states have adopted what may be termed *comprehensive charitable solicitation acts*. The remaining states—including the few that lack a charitable solicitation act altogether (and the District of Columbia)—have elected to regulate fundraising for charitable purposes by means of differing approaches.

The various state charitable acts are, to substantially understate the situation, diverse. The content of these laws is so disparate that any implication that it is possible to neatly generalize about their assorted terms, requirements, limitations, exceptions, and prohibitions would be misleading. Of even greater variance are the requirements imposed by the many regulations, rules, and forms promulgated to accompany and amplify the state statutes. Nonetheless, some basic commonalties can be found in the comprehensive charitable solicitation acts.

The fundamental features of many of these fundraising regulation laws are a series of definitions, registration or similar requirements for charitable organizations, annual reporting requirements for charitable organizations, exemption of certain charitable organizations from all or a portion of the statutory requirements, registration and reporting requirements for professional fundraisers, registration and reporting requirements for professional solicitors, requirements with respect to the conduct of charitable sales promotions (also known as commercial co-ventures), record-keeping and public information requirements, requirements regarding the contents of contracts involving fundraising charitable organizations, disclosure requirements, a range of prohibited acts, registered agent requirements, rules pertaining to reciprocal agreements, investigatory and injunctive authority vested in enforcement officials, civil and criminal penalties, and other sanctions.[29]

Meaning of Solicitation

Many terms in these charitable solicitation acts require definition. The most common ones are the organizations to which these laws apply (generically, *charitable entities*) and the transactions to which these laws apply (generically, *charitable contributions*). An aspect of these bodies of law that almost always guarantees inconsistency and confusion are the many meanings associated with the terms *professional fundraiser* and *professional solicitor*.

Yet, in the context of Internet communications, the key terms are the words *solicit* and *solicitation*. One of the principal questions of the day is this: When a charitable organization posts a message on its Web site that it is seeking contributions, is that a solicitation of charitable gifts? If that is a solicitation, then presumably the charity is soliciting gifts in every state, county, city, town, and hamlet in the United States (not to mention internationally). The regulatory implications associated with the answers to these questions are stupendous.

Before answering that question, a brief review of the law on the point is appropriate. The word *solicitation* in these statutes is broadly defined. This fact is evidenced not only by the express language of the definition but also by application of these acts to charitable solicitations conducted, in terminology that is common, "by any means whatsoever." A solicitation can be oral or written. It can take place by means of an in-person request, regular mail, facsimile, advertisement, other publication, radio, television, telephone, or other medium. Also, of course, charitable solicitations can occur over the Internet.

A most encompassing, yet typical, definition of the term reads as follows: The term *solicit* means any request, directly or indirectly, for money, credit, property, financial assistance, or other thing of any kind or value on the plea or representation that such money, property, and the like of any kind or value is to be used for a charitable purpose or benefit a charitable organization.

Usually the word *solicitation* is used in tandem with the word *contribution*. The term *solicitation* may, however, encompass the pursuit of a grant from a private foundation, other nonprofit organization, or government department or agency. About a dozen states exclude from the term *solicitation* the process of applying for a government grant. Occasionally state law will provide that the word *contribution* includes a grant from a government agency or will exclude the quest for a grant from a private foundation.

It is clear, although few charitable solicitation acts expressly address the point, that the definition of *solicitation* entails the seeking of a charitable gift. That is, there is no requirement that the solicitation be successful, which is to say that a *solicitation* can occur irrespective of whether the request actually results in the making of a gift.

One court created a definition of the term *solicit* in this setting, writing that the "theme running through all of these cases is that to solicit means "'to appeal for something,' to 'ask earnestly,' to 'make petition to,' to 'plead for,' to 'endeavor to obtain by asking,' and other similar expressions."[30]

With this as background, it can be seen that a message on the Web site of a charitable (or other nonprofit) organization seeking contributions from the public is, literally and plainly, a solicitation of those contributions. Likewise, and even more obvious, an e-mail message sent to a prospective donor is a solicitation of a gift. One does not have to be an expert in semantics or parlance, or retain the services of a logogogue, to readily conclude that these uses of the Internet are forms of communication that amount to gift solicitations.

Yet while this is the correct outcome as a matter of word definition, it can be an absurdity in terms of its real-life consequences. The presence of a message on a charity's Web site asking for contributions, taken literally, mandates registration and reporting by the charity in each of the states (as noted, most of them) that have a charitable solicitation act requiring this type of registration. It may mean that the charity is doing business in each of the states, requiring registration and reporting as a nonprofit corporation and/or trust. This can easily entail more than 100 annual registrations or reports. Such message also presumably means that the charity is soliciting gifts in thousands of counties, cities, and the like, all of which have ordinances purporting to regulate fundraising in their jurisdictions.[31] This level of compliance is not only beyond a reasonable person's ability to fathom, it would annihilate any semblance of a fundraising program.

It was because of the potential of these outcomes that the Charleston Principles were devised (see following section).

State Fundraising Regulation and the Internet

The Internet has greatly expanded the number of philanthropic organizations capable of carrying out, and actually engaged in the practice of, multistate solicitation activities. Essentially, to reach potential donors in all of the states, an organization needs nothing more than a computer and an account with an Internet service provider. Once established, the organization's charitable appeal can instantly be sent or made available to the entire Internet community. The large national and international charities with the resources necessary to assure compliance with the various state regulatory regimes are thus no longer the only ones affected by state charitable solicitation laws. Instead, even the smallest organizations, operating on shoestring budgets, are beginning to tap the national contributions market. Thus, the new technology indeed is altering the nature of communication in the charitable solicitations context—it renders communication inexpensive.

One of the most difficult of contemporary issues is whether fundraising by charitable organizations by means of the Internet constitutes fundraising in every state—

or, for that matter, in every locality. As discussed later in this chapter, current think-ing is that, technically, it does. If those states asserting jurisdiction over Internet fundraising are justified in doing so, the result will be that even the smallest organi-zations—those too small to afford multistate solicitation efforts by any other medium—will be required to register under numerous state charitable solicitation laws simply by virtue of utilizing the new communications technology to solicit contribu-tions. If they do not, or cannot, assure state-law compliance, they will be forced to de-cide between risking legal action in several foreign states or refraining from engaging in this form of speech altogether. The question, thus, is whether, under this new mix of facts, state laws enforced in this fashion impermissibly restrict speech protected by the First Amendment.

There is another, perhaps equally interesting question, that must first be addressed. From a legal perspective, should Internet fundraising appeals be treated any differently solely because they take place on the Internet? (For federal tax purposes, the answer from the IRS is, as noted, no.) That is, should communication over this newest medium be treated as anything other than communication, for which there already is a rich regulatory scheme?

To determine whether the various state charitable solicitation regimes unduly in-trude on the protected speech interest in this type of solicitation, the existing regula-tory framework must be applied to the new set of facts. The first step in this analysis is to ascertain whether the act of an organization in placing an appeal for funds in a document on a computer in one state subjects the organization to the jurisdiction of one or more foreign states. There is as yet no law directly on this subject. Nonetheless, while not directly on point, a court opinion may shed some light on the matter.

A federal court of appeals had the opportunity to discuss the legal status of computer-borne communications in the First Amendment context. Two individuals operated an adult-oriented bulletin board service from their home. The site was acces-sible to others around the nation via modems and telephone lines.

Working with the U.S. attorney's office in another state, a postal inspector pur-chased a membership in this bulletin board service and succeeded in downloading al-legedly obscene images from the bulletin board. The U.S. attorney's office filed criminal charges against these individuals for, among other things, transmitting obscenity over interstate telephone lines from their computer. By relatively conservative community standards, the images involved were found by a jury to constitute obscenity; the cou-ple was convicted.

On appeal, this federal appellate court affirmed the convictions, holding that the crime of "knowingly us[ing] a facility or means of interstate commerce for the pur-pose of distributing obscene materials" did not require proof that the defendants had specific knowledge of the destination of each transmittal at the time it occurred.[32] Of interest in the Internet setting, in determining that the crime occurred in the second state, rather than in the originating state, the court placed considerable weight on its finding that "substantial evidence introduced at trial demonstrated that the . . . [bul-letin board service] was set up so members located in other jurisdictions could access and order [obscene] files which would then be instantaneously transmitted in inter-state commerce."[33]

If the reasoning of this appellate court is followed by the state courts, it appears that communication via computer constitutes sufficient contact with the foreign state to subject the communicator to local law requirements. Applied in the charitable solicitation regulation context, then, the import of this court decision is clear: Soliciting funds by means of the Internet, where users download Web pages residing in foreign jurisdictions, in all likelihood will constitute sufficient contact to subject the organization to the jurisdiction of the foreign state or states and therefore to the foreign charitable solicitation regime or regimes.

It must next be determined whether interstate communication of this nature constitutes *solicitation* encompassed by the fundraising regulation laws of the states. Although no definite answer can be divined from the language of any one statute, a brief survey of some state statutes strongly indicates that Internet solicitation will be held in many jurisdictions to be subject to regulation. For example, in one state, solicitation covered by the charitable solicitation act is defined as the making of a fundraising request "through any medium," regardless of whether any contribution is received. In another state, the charitable solicitation law applies to all "request[s] of any kind for a contribution." In another state, the law embraces "each request for a contribution." The statutory scheme in another state applies to "any request, plea, entreaty, demand or invitation, or attempt thereof, to give money or property, in connection with which . . . any appeal is made for charitable purposes." In still another state, the law applies to organizations "soliciting or collecting by agents or solicitors, upon ways or in any other public places within the commonwealth to which the public have a right of access."

Certainly it is difficult to see how Internet fundraising is not caught by any of these strikingly broad provisions. As currently written, then, the statutes of at least five states can easily be construed to reach Internet charitable fundraising.

Indeed, it is likely that most, if not all, of the state charitable fundraising regulation regimes may be so construed and that those statutes that fail as currently written can be appropriately amended without much trouble.

Charleston Principles

If the assumption is that the solicitation of funds by charitable and other nonprofit organizations by means of the Internet constitutes fundraising in every state (and municipality), then, as suggested, the charitable community is facing an enormous burden. Some in the regulatory sector realize that, if this technically is the law, some form of relief for charities that solicit gifts is warranted.

To this end, the National Association of State Charity Officials (NASCO) developed guidelines to assist charitable organizations that solicit contributions, and their fundraisers, in deciding whether it is necessary to register fundraising efforts in the states when the solicitations are made by e-mail or on the organizations' Web sites. The guidelines are a product of discussion that was initiated at NASCO's 1999 annual conference in Charleston, South Carolina. Hence the guidelines are termed the *Charleston Principles (Principles)*.[34] The Principles are not law but rather, nonbinding guidance to NASCO members.[35]

The Charleston Principles rest on this true proposition: "Existing registration statutes generally, of their own terms, encompass and apply to Internet solicitations." An unstated proposition is that it is untenable to require registration of all charities soliciting gifts by means of the Internet, and their fundraisers, in all states with registration requirements. Thus, the scope of potential registration must be narrowed or, as the Principles put it, state charity officials should "address the issue of who has to register where."

The Principles differentiate between entities that are domiciled in a state and those that are domiciled outside the state. (An entity is domiciled in a state if its principal place of business is in that state.)

An entity that is domiciled in a state and uses the Internet to conduct charitable solicitations in that state must, according to the Principles, register in that state. This reflects the prevailing view that the Internet is a form of communication, and the law does not make a distinction between that form of communication and another (such as use of regular mail). The rule applies "without regard to whether the Internet solicitation methods it uses are passive or interactive, maintained by itself or another entity with which it contracts, or whether it conducts solicitations in any other manner."

Matters become more complex in cases where an entity is fundraising in a state in which it is not domiciled. Registration in the state is nonetheless required if:

- The organization's non-Internet activities alone are sufficient to require registration;
- It solicits contributions through an interactive Web site; and
- Either the entity
  - Specifically targets persons physically located in the state for solicitation, or
  - Receives contributions from donors in the state on a repeated and ongoing basis or a substantial basis through its Web site; or
  - The entity solicits contributions through a site that is not interactive but either specifically invites further offline activity to complete a contribution or establishes other contacts with that state, such as sending e-mail messages or other communications that promote the Web site, and the entity engages in one of the foregoing two activities.

Obviously, considerable line drawing will often be required in the actual application of these rules. The matter becomes even more interesting when some definitions are factored in.

An *interactive Web site* is a site that "permits a contributor to make a contribution, or purchase a product in connection with a charitable solicitation, by electronically completing the transaction, such as by submitting credit card information or authorizing an electronic funds transfer." These sites include those through which a donor "may complete a transaction online through any online mechanism processing a financial transaction even if completion requires the use of linked or redirected sites." A Web site is considered *interactive* if it has this capacity, irrespective of whether donors actually use it.

The phrase *specifically target persons physically located in the state for solicitation* means to engage in one of two practices:

1. Include on the Web site an express or implied reference to soliciting contributions from persons in that state; or
2. Otherwise affirmatively appeal to residents of the state, such as by advertising or sending messages to persons located in the state (electronically or otherwise) when the entity knows, or reasonably should know, that the recipient is physically located in the state.

Charities operating on a "purely local basis," or within a "limited geographic area," do not target states outside their operating area if their Web site makes clear in context that their fundraising focus is limited to that area, even if they receive contributions from outside that area on less than a repeated and ongoing basis or on a substantial basis.

To receive contributions from a state on a *repeated and ongoing basis* or a *substantial basis* means "receiving contributions within the entity's fiscal year, or relevant portion of a fiscal year, that are of sufficient volume to establish the regular or significant (as opposed to rare, isolated, or insubstantial) nature of these contributions."

States are encouraged to set, and communicate to the regulated entities, "numerical *[sic]* levels at which it *[sic]* will regard this criterion as satisfied." These levels should, the Principles say, define *repeated and ongoing* in terms of a number of contributions and *substantial* in terms of a total dollar amount of contributions or percentage of total contributions received by or on behalf of the charity. The meeting of one of these thresholds would give rise to a registration requirement but would not limit an enforcement action for deceptive solicitations.

Another Principle is that an entity that solicits via e-mail in a particular state is to be treated the same as one that solicits by means of telephone or direct mail, if the soliciting party knew or reasonably should have known that the recipient was a resident of or was physically located in that state.

The Principles address the circumstance as to whether a charity is required to register in a particular state when the operator of a Web site, through which contributions for that charity are solicited or received, is required to register but the charity does not independently satisfy the registration criteria. If the law of the state does not universally require the registration of all charities on whose behalf contributions are solicited or received through a commercial fundraiser, commercial co-venturer, or fundraising counsel who is required to register, then the state should independently apply the criteria to each charity and only require registration by charities that independently meet the tests. If, however, the law of the state universally requires registration of all charities under these circumstances, the state should consider whether, as a matter of "prosecutorial discretion, public policy, and the prioritized use of limited resources," it would take action to enforce registration requirements as to charities that do not independently meet the criteria.

Still another Principle is that solicitations for the sale of a product or service that include a representation that some portion of the price shall be devoted to a charitable organization or charitable purpose (commercial co-venturing, charitable sales promotion, or cause-related marketing) shall be governed by the same standards as otherwise set out in the Principles governing charitable solicitations.

There are two exclusions from the registration requirements (although they really are not exclusions at all). One is that maintaining or operating a Web site that does not contain a solicitation of contributions but merely provides program services by means of the Internet does not, by itself, invoke a requirement to register. This is the case even if unsolicited contributions are received.

The other exclusion is for entities that solely provide administrative, supportive, or technical services to charities without providing substantive content or advice concerning substantive content; they are not required to register. These entities include Internet service providers and organizations that do no more than process online transactions for a separate firm that operates a Web site or provides similar services. This exclusion does not, of course, encompass professional fundraisers, fundraising counsel, or commercial co-venturers.

The Principles provide that state charity officials "recognize that the burden of compliance by charitable organizations and their agents, professional fundraisers, commercial co-venturers and/or professional fundraising counsel should be kept reasonable in relation to the benefits to the public achieved by registration." Projects to create "common forms," such as the unified registration statement, are "strongly encouraged."

State charity offices are also "strongly encouraged" to publish their registration and reporting forms, their laws and regulations, and other related information on the Internet to facilitate registration and reporting by charitable organizations and their agents.

The Principles encourage development of information technology infrastructure to facilitate electronic registration and reporting. Also encouraged is Internet posting by charitable organizations of their application for recognition of exempt status, the IRS ruling, the most recent annual information returns, and their state registration statement(s). (This latter practice, of course, is also encouraged by the federal tax law, which obviates the need to provide hard copies of these federal documents to requestors when they are made available on the Internet.[36])

Internet Communications

There should be little doubt that those comprising the state regulatory community, and probably most in the local regulatory community, believe—at least as a matter of pure law—that fundraising by charitable and other nonprofit organizations by means of the Internet amounts to fundraising in every state and every locality. That is, the charities are soliciting contributions in those jurisdictions by means of this form of communication, whether it be by e-mail or Web site posting. The Charleston Principles, for example, say just that.

Although the deployment of the language is accurate and the logic impeccable, the outcome, of course, is, as a matter of real-world functioning, absurd. Only the largest of charities can afford to be and stay in compliance with such a massive regulatory system—and even in this setting, dollars are unnecessarily being diverted from charitable ends to the coffers of the regulators. The Charleston Principles are a nice first step, an attempt to frame a construct for enforcement of existing law. The Principles themselves are not, as noted, law, and there is no guarantee that a particular state will adhere, in whole or in part, to the guidelines.

There is another aspect of all this. The Principles do not reflect the fact that, once a person has contributed to a charitable organization by means of the Internet, that charity is almost certain to follow up that gift with a request for another one. That request may be by letter or telephone call, and not electronic, so that the Principles do not apply. At that point, of course, the charity is now soliciting in the states by other means—and would be required to register, annually report, and otherwise comply with charitable solicitation acts.

One remedial approach would be to jettison this statutory system, with its crazy-quilt of differing laws, and replace it with a federal rule. It is safe to say, however, that federal preemption of this or any other aspect of state law regulation of charitable fundraising is not imminent.[37] (In this setting, uniform statutes or uniform reports would not fully solve the problem, even if such miracles could be accomplished.)

Another approach would be to amend the state charitable solicitation acts to exempt Internet communications from regulation. That is, definitions of the term *solicit* could be trimmed to exclude gift solicitations by e-mail or Web site posting. There is no reasonable likelihood of that happening either.

There may be hope that some aspects of this matter can be resolved by the courts——holding that states (and localities) lack jurisdiction to regulate charities and fundraising professionals when the only nexus is Internet communications. As far as is known, the Commonwealth of Pennsylvania is the only state to have formally asserted, through its attorney general's office, that Internet fundraising may require registration and reporting in that jurisdiction by both the charitable organization involved and the Internet company facilitating the fundraising.

There has been one development in this regard. A federal district court held that a county ordinance regulating charitable fundraising is inapplicable to fundraising consultants who lack minimal contacts with the county.[38] (This decision does not pertain to charitable organizations that are the entities soliciting the contributions.) The case essentially concerns the matter of jurisdiction. The argument, which the court ultimately accepted, was that direct mail consultants do not have the requisite contact with citizens of the county.

This decision is a due process case. To be subject to jurisdiction of a government, a person has to have at least "minimum contacts" with that jurisdiction. As the appellate court stated the matter, the "regulated party must have performed some act by which it purposefully avails itself of the privilege of conducting activities within" the jurisdiction. The "unilateral act of a third party is not sufficient to create the requisite contacts."[39] Also: "An abstract, indirect, and unaimed level of involvement with the [c]ounty would not be sufficient for the [c]ounty to regulate" the fundraising consultants.[40]

The specific point of the case is that direct mail and comparable consultants, who are not involved in the solicitation of charitable gifts in a jurisdiction and do not have any contacts with that jurisdiction, cannot constitutionally be compelled to comply with the fundraising regulation law of that jurisdiction. The court agreed with the argument that the consultants "are not aware of where solicitations are mailed, they do not advise charities on where to send solicitations, and they do not control where solicitations are sent."[41] It was found that "no agency relationship exists" and that the consultants "do not exercise a sufficient level of control because the facts clearly indicate that the [charitable] client has final approval."[42] The court went on to find that the consultants "are not sufficiently involved in the solicitation process to justify [the county's] exercise of legislative jurisdiction" and that "sufficient contacts" do not exist between the consultants and the county.[43] This led to the conclusion that the county's application of the ordinance to the consultants is "unreasonable and violates due process."[44]

If this decision is correct, it means that individuals who and companies that consult with nonprofit organizations as to fundraising campaigns by mail are not subject to regulation by a government if they are not involved in the direction of the solicitations or control the fundraising program of the charitable organization. This rule of law applies equally where the government involved is a state, a county, or a city. It also should apply in the context of solicitations of charitable gifts by means of the Internet. Indeed, this rule of law may be extended to philanthropic organizations in the Internet setting.

Otherwise, assuming that the law cannot be meaningfully altered, the only feasible approach to resolution of this dilemma is to change the way the law is complied with. The power of the Internet can be harnessed to facilitate filing with the states by fundraising charities online. It does not appear that it would be that difficult, relatively speaking, to construct a system where charities could register with all of the states online. (This should be done irrespective of whether the charity is fundraising via the Internet.) Rather than regard Internet technology as exacerbating the problem, the technology should be seen as resolving it. All of this may have a turnout of some irony: The very technology (the Internet) that is bringing state fundraising regulation to the brink of collapse (if enforced) may be the very same technology that keeps it in place and enhances it.

CHARITABLE GIVING PROGRAMS ADMINISTRATION

As the nonprofit sector steadily grows and charitable giving steadily increases, federal and state law regulating the fundraising process steadily proliferates. One of the many aspects of this accretion of the law is a compounding of the burden of administering (other than gift solicitation efforts) a charitable giving program. The law that has developed, and is developing, in this area applies to charitable giving programs undertaken by means of the Internet.

Introduction

Abuses of the charitable contribution deduction are inflaming the IRS and Congress. One of the transgressions that is the genesis of much law is the transfer of money to a charitable organization in a transaction that is not a gift or is only partially a gift, where the transferor claims a charitable contribution deduction for all of the money paid over to the charity.

The IRS, for many years, has published its views on this subject, which are that (1) payments of this nature generally are not contributions at all (let alone deductible ones) and (2) if some portion of the payment is in excess of the value of a good or service received in exchange for the payment, only that excess component of the payment is a deductible gift.[45] Transactions of this nature are, however, difficult to detect, even in the context of an IRS audit, and the IRS did not have much in the way of sanctions to deploy when transgressions were found.[46]

Another issue in this regard is valuation of property. This matter can arise when a donor transfers property to a charitable organization and the issue becomes determination of the amount of the charitable deduction. On the flip side, there may have to be valuation of property received by a person in exchange for a payment, as part of the process of calculating the charitable deduction for the amount of the payment that exceeds the value of the property. Sometimes this valuation exercise was undertaken by the donor, patron, and/or charity, without benefit of assistance from a competent, independent appraiser.

A consequence of all of this is a battery of law, most of it fairly recent, designed to eliminate these abuses and punish them when they occur.

Substantiation Requirements

Law in General

Most transfers of money or property that are claimed to give rise to federal tax deductions have to be substantiated—that is, proved. Inasmuch as the burden of proof is on the taxpayer, the law requires the collection and retention of a certain amount of evidence to sustain the deduction should the IRS elect to examine it.

As to charitable contributions, however, special substantiation rules apply. Under these rules, donors who make a separate charitable contribution of $250 or more in a year, for which they claim a federal income tax charitable contribution deduction, must obtain written substantiation of the gift from the donee charitable organization. The sanction: If the substantiation is not timely provided, the donor is not entitled to the charitable deduction that would otherwise be available.

Specifically, the federal income tax charitable deduction is not allowed for a separate contribution of $250 or more unless the donor has written substantiation from the charitable donee of the contribution in the form of a contemporaneous written acknowledgment.[47] Thus, donors cannot rely solely on a canceled check as substantiation for a gift of $250 or more.

An acknowledgment meets this requirement if it includes the following information:

- The amount of money and a description (but not value) of any property other than money that was contributed
- Whether the donee organization provided any goods or services in consideration, in whole or in part, for any money or property contributed
- A description and good-faith estimate of the value of any goods or services involved or, if the goods or services consist solely of intangible religious benefits, a statement to that effect[48]

An acknowledgment is considered to be contemporaneous if the contributor obtains the acknowledgment on or before the earlier of (1) the date on which the donor filed a tax return for the tax year in which the contribution was made or (2) the due date (including any extension or extensions) for filing the return.[49] Even where a good or service is not provided to a donor, a statement to that effect must appear in the acknowledgment.

As noted, this substantiation rule applies with respect to separate payments. Separate payments generally are treated as separate contributions and are not aggregated for purposes of applying the $250 threshold. Where contributions are paid by withholding from wages and payment by the employer to a donee charitable organization, the deduction from each paycheck is treated as a separate payment.[50] Gifts of this nature may be substantiated by documents such as a pay receipt, Form W-2, or a pledge card.[51] The substantiation requirement does not apply to contributions made by means of payroll deduction unless the employer deducts $250 or more from a single paycheck for the purpose of making a charitable gift.

The written acknowledgment of a separate gift is not required to take any particular form. Thus, acknowledgments may be made by letter, post-card, or computer-generated form. A donee charitable organization may prepare a separate acknowledgment for each contribution or may provide donors with periodic (such as annual) acknowledgments that set forth the required information for each contribution of $250 or more made by the donor during the period.

A good faith estimate is the donee charitable organization's estimate of the fair market value of any goods or services, "without regard to the manner in which the organization in fact made that estimate."[52] The phrase *goods or services* means money, property, services, benefits, and privileges.[53]

A charitable organization is considered as providing goods or services in consideration for a person's payment if, at the time the person makes the payment, the person receives or expects to receive goods or services in exchange for the payment.[54] Goods or services a donee charity provides in consideration for a payment by a person includes goods or services provided in a year other than the year in which the payment is made.

If a partnership or S corporation makes a charitable contribution of $250 or more, the partnership or S corporation is treated as the taxpayer for gift substantiation purposes.[55] Therefore, the partnership or S corporation must substantiate the contribution with a contemporaneous written acknowledgment from the donee charity before reporting the contribution on its information return for the appropriate year and must maintain the contemporaneous written acknowledgment in its records. A partner in a partnership or a shareholder of an S corporation is not required to obtain any additional substantiation for his or her share of the partnership's or S corporation's charitable contribution.

If a person's payment to a charitable organization is matched, in whole or in part, by another payor, and the person received goods or services in consideration for the payment and some or all of the matched payment, the goods or services are treated as provided in consideration for the person's payment and not in consideration for the matching payment.[56]

It is the responsibility of the donor to obtain the substantiation document and maintain it in his or her records. (Again, as noted, the charitable contribution deduction is dependent on compliance with these rules.)

A charitable organization that knowingly provides a false written substantiation document to a donor may become subject to the penalty for aiding and abetting an understatement of tax liability.[57]

ePhilanthropy Rules

Clearly, the substantiation requirements apply with respect to contributions to charitable organizations made by means of the Internet. This is the case where (1) the gift is solicited by an Internet communication and paid or transferred to the charity in some other manner (such as by cash, check, or credit card), or (2) where the gift is both solicited and consummated by use of the Internet. In the latter circumstance, the charity may directly accept contributions by means of the Internet or do so through a third party that provides a secure connection for credit card transactions. Thus, a donor who makes a separate charitable contribution of $250 or more in a year, by means of the Internet, and intends to claim a federal income tax charitable contribution deduction, must obtain written substantiation of the gift from the charitable organization.

Inasmuch as all of the elements of these requirements are applicable in instances of gifts made by use of the Internet, the only aspect of these rules that was uncertain, until recently, was the matter of a *written* acknowledgment.

In any event, the IRS has attempted to resolve this matter. In early 2002, the agency—without fanfare or even notice—revised the online text of its publication on charitable contributions and the substantiation requirements.[58] In this publication, the IRS wrote that a charitable organization "can provide either a paper copy of the acknowledgment to the donor, or an organization can provide the acknowledgment electronically, such as via e-mail addressed to the donor."[59]

Quid Pro Quo Contribution Rules

Law in General

The federal tax law imposes certain disclosure requirements on charitable organizations that receive quid pro quo contributions. A quid pro quo contribution is a payment "made partly as a contribution and partly in consideration for goods or services provided to the payor by the donee organization."[60] The term does not include a payment to an organization, operated exclusively for religious purposes, in return for which the donor receives solely an intangible religious benefit that generally is not sold in a commercial transaction outside the donative context.[61]

Specifically, if a charitable organization receives a quid pro quo contribution in excess of $75, the organization must, in connection with the solicitation or receipt of the contribution, provide a written statement that:

- Informs the donor that the amount of the contribution that is deductible for federal income tax purposes is limited to the excess of the amount of any money and the value of any property other than money contributed by the donor over the value of the goods or services provided by the organization, and
- Provides the donor with a good-faith estimate of the value of the goods or services.[62]

It is intended that this disclosure be made in a manner that is reasonably likely to come to the attention of the donor. Therefore, immersion of the disclosure in fine print in a larger document is inadequate.

A charitable organization may use "any reasonable methodology in making a good-faith estimate, provided it applies the methodology in good faith."[63] A good-faith estimate of the value of goods or services that are not generally available in a commercial transaction may be determined by reference to the fair market value of similar or comparable goods or services. Goods or services may be similar or comparable even though they do not have the "unique qualities" of the goods or services that are being valued.[64]

No part of this type of payment can be considered a deductible charitable contribution unless two elements exist: [65]

1. The patron makes a payment in an amount that is in fact in excess of the fair market value of the goods or services received, and
2. The patron intends to make a payment in an amount that exceeds that fair market value.

This requirement of the element of intent may sometimes be relatively harmless, in that the patron is likely to know the charity's good-faith estimate amount in advance of the payment and thus cannot help but have this intent. Still, proving intent is not always easy.

There is a penalty, imposed on donee charitable organizations, for violation of these requirements. It is $10 for each contribution in respect of which the organization fails to make the required disclosure; the total penalty with respect to a particular fundraising event or mailing may not exceed $5,000.[66] This penalty may not be imposed if it is shown that the failure to disclose was due to reasonable cause.[67]

ePhilanthropy Regulation

Again, clearly, the rules as to quid pro quo contributions apply with respect to these contributions made by means of the Internet. These rules require that charitable organizations receiving these contributions provide written statements to payors containing certain information.

The IRS has asked whether a charitable organization meets the requirements as to quid pro quo contributions "with a Web page confirmation that may be printed out by the contributor or by sending a confirmation e-mail [message] to the donor."[68] This is, in essence, the same question that was asked in the gift substantiation context.

The same considerations apply in this context as in the setting of the gift substantiation rules. That is, the IRS possesses the authority to regard printed Web page confirmations and copies of e-mail messages as writings for purposes of the quid pro quo contribution rules. In the modern era, it should be expected. In any event, this conclusion is also compelled by the Electronic Signatures Act. Nonetheless, although the IRS has approved the use of electronic messages in the context of charitable gift substantiation, the agency has yet to make a similar announcement as to quid pro quo disclosures.

Vehicle Donation Programs

The IRS wrote that "[i]t is now common to turn on your radio, television or the [I]nternet and be exposed to an advertisement encouraging you to donate your car to charity."[69] Thus, it is clear—it would be in any event—that vehicle donation programs involving Internet communications are subject to the same bodies of law that pertain to these types of gifts made otherwise.

There is nothing inherently improper in the solicitation of contributions of used automobiles, other motor vehicles, boats, and the like by philanthropic organizations. Nonetheless, the IRS is concerned about "certain practices that occur in some car donation programs"—indeed, the agency has proclaimed this to be a "growing area of noncompliance."[70]

The IRS has said that it is not concerned about charities that solicit these vehicles for use in their programs (such as sheltered workshops and programs for refurbishment of cars to be given to the needy). The IRS also is not concerned with small charities that receive a few cars and resell them. The focus of the IRS is on organizations "who have permitted third party entrepreneurs to use their names to solicit contributions of cars; to plan and place advertising for donations; to take delivery on the cars (or pick them up) if they are not in running condition; to complete the legal paper work; and to sell them typically at auction or to junk yards or to scrap dealers." The IRS is dismayed that some charities "perform no oversight" in this process; they have "abdicated responsibility for the things that are done in their names." The IRS refers to these practices as "suspect vehicle donation plans or programs."

One of the principal issues in this area is a fact one, not a law one: valuation. The IRS is deeply troubled by advertisements that state or suggest that donors will be entitled to a deduction based on the full fair market value of the vehicle, such as the value stated in the Blue Book, when the vehicle is in poor or perhaps nonoperating condition. The IRS wrote that valuation methods "presume that the car is running and then evaluate it according to its condition, mileage, etc."

Therefore, the value of a used vehicle is, like the value of any item of property, based on its true condition. There may be a mere modicum of value—and hence not much of a charitable deduction. Philanthropic organizations need to be cautious and avoid an overstated tax deduction for the gift of a vehicle or similar property. The IRS issued guidance as to this valuation process.[71]

A contribution of a used vehicle to a charitable organization is likely to trigger the substantiation requirements. The recipient philanthropic organization must provide the donor with a contemporaneous written acknowledgment, which, although it does not have to assign a value to the vehicle, must be truthful and sufficient so as to provide the appropriate descriptive basis for determining that value. As the IRS indelicately noted, the charity involved "must ensure that this paperwork is done accurately because there are penalties for aiding and abetting in the preparation of a false return."[72]

A contribution of a used vehicle to a philanthropic organization may well require application of the appraisal requirements (see following section). The IRS's observation that the philanthropic involved "must ensure that this paperwork is done accurately because there are penalties for aiding and abetting in the preparation of a false return" was also offered up in the context of the appraisal rules.

Other Requirements

Contributions of most items of charitable deduction property that have a value of more than $5,000 are subject to certain appraisal requirements.[73] These requirements are applicable in situations where property is contributed to a charitable organization in a transaction involving an Internet communication.

The determination of a federal income tax charitable contribution deduction for a gift of property to charity requires valuation of the property. This requirement pertains in situations where property is contributed to a charitable organization in a transaction involving an Internet communication.

Charitable donees that make dispositions of contributed property are required to file an information return with the IRS.[74] This requirement applies to original and successor donees.[75] The property that is involved generally consists of items or groups of similar items for which the donor claimed a charitable deduction of more than $5,000 and was included in an appraisal summary.[76]

OTHER BODIES OF LAW

Philanthropic organizations should be cognizant of other bodies of federal tax law that can be applicable in the ePhilanthropy context. They are the private inurement doctrine, the benefit doctrine, the intermediate sanctions rules, the royalty exception, the accuracy-related penalties, and emerging principles of privacy.

Private Inurement Doctrine

Philanthropic organizations should remain cognizant of the private inurement doctrine.[77] Pursuant to this doctrine, a transaction between the organization and a person who is an insider with respect to it can, if the terms and conditions of the transaction are not reasonable, cause the organization to lose or be denied federal tax-exempt status. An illustration of this is payment of excessive compensation to a key employee.

Private Benefit Doctrine

A philanthropic organization may not serve private interests, other than incidentally. This rule of law is the *private benefit doctrine*.[78] The word *incidental* in this context has a qualitative and a quantitative meaning. To be incidental in a qualitative sense, the benefit to the public cannot be achieved without necessarily benefiting certain private individuals. Also, if an organization's activity provides a substantial benefit to private interests, even indirectly, it will negate charitability and thus tax-exempt status. The substantiality of the private benefit is measured in the context of the overall public benefit conferred by the activity. This doctrine can be triggered, even if an insider is not involved. Again, the sanction is revocation or denial of tax-exempt status.

Intermediate Sanctions

The intermediate sanctions rules apply in this context as well. These rules parallel the private inurement doctrine rules, the main difference being that the penalties fall on the insider (termed, in this context, a disqualified person). The private inurement transaction is called an *excess benefit transaction*, triggering tax penalties and correction obligations on the part of the disqualified person.[79]

Royalty Exception

Royalties paid to a tax-exempt organization are not subject to the unrelated business income tax.[80] Thus, philanthropic organizations often try to structure certain types of fundraising arrangements, unrelated business transactions, and other relationships so that the resulting income flows to the organization as a royalty.

Penalties

The federal tax law contains a variety of penalties that can be applied for violation of various aspects of the law of fundraising and charitable giving. These penalties are part of a broader range of *accuracy-related penalties*.[81]

The accuracy-related penalty is determined as an amount to be added to the income tax equal to 20 percent of the portion of the underpayment.[82] This body of law relates to the portion of any underpayment that is attributable to one or more specified acts, including negligence, disregard of rules or regulations, any substantial understatement of income tax, any substantial income tax valuation misstatement, or any substantial estate or gift tax valuation understatement.[83]

Additional penalties may be applied in the context of charitable giving. One of them is the penalty for the promotion of a tax shelter.[84] Another penalty—one that the

IRS has often threatened philanthropic organizations with—is the penalty for aiding and abetting an understatement of tax liability.[85]

Privacy Principles

ePhilanthropy will struggle against existing and emerging principles of law concerning personal privacy. The ease of gathering and transmitting personal information electronically is astonishing. The relatively new concept of identity theft has become a part of national discourse. The difficulties the health care field is having coping with the health information privacy regulations issued by direction of the Health Insurance Portability and Accountability Act are illustrative of the future in this regard for philanthropic organizations in general.

CONCLUSION

The age of ePhilanthropy regulation is dawning. Ahead lies a vast range of legislation, regulations, rules, forms, instructions, and court opinions. Since almost all of this law and regulation is only in the future, fundraisers must cope with the daunting task of simultaneously generating charitable contributions and complying with the law—in a regulatory environment the contours of which are just emerging.

ABOUT THE AUTHOR

Bruce R. Hopkins is the country's leading authority on tax-exempt organizations and is a lawyer with the firm Polsinelli, Shalton Welte, Suelthaus P.C. He is also the author of more than 16 books, including *The Law of Intermediate Sanctions, The Legal Answer Book for Private Foundations, The Legal Answer Book for Nonprofit Organizations, The Law of Tax-Exempt Organizations, 8e, Private Foundations: Tax Law and Compliance, 2e,* and *Starting and Managing a Nonprofit Organization: A Legal Guide, 4e,* as well as the newsletter *Bruce R. Hopkins' Nonprofit Counsel,* all published by Wiley.

Specializing in the areas of corporate law and taxation, Bruce emphasizes the representation of nonprofit organizations. His clients include charitable and educational organizations, associations, colleges, universities, hospitals, other health care providers, religious organizations, business and professional associations, and private foundations. He serves many nonprofit organizations as general counsel; others use his services as special tax and/or fundraising counsel.

Hopkins's experience includes the establishment and qualification for tax exemption of nonprofit organizations, the establishment and operation of charitable and fundraising programs, and advice on matters such as public charity/private foundation qualification, intermediate sanctions, lobbying, political activities, the unrelated business income rules, and the involvement of nonprofits in partnerships and other joint ventures. His practice also encompasses collateral areas of law, such as postal laws and charitable fundraising regulation.

ENDNOTES

1. Some hints as to the areas of the federal tax law that will be the subject of ePhilanthropy regulation are found in a fascinating announcement issued by the IRS in 2000 requesting comments on a series of questions it posed (Ann. 2000-84, 2000-2 C.B. 385).
2. An attempt at this exercise is Hopkins, *The Nonprofits' Guide to Internet Communications Law* (New York: John Wiley & Sons, Inc., 2003).
3. "Tax-Exempt Organizations and Worldwide Web Fundraising and Advertising on the Internet," in the IRS's tax-exempt organizations continuing professional education technical instruction program textbook for the government's fiscal year 2000 ("IRS FY 2000 CPE Text on Exempt Organizations and Internet Use") at 64.
4. Tax Regulations ("Reg.") section ("§") 1.513-4 (concerning the corporate sponsorship rules).
5. Internal Revenue Code ("IRC") § 513(i).
6. IRS FY 2000 CPE Text at 74.
7. *Id*. at 70.
8. IRC § 513(c).
9. *United States v. American College of Physicians*, 475 U.S. 834, 849 (1986).
10. *Id*. at 849-850.
11. IRS Private Letter Ruling 9723046, where it was written that "[a]dvertising spots differ from mere expressions of recognition in that they may contain additional information about an advertiser's product, services or facilities, or function as a hypertext link to the advertiser."
12. IRS FY 2000 CPE Text at 74. All quotations of the IRS in this section are from this text.
13. E.g., Technical Advice Memorandum 9720002.
14. These generally are organizations that are tax-exempt pursuant to IRC § 501(a) by reason of description in IRC § 501(c) (6).
15. IRC § 513(i)(2)(B)(ii)(I).
16. *Id.*
17. IRC § 513(i)(2)(B)(ii)(I).
18. Reg. § 1.513-4(b).
19. Reg. § 1.512(a)-1(a).
20. *Id.*
21. Reg. § 1.512(a)-1(c).
22. E.g., *Rensselaer Polytechnic Institute v. Commissioner*, 732 F.2d 1058 (2d Cir. 1984).
23. Reg. § 1.512(a)-(d).
24. Although the rules are not *law*, these approaches are also reflected in standards promulgated by the Financial Accounting Standards Board and guidelines published by the American Institute of Certified Public Accountants.
25. *United States v. American Bar Endowment*, 477 U.S. 105 (1986).
26. *American Bar Endowment v. United States*, 84-1 U.S.T.C. 9204 (Ct. Cl. 1984).
27. *Id*. at 83,350. Indeed, the court observed (seemingly with the Internet in mind) that, "[o]ver the years, charities have adopted fundraising schemes that are increasingly complex and sophisticated, relying on many business techniques" (id.)
28. *Id.*
29. In general, Hopkins, *The Law of Fundraising, Third Edition* (New York: John Wiley & Sons, Inc., 2002), particularly Chapters 3 and 4.
30. State v. Blakney, 361 N.E. 2d 567, 568 (Ohio 1975).
31. Moreover, fundraising by means of the Internet involves solicitation of contributions *internationally*, with all of the potential of country-by-country regulation of the process.
32. *United States v. Thomas*, 74 F2d 701 (6th Cir. 1996).
33. *Id*. at 709.

34. The text of the Principles is available at *www.nasconet.org.*
35. Nonetheless, the concept underlying the Principles is similar to the "sliding scale" analysis, by which Web sites were characterized on a continuum from active to passive, used in *Zippo Mfg. Co. v. Zippo Dot Com, Inc.*, 952 F. Supp. 1119 (WD. Pa. 1997).
36. IRC § 6104(d)(4).
37. It is interesting to compare this set of circumstances with those prevailing before the Electronic Signatures Act was enacted. In the latter case, Congress smartly—under comparable and compelling conditions-preempted state law except where a certain form of uniform act was in place. This approach lends itself nicely as a solution to the burdens imposed by the multifarious state charitable solicitation acts.
38. *American Charities for Reasonable Fundraising Regulation, Inc. et al. v. Pinellas County*, 189 E Supp. 2d 1319 (M.D. Fla. 2001), on remand, 221 F3d 1211 (11th Cir. 2000).
39. *Id.*, 221 E.3d at 1216.
40. *Id.* at 1217.
41. *Id.*, 189 F. Supp. 2d at 1329.
42. *Id.* at 1331.
43. *Id.*
44. *Id.*
45. E.g., Rev. Rul. 67-246, 1967-2 C.B. 104.
46. The IRS conceded that there were no sanctions for violations of its disclosure requirements (Private Letter Ruling 8832003).
47. IRC § 170(f)(8)(A).
48. IRC § 170(f)(8)(B); Reg. § 1.170A-13(f)(2).
49. IRC § 170(f)(8) (C); Reg. § 1.170A-13(f)(3).
50. Reg. § 1.170A-13(f)(11)(ii).
51. Reg. § 1.170A-13(f)(11)(i).
52. Reg. § 1.170A-13(f)(7).
53. Reg. § 1.170A-13(f)(5).
54. Reg. § 1.170A-13(f)(6).
55. Reg. § 1.170A-13(f)(15).
56. Reg. § 1.170A-13(f)(17).
57. IRC § 6701.
58. Charitable Contributions—Substantiation and Disclosure Requirements (IRS Pub. 1771) (revised in March, 2002).
59. This rule is also stated in IRS Notice 2002-25, 2002-15 I.R.B. 743.
60. IRC § 6115.
61. *Id.*
62. IRC § 6115(a).
63. Reg. § 1.6115-1(a)(1).
64. Reg. § 1.6115-1(a)(2).
65. Reg. § 1.170A-1(h)(1).
66. IRC § 6714(a).
67. IRC § 6714(b).
68. Ann. 2000-84, *supra* note 1.
69. IRS FY 2000 CPE Text.
70. IRS FY 2000 CPE Text, Section T, Part I. All quotations from the IRS in this section are from this CPE Text article.
71. Rev. Rul. 2002-67, 2002-47 I.R.B. 873.
72. This penalty is the subject of IRC § 6701. In a relevant application of this penalty, it was assessed against an individual who had a practice, in his capacity of president of a charitable organization, of providing donors of used vehicles with documentation supporting a charitable deduction based on full fair market value when in fact he knew that "many of

the donated vehicles could only be sold for salvage or scrap" (Technical Advice Memorandum 200243057).
73. Reg. § 1.170A-13(c).
74. Form 8282.
75. IRC § 6050L.
76. Form 8283. These rules do not apply to gifts of money or certain publicly traded securities.
77. See Hopkins, *The Law of Tax-Exempt Organizations, Eighth Edition* (New York: John Wiley & Sons, Inc., 2003) §§ 19.1-19.4.
78. *Id.* § 19.10.
79. In general, see Hopkins, *The Law of Intermediate Sanctions: A Guide for Nonprofits* (New York: John Wiley & Sons, Inc., 2003).
80. IRC § 512(b)(2).
81. IRC § 6662.
82. IRC § 6662(a).
83. IRC § 6662(b).
84. IRC § 6700.
85. IRC § 6701.

CHAPTER 19

Evaluating ePhilanthropy Programs

James M. Greenfield, ACFRE, FAHP
J.M. Greenfield & Associates

A charities Web site has to provide the opportunity for relationship-building. It must provide communication. It must be entertainingly interactive, and it must provide an opportunity to give.[1]

—Paul Clolery, 1999

INTRODUCTION TO NONPROFIT PERFORMANCE MEASUREMENT

This chapter is about how to evaluate the intriguing and inventive Internet strategies described in this book for marketing, communications, and fundraising purposes. To be evaluated for success, each must be able to demonstrate how it builds and enhances relationships with those being served by nonprofit organizations, as well as demonstrate that its performance has been efficient as well as cost-effective. In a word, *accountability*. Accountability is a big, scary word, and more of it is required of every nonprofit organization today in their use of *ePhilanthropy* or not. Accountability is about reporting quantitative as well as qualitative results of outputs realized, defining success factors, and measuring outcomes achieved for the common good, each a calculable benefit that the organization has been entrusted to perform. "Not only is it [accountability] important for nonprofit organizations, especially philanthropic ones, to be open about the things they do, and how and why they do them, it is also important that they be ready to explain and generally be accountable for their choices. This is an extension of the implicit social contract of privilege and trust these organizations enjoy in our society."[2] Good faith, public confidence, and trust are all implied. Today, good works have to be visible, quantifiable, and the organizations transparent.

Internet technology abounds as does its methods for measurement. What any organization must do, to begin its assessments, is identify clear objectives for use of this technology. Exhibit 19.1 provides a list of valuable criteria, along with a means to score each for their application. Each element is measurable, and while all are capable of unique insight into performance characteristics, some priority must be assigned to

EXHIBIT 19.1   Assessment Criteria for Marketing and Communications

	Score				
	Low			High	
Broadened base of support	1	2	3	4	5
Comprehensive online strategy	1	2	3	4	5
Constituent relationship management	1	2	3	4	5
Events management	1	2	3	4	5
Improved delivery of services	1	2	3	4	5
Improved donations	1	2	3	4	5
Improved Web site	1	2	3	4	5
Increased access to supporters	1	2	3	4	5
Increased advocacy	1	2	3	4	5
Increased involvement	1	2	3	4	5
Increased outreach	1	2	3	4	5
Increased support base	1	2	3	4	5
Mobilized supporters	1	2	3	4	5
Personalized communications	1	2	3	4	5
Reduced costs	1	2	3	4	5
Reports of results and outcomes	1	2	3	4	5
Synchronized data	1	2	3	4	5
Time utilization and cost savings	1	2	3	4	5
Median Score:					

Source: With appreciation to Vinay Bhagat and CONVIO for sharing this list of assessment benefits.

those the organization seeks to track as most important to its Internet use. *Data mining* is a term that refers to both tracking and reporting methods as well as depth of analysis.

Nonprofit organizations, their boards, administrators, and public affairs staff must also be able to prove, using valid measurement tools, that each of their Internet applications used for marketing, communication, and fundraising strategies is creative, convincing, ethical, resourceful, and successful. They also must be able to demonstrate how these three outreach functions, with the addition of ePhilanthropy technology, are valuable as aids that enhance the mission, vision, and values of the organization, improve its relationships with donors, and advance the cause. This chapter attempts to offer how this measurement can be performed.

The challenge of successful coordination of day-to-day activities in traditional marketing, communications, and solicitation activities using online and offline options in concert requires a new look at evaluation techniques. Several performance measurements are needed to evaluate how all three can and should work together in all avenues of public affairs. Desired outcomes also must be defined to establish success factors, to quantify what results are to be measured, and to be able to demonstrate whether they achieved designed objectives or made any difference. Although achieving such proof might require some honest work internally, methods and tools must be found in order for these assessments to be conducted with consistency to be accepted by board members, administrators, donors, volunteers, and the general public. Only with good tools, good data, and a fair and open-minded analysis can reasonable men and women evaluate results, consider improvements, and reach good decisions about their continued and expanded usage to deliver benefits to their community in accordance with their mission. And, when limited budget and staff resources are involved, decisions also must be able to illustrate that they are both effective and cost-efficient.

Several challenges exist in how to demonstrate value as well as beneficial outcomes of any nonprofit organization. "Accountability in the voluntary sector is multilayered—to different audiences, for a variety of activities and outcomes, through many different means. This multidimensional nature is the principle complexity of accountability in the voluntary sector."[3] Further adding to this challenge are the realities that "models are imperfect, assumptions can be varied, uncertainty is pervasive."[4] To begin the process of demonstrating value and beneficial outcomes using ePhilanthropy, one needs to appreciate that nonprofit organizations are not the same in how they conduct their public affairs activities. Much depends on multiple intangibles such as geographic location, demographic client mix, financial strength, image and reputation, local political and regulatory restrictions, and more, all of which influence how they apply Internet technology in their ePhilanthropy marketing, communications, and fundraising activities. It is also true that public affairs programs do not and will not perform the same for every organization using these methods. The reasons are simple: Nonprofit organizations exist for a range of purposes, have long or short histories with varying accomplishments, serve a vast array of public needs, have varying leadership styles, and exist in communities of all sizes and locations. They also cannot invest in technology at the same budget levels as others, especially for-profit enterprises, nor can they keep pace with its constantly evolving enhancements. Thus, efforts to compare the ePhilanthropy results of one nonprofit with another is extremely problematic and likely to be unproductive and misleading given such disparity in causes, geography, history, leadership, reporting methods, local environmental and economic conditions, and (most significantly), applications in technology. There also is, at present, an absence of unique guidelines or standards for nonprofit technology applications, including criteria for performance measurement, standards for evaluation, uniform success factors for self-assessment, and more.

To begin this evaluation, each of these three internal management areas ought to be scrutinized against the specific operational objectives they are charged to fulfill in order to define and measure their success. They each have separate goals and different evaluation criteria (see Exhibit 19.2, where an average score of 3.0 to 3.5 in each area is commendable). They also must coordinate, cooperate, and communicate together. Such unity is not easily accomplished but well worth the effort because there are efficiencies and effectiveness benefits plus consistency of messages delivered to desired audiences. One of the best applications of Internet technology is its volume and variety of message opportunities, plus its "live" personal interactions. Each form of use can and ought to be assessed for its service to and support of the organization's mission, vision, and values, as well as facilitating the desired responses each tactic is charged to achieve. "Evaluations must be able to analyze results, assess strengths and weaknesses, and audit all systems related to overall performance. Measuring results at regular intervals provides the advantage to make decisions, to modify plans, to guard against errors, and to improve results. Performance studies illustrate productivity, profitability, and progress according to plans . . . [r]esults ought to be fully accountable for positive returns based on the application of principles of professional practice."[5]

EXHIBIT 19.2   Analysis of Coordination of Marketing, Communications, and Fund Development Goals and Objectives

		Score			
	Low			High	
Marketing Objectives					
Identify target markets	1	2	3	4	5
Establish an image	1	2	3	4	5
Create clients for programs	1	2	3	4	5
Elicit a positive response	1	2	3	4	5
Stimulate the public to act	1	2	3	4	5
Subtotal:					
Communications Objectives					
Inform and educate	1	2	3	4	5
Tell a story; repeat it often	1	2	3	4	5
Report results, deeds, outcomes	1	2	3	4	5
Build confidence and trust	1	2	3	4	5
Build community consensus	1	2	3	4	5
Fund Development Objectives					
Friend raising and relationship building	1	2	3	4	5
Develop a willingness to volunteer	1	2	3	4	5
Develop a willingness to give	1	2	3	4	5
Develop gifts to meet priority needs	1	2	3	4	5
Provide continuous contact with donors	1	2	3	4	5
Subtotal:					
Grand Total:					

Source: James M. Greenfield, *Fund Raising: Evaluating and Managing the Fund Development Process,* 2nd ed. (New York: John Wiley & Sons, Inc., 1999), 60. Used with permission.

Marketing, communications, and fundraising are, first, among all other operational criteria for success, time-tested methods and proven techniques for the exchange of information with a variety of publics for multiple purposes and to stimulate responses. Each is designed to broaden public awareness, develop consensus of value, recruit friends and supporters, and build lasting relationships between people and causes. ePhilanthropy is the newest and best method to aid in achieving these objectives. Nonprofit organizations and their leaders should accept the challenge of making the best use of ePhilanthropy to build up and expand upon their corps of informed, enthusiastic, and committed advocates, volunteers, and donors, as well as satisfied clients, customers, students, and patients. Organizations also need people and institutions that will give generously to improve humanity, help to save lives, advocate the environment, deliver benefits to those in need, and more. The overall goal is to achieve consensus among the many who, convinced of the value of these efforts, will step forward to ensure that support in time, talent, and treasure will be delivered where and when it is needed. How to evaluate these results and to answer fully the public's accountability questions is the subject of this chapter.

INTERNET SUPPORT TO PUBLIC AFFAIRS MANAGEMENT

There are five main areas where ePhilanthropy is best deployed to support the mission, vision, and values of every nonprofit organization. They are *access to information, marketing, communications, fundraising,* and *stewardship.* The Internet, today's preferred *information superhighway,* is an open transportation system that multiplies an organization's ability to chronicle its cause and to be fully open and accessible at the same time, globally. That's an enormous first! That's ePhilanthropy. All five areas also are available at the same time for unlimited research, promotion, information and education, solicitation, and accountability—another remarkable achievement, and one filled with opportunity.

Now come the questions: How best to apply them for their own ultimate purposes by adding ePhilanthropy? How best to use them together, strategically and tactically? How best to use them ethically? And, how best to evaluate their results?

- *Access to information: research.* Information is knowledge, and access to it is open to all on the Internet. Separate from the dictum to *seek only what you must and use only what you need,* research is a tool that consumes time and money unless guided with precision. Among its many ePhilanthropy uses are acquisition and analysis of data for decisions (market intelligence) along with prospect identification, background, and qualification of those best able to make gifts, grants, and contributions.
- *Marketing: promotion.* " . . . [T]he ultimate objective of any marketing effort is influencing behavior."[6] Not to imply manipulation, but audience behavior modification is permissible to promote a desired public benefit objective (e.g., stop smoking). Promotions target audiences for specific messages to encourage actions or to benefit others toward a common objective (better health).
- *Communications: information and education.* Integrating existing stand-alone publications onto a Web site is a passive first step. Proactive communications aim to inform and educate all to the organization's mission, vision, and values as well as to report on its current activities and results. This effort requires strategies for audience selection, message fit, timing, media form, and close coordination with all other outbound messages.
- *Fundraising: solicitation.* Gifts result from asking, a *contact sport* all nonprofits must engage in to raise money. Whether by mail, telephone, radio, television, fax, the Internet, e-mail, or in person, one-on-one contact is the best strategy to build relationships; money follows people who believe and who care. Personalization makes all the difference, and the best use of the Internet is as a personal medium.
- *Stewardship: accountability.* Nonprofit organizations are duty-bound to honor and respect their customers, clients, patients, or students and to be accountable for using all its resources to benefit these same individuals or causes. Codes of ethical and professional practice, privacy policies, donor's rights, and so on, are more than guides; they are standards of professional practice to be observed at all times.

As a general guideline for the optimal design and application of ePhilanthropy in marketing, communications, and fundraising strategies, first develop an understanding of how each can and ought to be put to best use on the Internet, as described in preceding chapters. Then, utilizing each for multiple purposes as well as working closely together in a spirit of coordination, cooperation, and communication, make every effort to ensure that all three can define their success factors and, where possible, to demonstrate that they are effective and cost-efficient. Among the ePhilanthropy goals nonprofit organizations ought to set for themselves is that "By promoting on-line resources and services through integration with traditional marketing and communication channels, organizations significantly increase the effectiveness of overall operations while providing additional options to their supporters."[7]

ePHILANTHROPY STRATEGIES FOR MARKETING AND COMMUNICATIONS

As marketing is about exchanges and nonprofit marketing is about social exchanges, a recent definition will refocus what marketing and communications are designed to achieve today: "[T]he process of planning and executing the conception, pricing, promotion, and distribution of ideas, goods, and services to create exchanges that satisfy individual and organizational goals. In the nonprofit world, products are services, are cause-related and mission driven, are intangible, perishable, simultaneous, and heterogeneous."[8] Given such criteria, results analysis needs to be detected and measured, especially to quantify how and how well these activities have had an impact on the quality of life in the community. "Unfortunately, the combination of that measurement difficulty and the glare of public accountability that faces many nonprofits leads managers too often to seek to achieve what is measurable rather than what is important."[9]

Internet use of marketing and communications applications requires careful planning and thorough preparation. "When formulating marketing objectives, there are several guidelines to follow. Most important, marketing objectives must be specific; an objective must be a precise statement of what is to be accomplished by the organization's marketing efforts. Objectives should be stated in simple, understandable terms, so that everyone involved in marketing knows exactly what is to be done. Further, objectives should be measurable—that is, they should be stated in quantitative terms. Finally, marketing objectives should be related to time, so that everyone knows when the objectives should be achieved."[10] Designing and following a clear strategy permits progress assessments during all phases of implementation, not only to redirect media, messages, methods, audiences and/or timing, but also to maximize limited budget and staff resources. What are the purposes, goals, and objectives that define success in a marketing and communications campaign? Is it reaching the right people, crafting the right message, or delivering at the right time? Or is it more strategic, seeking to enhance public awareness, improve image and reputation, influence public behavior, invite public participation, or cultivate public consensus. More than likely, the answer in each instance is . . . all of the above.

> *Any online marketing strategies should do three vital things: (1) Protect your brand, (2) increase traffic to the giving sections of your Web site, and 3) plan, test, and track results.*[11]

When designing this strategy, add how it will define how it is to be evaluated. Build into its plans checkpoints and analysis criteria, as well as frequent progress reports on the results achieved. Marketing and communications objectives must address identification of target markets, market segmentation, message fit, response rates, timing, use of media forms, and coordination with all other messages along with budget and results analysis. Additionally, issues of client retention and service quality go hand in hand with perceived or altered image and reputation, all of which need to be factored in as quantifiable criteria for measurement against the plan. In today's global world of instant access, competition, and message overload, the task of collecting copious amounts of measurable data to be evaluated against defined success factors is as important as analysis of the results.

EVALUATING ePHILANTHROPY MARKETING AND COMMUNICATIONS

Although the use of ePhilanthropy for marketing and communications purposes is still a reasonably new application, a variety of methods are available to measure and monitor its results. Quantifiable data for analysis are readily available from online market research surveys such as *click-through rates, traffic spikes, Web metrics,* and other tracking methods provided by network monitors, single-pixel solutions, and HTTP server log analysis. Several ePhilanthropy technology vendors can provide performance evaluations, including online response data such as

- Return receipt key
- E-mail addressees
- Who opened the message
- Who drilled down
- Which attachments were opened
- What portions of the text were viewed
- How long the visitor remained on the site

All of this is valuable information regarding the type of usage as well as individual use details. Also available are data on each visitor, their profile, date of last visit, average visit duration, and number of repeat visits, all of which provide options for responses to enhance communications, information exchanges, and personal relationships.

Key information to capture is data to segregate what's happening along with performance, beginning with collecting information in two broad areas to be measured against success factors and defined strategic goals and objectives:

External Environment	Valid Analysis Areas
Current market strategy	Mission and vision awareness
Key messages	Building confidence and trust
Marketing goals	Image changes, stimulates action
Communications objectives	Public awareness and consensus
Target audiences	Responses of all types

Based on this information, the challenge is to select just what specific data are needed, how to get these data (and how much of it), and how to interpret the results. Good evaluation depends on what you're looking for. Setting specific goals and objectives ahead of time as assessment criteria directs how the analysis will be performed later. After the results are tabulated, analyzed, and understood, the true purpose of measurement emerges—what to do about it. Results should point to actionable options and recommendations, timeline schedules, and budget requirements along with progress reports to monitor success.

The objective in evaluating ePhilanthropy use for marketing and communications purposes is to understand the results of their active Internet usage along with their success in integrating marketing and communications means. Measurements of fundraising results may appear to be easier because they are quantifiable using simple criteria (i.e., number of donors, amount of money received, average gift size), which can be compared with budgets spent to acquire them in cost-benefit analysis. Marketing and communications activities also can be evaluated with similar hard figures. Among the more easily available areas to track are the following:

- Analysis of defined success factors
- Market research surveys to periodically assess attitudes and opinions among select audiences
- Evaluations of how marketing and communications appeals, information, promotions, and other messages have altered public views of image and reputation
- Increased awareness of programs offered
- Quality measurements of services provided
- Increased Web site and e-mail traffic
- Tracking Web site use and responses
- Appointments made
- Information requests

Offline methods (i.e., tallying copy inches or "air time") will count messages delivered to the extent that news releases, interviews, benefit event coverage and other reports, once published, add up as circulation achieved (however imprecisely) to intended audiences. Media assessments, when carefully tracked, can reveal which ePhilanthropy applications added improved perceptions, found new clients, increased site visits, raised more money, or sparked "contact us" requests for additional information. Beyond these forms of assessment, there is also the opportunity to evaluate public opinion with some precision and analyze the results of ePhilanthropy marketing and communications strategies. To that end, multiyear definitive success factors will be helpful to guide online and offline marketing and communications strategies in future applications.

In addition to data analysis, there also are legal regulations, privacy protection guidelines, the *ePhilanthropy Code of Ethical Online Philanthropic Practices*,[12] the *Donor Bill of Rights*, and other ethical standards and behavior guidelines. Although every nonprofit organization must respect and follow these requirements, there are no specific performance guidelines on ePhilanthropy use for marketing and communications strategies. "Unlike direct mail, telemarketing, or other established channels for fundraising and communications, the online medium does not have mature and broadly accepted standards for data collection and metrics for measuring success."[13]

Notwithstanding, ePhilanthropy use continues to grow within nonprofit organizations and evaluation tools are being added to guide Internet marketing and communications programs toward their best use that will establish levels for maximum effectiveness and efficiency assessment. It is also true that there can be no value given for limp excuses or faulty logic models, such as a "look good—avoid blame"[14] mind-set or defensive posture, in an attempt to avoid open and full disclosure of actual performance results.

The Challenge of Joint-Cost Accounting

Adding to the analysis challenge is joint-cost accounting, or how to segregate accurately all expenses between programs and services, administration and general, and fundraising. Is marketing an integral part of an organization's programs and services for clients, or is it an administrative activity in direct support of its programs and services? In the same vein, are brochures, newsletters, and other publications prepared for client and media use, or are they administrative functions designed primarily for promotion and image enhancement? Further, can expenses be isolated between marketing and communications in order to track responses against production costs? American standards of accounting promulgated by the Financial Accounting Standards Board (FASB) and audit guidelines published by the American Institute of Certified Public Accountants (AICPA) were not written for Internet applications, with the result that how to report joint-cost expenses in these areas is left to the discretion and interpretation of the organization's finance and business officers and their auditors. The result is not surprising; no single methodology exists or is followed for joint-cost allocation. The search for established standards in performance measurement is likely to remain incomplete and unresolved.

What's to be done? What kinds of evaluations can be made? Are there other report methodologies that can be applied to Internet and ePhilanthropy analysis? Can the balanced scorecard be adapted to provide the answers? Perhaps some new invention is required to define the attributes, criteria, and scope of assessment needs that can be framed, beginning with three areas: Who is being evaluated? What is being evaluated? And how are they being evaluated?

STRATEGIES FOR ePHILANTHROPY FUNDRAISING

Although most nonprofit organizations have now begun to embrace the Internet for active fundraising purposes, most offer only donation icons with single-page response forms on their Web site, all quite passive solicitation techniques. Although useful in a full-service ePhilanthropy application, the many opportunities described in this book can and will expand the variety of pro-active solicitation techniques into direct contacts with prospects, donors, and volunteers as well as those who benefit from programs and services offered. The first layer of add-on applications is to reinforce primary solicitation methods with Web site information (e.g., virtual brochures, newsletters, reports, and more), adding details about operational program and service activities that benefit from annual and major gift campaigns, estate planning activities, and ending with progress reports, volunteer leadership profiles, and donor testimonials. Next, when accurate e-mail addresses of prior donors and prospects are available, they should be integrated with traditional offline solicitations.

An e-mail message in advance of a letter or phone call—or following it—adds a form of personal conversation, definitely a high-touch extra contact. Membership organizations and donor club involvement can be enhanced by a donor's access to full information on the organization's Web page using members-only passwords. Research access to corporation and foundation information helps to find the necessary match with priority programs that both seek to fund; it also allows corporations and foundations to search each applicant's Web page to aid in their personal evaluations. Invitations and reservations for activities, benefits, and special events are only a click of a mouse away. Volunteer recruitment, training, supervision, motivation, coordination, and recognition are all available online. Enhanced donor relations with instant thank-you messages can engage donors in recognition activities, including access to donor benefits and privileges.[15]

Adding follow-up notices as a first or second contact, to confirm an appointment or to seek details from grant makers on proposal contents, deadlines, and more (see Exhibit 19.3) will be efficient and cost-effective. Multimedia solicitations among traditional fundraising methods have long proven successful (e.g., mail-phone or phone-mail) because they are the most *personalized* approach short of a face-to-face visit.[16] "Discourse" is the key in telephone conversations and the same result can be achieved with e-mail and chat room techniques—it's all about building and enhancing relationships, that essential feature for success in every fund development program.

EXHIBIT 19.3   ePhilanthropy Additions to Traditional Solicitation Methods

Group A: Annual Giving Solicitation Methods

Traditional Methods	Additions Using E-Mail Addresses
Direct mail acquisition	1st or 2nd contact at no print/postage costs
Direct mail renewal/upgrade	1st or 2nd contact at no print/postage costs
Membership programs	1st or 2nd contact at no print/postage costs
Donor club programs	1st or 2nd contact at no print/postage costs
Telephone campaigns	1st contact to schedule telephone appointment
Groups and guilds	2nd contact to invite or renew membership
Benefit events	1st or 2nd contact to sell sponsorships and tickets
Tribute giving	1st or 2nd contact to confirm details and to thank
Federated campaigns	2nd contact to reinforce campaign strategies
Volunteer solicitations	2nd contact to confirm appointments, schedule meetings, post progress reports, and more

Group B: Major Giving, Campaigns, and Planned Giving Methods

Corporations	Visit Web site for information; ask questions
Cause-related marketing	Add corporate partner campaign data to Web site
Foundations	Visit Web site for information; ask questions
Individuals	Confirm cultivation events and appointments; send progress reports and invitations; convey appreciation
Capital campaigns	Report progress; pledge status; recognition
Planned giving	Recognition; report investment performance

The best ePhilanthropy use for relationship building is direct communications. Consider the following actions as multiple opportunities for personal contact with prospects, donors, and volunteers:

Prospects	Volunteers	Donors
Identify	Educate	Inform
Inform	Involve	Educate
Contact	Renew	Motivate
Solicit	Upgrade	Renew
Acknowledge	Reward	Recognize
Thank	Thank	Thank

Outbound message opportunities are available multiple times each year, and each should encourage replies and discussion. Maintaining a high level of personal communications requires careful preparation and supervision by the organization, well worth the time and effort when gift renewal and other forms of active participation are invited. Advantaged message opportunities occur when information on specific programs and services are offered. As an example, a hospital adds a newly approved screening test for heart disease and seeks to report its availability to the community it serves. An e-mail announcement to all current and prior heart patients as well as volunteers, donors, and prospects is released at the same time to the media. Not only does it provide each key constituent with privileged information, but also the message is personalized and received prior to any published media coverage. Relationships are built on service; lasting relationships are built on *personalized* service. The ease of transmitting special announcements, newsletters, event invitations, magazines, annual reports, and more, are all possible on the Internet with exceptional budget savings over print and postage costs.

EVALUATING ePHILANTHROPY FUNDRAISING PROGRAMS

The evaluation problem is *not* how to assess fundraising activities; the continuing problem is the *absence* of uniform guidelines or standards for evaluating results. The Council for Advancement and Support of Education (CASE) has published several guidelines to aid this benchmarking problem. The CASE reporting standards on how to count contributions and report their sources, for colleges, universities, and schools and for other nonprofit organizations advocate uniform reporting methods.[17] Adding a variety of self-assessment studies using each organization's prior results can be their most reliable indicator for interpretation of their own performance and provide a basis for estimating future results with some reliability. Prior fundraising results are the best indicators of where weaknesses lie, as well as where improvements can be discovered. Results data have the advantage of the organization's staff and volunteers knowledge of who did what, when it happened, who helped, what it cost, what problems were encountered, what the results were, and more. Further, self-assessment has the dual advantage of aiding in reliable forecasting for future results and for setting realistic expectations and performance standards based on internal realities, not external myths or untested expectations. To achieve reliable credibility requires honest homework in budget preparation, expense allocation, coded replies to match solicitation methods, tracking direct costs, staff time, and other indirect and overhead costs. These assessments are quite possible using computers and available software, if there is the will to do the required homework.

Given that preamble, prepare to measure each solicitation method and its separate budget of time, staff, systems, and other costs with the results of each solicitation each time the method is used. For example, offering credit card automated bank transfer, or Electronic Funds Transfer(EFT) options on the Web site donation page can track sources of gifts, number of gifts received, gift values, and average gift size (see Exhibit 19.4), along with details of cash received and pledges outstanding. Outgoing or "outbound" e-mail tracking also can report who received the message, who opened it, and who accessed which attachments, how long they stayed on site, and more—key features when comparing ePhilanthropy results with direct-mail solicitations where only replies (with or without money) are an indication of actual receipt. Analysis of each donor's prior gift history may reveal a willingness to convert to electronic giving, whether by e-mail or EFTto invite an increase in gift levels, or to improve the donor's pledge fulfillment records.

It also is possible to learn a volume of details from a host site, charity channel, network monitor, or Internet service provider (ISP), provided donors agreed to share the response information with its details. Results comparisons between these sites also may reveal donor preferences of where and how they choose to give in order to stimulate increased responses. Where there may be no visible change in gift revenue, these analyses can help to clarify whether privacy and/or security may be the issue with some donors by evaluating variances in their giving methods, such as site choices and site functions visited along with options such as credit card versus EFT, pledge versus on-time payment, or mailed-in check versus online virtual giving.

Some of the non-traditional fundraising methods also are available for ePhilanthropy use. These include online auctions, product sales, and cause-related marketing. Although these data are not easy to capture when the results reside with vendors outside the nonprofit organization, they can be a useful addition to assessing the stan-

EXHIBIT 19.4   ePhilanthropy Web Site Annual Gift Results

Sources of Gifts	Number	Gift Values	Average Gift Size
Gift responses:			
Gift pledges paid	4,669	$210,475	$25.80
Gift pledges outstanding	5,700	186,164	32.66
Subtotal	10,369	$306.639	$29.57
Payment method			
Credit card payments	8,754	250,114	28.57
EFT gifts authorized	1,615	56,525	35.00
Subtotal	10,369	$306,639	$29.57
Other responses			
Planned gift inquiries	211	?	?
Planned gift follow-up contacts	167	?	?
New planned gifts written	2	25,000	12,500
Total responses	10,749	$331,639	$30.85

dard menu of solicitation and giving options and their results. Where available, self-assessment measurements are recommended to evaluate their performance, comparing past experience with the organization's recent results alongside other solicitation methods in use at the same time. These assessments help determine which has greater value, be it higher donor acceptance, increased net income, greater numbers of donors, higher percent participation, and/or increased average gift size. First-time usage of any solicitation tactic, when used alone, also benefits from a thorough investigation for its "fit" within the organization's active levels of ongoing marketing, communications and fundraising strategies and tactics, by tracking the success of each method with different audiences, messages, timing, response rates, and more. On occasion, further research to learn what experiences other organizations may have achieved when using these methods will be useful. Such comparisons as launch problems, policy issues, public reactions, and more are applicable in comparative analysis. However, another's results are no predictor of one's own organization's returns.

Fundraising Cost-Effectiveness and Return on Investment

As Internet technology continues to add features, nonprofit organizations need to examine how well these new applications add to and are appropriate for their mission, vision, and values. Common elements that lend themselves to useful analysis, including "open rates, click-throughs, opt-out rates, conversion rates, average on-line gift size, etc.,"[18] are valuable in understanding prospect and donor acceptance and preferences. Much harder to evaluate will be the fundraising cost-effectiveness measurement and return on investment (ROI) analysis. Adding to the challenge of how best to conduct these assessments is the lack of meaningful statistics or financial models for comparison, which leads us back to the available option of self-assessment once again. One set of measurements for fundraising performance is the Nine-Point Performance Index (see Exhibit 19.5). While this index is applicable to each of the traditional offline solicitation methods, some criteria may fail in ePhilanthropy analysis due to the absence of budget and expense details. There is little to no direct costs for Internet solicitation

EXHIBIT 19.5   Nine-Point Performance Index

Basic Data

1. Participants   = Numbers of donors responding with gifts
2. Income   = Gross contributions
3. Expense   = Fundraising costs

Performance Measurements

4. Percent participation = Divide participants by total solicitation made
5. Average gift size   = Divide income received by participants
6. Net income   = Subtract expenses from income received
7. Average cost per gift = Divide expenses by participants
8. Fundraising cost   = Divide expenses by income received
9. Return   = Divide net income by expenses; multiply by 100 for percentage

Source: James M. Greenfield, *Fund-Raising Cost Effectiveness: A Self-Assessment Workbook* (New York: John Wiley & Sons, Inc., 1996), 31. Used with permission.

once the one-time expense of equipment and software are in place. Direct costs for office supplies, computer equipment, software and vendor costs, data entry and tracking will be incurred along with indirect and overhead expenses for employee salaries and benefits, gift acknowledgments (receipts, envelopes, postage), donor communications, donor recognition, and more, all normal expenses in support of routine solicitation activities. While real expenses, their actual costs may be difficult to segregate, as ePhilanthropy expenses only, from other, day-to-day back-office support activities. The method to calculate all these costs may require the laborious work of a yearlong staff time analysis study along with detailed cost accounting to segregate the areas of ePhilanthropy expenses for each of the other individual solicitation methods in use. This level of detailed office work is unpopular with fundraising staff and seldom engaged as a result ("I'm supposed to use my time to raise money"), a behavior that must be modified to meet the increased demands for added accountability being required today of all nonprofit organizations on their performance, including their fundraising performance.

Internal self-analysis often leads to an improved and informed understanding of key fundraising performance areas. One such evaluation is to measure growth in giving where the focus is on adding numbers of renewing donors and tracking multiyear performance levels of net income along with bottom-line attention to fundraising costs and return on expenses in a cost-benefit ratio analysis (see the example in Exhibit 19.6). Such multiyear performance aids board members, administrators, volunteers, and donors in appreciating consistent solicitation results from current fundraising activities collected together in a summary analysis. This summary format also represents a valid methodology and worksheet framework to examine each fundraising method used. Further, it allows for reasonably reliable forecasts of future performance based on a three-year examination of each solicitation method and their integration with

EXHIBIT 19.6   Report on Overall Rate of Growth in Giving using Nine-Point Performance Index

	Two Years Ago	Last Year	Annual Rate of Growth (%)	This Year	Annual Rate of Growth (%)	Cumulative Rate of Growth (%)
Participation	1,355	1,605	18	1,799	12	31
Income	$448,765	$507,855	13	$571,235	12	26
Expenses	$116,550	$123,540	6	$131,850	7	13
Participation (%)	39	44	13	52	18	31
Average gift size	$331	$316	−4	$318	0.4	4
Net income	$332,215	$384,315	16	$439,385	14	30
Average cost per gift	$86.01	$76.97	−11	$73.29	−5	−15
Cost of fundraising	$0.26	$0.24	−6	$0.23	−5	−11
Return (%)	285	311	9	333	7	16

Source: James M. Greenfield, *Fund Raising Fundamentals: A Guide to Annual Giving for Professionals and Volunteers,* 2nd ed. The AFP Fund Development Series (New York: John Wiley & Sons, Inc., 2003), p. 491. Used with permission.

other techniques. More important, perhaps, is that this model illustrates where an additional budget investment in one or more of these proven cost-effective and profitable fundraising methods could yield a reliable increase in net income of as much as three to four times the expense required. Conversely, if budget cuts are mandated, an estimate of lost revenue also can be clearly calculated. However, if this evidence clearly demonstrates where increased profits are possible, can the organization ignore this opportunity and choose not to make the necessary investment? Yes, it can, even if the figures prove the net income profit potential, because nonprofit leaders are obligated to invest first in public service programs rather than risk investing in spending scarce funds on the promise of increased net revenues from fundraising. This conclusion will be true even when the actual direct costs will be fully recovered and profits are delivered within 12 months or less.

SUGGESTED GUIDELINES FOR ePHILANTHROPY PERFORMANCE

Several evaluation areas for measurement of marketing, communications, and fundraising have been offered in this chapter. Begin with a review of how well the original purposes, design objectives, and definitive success factors for each strategy have performed. Evaluations also must consider the internal and external environments that impact upon each organization's ability to fulfill its mission and carry out its operating activities. However, there remains a lack of faith in some measurement tools now available, which can be a handicap to nonprofit board members and administrators' decisions. And, even if tools to conduct performance evaluations were available, the preference often is to attempt to validate performance using comparative analysis data between like and/or local organizations, a common for-profit assessment methodology. For nonprofit organizations, these attempts can result in misleading and misguided answers, as no two organizations are so alike in their public affairs strategies and tactics, audiences, and timing to render comparisons realistic or credible.

One area that can yield immediate analysis is to examine a nonprofit's own Web site for being up to date with available technological improvements. For example, evaluating its Web *presence* will be indicative of organizational commitment to best use of the Internet. *Presence* means a focus on audience interest and content development, meeting their needs first, caring about their relationships. The Internet is a medium for both outreach and advocacy, which is where online marketing, communications, and fundraising overlap with the organization's strategic plans.[19] Integrating message objectives for each target audience that is essential to the organization requires close coordination and cooperation between marketing, communications, and fundraising staff. After all, the audiences for each are often identical. As the Internet is best used as the total message medium for marketing, communications, and fundraising purposes, Exhibit 19.7 can be used to evaluate their combined as well as interconnected performances (a median score of 3.5 or better will be excellent).

INTERNET PERFORMANCE WATCHDOGS

Hosts of self-appointed evaluators or *watchdogs* have invented a variety of evaluation criteria to measure nonprofit organizations' performance and to offer their analysis in the form of ratings, and to broadcast their scores on the Internet. These measurement

EXHIBIT 19.7 Measuring ePhilanthropy Overall Performance

	Score				
	Low			High	
Advocacy of the cause	1	2	3	4	5
Branding identity for public confidence and trust	1	2	3	4	5
Collaborating to meet defined community needs	1	2	3	4	5
Communicating the mission, vision, and values	1	2	3	4	5
Distance learning to share knowledge	1	2	3	4	5
Electronic commerce to facilitate support	1	2	3	4	5
Fundraising to invite and renew gift support	1	2	3	4	5
Information access for open and full disclosure	1	2	3	4	5
Marketing programs and services to those in need	1	2	3	4	5
Promoting access to programs and services	1	2	3	4	5
Recognition of donors and volunteers	1	2	3	4	5
Research to understand local environments	1	2	3	4	5
Stewardship of past gifts, grants, and contributions support	1	2	3	4	5
Surveys to monitor and measure progress	1	2	3	4	5
Testing to demonstrate being effective and efficient	1	2	3	4	5
Median Score:					

criteria include accountability, best practices, return on investment, efficiency and effectiveness, disclosure, transparency, outcomes, and fundraising costs. Their main source of data for all these evaluations is the Return of Organization Exempt from Income Tax (IRS Form 990). Some of these observer entities also collect audited financial statements, annual reports, and other documentation for their assessments. Unfortunately, these enterprises have promulgated separate ratings and scores that are confusing and sometimes contradictory (see Exhibit 19.8 for a partial list of agencies that rate nonprofits).

This use of the Internet to support a new classification system fails due to their contradictory measurement criteria, which significantly limits their value to provide the public with consistent, verifiable information on the charities they wish to support. The time-tested and most respected of these enterprises is the Better Business Bureau's "Wise Giving Guide." Their analysis is focused on four main issues: how the organization is governed, how it spends its money, the truthfulness of its representations, and its willingness to disclose basic information to the public. In their recent release of new *Charity Accountability Standards* (effective beginning March 3, 2004), the BBB has reconfirmed four key financial guidelines. These included Standard B:3 "Spend a reasonable percentage, not exceeding 35%, of related contributions on fund raising," and Standard B:4 "Spend a reasonable percentage, not exceeding 50%, of total income on fund raising and administrative costs."[20] Simple enough except for the difficulty of how to allocate the joint costs involved. Other reviewers, for there own purposes, have departed from the Better Business Bureau's standards and have issued a variety of divergent guidelines, which is unfortunate. Three of these better known, active watchdogs and their evaluation criteria are:

1. *American Institute of Philanthropy.* Percent spent on charitable purpose, cost to raise $100, years of available assets.

EXHIBIT 19.8 Agencies that Rate Nonprofit Organizations

Internet Sites	Internet Addresses
American Institute of Philanthropy	http://www.charitywatch.org
Benefice Information Center	http://www.benefice.com/html/in_center.html
Better Business Bureau	http://www.give.org
Charitable Choices	http://www.charitablechoices.org/index.htm
Charities Aid Foundation (UK)	http://www.cafonline.org
Charities USA	http://www.charitiesusa.com/
Charity Canada	http://www.charity.ca
Charity Guide	http://www.charityguide.org/charity/ charityratings.htm
Charity Navigator	http://www.charitynavigator.org
Charity North	http://www.charitynorth.com
Charity Registration Offices	gopher://people.human.com/00/inc.data/states
Charity Regulation in Other States	http://www.sos.state.med.us/sos/charity/ html/otstates.html
GiveforChange.com	http://www.uic.edu:80/1mhurst/donors/
Give Spot	http://www.givespot.org
GuideStar	http://www.guidestar.org/
Guide to Cruelty Free Giving	http://www/neavs.org/info/charities.html
Idealist	http://www.idealist.org
Independent Charities of America	http://www.independentcharities.org
Kansas Charity Check	http://kscharitycheck.org
Kimberly Chapman	http://kimberlychapman.com
National Association of State Charity Officials (NASC)	http://nasconet.org
National Commission on Philanthropy and Civic Renewal (NCPCR)	http://www.ncpcr.org
Rate It All: The Opinion Network	http://www.rateitall/com
Society Guardian (UK)	http://www.society.guardian.co.uk/charityreform
Wise Giving to Charities	http://www.heartsandminds.org

Media Rating Participants

Chronicle of Philanthropy	"Top 400 List," based on amount of money they raise from individuals, foundations, and corporations.
Money Magazine	Selects a few national charities as a benchmark for evaluating other worthy groups. Criteria include devoting a high portion of its income to programs, keeping fundraising costs low, and the organization's A+ rating by The American Institute of Philanthropy.
The Nonprofit Times	"NPT 100" list, based on amount of funding received from public sources (must be at least 10 percent of total revenue).
Smart Money magazine	Ranks organizations primarily based on how much money they spend on programs but takes into account efficiency in fundraising.
Worth magazine	Lists 100 top charities, based on worthiness of goal and mission, effectiveness of its spending, and its reputation among other nonprofits.

2. *Charity Navigator.* Fundraising efficiency, fundraising expenses, program expenses, administrative expenses; primary revenue growth, program expenses growth, working capital ratio; and summation scores
3. *GuideStar.* Accountable payable aging indicator, contributions and grants ratio, debt ratio, and fundraising ratio

Although the apparent intent of these watchdogs might be to encourage wider public access to and awareness of nonprofit performance, their basic weakness is too much focus only on financial and fundraising details, with no review or analysis of the organization's effectiveness or efficiency in delivery of its programs and services, management processes, adherence to all laws and regulations, observance of stated plans, or faithful fulfillment of its mission, vision, and values. Further, and more significant to defining a quality measurement standard, is the fact that there is, as yet, no research to support the claim that meeting their standards is related to any level of outcome performance of benefit to the public.[21]

CONCLUSION

Where does this call for analysis lead? One cannot be confident in making predictions given the rapid evolution in technological advances that fuel the Internet daily. Certainly, nonprofit organizations need to be fully engaged in documenting their activities and become more open and accountable. Those who seek to use a nonprofit's programs along with those who support it will become more adept at Internet usage when choosing these services. They also should expect their favorite organizations to be prepared to provide full information, as well as to interact easily with them in an open and full disclosure manner. Nonprofit boards of directors and administrators will likely struggle to invest more budget in their ePhilanthropy technology because each investment dollar must compete with program and service priorities, staff salaries, and employee benefits. Given the scarcity of budget and necessity to measure all budgets as investment decisions that expect performance returns, these hard decisions can best be made when based on solid, demonstrated results. One prediction may be reasonably safe—decisions about nonprofit marketing, communications, and fundraising utilization will continue to be a valid and valued means to meet public demands for greater accountability. All who appreciate the message behind this question, "What's private about a public benefit corporation?" will become as open and accountable as possible and willing to disclose operational details, including financial information.

Nonprofit organizations must be able to document their results using quantifiable as well as qualitative data in performance measurements. These results also should be reported as beneficial outcomes delivered back to the community. These outcomes answer what their mission statements declared to be their purposes, which is what their performance analysis should disclose. There is no better way to create and enhance the public's trust in what nonprofit organizations do with the public's money and what they say are their outcomes than to openly reveal how they have directly benefited others in fulfillment of their mission.

ABOUT THE AUTHOR

Jim M. Greenfield, ACFRE, FAHP, retired in February 2001, after completing 40 years as a fundraising professional at five hospitals and three universities. Following retirement, Jim continues speaking, teaching, and writing plus aiding nonprofit organizations with a fundraising management consulting service. He and his wife, Karen, continue to live in Newport Beach, California.

Jim has written and edited eight books on fundraising management including *Fund Raising Fundamentals: A Guide to Annual Giving for Professionals and Volunteers* (2nd ed., 2002), *Fund Raising: Evaluating and Managing the Fund Development Process,* (2nd ed. 1999), *Fund-Raising Cost Effectiveness: A Self-Assessment Workbook* (1996), and is editor of *The Nonprofit Handbook: Fund Raising,* Third Edition (2001). You can e-mail Jim at fundrazer@cox.net.

ENDNOTES

1. Paul Clolery, editor-in-chief, *The Nonprofit Times*, in Michael Johnston, *The Fund Raiser's Guide to the Internet,* The NSFRE/Wiley Fund Development Series (New York: John Wiley & Sons, Inc., 1999), p. xii (Foreword).
2. Thomas H. Jeavons, "Ethics in Nonprofit Management: Creating a Culture of Integrity" in Robert D. Herman & Associates, eds., *The Jossey-Bass Handbook of Nonprofit Leadership and Management,* The Jossey-Bass Nonprofit Sector Series (San Francisco: Jossey-Bass, Inc., 1994), p. 197.
3. *Building Strength: Improving Governance and Accountability in Canada's Voluntary Sector,* panel on accountability and governance in the voluntary sector, Ottawa, 1999, p. 14.
4. James Cutt and Victor Murray, *Accountability and Effectiveness Evaluation in Non-Profit Organizations* (New York: Routledge, 2000), p. 14.
5. James M. Greenfield, *Fund-Raising Cost Effectiveness: A Self-Assessment Workbook* (New York: John Wiley & Sons, Inc., 1996), p. xiv.
6. Alan R. Andreason and Philip Kotler, *Strategic Marketing for Nonprofit Organizations,* 6th ed. (Prentice-Hall, 2003), p. 503.
7. Theodore R. Hart, "The Internet as a Fund Raising Vehicle" in Eugene R. Tempel, ed., *Achieving Excellence in Fund Raising.* 2nd ed., Henry A. Rosso & Associates (San Francisco: Jossey-Bass, 2003), p. 265.
8. American Marketing Association, as found in Eugene M. Johnson and M. Venkatesan, "Marketing," in Tracy Daniel Connors, ed., *The Nonprofit Handbook: Management,* 3rd ed. (New York: John Wiley & Sons, Inc., 2001), pp. 130, 132–133.
9. Andreason and Kotler, *Strategic Marketing for Nonprofit Organizations,* p. 26.
10. Eugene M. Johnson and M. Venkatesan, *Strategic Marketing for Nonprofit Organizations,* p. 144.
11. Michael Johnston, "Fund Raising on the Net" in James M. Greenfield, ed., *The Nonprofit Handbook: Fund Raising,* 3rd ed., The AFP/Wiley Fund Development Series (New York: John Wiley & Sons, Inc., 2001), p. 535.
12. Mal Warwick, Ted Hart, and Nick Allen, *Fundraising on the Internet: The ePhilanthropy Foundation.Org's Guide to Success Online,* 2nd ed. (San Francisco: Jossey-Bass, 2002), pp. 259–260.

13. Warwick, et al, *Fundraising on the Internet: The ePhilanthropyFoundation.Org's Guide to Success Online,* p. 33.

14. James Cutt and Victor Murray, *Accountability and Effectiveness Evaluation in Non-Profit Organizations,* pp. 39–41.

15. James M. Greenfield, *Fund Raising Fundamentals: A Guide to Annual Giving for Professionals and Volunteers,* 2nd ed. (New York: John Wiley & Sons, Inc., 2002), p. 321.

16. William Freyd and Diane M. Carlson, "Telemarketing" in James M. Greenfield, ed., *The Nonprofit Handbook: Fund Raising, Third Edition,* The AFP/Wiley Fund Development Series (New York: John Wiley & Sons, Inc., 2001), p. 568.

17. Council for Advancement and Support of Education, *Case Management Reporting Standards: Standards for Annual Giving and Campaigns in Educational Fund Raising* (Washington, DC: Council for Advancement and Support of Education, 1996); and *Fund-Raising Standards for Annual Giving and Campaign Report for Not-for-Profit Organizations other than Colleges, Universities, and Schools,* 1998.

18. "Return on Investment Analysis" in *ePhilanthroply Business Plans* at *http://www.charity.ca.*

19. Michael Stein, "Nonprofit Success on the Internet: Creating an Effective Online Presence" in James M. Greenfield, ed., *The Nonprofit Handbook: Fund Raising,* 3rd ed., The AFP/Wiley Fund Development Series (New York: John Wiley & Sons, Inc., 2001), pp. 225, 239.

20. "Standards for Charity Accountability" in *BBC Wise Giving Guide* (Arlington, VA: BBC Wise Giving Alliance, 2003).

21. James Cutt and Vic Murray, *Accountability and Effectiveness Evaluation in Non-Profit Organizations,* pp. 115–119.

CHAPTER 20

The Future of ePhilanthropy: Final Thoughts

Michael Johnston, ePMT
HJC New Media

Difficult to see. Always in motion is the future.

—Yoda, 800-year-old Jedi Master

WHERE WE'VE COME FROM—A TEN-YEAR ePHILANTHROPY JOURNEY

In the fall of 1995, I made a presentation to 150 nonprofit managers at the Trade Union Congress in London, England. It was an unseasonably hot day, and everyone was struggling to see this peculiar new nonprofit environment—the Internet—on a screen that was washed out by sunlight streaming through stained-glass windows. We eventually solved the sunshine problem by having someone climb a rickety ladder and hammer long pieces of cloth over the windows.

It was the shock of seeing for the first time, this new medium at work—and the nonprofit participants were all wondering just what this would mean to their organizations. We didn't know the answer then, and we still aren't sure now, but the intervening years have revealed some of what this new medium means to nonprofit organizations, both now and in the future.

Late that same year, we ran a similar session for more than 100 nonprofit managers at Seton Hall University in New Jersey. Like that first session in the United Kingdom, the U.S. nonprofit crowd was simultaneously awed and highly skeptical. The content of those first sessions was rudimentary. I started by showing a cartoon to make everyone feel comfortable—it portrayed someone admitting that they didn't know what the Internet was, and that's exactly where most of the nonprofit participants were at in their understanding of the Internet (see Exhibit 20.1).

In those early years, we explained what the Internet was—how the U.S. Department of Defense created an electronic communication system that was modular. It could survive even if one of the nodes was destroyed by a nuclear attack by simply rerouting through another city anywhere in the world that was connected to this evolving electronic network.

EXHIBIT 20.1 Early ePhilanthropy

I also remember explaining other concepts like e-mail, e-mail subscription lists, Web sites, URLs, and other basics. When I think about what information this book explains—ASP services; electronic customer management; and electronic strategies for major gifts and planned gifts—I know that this medium is here to stay.

At the beginning of the Internet era for nonprofits (which I'll arbitrarily put at 1995), there was very little online fundraising and mostly online awareness campaigns. At that time, I had just run my first online campaign, gathering e-mail addresses for a virtual petition campaign to save the life of the imprisoned Nigerian writer and activist, Ken Saro-Wiwa.

In 1995, Ken Saro-Wiwa was imprisoned by a kangaroo court for leading a protest against the exploitation of his people's land by Shell Oil and the Nigerian dictatorship. The international cosmetics retailer, The Body Shop International, began to campaign for Ken's release in the United Kingdom, Canada, and a number of other countries where it had retail shops. At the time, we realized that this was a truly global human rights campaign and wondered if this new technology, the fledgling World Wide Web and the Internet, could help us out.

We designed a campaign area on The Body Shop International Web site that allowed concerned global citizens to sign a petition. After a few weeks, we'd gathered more than 10,000 names online (including the support of a highly placed oil executive!). Those names were printed out, and sacks of petitions were filled and delivered to the British Foreign and Commonwealth Office in London. If the reader hasn't had a chance, please go to Vinay Bhagat's chapter (see Chapter 10), to see how far we've come from this 1995 campaign.

I believe this experiment helped us understand the potential power of the Internet for the nonprofit sector, so we took our work one step farther. We had The Body Shop Canada send a computer to MOSOP (The Movement for the Survival of the Ogoni

People) in Port Harcourt, Nigeria. With Ken's imprisonment, the office of MOSOP had been shut down and his people besieged by a brutal military governorship. They needed access to the outside world. This one computer, which was able to connect to the Internet, was their one reliable connection with the outside world. MOSOP was able to send out e-mails that gave an accurate, but desperate, view of their situation. They were also able to receive e-mails from supportive nonprofits and citizens from around the world.

Was it a success? Margot Fransen, CEO of The Body Shop Canada, said, "Not only did the that Internet access help shine a light on the unfair trial of Ken, it most likely saved thousands of lives." But if the reader would like to delve deeper into how to evaluate online success, then read Jim Greenfield's excellent chapter, "Evaluating ePhilanthropy Programs" (Chapter 19).

Sadly, the campaigning didn't save the life of Ken Saro-Wiwa, but this early Internet campaign showed its power to motivate citizens located all around the planet. Did the campaign raise money? Very little. A few hundred dollars were raised directly from the online campaign. It would have raised more, but the Web site also asked potential supporters to contact Greenpeace and Amnesty International to make donations to their Nigeria campaigns.

It was a rudimentary beginning for online fundraising, and far away from where we're at now. When readers delve into Chapter 15, they will uncover how powerful automated fundraising tools have become. A donor doesn't have to print off a donation form and mail it in, or see a phone number and pick up the phone. Instead, the prospective online donors can choose automatic debit from their bank accounts or make use of their credit cards—both automatically verified with an instantaneous thank you. They can even receive an electronic tax receipt in some countries.

The mid-1990s were a time when the number of nonprofit organizations raising money online could be counted on two hands—and that would cover the whole world.

Although the nonprofit sector had a relatively small online presence through the late 1990s, I could detect a deeper influence by the spring of 2000, when I walked into the office of a staff person at North York General Hospital Foundation. He and I talked about the possibilities of online fundraising for the Foundation. It was a stimulating one-hour conversation. Near the end, I was ready to leave, hoping that we could work together. We exchanged business cards, and when I looked down at his I couldn't believe it—his card said that he was director of ePhilanthropy (see Exhibit 20.2).

This new fundraising medium, still young in 2000, had shown enough potential for nonprofit organizations to hire individuals to manage this area of giving. I knew around that time that the medium was more than a passing fancy, as I witnessed the human resource developments across the sector. Chapter 4 offers the reader a great review of how to meet ePhilanthropy staffing needs.

From the mid 1990s through the end of the twentieth century, there was little complexity in the campaigns, plans, and tools used to conduct online fundraising. Most organizations had just gotten their first Web sites up and had simply translated their paper assets to the online environment. Some people called these sites *brochureware*. The Web sites were static and did not give visitors a chance to interact with the organization.

However, a few organizations were beginning to realize that this new medium had more to offer than just a few static words and images. In 1999, Amnesty International

4001 Leslie Street
Toronto, Ontario M2K 1E1
Tel: (416) 756-6717
Fax: (416) 756-9047

NORTH YORK GENERAL HOSPITAL
FOUNDATION

Director of
E-Philanthropy

Taking pride in taking care

Registered Canadian
Charitable Organisation
88875 1245 RR0001

EXHIBIT 20.2   Director of ePhilanthropy

in the United Kingdom created one of the first examples of how the online medium could combine text, programming, images, and sound to make interactive and persuasive online fundraising.

A landing page was created that used both animation and sound to animate the story of Maria, a young woman imprisoned and brutally tortured by an oppressive regime. Please look at Exhibit 20.3 and imagine listening to a woman's screams as you land on the page.

Not only was Amnesty introducing the multimedia power of the Internet to its online fundraising, it was also applying the tried and true principle of testing different creative approaches to see which was most effective in garnering donations. When entering the support area from the home page, the site visitor was given one of three randomly generated appeals. These three creative approaches tested both creative and technological sophistication:

1. The first appeal told a good-news story of an individual released from prison because of the letters sent by Amnesty supporters worldwide.
2. The second appeal invited the visitor to click on a series of yes/no boxes to answer questions (it might be compared to a questionnaire mailing) such as, have you ever read a book? or would you defend your family?
3. The third appeal was the hard-hitting animation and sound of Maria's story.

In each appeal, the giving method was made simple by presenting the phrase "Click the candle (the Amnesty logo) to make a donation."

The best offline fundraising often relies on the powerful, personal stories to raise significant funds. With the success of the Maria story, this new medium was beginning to prove that there were similarities between offline and online fundraising success. If you haven't already read it, then you should turn back to Chapter 9 to re-

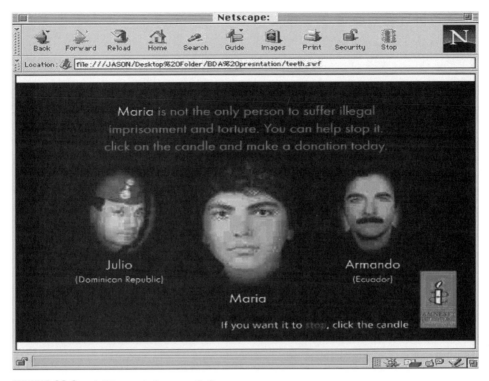

EXHIBIT 20.3 A Woman's Scream Online

mind yourself about the incredible storytelling and fundraising potential of the on-line environment.

Then, as the nonprofit sector moved into the beginning of the twentieth century, it began to make real progress with online fundraising. It started to push past brochure-ware and move into more interactive uses of the medium to motivate online donors.

SEPTEMBER 11, 2001 AND ONLINE FUNDRAISING

The tragedy of the terrorist attacks on the United States on September 11, 2001, had a powerful effect on the culture of online giving. The president of the United States, in his address to the world shortly after the attacks, made reference to an online giving site, *www.libertyunites.org*. That hastily constructed Web site—supported by a num-ber of large and capable corporations—collected more money online than any Web site could have imagined before those terrible events.

This moment marked a change in giving culture. An important political leader, in a high profile event, centered media attention on online giving in a way that had never happened before. The reference to the Web site was the key legitimizing event in the history of ePhilanthropy.

And it was during this short, intense period of online giving that the medium proved itself capable of raising money efficiently and effectively. It was a time when the ideas of fundraising integration came into their own. For a more detailed examination of truly integrated (offline and online) fundraising, the reader should turn to Chapter 3.

The United Way of New York desperately needed funds to provide service in the aftermath of the September 11 attacks. The United Way of Toronto wanted to help, and it found a way through the Tribute to Heroes Telethon. The telethon was simultaneously broadcast in Canada as it went to air in the United States. However, Canadians couldn't call the 800 number that would appear on the U.S. broadcast. The United Way of Toronto decided to quickly implement an offline/online solution:

1. Use a Canadian 800 number for Canadians to call in to the United Way of Toronto donation center.
2. When donors called in, the in-bound telephone volunteers would have a computer screen with the United Way of Toronto Web site giving form ready to process the gift.
3. Once the credit card was processed automatically through the Web page, the telephone volunteer would ask for the donor's e-mail address and tell the donor that they could receive an electronic tax receipt attached to their e-mail (in Canada, every donation over $10 must be officially receipted).

In 48 hours, the whole system was set up, over 6,000 online gifts were processed totaling more than $500,000 (with an average gift of $81) and the majority of the callers received their tax receipt via e-mail within 24 hours. This was an incredibly elegant integration of offline and online media.

But even if the creative and integrated approaches and underlying technology are changing and improving, has the demographic profile of the online donor changed as well? The only rolling study of online giving in one organization has been conducted by Greenpeace Canada: three times over a six-year period. In 1998, 2000, and again in 2002, the organization surveyed, through telephone and e-mail, online donors for those years (see Exhibit 20.4).

The results of this rolling study show some broad trends:

■ The predominant position of younger donors in 1998, for this organization, has fallen in importance.
■ Middle-aged donors have begun to give in larger numbers.
■ And finally, older donors, not represented at all in 1998, have become more comfortable and are giving in larger numbers.

This is only one study, but an intriguing one. It points to a trend that most nonprofit organizations see in online giving—the fact that it's no longer the domain of young people, but a medium being adopted by older individuals as well.

To back up the fact that most organizations are finding more and more older online donors, here is another online giving study conducted at the start of 2003 for the relief organization, Doctors Without Borders (or Medcins Sans Frontieres). A total of 900 online donors (out of 3,000 2002 donors) responded to an online survey (see Exhibit 20.5).

The reader may be a bit surprised by the fact that more than 50 percent of the Doctors Without Borders donors are over 50 years old. But the reader shouldn't be. As

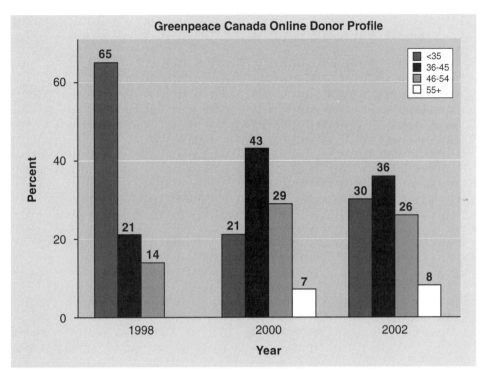

EXHIBIT 20.4 The Changing Demographics of Online Donors

middle-aged people and seniors adopt online technologies they become more comfortable with them—perhaps making their first commercial purchases, then philanthropic ones, and finally telling their peers about this effective way to donate.

The Greenpeace and Doctors Without Borders demographic surveys should remind the reader that as nonprofit organizations have been testing and improving their use of the Internet, there has been a parallel development in the demographic profile of the online donor. For example, as older donors come online, they demand more stable, more straightforward, less technical interfaces to conduct their business online. Nonprofit organizations, learning more and more about powerful online tools and their potential, listen to the demands from customers and ask vendors to deliver a better online giving product.

If it's true that a more representative sample of different age subsets have been giving online over the last six years, then how many organizations are they giving to?

Very few studies can show us. An August 2003 study of online donors conducted by *www.canadahelps.org* sampled a few hundred nonprofit organizations, ranging from large to small, from health charities to environment groups to battered woman's shelters. It was a broad and shallow survey of online donors who had given in 2003 (see Exhibit 20.6).

The majority of the respondents indicated that they had given online to one or two charities in the past year. How does that compare to direct-mail donors? A 2003 survey of American and Canadian direct-mail donors conducted by Mal Warwick and Associates and The FLA Group, found that direct-mail donors gave on average to 10 or more charities.[1] So it seems that the online fundraising space is much less cluttered

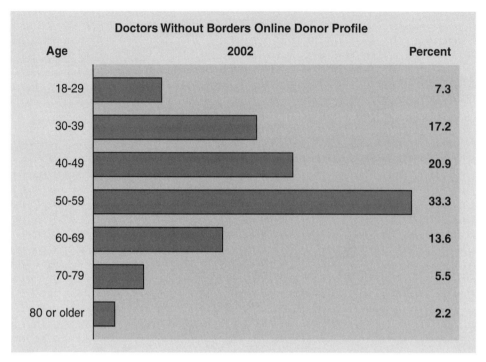

EXHIBIT 20.5   Older Donors Are Becoming an Important Source of Online Gifts

than the offline direct response world. Online donors generally give to between one and five charities and very few give to more than that.

This may change as the medium matures, but for now, there are less charities competing online for the loyalties of online donors. It might also be true that online donors aren't comfortable enough with the medium to give to more than just a few charities.

Not only are readers wondering about the demographic composition of the online donor, they may also be wondering about their technical capabilities. Exactly what does an online donor understand of the medium—and what kind of connection to the Internet do they have?

A description of the average online donor and their attitudes can be best understood through a telephone survey conducted by the U.S. fundraising firm, Craver, Matthews, Smith & Company in October of 2001 (733 donors participated). The reader can compare it to a similar Canadian study conducted in 2002.[2] Some of the highlights can be seen in the following list:

	Canada	**United States**
	%	%
Broadband access	71	36
Online at least 4 years	71	73
Online every day	87	80
Online banking	70	56

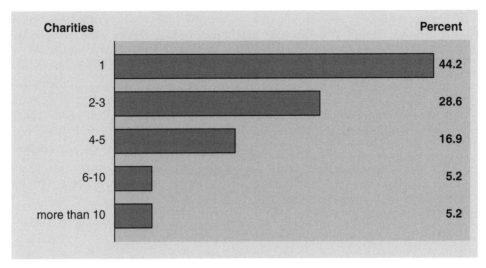

Charities		Percent
1		44.2
2-3		28.6
4-5		16.9
6-10		5.2
more than 10		5.2

EXHIBIT 20.6   Online Donors Still Have Few Divided Loyalties

In both studies, it became clear that younger online donors—individuals in their thirties—were the biggest e-bankers, with approximately 31 percent of Internet users aged 30 to 39 using it for this activity.

Therefore, online donor surveys indicate a reasonable proportion of individuals with high-speed access (this has greatly increased since the 2001 and 2002 surveys) which means these donors can see content that demands a faster Internet connection. This means that online donors will have less and less problems viewing online video appeals.

THE FUTURE OF NEW TECHNOLOGY FUNDRAISING

If you retrace the steps offered in Chapters 1, 2, and 13 about ePhilanthropy and fundraising strategies, an organization can gather clues about the most effective and efficient deployment of what new technologies might offer, either tomorrow or even two years from now.

Will the Web and e-mail be the future of ePhilanthropy? Yes and no. Some of the elements of ePhilanthropy from the past decade—like e-mail and the Web—will be reinvented in different formats like SMS text messaging via cellular phones and other wireless devices.

So let's take a look at what forward-thinking nonprofit organizations are doing now. It might just give us a window on the future of ePhilanthropy.

Wireless Devices

In the commercial sector, handheld devices that allow credit cards to be swiped for a product or service is something that car rental companies and others have been using for a number of years. Now, the nonprofit sector is investigating the effectiveness of using wireless devices for donations at events and for public canvassing.

Nonprofit organizations should seek out the financial services vendors that provide these devices and find out how they can be used to raise money. One such vendor is Moneris, which can be found at *www.moneris.com* or *www.monerisusa.com*.

For Trent University, *www.trentuniversity.ca*, the rental of a Moneris device allowed their fundraisers to process $60,000 on one machine, in one day, at their convocation. That is one heck of a good return on a $135.00 investment.

Imagine an organization has a special event that includes both silent and live auctions. There could be trained volunteers walking around the event. Staff could not only take donations but could make sure other financial transactions like auction purchases are processed immediately.

Though costs vary, an organization should expect to pay approximately the following:

Credit card transaction fee:	1.68% (varies slightly)
Debit transaction fee:	$0.15 / transaction
Terminal pin pad fee:	$54.00 (wireless) / month
One-time activation fee:	$135.00

In the right location, with the right training, and the right event, a nonprofit could make thousands and thousands of dollars with a wireless device that can process gifts immediately.

If more fundraising in the future—whether the first contact is at the mall or elsewhere—will rely on electronic media for future appeals and correspondence, then organizations must see electronic media as the sharp end of the stick in communications and stewarding donors. The use of the electronic environment to build a long-lasting relationship will be vital, and Chapter 12 provides an excellent case study about why online relationships have to be properly planned, tested, and supported with both human resources and technology.

E-Stewardship

New technologies can help improve the efficiencies of capturing the first gift and making sure information about the donor is properly entered into the donor database. The twenty-first century will be the century in which we know more about our donors—and can manipulate that data to the benefit of both the donor and the nonprofit organization.

By using that data in a structured stewardship cycle, nonprofit organizations will be truly taking advantage of new technologies to build better relationships online—and offline.

In many ways, creating an online stewardship plan is a way to make communication as efficient as possible—and free up more time for fundraising staff to spend 'face time' with as many donors as possible. In the future, a nonprofit organization will want to provide electronic communication to donors in order to do the following:

- *Improve renewal rates, and/or increase* (see Chapter 13) their regular gift in comparison to donors who receive mail and/or phone contact
- *Allow donors to use viral marketing* (see Chapter 6) tools to tell friends and family about the organization they support

- *Allow donors to use online event tools* (see Chapter 14) to participate in other fundraising activities like a walk or run for the organization they already support with a regular gift
- *Allow donors to use online tools to manage their own contact information* (see Chapter 11) and give the organization more accurate contact data
- *Allow donors to use online advocacy tools* (see Chapter 9)

The Cellular Phone

The cellular (or mobile) phone is becoming an important, and convergent, piece of technology for consumers—and subsequently—nonprofit organizations.

In many parts of the world, the cellular phone is becoming an important communication vehicle for politics, leisure, friends and family, and now, fundraising. They are also becoming incredibly sophisticated machines: they can receive and take pictures and video, access e-mail and the Web, and run multiple software programs.

It's not just for fundraising but a holistic connection of communications, marketing, and fundraising.

Political parties are starting to use text messaging on cellular phones to do a number of things:

- Ask individuals who see a TV ad to enter a series of numbers to agree or disagree with a position
- Ask individuals to enter a number code to donate to the party
- After building a list of cell phone numbers—sending text messages immediately after a TV debate—ask them to vote on the winner or one particular issue from the debate with instant results
- Polling could be done from one phone—even done by the political leader—and the results instantly sent back and shown to the press
- For nonprofit organizations that have advocacy as part of their mission, the instantaneous, broad polling available through cellular phones is an important future possibility.

PUTTING IT ALL TOGETHER—WHAT CAN THE FUTURE HOLD?

First, it's most likely going to involve new ways to acquire donors. As the phone and the mail become less important to the next generation of donors, new acquisition techniques—like mall fundraising—will appear.

In the mall, fundraisers may be presenting riveting video material on giant screens—or on handheld computers—engaging interested citizens. When someone is interesting in giving, the fundraiser will take down the information instantly on a small computer—and process a credit card or EFT gift—with confirmation within seconds. Then, they'll be asked if they'd like to keep in touch during urgent times by sharing their cellular phone number. That way, the next time a crisis appeal goes out, it arrives on someone's cellular phone—a piece of video and a function allowing for instant donations.

Current technology allows wireless cell-phone video reception and may soon add wireless disc players with this capability. Think what an organization can do with linking live transmissions to individuals or groups via both the Internet, telephone, and other hand-held devices. How about colleges broadcasting athletic events, lectures, public ceremonies? Or arts organizations' time-delay interviews with current performers? Or hospitals sharing new medical applications and promoting advanced healthcare directives? Even small nonprofits can produce CDs (normal size and the smaller shape) on a variety of topics, program and service-oriented, as well as uses for marketing, communications, and fundraising purposes.

Of course, this will all require the proper human resources to manage a twenty-first century campaign, and Chapter 4 does a good job to prepare you for what online and new technology fundraising will require.

PUTTING THE FUTURE OF ePHILANTHROPY IN PERSPECTIVE

Over the last 10 years, the pace of technological innovation in fundraising—and especially online fundraising—has been ferocious. It's going to be difficult to stay on top of the pace of change.

The author hopes that the final part of this chapter will give some human perspective on ePhilanthropy.

> *During the early 1970s, running water was installed in the houses of Ibieca, a small village in northeast Spain. With pipes running directly to their homes, Ibiecans no longer had to fetch water from the village fountain. Families gradually purchased washing machines and women stopped gathering to scrub laundry by hand at the village washbasin.*
>
> *Arduous tasks were rendered technologically superfluous, but village social life unexpectedly changed. The public fountain and washbasin, once scenes of vigorous social interaction, became nearly deserted. Men began losing their sense of familiarity with the children and the donkeys that had once helped them to haul water. Women stopped congregating at the washbasin to intermix their scrubbing with politically empowering gossip about village life.*
>
> *In hindsight, the installation of running water helped break down the Ibiecans' strong bonds—with one another, with their animals, and with the land—that had knit them together as a community.*[3]

Is this a parable for fundraising in the twenty-first century nonprofit sector? Like Ibiecans, we seem to acquiesce quietly to seemingly innocuous technological changes. We adopt more advanced databases, more powerful computers and their networks, e-mail, and Internet solutions—mostly without question.

Have we thought clearly about the implications of these technologies for our sector and on the constituencies we serve?

If we think that technology can have a profound impact on our sector, then the pace of technological change should make us pay even more attention. It took more than 20 years for radio to reach 50 million households in North America—50 million being a benchmark indicating mass communication maturity. It took just 12 years for television to reach the same saturation level and only 4 years for the World Wide Web to do it.

If technological advances are reaching more people, faster, then we need to study these new technologies more thoroughly in order to decide how to adapt them to the nonprofit sector.

Are technologies improving the ability of the nonprofit sector to fundraise more effectively—to better manage donor information and relationships? I would say a cautious yes, but we need to proceed carefully as we invest in new technologies (like an Internet presence and the further computerization of fundraising).

We need to be aware of something called the *Productivity Paradox*—a concept that has emerged out of studies proving that worker productivity since the introduction of computers has either flatlined or declined. It's also been called the *Solow Effect*. With all of the incredible investment in computers we're still about as productive as before their introduction. There is one area where we're much more productive—the manufacturing of computers themselves.

I know many readers will say that the Productivity Paradox cannot be true when you consider how computers have allowed your nonprofit organizations to keep better track of donors, authorize donations, organize files, and communicate between staff, volunteer, and donors. While all that may be true, computers and their accompanying technologies can be incredibly difficult to manage and have unintended consequences.

Now more than ever, we are being challenged by management issues arising from Internet use in the office. How do we craft an effective privacy policy? How can we create an e-mail usage policy that respects every worker by keeping management informed but allowing for everyone to fully utilize the Internet? How do we create effective job descriptions and management structures to deal with the introduction of greater Internet fundraising responsibilities? What does the Productivity Paradox mean to ePhilanthropy? It reminds us that computers are an incredibly powerful technology that needs precise and careful management to allow us to do our work more effectively and efficiently.

THE HUMAN MOMENT

Beyond the Productivity Paradox, the author believes there are other reasons for the nonprofit sector to be cautious about ePhilanthropy and the potent mix of associated new technologies (which will take forms like wireless, plasma screen, cellular phone, and mall fundraisers). Studies are beginning to show that the Internet could have detrimental effects on community and the social well-being of citizens. A Carnegie-Mellon study indicated that people who spend time online exhibited increased levels of depression and loneliness even when only connected a few hours a week.

What this study tells us is that our sector needs to know more about the impact of these coalescing technologies on our nonprofit organizations and our relationships with online donors.

TAKING A HARDER LOOK

Although governments, private sector interests, and nonprofits are pouring more money into new technologies for the sector, there is very little study being done on the impact of these technologies on online giving.

Technology philosopher Ursula Franklin, in a recent lecture, mentioned this possibility:

> *The Internet will make it easier to give to an earthquake victim half-way around the world, but it makes it easier to forget about the homeless person on our own street. Will the Internet dislocate time and space when it comes to our caring for others in our own community?*[4]

It would be a wise decision by foundations and government bodies to fund studies of online donors to determine the positive or negative social impact of this new philanthropic endeavor. No data currently exist, and studies would help citizens, nonprofits, and governments to begin to understand the social impact of online giving now and in the future.

Similarly, we should be studying the impact that the online environment is having on other parts of the nonprofit organization. Are new technologies creating more stress within nonprofit organizations? Are they creating dislocation between nonprofits and the people they serve?

We need answers to these questions as we move forward with these new fundraising technologies. The nonprofit sector is being told to adopt these technologies by government and business without fully understanding the implications of doing so.

This is also a time of incredible pressure for nonprofit organizations. They are being asked to do more in an increasingly competitive environment.

In this chapter, there was a reference to the town of Ibieca and its adoption of running water. The reader should wonder if that story could be the parable for the nonprofit sector's use of online fundraising at the start of the twenty-first century.

ABOUT THE AUTHOR

Michael Johnston, president of HJC, is an expert in fundraising and the use of the Internet by nonprofit agencies. Mike has worked with more than 100 nonprofit organizations ranging from third-world development organizations, to hospitals, to peace and disarmament groups, in Canada, the United States, and the United Kingdom. He gained considerable experience as a senior consultant and director with Stephen Thomas Associates, one of the first fundraising firms in Canada to work exclusively with NGOs. He has been a past member of the ethics committee of the Canadian Society of Fund-Raising Executives (CSFRE) and was a volunteer fundraising leader with the United Way in its Management Assistance Program. Mike is also a past board member and current member of the Association of Fundraising Professionals (AFP) and sits on the AFP's Volunteer Online Council in Alexandria, Virginia. He has recently joined the board of directors of the U.S.-based ePhilanthropy Foundation. Mike sits on the executive committee and is the chairman of the product development and education committee.

Mike is a skilled communicator, and his skills are known throughout the nonprofit community. He is the author of *The Fund Raiser's Guide to the Internet* and *The Nonprofit Guide to the Internet* and is the editor of *Direct Response Fund Raising,* all published by John Wiley & Sons. He has worked with a range of educational institutions, lecturing on the Internet and the nonprofit sector and has spoken at five AFP International Conferences, teaching both full-day seminars and short workshops. From his seminars to television appearances to his published articles, Mike has been able to analyze the implications of the Internet for thousands of people in the nonprofit sector. Michael Johnston is committed to the nonprofit sector and dedicated to helping organizations reach their charitable goals. You can e-mail Mike at mjohnston@hjcnewmedia.com

ENDNOTES

1. The complete survey results can be found at *www.theflagroupinc.com.*
2. An online survey of 2002 online donors to Amnesty International Canada.
3. Richard E. Sclove, *Democracy and Technology* (New York: The Guildford Press, 1995), p. 3.
4. Ursula Franklin, lecture, *The Real World of Technology Revisited,* Ursula Franklin High School, May 10, 1999.

ePhilanthropy Code of Ethical Online Philanthropic Practices

The ePhilanthropy Foundation exists to foster the effective and safe use of the Internet for philanthropic purposes. In its effort to promote high ethical standards in online fundraising and to build trust among contributors in making online transactions and contributions with the charity of their choice, this code is being offered as a guide to all who share this goal. Contributors are encouraged to be aware of non-internet-related fundraising practices that fall outside the scope of this code.

Ethical online practices and practitioners will:

Section A: Philanthropic Experience
- Clearly and specifically display and describe the organization's identity on the organization's Web site
- Employ practices on the Web site that exhibit integrity, honesty, and truthfulness and seek to safeguard the public trust

Section B: Privacy and Security
- Seek to inspire trust in every online transaction
- Prominently display the opportunity for supporters to have their names removed from lists that are sold to, rented to, or exchanged with other organizations
- Conduct online transactions through a system that employs high-level security technology to protect the donor's personal information for both internal and external authorized use
- Provide either an opt-in or opt-out mechanism to prevent unsolicited communications or solicitations by organizations that obtain e-mail addresses directly from the donor. Should lists be rented or exchanged, only those verified as having been obtained through donors or prospects opting in will be used by a charity
- Protect the interests and privacy of individuals interacting with their Web site
- Provide a clear, prominent, and easily accessible privacy policy on its Web site telling visitors, at a minimum, what information is being collected, how this information will be used, and who has access to the data

---

Section C: Disclosures

- Disclose the identity of the organization or provider processing an online transaction
- Guarantee that the name, logo, and likeness of all parties to an online transaction belong to the party and will not be used without express permission
- Maintain all appropriate governmental and regulatory designations or certifications
- Provide both online and offline contact information

Section D: Complaints

- Provide protection to hold the donor harmless of any problem arising from a transaction conducted through the organization's Web site
- Promptly respond to all customer complaints and to employ best efforts to fairly resolve all legitimate complaints in a timely fashion

Section E: Transactions

- Ensure contributions are used to support the activities of the organization to which they were donated
- Ensure that legal control of contributions or proceeds from online transactions are transferred directly to the charity or expedited in the fastest possible way
- Companies providing online services to charities will provide clear and full communication with the charity on all aspects of donor transactions, including the accurate and timely transmission of data related to online transactions
- Stay informed regarding the best methods to ensure the ethical, secure, and private nature of online ePhilanthropy transactions
- Adhere to the spirit as well as the letter of all applicable laws and regulations, including, but not limited to, charity solicitation and tax laws
- Ensure that all services, recognition, and other transactions promised on a Web site, in consideration of gift or transaction, will be fulfilled on a timely basis
- Disclose to the donor the nature of the relationship between the organization processing the gift or transaction and the charity intended to benefit from the gift

The Ten Rules of ePhilanthropy Every Nonprofit Must Know

1. DON'T BECOME INVISIBLE

If you build it, they won't just come. Building an online brand is just as important and just as difficult as building an off-line brand.

2. IT TAKES "KNOW HOW" AND VISION

Your organization's Web site is a marketing and fundraising tool, not a technology tool. Fundraisers and marketers need to be driving the content, not the Web developer.

3. IT'S ALL ABOUT THE DONOR

Put the Donor First! Know your contributors; let them get to know you.

4. KEEP SAVVY DONORS; STAY FRESH AND CURRENT

Make online giving enjoyable and easy. Give the donor options. Use the latest technology. Show your donor how their funds are being used.

5. INTEGRATE INTO EVERYTHING YOU DO

Your Web site alone will do nothing. Every activity you have should drive traffic to your site.

6. DON'T TRADE YOUR MISSION FOR A SHOPPING MALL

Many nonprofit Web sites fail to emphasize mission, instead turning themselves into online shopping malls, without even knowing why.

Reprinted with permission from the ePhilanthropyFoundation.org © 2005.

7. ETHICS, PRIVACY AND SECURITY ARE NOT BUZZWORDS

Many donors are just now deciding to make their first online contribution. They will expect that your organization maintain the highest standards of ethics, privacy, and security.

8. IT TAKES THE INTERNET TO BUILD A COMMUNITY

Many nonprofits (particularly smaller ones) lack the resources to communicate effectively. The Internet offers the opportunity to cost effectively build a community of supporters.

9. SUCCESS ONLINE MEANS BEING TARGETED

The Web site alone is not enough. You must target your audience and drive their attention to the wealth of information and services offered by your Web site. Permission must be sought before you begin direct communication via the Internet.

10. ePHILANTHROPY IS MORE THAN JUST E-MONEY

ePhilanthropy is a tool to be used in your fund raising strategy. It should not be viewed as quick money. There are no short cuts to building effective relationships, but the Internet will enhance your efforts.

APRA Statement of Ethics

A ssociation of Professional Researchers for Advancement (APRA) members shall support and further the individual's fundamental right to privacy and protect the confidential information of their institutions. APRA members are committed to the ethical collection and use of information. Members shall follow all applicable national, state, and local laws, as well as institutional policies, governing the collection, use, maintenance, and dissemination of information in the pursuit of the missions of their institutions.

CODE OF ETHICS

Advancement researchers must balance an individual's right to privacy with the needs of their institutions to collect, analyze, record, maintain, use, and disseminate information. This balance is not always easy to maintain. To guide researchers, the following ethical principles apply:

I. **Fundamental Principles**

A. **Confidentiality**

Confidential information about constituents (donors and non-donors), as well as confidential information of the institutions in oral form or on electronic, magnetic, or print media are protected in order to foster a trusting relationship between the constituent and the institution. This means that the information is not available for anyone except development professionals, and their agents, to see.

B. **Accuracy**

Advancement researchers shall record all data accurately. Such information shall include attribution. Data analyses and their by-products should be without personal prejudices or biases.

C. Relevance

Advancement researchers shall seek and record only information that is relevant to the cultivation, solicitation, and/or stewardship strategy with the prospect.

D. Self-responsibility

Advancement researchers often play a significant role in developing and monitoring advancement department policies on information storage and confidentiality. It is important that advancement researchers lead by example. First, advancement researchers should develop clear policies and procedures for the prospect research department on the collection, storage, and distribution of constituent information and analysis. Second, when possible, advancement researchers should advocate for the development and adoption of institution wide ethics guidelines and privacy policies which are at least as complete as the APRA Statement of Ethics.

E. Honesty

Advancement researchers shall be truthful with regard to their identities and purpose, and the identity of their institutions during the course of their work.

F. Conflict of Interest

Advancement researchers should be careful to avoid conflicts of interest. Prospect research consultants should have explicit policies which outline how they will deal with conflicts of interest between clients. Advancement researchers who are employed full-time for an institution and also perform consulting services should be certain that the consulting services do not represent a conflict of interest with their primary employer.

II. Standards of Practice

A. Collection

1. The collection of information should be done lawfully, respecting applicable laws and institutional policies.
2. Advancement researchers should be experts on the reliability of sources (print, electronic, and otherwise), as well as the sources utilized by third parties to gather information on their behalf.
3. Advancement researchers should not evade or avoid questions about their affiliations or purpose when requesting information in person, over the phone, electronically, or in writing. It is recommended that requests for public information be made on institutional stationery and that these requests clearly identify the requestor.
4. Advancement researchers should use the usual and customary methods of payment or reimbursement for products or services purchased on behalf of their institutions.

5. Advancement researchers who are employed full-time for an institution and also perform consulting services should develop clear understandings with their primary employers about the use of the employers' financial and human resources.

B. Recording and Maintenance

1. Advancement researchers shall present information in an objective and factual manner; note attribution, and clearly identify information which is conjecture or analysis. Where there is conflicting information, advancement researchers should objectively present the multiple versions and state any reason for preferring one version over another.

2. Advancement researchers should develop security measures to protect the constituent information to which they have access from access by unauthorized persons. When possible, these measures should include locking offices and/or file cabinets and secure and frequently changed passwords to electronic databases. Advancement researchers should also advocate institution-wide policies which promote the careful handling of constituent information so that constituent privacy is protected. The use of constituent databases over a wireless Internet connection is not recommended.

3. Where advancement researchers are also responsible for donor giving records and their maintenance, they should develop security measures to provide very limited access to the giving records of anonymous donors. Access to these records should be limited to only those staff who need the information to successfully cultivate, solicit, or steward said donor.

4. Where there is no existing case law which outlines clearly the rights of a donor in accessing advancement files (paper and/or electronic), advancement researchers should work with their institution's legal counsel to develop an institution specific policy regarding this access. This policy should be put in writing, approved by the President/CEO, and distributed to any advancement professionals who might field a request for such access.

5. When electronic or paper documents pertaining to constituents must be disposed, they should be disposed in a fashion which lessens the danger of a privacy breach. Shredding of paper documents is recommended.

C. Use and Distribution

1. Researchers shall adhere to all applicable laws, as well as to institutional policies, regarding the use and distribution of confidential constituent information. Careful consideration should be given to the use of electronic mail and faxes for the delivery of constituent information.

2. Constituent information is the property of the institution for which it was collected and shall not be given to persons other than those

who are involved with the cultivation or solicitation effort or those who need that information in the performance of their duties for that institution.

3. Constituent information for one institution shall not be taken to another institution.

4. Research documents containing constituent information that is to be used outside research offices shall be clearly marked confidential.

5. Vendors, consultants, and other external entities shall understand and agree to comply with the institution's confidentiality policies before gaining access to institutional data.

6. Advancement researchers, with the assistance of institutional counsel and the advancement chief officer, should develop policies which address the sharing of directory information on their constituents with other institutions. Constituent requests to withhold directory information should be respected in all cases.

The Gilbert E-Mail Manifesto for Nonprofits

E-mail is more important than my Web site!

—Michael Gilbert

I can't stand it any more . . . I've listened to too many four-hour workshops about online fundraising in which it's all about Web sites, Web sites, Web sites. I've been to too many technical assistance sites that have class after class on web design. I've heard too many nonprofits obsess about their Web sites.

I ask leaders of nonprofit organizations if they have an e-mail strategy and their usual response is something on the order of "huh?" They are spending enormous amounts of money and staff time on their web sites and it's the rare exception that the organization even has enough of an e-mail strategy to have a newsletter.

They are wasting their money. I'm serious.

Why is this happening? Is it because Web sites are pretty and e-mail is mostly text? Is it because people love graphic design? Is it because this is the approach that is pushed by the consulting firms? Or is it perhaps because thinking about e-mail is a little more difficult, as it is a constantly moving target?

I don't know the reasons for sure, but I do know that something can be done. I have been recommending "Three Rules of E-mail" to help nonprofit organizations develop a genuine Internet strategy and avoid being seduced by their own Web presence:

Rule #1: Resources spent on e-mail strategies are more valuable than the same resources spent on Web strategies.

Rule #2: A Web site built around an e-mail strategy is more valuable than a Web site that is built around itself.

Rule #3: E-mail oriented thinking will yield better strategic thinking overall.

The Gilbert Center is an incubator, research institute, consulting firm, and publishing house working to support and empower the people and organizations changing the world for the better. The expertise of the founder, Michael Gilbert, and company lie primarily in the area of communication, whether for internal organizational health and renewal, for successful outreach to members, funders, or the public, or for the dramatic opportunities presented by online communication.

Nonprofits that truly embrace these three rules will reach a genuine breakthrough in their online presence. They will seize the initiative from technologists and guide their own technology on their terms. Let me elaborate. For each of these principles I will scratch the surface as to why it's true and how it might be applied. Each of these is worthy of several workshops in their own right.

RULE #1: RESOURCES SPENT ON E-MAIL STRATEGIES ARE MORE VALUABLE THAN THE SAME RESOURCES SPENT ON WEB STRATEGIES.

However unglamorous it might be, e-mail is the killer application of the Internet. It is person-to-person communication, and the one thing that breaks down barriers faster than anything else on the net. Consider these facts:

- Everybody on the net has e-mail and most of them read most of their messages.
- People visit far fewer Web sites than they get e-mail messages.
- E-mail messages are treated as To Do items, while bookmarks are often forgotten.
- E-mail is always a call to action.
- E-mail is handled within a familiar user interface, whereas each Web site has to teach a new interface.
- E-mail is a very personal medium.
- Stop obsessing about how many hits your Web site gets and start counting how much e-mail interaction you have with your stakeholders.

RULE #2: A WEB SITE BUILT AROUND AN E-MAIL STRATEGY IS MORE VALUABLE THAN A WEB SITE THAT IS BUILT AROUND ITSELF.

On some nonprofit list, somewhere, someone right now is asking how they can get more traffic on their Web site. And someone is answering by telling them how to put META tags in their site so they will get listed in search engines. This is so tired. . . .

My answer to this tired question is simple: Send them there with e-mail!

Obviously this means there has to be a purpose for them to go to the Web site that cannot be fulfilled with the e-mail message itself. Some of the obvious ways that a Web site can supplement your e-mail strategy include:

- Gathering e-mail addresses in the first place
- Archiving your relationships with stakeholders (ex: collecting the results of surveys)
- Serving as a library to back up your smaller e-mail communications
- Providing actual online tools for your stakeholders
- Providing Web forms that allow you to structure your communication and pull it into databases

RULE #3: E-MAIL ORIENTED THINKING WILL YIELD BETTER STRATEGIC THINKING OVERALL.

Last year, the most common question I was asked by journalists reporting on the Internet and nonprofits was about the role of the Internet in fundraising. My response was always the same:

> *The ability to process credit card transactions is the equivalent of having a checking account. It's not very interesting, and it's not actually fundraising. The true power of the Internet for fundraising (or any other stakeholder relationship) is the power of personal communication combined with the power of scale.*

Nonprofits know how to mobilize people on a personal level. By using the Internet appropriately, they can do so on a scale never before possible.

Understanding e-mail will make this possible. True, not all personal, online communication takes place through e-mail, but e-mail is the canonical "closed loop relationship" that direct marketing managers understand so well. Applied well, it will allow nonprofits to succeed on a whole new level.

Repeat after me: "E-mail is more important than my Web site!"

Glossary of Terms

Acrobat   Acrobat is a program made by Adobe that allows you to convert any document to a portable document format (PDF) file, which is a type of file that is commonly posted on the Web for download. Anyone can then open your document across a broad range of hardware and software, and it will look exactly as you intended—with layout, fonts, links, and images intact. Source: Adobe.com

Applet   An applet is a small program that can be included in an HTML page, just like an image is included. Java applets can perform interactive animations, immediate calculations, or other simple tasks without having to send a user request back to the server. Source: Sun.com

ASCII   American Standard Code for Information Interchange (ASCII) is a 7-bit code that represents the most basic letters of the Roman alphabet, numbers, and other characters used in computing. ASCII characters allow us to communicate with computers, which use their own language called "binary" (made up of 0s and 1s). When we type ASCII characters from the keyboard (which looks like words to us), the computer interprets them as binary so they can be read, manipulated, stored, and retrieved. Source: Learnthenet.com

ASP   Application service providers (ASPs) are third-party entities that manage and distribute software-based services and solutions to customers across a wide area network from a central data center. ASPs may be commercial ventures that cater to customers, or not-for-profit or government organizations, providing service and support to end-users. Source: ASPNews.com

Bandwidth   Bandwidth is the maximum amount of data that can travel a communications path in a given time, usually measured in seconds. For digital devices, the bandwidth is usually expressed in bits per second (bps) or bytes per second. Source: Webopaedia.com

Banner   Depending on how it's used, a banner is either a graphic image that announces the name or identity of a site (and often is spread across the width of the Web page) or is an advertising image. Advertisers sometimes count banner "views," or the number of times a banner graphic image was downloaded over a period of time. Source: SearchWebManagement.com

---

This glossary of terms has been compiled from a variety of sources (noted following each entry) by the ePhilanthropyFoundation.org. Reprinted with permission from the ePhilanthropyFoundation.org ©2005.

Blog   With newsgroups and Web sites, people all around the world easily and inexpensively express themselves online. Weblogs, commonly referred to as blogs, are a relatively new form of personal publishing. In the last few years the Web has witnessed a veritable explosion of blogs. A blog is similar to an electronic journal or diary. Source: Learnthenet.com

Blogger   The writer, known as a blogger, makes periodic entries, sometimes as frequently as a few times a day. Blogs can be on any subject, for instance, politics, relationships, or daily observations while driving to work. These musings may be of interest only to the blogger's family and friends or they can command the attention of a global audience. It all depends on how thoughtful and compelling it is. What distinguishes blogs from other online content is that it is highly personal, reflecting the point of view of the blogger. Source: Learnthenet.com

Bobby-Approved Web Site   A Web site that has been tested and approved by Bobby (located at *http://bobby.cast.org/bobby/html/en/index.jsp*), a Web-based tool that evaluates the accessibility of Web sites for people with disabilities.

Bookmark   Using a World Wide Web browser, a bookmark is a saved link to a Web page that has been added to a list of saved links. When you are looking at a particular Web site or home page and want to be able to quickly get back to it later, you can create a bookmark for it. Netscape and some other browsers use the bookmark idea. Microsoft's Internet Explorer uses the term "favorite." Source: Whatis.com

Bounce   An electronic mail message returned with a notice indicating the transmission failed, either because the message was misaddressed or a connection failed. Source: Computeruser.com

Browser   A software program that allows you to surf the Web. The most popular Web browsers right now are Netscape Navigator and Internet Explorer. Source: Webguest.com

Cascading Style Sheets (CSS)   An extension to HTML to allow styles (e.g., color, font, size) to be specified for certain elements of a hypertext document. Style information can be included in-line in the HTML file or in a separate CSS file (which can then be easily shared by multiple HTML files). Multiple levels of CSS can be used to allow selective overriding of styles. Source: Instantweb.com

CGI   Common gateway interface (CGI) is a standard for running external programs from a World Wide Web HTTP server. The CGI program can, for example, access information in a database and format the results as HTML. A CGI program can be any program that can accept command line arguments. Source: Instantweb.com

Cookie   A small piece of information that a Web server sends to your computer hard disk via your browser. Cookies contain information such as login or registration information, online shopping cart information, user preferences, and so on. This information can be retrieved by other Web pages on the site, so that this site can be customized. Source: Webguest.com

CRM   Customer relationship management (CRM) is the same as one-to-one marketing. This customer-focused business model also goes by the names relationship marketing, real-time marketing, customer intimacy, and a variety of other terms. But the idea is the same: establish relationships with customers on an individual basis, and then use the information you gather to treat different customers differently. The exchange between a customer and a company becomes mutually beneficial, as customers give information in return for personalized service that meets their individual needs. Source: 1to1.com

Digest   A periodical collection of messages that have been posted to a newsgroup or mailing list. A digest is prepared by a moderator who selects articles from the group or list, formats them and adds a contents list. Source: Instantweb.com

Domain Name System (DNS)   A general-purpose distributed, replicated, data query service chiefly used on Internet for translating hostnames (ephilanthopy.org) into Internet addresses (233.444.213.121). Also, the style of hostname used on the Internet, though such a name is properly called a fully qualified domain name. DNS can be configured to use a sequence of name servers, based on the domains in the name being looked for, until a match is found. Source: Instantweb.com

eCRM   Online constituent relationship management (eCRM) is the strategy of using the Internet to develop constituent relationships. Source: Convio, Inc.

EDI   Electronic data interchange (EDI) is the exchange of standardized document forms between computer systems for business use. Source: Instantweb.com

Encryption   A way of coding the information in a file or e-mail message so that if it is intercepted by a third party as it travels over a network it cannot be read. Only the person or persons that have the right type of decoding software can unscramble the message. Source: Learnthenet.com

ePhilanthropy   The building and enhancing of relationships with supporters of nonprofit organizations using an Internet-based platform, the online contribution of cash or real property or the purchase of products or services to benefit a nonprofit organization, and the storage of and usage of electronic data or use of electronic methods to support fund raising activities. Source: ePhilanthropyFoundation.org

Firewall   A firewall is a combination hardware and software buffer that many companies or organizations have in place between their internal networks and the Internet. A firewall allows only specific kinds of messages from the Internet to flow in and out of the internal network. This protects the internal network from intruders or hackers who might try to use the Internet to break into those systems. Source: Learnthenet.com

FTP   File transfer protocol (FTP) is a client-server protocol that allows a user on one computer to transfer files to and from another computer. Source: Instantweb.com

HTML   Hypertext markup language (HTML) is the computer language used to create hypertext documents. HTML uses a finite list of tags that describe the general structure of various kinds of documents linked together on the World Wide Web. Source: Learnthenet.com

HTTP   Hypertext transfer protocol (HTTP) is the method used to transfer hypertext files across the Internet. On the World Wide Web, pages written in HTML use hypertext to link to other documents. When you click on hypertext, you jump to another Web page, sound file, or graphic. Source: Learnthenet.com

Hyperlink   A highlighted word (or graphic) within a hypertext document (Web page). When you click a hyperlink, it will take you to another place within the same page, or to another page. Source: Webguest.com

IP Address   An Internet protocol (IP) address is the 32-bit numeric address that serves as an identifier for a computer; information is routed based on the IP address of the destination. The IP address is written as four numbers separated by periods. For example 207.158.192.40 could be an IP address. Each of the four numbers (which can be from zero to 255) is used in different ways to identify a particular network and a host on that network. Source: About.com

ISP   An Internet service provider (ISP) is a company that provides access to the Internet. For a monthly fee, the service provider gives you a software package, username, password, and access phone number. Equipped with a modem, you can then log on to the Internet, browse the World Wide Web, and send and receive e-mail. Source: Webopaedia.com

Listserv   Listserv is a small program that automatically redistributes e-mail to names on a mailing list. Users can subscribe to a mailing list by sending an email note to a mailing list they learn about; listserv will automatically add the name and distribute future e-mail postings to every subscriber. (Requests to subscribe and unsubscribe are sent to a special address so that all subscribers do not see these requests.) Source: Searchvb.com

NGO   A non-governmental organization (NGO) is any non-profit, voluntary citizens' group that is organized on a local, national, or international level. Task-oriented and driven by people with a common interest, NGOs perform a variety of services and humanitarian functions, bring citizens' concerns to governments, monitor policies, and encourage political participation at the community level. They provide analysis and expertise, serve as early warning mechanisms, and help monitor and implement international agreements. Some are organized around specific issues, such as human rights, the environment, or health. Source: UN.org

Perl   Practical extraction and report language (Perl) is a general-purpose language that is often used for scanning text and printing formatted reports. The use of Perl has grown significantly since its adoption as the language of choice of many World Wide Web developers. Source: Instantweb.com

POP3   Post office protocol, version 3 (POP3) is a publication that standardizes the way computers on the Internet send and receive email messages. The computers that do the sending and receiving are called servers. Source: Instantweb.com

RGB   Red, green, blue (RGB) are the three colors of light that can be mixed to produce any other color. Colored images are often stored as a sequence of RGB triplets or as separate red, green, and blue overlays. Often used as a synonym for color, as in "RGB monitor," as opposed to monochrome (black and white). Source: Instantweb.com

Search engine   A search engine is a type of software that creates indexes of databases or Internet sites based on the titles of files, keywords, or the full text of files. The search engine has an interface that allows you to type what you're looking for into a blank field. It then gives you a list of the results of the search. When you use a search engine on the Web, the results are presented to you in hypertext, which means you can click on any item in the list to get the actual file. Source: LearntheNet.com

Split-Cell Test   The process of sending two different e-mails to similar segments to compare results. Source: Convio, Inc.

SQL An industry-standard language for creating, updating, and querying relational database management systems. Source: Instantweb.com

SSL Secure sockets layer (SSL) is a protocol designed by Netscape Communications Corporation to provide encrypted communications on the Internet. Source: Instant web.com

TCP/IP Transmission control protocol/Internet protocol (TCP/IP) is the basic communication language or protocol of the Internet. It can also be used as a communications protocol in the private networks called intranets and in extranets. When you are set up with direct access to the Internet, your computer is provided with a copy of the TCP/IP program just as every other computer that you may send messages to or get information from also has a copy of TCP/IP. Source: Whatis.com

Top-Level Domain .COM, .NET, and .ORG are top-level domains in the hierarchical Internet Domain Name System. These top-level domains are just underneath the "root", which is the start of the hierarchy. Anyone may register Web addresses in .COM, .NET, and .ORG. Source: NetworkSolutions.com

URL Uniform (previously "universal") resource locator (URL) is a draft standard for specifying the location of an object on the Internet, such as a file or a newsgroup. URLs are used extensively on the World Wide Web. They are used in HTML documents to specify the target of a hyperlink that is often another HTML document (possibly stored on another computer). Source: Instantweb.com

Viral Marketing Method of leveraging existing audience to forward e-mails, site content, and other online elements via tell-a-friend features. Most often, this is implemented in e-mail newsletters or entertaining/educational Flash animations that ask you to forward to friends. Source: Vervos.com

WWW A system of Internet servers that support specially formatted documents. The documents are formatted in HTML that supports links to other documents, as well as graphics, audio, and video files. This means you can jump from one document to another simply by clicking on hot spots. Not all Internet servers are part of the World Wide Web. Source: Webopaedia.com

XML Extensible markup language (XML) is a simple, very flexible text format. Originally designed to meet the challenges of large-scale electronic publishing, XML is also playing an increasingly important role in the exchange of a wide variety of data on the Web. Source: W3.org